CAMBRIDGE STUDIES IN

General Editors: B. COMRIE, C. J. FILL
R. B. LE PAGE, J. LYONS, P. H. MATTH
R. POSNER, S. ROMAINE, N. V. SMITH, J. L. M. TRIM, A. ZWICKY

Predication theory

A case study for indexing theory

UNIVERSITY OF CAMBRIDGE
RESEARCH CENTRE FOR ENGLISH
AND APPLIED LINGUISTICS
ENGLISH FACULTY BUILDING
9 WEST ROAD, CAMBRIDGE CB3 9DP

Donated by John Trim

In this series

Supplementary Volumes

* *Issued in hard covers and as a paperback*
  Earlier titles not listed are also available

PREDICATION THEORY

A CASE STUDY
FOR INDEXING THEORY

DONNA JO NAPOLI

Program in Linguistics, Swarthmore College

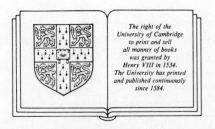

The right of the
University of Cambridge
to print and sell
all manner of books
was granted by
Henry VIII in 1534.
The University has printed
and published continuously
since 1584.

CAMBRIDGE UNIVERSITY PRESS

CAMBRIDGE   NEW YORK   NEW ROCHELLE
MELBOURNE   SYDNEY

Published by the Press Syndicate of the University of Cambridge
The Pitt Building, Trumpington Street, Cambridge CB2 1RP
32 East 57th Street, New York, NY 10022, USA
10 Stamford Road, Oakleigh, Melbourne 3166, Australia

© Cambridge University Press 1989

First published 1989

Printed in Great Britain at the University Press, Cambridge

British Library cataloguing in publication data

Napoli, Donna Jo
Predication theory: a case study for indexing theory.–(Cambridge studies in linguistics).
1. Language. Predication
I. Title
400

Library of Congress cataloguing in publication data

Napoli, Donna Jo, 1948–
Predication theory: a case study for indexing theory / Donna Jo
Napoli   p.   cm. – (Cambridge studies in linguistics: 50)
Bibliography.
Includes indexes.
ISBN 0 521 35298 3   ISBN 0 521 36820 0
1. Grammar, Comparative and general – Verb phrase. 2. Government-
binding theory (Linguistics) 3. Index theory (Mathematics)
4. Anaphora (Linguistics)   I. Title.   II. Series.
P281 N37 1988
415–dc19   88–11988 CIP

ISBN 0 521 35298 3 hard covers
ISBN 0 521 36820 0 paperback

Contents

Acknowledgements

For a sabbatical leave in winter, 1987, I thank the University of Michigan. For a stimulating and still peaceful environment to work in, I thank Swarthmore College.

For help with chapter 1, I thank Pete Becker, Dwight Bolinger, Jennifer Cole, Bill Croft, Rod Johnson, John Myhill, and Hala Talaat; chapter 2, Pete Becker, John Myhill, and Haj Ross; chapters 3 and 4, Josh Ard, Ivonne Bordelois, Marcel Danesi, Peter Hook, Giulio Lepschy, Marina Nespor, and John Swales; chapter 5, Dwight Bolinger and Becky Brys; chapter 6, Mutsuko Simon. A preliminary version of chapter 3 was presented at the Sixteenth Linguistic Symposium on Romance Languages at Austin, Texas, in March 1986, and appears as Napoli (1987b). For discussions about data, I thank Frank Casa, Barbara Mazzola, Maurizio Pacifici, Melina Scholler, Franco Sciannameo, Nicoletta Sonnega, and Raffaella Zanuttini. And for proofreading the final version, I thank Dorcas Allen.

For comments on earlier versions of this entire book, I am grateful to Greg Carlson, Stuart Davis, Jacqueline Guéron, Ken Hale, Dick Hudson, Ray Jackendoff, Andrew Radford, and Raffaella Zanuttini. Often in this book I point out examples and arguments they have offered to me. But much more often their contributions are hidden in the fact that what they taught me led to cutting out faulty arguments and irrelevant data. I am indebted to all of them.

My greatest academic debt is to Barry Miller, without whose constant criticism, encouragement, and insights this book would never have been written – this in spite of the fact that he has never read through a single version of this book. May every professor of linguistics be blessed with students of his intelligence and obstinacy.

And, finally, I thank the people who helped me spiritually. I thank Pete Becker, Dwight Bolinger, and Ken Hale, who helped me to realize there is no shame in raising questions I cannot answer. And I thank Barry, Elena, Michael, Nicholas, Eva, and Robert Furrow, who helped me to see that life goes on whether one understands predication or not. This book is dedicated to my spiritual helpers.

Introduction

Predication, by definition, has been an issue of interest to philosophers and linguists since what we might call the beginning of these disciplines. Only recently, however, have developments in modern linguistics allowed the questions relating to the nature of predication to take on a distinctly non-semantic flavor. For instance, current debates on predication within the Theory of Government and Binding (allowing the GB rubric to envelop many varieties of generative theories that share common properties, such as modularity) often discuss only or primarily the configurational properties of the phrases involved.

The present work, framed in a gently modified version of GB but written with the hope that it will be accessible and useful to linguists of all theoretical bents who have a familiarity with GB, is in part an attempt to pull linguistic discussions of predication back into the arena of semantics, and it has been made possible, perhaps paradoxically, by Noam Chomsky's *Barriers* (1986a). Chapter 1 outlines a theory of theta assignment and develops an approach to predication based on events and role players in those events. This approach recognizes predicates and role players as primitives that are not configurationally defined. Chapter 2 offers principles of coindexing between a predicate and its subject role player which revolve around theta role assignment. The types of data typically used to support configurational approaches to the coindexing of a predicate and its subject role player are examined, and the empirical inadequacy of these approaches is uncovered. In contrast, the theta-based theory of predication offered here is shown to handle the traditional data well and to make correct predictions about new data. This chapter does not give a comprehensive point-by-point comparison of the theta-based theory with other theories. Instead, it points out major differences where relevant and avoids discussions of details which lead to no new insights into predication theory.

Chapters 3, 4, and 5 look at other constructions which have not to my knowledge been treated at all (or, if they have, only in passing) in the literature on predication. These chapters show how the constructions studied there offer support for the theta-based theory of predication over other theories.

Once having established the theta-based theory of predication, our attention turns to the second major task of this work: extending the predication coindexing principles arrived at in chapter 2 into a general indexing theory. I propose that the principles needed to account for coindexing between a predicate and its subject role player should and can be extended to handle the coindexing between an anaphor and its antecedent. This proposal grows naturally out of the work of Safir (1985), as an attempt to follow his Unity of Indexing Hypothesis. And this proposal is not without problems, some of which are grave, as I point out in chapter 6. Still, even if the extension of the coindexing of chapter 2 to binding in chapter 6 is shown eventually to be wrong, it is an important and enlightening exercise to push the hypothesis as far as it will go: many similarities between anaphors and predicates are brought to light in chapter 6 and demand a theory which will account for these similarities.

The central goal of this book is to arrive at the coindexing principles. Thus while I develop principles for theta assignment, I do not investigate event structure. That is, I do not delve into the semantic basis for different theta roles. At several points in chapters 1 and 2, particularly, I refer the reader to works that do just that.

In chapter 1 an informal approach to the notions of argument, role player, and predicate is developed. No formal definition of any of these appears in this book. Arguments against the feasibility and desirability of a formal definition of predicate appear in chapter 1, section 5.

Throughout, I assume a restrictive version of X-bar theory, incorporating only two phrase-structure rules for the lexical categories of N(oun), V(erb), A(djective), and P(reposition) (as in Stowell 1981):

$$X'' \rightarrow \text{spec } X' \ X'$$
$$X' \rightarrow X \ Y''^*$$

X'' is the maximal projection of X (otherwise known as XP – and I will use X'' and XP interchangeably throughout this book). X' is an intermediary phrasal projection of X which can appear with a single sister: its specifier. And X is the lexical projection, the head of the phrase, which can appear with multiple phrasal sisters (as the asterisk on Y'' in the phrase-structure expansion rule above indicates). I also allow any projection of X to have a coordinated identical projection of X. I leave open the possibility that the categories of I (for Inflection) and C (for Complementizer) can take sisters (such as modifiers) at the phrasal levels, in contrast to the categories N, V, A, and P (and see ch. 2, secs. 5 and 7, ch. 5, sec. 5, and ch. 6, sec. 3).

This is not the X-bar theory that many recent works in linguistics assume. However, it is the X-bar theory offered in Chomsky 1981 and revised in Chomsky 1986a (with the exception of my leaving open the question of whether phrasal projections of I and C can take sister modifiers). I assume the stance that this restrictive version of X-bar theory is the one we should adopt unless we are forced to abandon it in favor of a more powerful version on the grounds of empirical inadequacy. At various points in this book, whether or not an element is a syntactic sister to another element will be important. At those points I argue for the structure on independent syntactic grounds. Never is my adopted version of X-bar theory the only basis for a syntactic analysis. We will see that for an adequate analysis of the data handled in this book no appeal to a less restrictive version of X-bar theory is necessary.

I suggest that this restrictive version of X-bar theory is, in fact, the only justifiable version. Much of the argumentation for more elaborate versions, with (non-conjunct and non-specifier) sisters to X′ and even sisters to X″, where X is any category, is based on semantic factors. And even works that strive to simplify and restrict X-bar theory appeal to semantic considerations in determining constituency. For example, Stuurman (1985), who gives a comprehensive history of the expansion and retrenchment phases in the development of X-bar theory, uses the interpretation of the pronoun "one" as a test for constituency, thus allowing X′ to be recursive. The result is that, except for the specifier system (which I believe Stuurman truly improves upon), the internal branching Stuurman assigns to most phrases is as hierarchically complex as that of many others (such as the classic work of Jackendoff 1977). Others claim that whether an item is an argument or a modifier of a lexical head is relevant to which node that item is a sister to (see the discussion and references in Speas 1986). And some go so far as to say that different kinds of modifiers (different by semantic criteria) can have different syntactic relations to the items they modify.

I object strenuously to the use of semantic criteria (such as those mentioned above) for syntactic constituency. In particular, just because an element is semantically peripheral or circumstantial is not a reason to posit that it is a nonsister to the head, nor to claim that there are sisters to both the X' and X" levels (and see van Gestel 1986 and Spooren 1981 for arguments that Dutch restrictive and non-restrictive relative clauses have identical structure; see also Jackendoff 1987b, who argues that the distinction between arguments and adjuncts is not structural in syntax or semantics, but rather "a distinction in what kind of correspondence rule achieves the match between the two" (p. 74); and see the evidence in chapter 3 of this book that modifiers of N in Italian are sisters to the N, based on the fact that they can (and sometimes must) come linearly between the N and arguments of the N). Furthermore, the interpretation of pro-forms (such as "one") has never convincingly been shown to be related to syntactic constituency.

One of the conclusions reached repeatedly in this book is that semantic systems are not isomorphic to syntactic systems. Hence arguments for syntactic structure must be based solely on syntactic data. With such a guideline, I hope to have avoided the pitfall of proposing more and more elaborate syntactic structures without looking for genuinely explanatory accounts, the pitfall that the earlier work of Stuurman (1983) warns against.

One may well ask why, given that I will lead us into a nonconfigurational theory of predication, I have chosen to frame the present work in GB, a theory founded on the configurational notion of government. My answer is that by working within GB, a theory in which configurational solutions are available, I hope to show that it is the nature of predication itself, not the particular theory one works within, that forces us to adopt a nonconfigurational approach. It would be a simple matter (with unsurprising results) to offer a nonconfigurational theory of predication within a nonconfigurational theory. It is quite a different matter (and one with surprising results) to offer a nonconfigurational theory of predication within GB. But I maintain that such an approach is not only possible, but empirically necessary.

Much of the work here flies in the face of a great deal of recent linguistic literature. But, although I will be offering arguments against many such works and although I will not even be discussing others, my debt to these works is enormous. They include Farmer (1984), who forced even people outside lexical semantics to look at argument structure; Bresnan (1982a), who made obvious the hopelessness of configurational approaches to predication; Marantz (1984), who placed the problem correctly in the middle of theta theory; Gruber (1965) and Jackendoff (1972), who did the ground work that allowed Marantz, Farmer, and others to explore thematic relations; Rothstein (1983), who let us see the potential of a system that distinguished between primary and secondary predication; Chomsky, in all his work, who laid the groundwork without which none of these issues would have become clear so quickly and whose infectious enthusiasm has spurred the inquiry of others; and, especially, Williams (1980 and after), who made everyone (including, finally, Chomsky (1986b)) admit that a predication relationship did not entail a clause structure and who gave us a model for an explicit theory of predication.

While I expect this entire book to be controversial, I offer it in the spirit of scientific inquiry. That is, what would happen if we were to take an approach to predication that lets theta-role assignment be the key to the subject–predicate relationship and that recognizes barriers (in the sense of Chomsky 1986a) as boundaries that predication coindexing is sensitive to? This book is an exploration of the answer to that question. And, not surprisingly, it raises more questions than it answers. My hope is that the recognition of the questions before us will contribute to an eventual understanding of predication.

The data are taken from Italian and English and the conclusions are meant to hold for all configurational languages. And, finally, since the notion of argument ladder should have its counterpart in nonconfigurational languages, at least Principle I of indexing theory (given in example (6–200)) should hold for all languages.

1 *Predicates and theta-role assignment*

In this chapter I offer a definition of predicate and a theory of theta-role assignment, and I distinguish arguments of a lexical item from role players of a predicate. What follows is an aformal discussion that will lay the necessary foundation for chapter 2 and the rest of this book. It will be easy for the reader to find formal approaches to these issues in the linguistic literature. The reason for an aformal discussion will become apparent as the relevant issues are examined.

This chapter will establish three major points:

(A) Predicates are semantic entities that need not have any particular syntactic characteristics;

(B) The relationship of a predicate to its role players is distinct from, although highly coincidental with, theta role assignment from a lexical item to its arguments. I modify a term from Marantz (1984) and say that predicates assign Semantic Roles to their role players. The schema I will defend is the following:

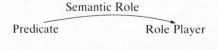

Semantic Role

Predicate   Role Player

Theta Role

Lexical Item   Argument

where the arrow represents the direction of assignment of the Semantic Role or Theta Role;

(C) Typically the lexical heads N (noun), A (adjective), and V (verb) head a predicate, although there are uses in which P (preposition) may also head a predicate.

1 An event-structure approach to predicates

A clause typically corresponds to the semantic notion of proposition, in which we have some state or action expressed and a group (which may consist of one or more) of participants or role players in that state or action. (For a discussion of what a STATE word and an ACTION word are, see Jackendoff 1983.) I lump together states and actions under the term "event". In (1–1), for example, the event is the action of lending and the role players are a lender, an object lent, and someone who has received the object lent.

(1–1)   Jean **lent** Mary books.

In this book I analyze a sentence such as (1–1) as containing the predicate *lent* (marked in boldface in (1–1)) and the three role players for that predicate: *Jean*, *Mary*, and *books* (and see Halliday 1970 and Matthews 1981, among many others, for a similar event structure analysis of propositional structure). Immediately, then, we can see a first formulation of an informal definition of predicate: an event word which takes one or more role players, where the term "event" covers both states and actions. (In sec. 1.5 below I discuss the necessity for at least one role player per predicate.)

Certainly there are other ways to analyze (1–1), still thinking of it in terms of an event and role players. For example, we could view the event as being one of lending books. With that idea in mind, the predicate would be the discontinuous string *lent . . . books* and there would be only two role players: *Jean* and *Mary*. (That predicates can be discontinuous strings is shown below in sec. 1.2.) We could as easily view the event as being one of Jean lending to Mary, in which case the predicate would be the string *Jean lent Mary* and the role player would be *books*. Or we could view *lent Mary* as an event and see *Jean* and *books* as the role players. And so on. That is, we could view *lent* alone or in combination with any one or more nominal in (1–1) as a predicate, so long as there is at least one role player.

So far as I can see, there is no *a priori* basis upon which to choose between these possibilities. (We will see ample evidence against the claim that a predicate must be a maximal projection below in secs. 2.5 and 2.6 and in ch. 2, secs. 3 and 4.) Thus we must look to how language treats the syntactic entities that participate in the make-up of a semantic proposition when determining which entities correspond to a predicate and which entities correspond to role players. That is, we must base our analysis on the syntactic and semantic behavior of these entities.

In this chapter I argue that an event lexical item is the "head" (as I will define the term below) of a predicate and that the event lexical item assigns a thematic (theta) role to the role players. Theta assignment will be seen to treat all role players equally (see, in particular, sec. 2.5, where I argue against the claim that VP assigns a theta role to the item in syntactic subject position). It is primarily upon the basis of theta-role assignment behavior that I have decided to analyze a sentence like (1–1) as having only *lent* be the predicate, with all the nominals being role players (but we will see in sec. 3 below that items other than nominals may be role players).

There is at least one instance, however, in which I believe it makes sense (from an empirical point of view – since, as I said above, from a theoretical point of view a wide range of analyses of (1–1) can be argued to be valid) to analyze strings like *Jean lent Mary* or *Jean lent . . . book* or *lent Mary books* as a predicate. And that is when there is a variable present in the clause in the "missing" role-player slot. The item that binds that variable could be considered the single role player, and the clause with the variable could be considered a predicate clause. I will call such clauses "open," and I will return to a brief discussion of them in section 2.6 below and in chapter 5, section 5.

We will here proceed, then (laying aside until later the discussion of open-clause predicates), with this very simple first formulation of the notion of predicate as an event word which takes one or more role players. With this formulation we can rule out closed clauses (clauses without variables) from the class of potential predicates: closed clauses are not just events, but events plus all their role players. Thus closed clauses correspond to propositions. With this formulation we can also rule out anything but the phrasal level as a level for role players that are nominal (but we will see in sec. 1.4 below and in ch. 2, sec. 14 that we may have to allow nonphrasal role players that are non-nominal). This is because if a role player is referential, the entire reference (not just the sense) of an item tells us who or what the role player is. But N″ is the referential level. For example, in an N″ like *the dangerous dog*, the head N tells us only the sense of the nominal, but all the elements (*the, dangerous,* and *dog*) contribute to helping us pick out the referent. Thus N″ is the referential level of nominals. Therefore N″ can be a role player, but N or N′ cannot.

In (1–1) the boldface predicate is an action; in (1–2) it is a state.

(1–2)   The man who marries young is **happy**.

In (1–2) *happy* alone, not *is happy*, is the predicate. I follow Emonds (1985) in calling the copula here a grammatical word. *Is* is present in (1–2) purely to satisfy needs of the syntax and does not contribute to the semantic interpretation of the sentence in the same way semantically full lexical items do. (One of the functions of *is* in (1–2) is to carry the tense of the sentence, for example.) Notice that the same semantic relationship of predication holds between *the man who marries young* and *happy* in (1–3), without any copula, as in (1–2) above, with the copula. (Examples of the first type in (1–3) were pointed out to me in this regard by Andrew Radford (personal communication).)

(1–3)   **Happy** the man who marries young!
I consider **happy** the man who marries young.

The fact that the predication between *the man who marries young* and *happy* in (1–2) and (1–3) is the same is evidence that the copula in (1–2) is not part of the predicate, but a grammatical word only.

Predicates, whether of the action or state type, can take as few as one role player, as in (1–2) above for states and (1–4) below for actions:

(1–4)   Jean **ran**.

And predicates can take more than one role player, as in (1–1) above for actions and (1–5) below for states:

(1–5)   Jean is **talented** at the piano.

In (1–5) the role players are *Jean* and *the piano*. The predicate is *talented*, which lexically selects the preposition *at* to introduce one of its role players (see sec. 2.1 below for discussion).

The preceding first glance at predicates is quite distinct from most linguistic definitions today, in which typically the subject role player is singled out and the rest of the material is the predicate. I will argue in section 2.6 below against any analysis of predication in terms of VP (verb phrase) versus the syntactic subject. But the argumentation will depend upon an understanding of lexical argument structure; thus it must be postponed until after the relevant discussion. I will return to this issue from another perspective in chapter 2, section 3.

One immediate advantage of the event-structure definition of predicate developed in this chapter is that such a definition can carry over to languages which lack a VP (the so-called nonconfigurational languages, such as Tagalog – as argued in Miller (1988)).

1.1   Modifiers and specifiers as part of the predicate

The sentences used to exemplify predications above, with the exception of that in (1–3), consist of a single clause with predicates that consist of a single word, all the remaining words of the sentence being phrases that function as role players in the event. The sentences of natural language, however, do not always lend themselves to such a neat analysis.

(1–6)   Jean **almost lent** Mary books.

(1–7)   Jean **lent** Mary books **frequently**.

In (1–6) and (1–7) the words *almost* and *frequently* call for analysis. They are not role players in any event. We might, then, ask if they are themselves events, i.e. predicates. That is, are (1–6) and (1–7) best analyzed as representations of a proposition in which there is a predicate roughly paraphrased as "almost happened" and "frequently happened" with a propositional role player roughly paraphrased as "Jean lent Mary books"?

Certainly scholars have argued that adverbials are predicates (see Davidson 1975, Rothstein 1983, Abney 1986, among others), where I use the term "adverbial" to cover the functional notion of modifier of a non-nominal. Thus the analysis of adverbials as predicates is not a strawman, and such an analysis has significant effects on the semantic representation of sentences. For example, (1–8) would be analyzed as having three predicates (each in boldface here):

(1–8)   Jean **almost lent** Mary books **frequently**.

And the different readings of whether it was a frequent occurrence that Jean almost lent Mary books or (the more bizarre reading) that it was almost the case that Jean frequently lent Mary books could be represented by having either *frequently* or *almost* as the highest (i.e., least embedded) predicate. That is, at LF (Logical Form) the arrangement of predicates would encode scope relations.

An analysis with adverbials as predicates, however, would meet resistance in a theory that requires role players to be phrasal. For example, in (1–6) the putative predicate *almost* would take a single role player (the whole sentence minus *almost*) that does not form even a constituent, much less a phrasal level of one. Most theories of predication that I know of require role players to be phrasal – thus one might balk at giving up this requirement on role players easily. Still, the requirement that role players be phrasal is as stipulative as any other claim about role players, at least so far as non-nominal role players are concerned. (Recall that it was argued above that nominal role players must be N″, since N″ is the referential projection.) And we will see in various places in this book (including ch. 2, sec. 14) that non-nominal role players may well not be phrasal. We must therefore consider this objection in that light. And if this were the only objection to a predicate analysis of adverbials, and if such an analysis seemed otherwise to be the most nearly adequate one, I would be led to propose that these adverbials offer one more piece of evidence against the requirement that all role players be phrasal. However, this is not, in my opinion, the most nearly adequate analysis of adverbials.

There are alternative analyses of (1–6) and (1–7) that lead to simpler semantic representations of sentences like (1–8). One is the analysis linguists traditionally have given such sentences, in which *almost* and *frequently* are taken to modify other parts of the sentence rather than to predicate of them. This analysis, of course, assumes a distinction between "modification" and "predication," a distinction that I return to and defend in section 1.4 below. With this kind of analysis the varying interpretations of (1–8) would be handled as scope phenomena.

An alternative midway between the two above is to call an adverb like *frequently* a predicate but an adverb like *almost* a modifier (where the term "adverb" is a category label, although these adverbs are adverbial in function, as well). The relevant distinction here would be that (1–6) does not entail (1–1), but (1–7) does. (See Davidson 1970, Clark 1970, Thomson 1977 for a discussion of the entailment of sentences like (1–1) from sentences like (1–7).)

None of these analyses seems quite right to me, although the last one discussed above seems less obviously incorrect than the others. Consider *almost* in (1–6). Rather than being an event in itself in any obvious way, it acts as a degree word, telling us that some independent event (independent of the concept of "almost") did not occur but came very close to occurring. As a degree word it is similar in function to the italicized words in:

(1–9)   Sally is *very* tall.

(1–10)   Sally is *so* smart.

(1–11)   That is *quite* a possibility.

(1–12)   She's *a little bit* nice.

And like these degree words, *almost* modulates an event by placing it somewhere on the scale from negative to positive with respect to the occurrence or extent of the event; *almost* is an intrinsic part of which event actually occurs. I therefore analyze the predicate in (1–6) as consisting of the two words (which do not form a syntactic constituent) *almost lent*. In other words, I take *almost* to be a modifier which combines with an event word to form a new event, and, thus, a new predicate.

Let me point out that if I were to accept *almost* as a predicate, I can see no clear reason for not also analyzing the italicized words in (1–9) through (1–12) as predicates. But then the notion of predicate would get ever more distant from the event structure notion I develop in this section (in which predicate is an event word or words that takes at least one role player). Thus, while a more abstract approach to the concept of predicate might well allow an analysis of *almost* as a predicate, I will here stick to a limited sense of predicate that excludes degree words from qualifying for predicate status.

Given that I am analyzing some adverbials (the degree adverbials) as parts of predicates, I will generalize and analyze all adverbials that are not themselves role players (and see McConnell-Ginet 1980, who argues that some manner adverbials are role players (in our terms) with certain predicates, as well as secs. 1.6, 2.4, and 3 below) as parts of predicates. That is, my predication theory will not distinguish between types of adverbials unless such distinctions are required for explanatory or theoretical adequacy. And, so far as I can see, such distinctions are not required. Therefore, even adverbials such as *frequently* in (1–7) will be analyzed here as parts of predicates. In sum, modifiers of an event word are parts of the predicate that the event word is part of.

Let me point out that my adopted position that manner adverbials like *frequently* are part of the predicate, rather than predicates themselves, is not a strong one. It is quite possible that adverbials do, in fact, split into two groups, where some form part of the predicate and others are separate predicates which predicate of the predicate (or, perhaps, of the entire proposition minus the adverbial). That is, I recognize that *frequently* might best be analyzed as an event unto itself. In fact, as I point out below with respect to (1–34), there are uses in which even degree adverbs seem much more open to an analysis as predicates than *almost* does in (1–6). Still, throughout this study I will continue to analyze adverbials that are not role players as part of the predicate they co-occur with for ease of exposition. The theory to be developed here, however, does not hang on this choice of analysis. In fact, no claim in this book is based solely on the analysis of adverbials as parts of predicates. Thus, if one were to analyze adverbials as predicates themselves, the theory of predication given in this work would hold unchanged.

Like adverbial modifiers, I contend, are the auxiliaries. That is, the auxiliaries, by giving the information of aspect, modality, and voice, are an intrinsic part of the event and should be analyzed as part of the predicate (and see Napoli 1981 for a discussion of the semantic contribution of an auxiliary to the predicate).

One important result of the analysis of adverbial modifiers and auxiliaries as part of the predicate is that we will not be able to recognize predicates in the lexicon. (But, as mentioned above, this result will follow also from other data. These data are given in secs. 1.2 and 2.4 below.) Instead, we need to see which words go together in a sentence before we can pick out the predicate. This fact means that we must make a distinction between lexical items and predicates and between the semantic relationship between a lexical item and its arguments as opposed to the semantic relationship between a predicate and its role players. We will turn to this distinction in section 1.6 below.

At this point, we can alter our working definition of predicate to be an event word plus or minus modifiers and auxiliaries, taking one or more role players.

Finally, up to this point in this subsection the predicates whose auxiliaries and modifiers we have discussed have been verbs. We will see repeatedly in this chapter (particularly in sec. 2 below) that we can have predicates that do not contain verbs (and we already have seen an example of one in (1–3) above). I propose to generalize the findings of this subsection to all categories that can be predicates. Thus not only auxiliaries, which are specifiers of V', but specifiers of any category can be part of a predicate (though they need not be – as in the case where a specifier of N' is a role player of a predicative N – see sec. 2.3 below). And not only adverbials (which I have defined as modifiers of non-nominals), but modifiers of any category can be part of a predicate. In the examples below, the predicates are in bold face.

(1–13) I am **very fond** of Sue.

(1–14)   She is **a terrific scholar** of Dante.

(1–15)   She's **absolutely into** Greek art.

In section 1.6 I argue that all role players of a predicate are arguments of a theta assigner that is (part of) the predicate. The theta assigner turns out to be the event lexical item of the predicate. For the moment let us assume this. We can now define the concept "head of a predicate," which will be useful to us in later discussion:

(1–16)   *Head of a predicate*: The lexical item which assigns a theta role to the role players of a predicate containing that lexical item is the head of that predicate.

To see what this definition means, consider:

(1–17)   Jean **lent** Mary the books **in great haste**.

In (1–17) the predicate consists of the discontinuous string *lent . . . in great haste* (that is, an event word plus an adverbial). There are two lexical heads which are parts of this predicate: *lent* and *haste*. But of them only *lent* assigns a theta role to the role players of the predicate, so *lent* is the head of the predicate.

In (1–16) "containing" is not to be read as properly containing. Thus the word *lent* in (1–1), for example, is a part of the predicate and is, in fact, the entire predicate. Here *lent* heads the predicate that it is (part of).

1.2   Nonconstituent predicates

In (1–6) the continuous string *almost lent* is a predicate, although it does not form a syntactic constituent. Thus analyzing modifiers and specifiers as part of the predicate requires that I admit predicates which do not form syntactic constituents. We would hope that other factors besides the analysis of modifiers and specifiers would lead us to the conclusion that predicates do not have to form syntactic constituents, for, if not, our analysis of modifiers and specifiers as potentially being part of the predicate could be seen as too expensive to the grammar.

In fact, there is strong evidence independent of the analysis of modifiers and specifiers that predicates need not form syntactic constituents. Consider predicates consisting of fixed or idiomatic sayings. Such sayings need not form syntactic constituents, as in:

(1–18)   Mary **took** the students **to task**.
         Mary **took** the students **on an outing**.

Both *took . . . to task* and *took . . . on an outing* are predicates and neither forms syntactic constituents or even continuous strings (and see Emonds 1976 and Larson 1987 for more such examples). There are many such idiomatic predicates, a great number of which involve a verb plus a preposition, as in *look after* in the sense of "take care of." The approach to predication developed here can analyze these strings as predicates without calling for any kind of syntactic restructuring of a V plus a P into a new constituent (compare Hornstein and Weinberg 1981, for example, and see the refutation of this kind of syntactic restructuring in ch. 2, sec. 3).

Of course, a predicate certainly can be a syntactic constituent, as with an idiomatic P(repositional) P(hrase) (hereafter PP) and V(erb) P(hrase) (hereafter VP):

(1–19)a. Bill is **out of his mind**.
     b. Bill **lost his cool**.

Here the entire PP *out of his mind* and the entire VP *lost his cool* are the predicates. (And see Maling (1982) for discussion of idiomatic PPs).

Example (1–19) can be used to point out another important fact: not all predicates need have a head that is a single word, in the sense of (1–16) above. In (1–19)a, for example, both *out* and *mind* are lexical heads that are part of the predicate, but neither of them is an event word in this usage, thus neither of them is a theta assigner here. This predicate, then, is a phrasal lexical item. I will argue in section 1.6 that the whole phrase is a theta assigner. Therefore the whole phrase is the head of the predicate (as well as filling the entire predicate).

At this point one of the most important results of this chapter is apparent: predicates are semantic primitives which are not definable either as lexical units (and see sec. 1.1 above) or as syntactic units. Thus the concept of predicate, which is best defined by considering the semantic concepts of events and role players, must be admitted into the grammar of natural language.

1.3 Predication versus unanalyzable idioms, identification, and nonpredicative verbs

So far we have examined single-clause sentences in which it is clear that a single event occurs and that event has at least one role player. Here I ask the question of whether every clause must have a predicate.

The answer is clearly no. Several types of clauses do not involve predication. The sentences in (1–20), for example, cannot be analyzed as consisting of an event plus role players in that event.

(1–20)   Mum's the word.
          The jig's up.

These are semantically unanalyzable idioms (in the sense of Napoli 1987a), and the entire clause forms a single semantic unit that cannot be broken down into semantic subparts (although, of course, these sentences are syntactically analyzable).

In fact, it has been claimed in the literature that many types of clauses do not involve predicates in the sense I am developing here, such as sentences expressing weather and time. That is, some claim that these expressions involve actions or states, but fail to have role players. In Napoli 1987a I argue that weather and time expressions in English (although this is not so in many other languages) are, after all, examples of predication structures, and do, in fact, involve role players. For example, weather *it* can control PRO, as in *It got cold enough [PRO to snow]*, where event control (as in Lasnik 1984 and Williams 1985) is not possible: the event of getting cold does not snow. Thus if only arguments can control PRO (as in Chomsky 1981), then weather *it* is an argument and "weather words" are predicates. (See Napoli 1987a for further arguments for the thematic status of weather and time *it*.)

There are other kinds of clauses which have been argued not to involve predication, such as purely identificational sentences of the type seen in (1–21). (See Williams 1983b, among others, where the linguistic tradition is quite distinct from that found in the more philosophical literature.)

(1–21)   My aunt is Miss Prothero.

Actually, the determination of whether a sentence like (1–21) is an identificational sentence or a predicational sentence is highly dependent upon context. With a sentence of the form NP_1–copula–NP_2 (where NP = Noun Phrase) the likelihood of NP_2's being understood as a predicate correlates inversely with the likelihood of NP_2's being understood as a totally referential NP. Thus if we are offering two different names for the same person, (1–21) is an equational or identificational sentence and has no predicate and no role player. In that situation, the sentence should be symmetrical. That is, if we reversed the order of the NPs, we still would be giving the same information. But in another context NP_2 could be understood to be assigning a semantic role to NP_1; it can be telling us that NP_1 has the property described by NP_2. Such a context is found in:

(1–22)   We all know that a woman named Miss Prothero asked the firemen if they wanted anything to read. But what you haven't figured out yet is that my own aunt, our dear friend, is Miss Prothero.

Here *Miss Prothero* is a predicate taking *my own aunt* as its role player.

While English does not morphologically signal the difference in semantic function between the NP *Miss Prothero* in (1–21) and in (1–22), other languages may. John Myhill (personal communication) has pointed out to me that (1–21) would be rendered differently from (1–22) in Indonesian, where the predicative status of the relevant NP in (1–22) would be clearly marked. The linguist studying predication in English is nowhere near so lucky, however, and must rely primarily on context for recognizing instances of predication in copular sentences.

Still, there are other clues that help us distinguish between predication and identification. As Rothstein (1983, p. 104) points out, in general the more evaluative material there is in the NP to the right of the copula, the more likely we are to interpret that NP as predicative. (See also Strawson 1950, Wiggins 1970, Donnellan 1966, Geach 1950, 1968, Halliday 1967a and b, Fodor 1970, Hawkins 1978, Higgins 1979, Williams 1980, Woisetschlaeger 1983, and Safir 1985 (pp. 169–70) for a discussion of definite NPs as predicates.) Many have noted that superlative NPs can be predicates, whereas usually a definite specifier closes an NP so that it cannot be a predicate – see Higginbotham 1985. (For other ways in which superlatives behave like indefinite NPs, see Rando and Napoli 1978 and the references given there.)

Higgins (1979) offers tests for predicate nominals, such as whether or not they can be questioned with *what* (the operator binding a predicate NP position) rather than *who* (the operator binding a referential [+human] NP position). (See also Williams 1983b, who makes use of this question test.) By that test the NP to the right of the copula in (1–21) is not a predicate. Thus (1–21) is not an appropriate response to (1–23):

(1–23)   What is your aunt?

But the NP to the right of the copula in (1–24) is a predicate, as we can see by the fact that (1–24) can be an appropriate response to (1–23).

(1–24)   My aunt is a doctor.

Nominals that function as identifications also have a distinct distribution from nominal predicates, as noted by Stuurman (1985, p. 242) and Napoli (1987a). (But see Jackendoff 1983, who argues that identification and predication are essentially the same in conceptual structure – and see my remarks on coindexing in identificational sentences in ch. 2, sec. 2, as well as the NPs analyzed in ch. 5, sec. 1.)

Still another candidate for a clause that does not contain a predicate is a clause with the main verbs *seem, happen, begin, continue,* and other so-called aspectual verbs (see Newmeyer 1975, and Napoli and Rando 1979, ch. 1), as in:

(1–25)   It happens now and then that cats can't meow.

(1–26)   Jack began [t to cry].

When these verbs take an infinitival complement, I analyze them in the standard GB way as involving NP movement. The "t" in (1–26), then, is the trace of the moved NP *Jack.* The question is whether these verbs head predicates.

Given the semantic definition of predicate developed thus far, we are led to conclude that these verbs are not predicates. Instead, like *almost* (see sec. 1.1 above) and the auxiliaries, these verbs give information in such a way that they are intrinsic parts of some event but do not denote events in themselves. Thus *happens* in (1–25) forms a predicate with the discontinuous string *now and then . . . can't meow.* And *began* in (1–26) forms a predicate with *to cry.* Likewise, the modal verbs and aspectual verbs of Italian (which are main verbs syntactically; see Napoli 1974b) would not be predicates in themselves, but parts of predicates (as in Napoli 1981, who draws syntactic as well as semantic parallels between these verbs and the auxiliaries *avere* ('have') and *essere* ('be') in Italian).

One might object to this analysis on two different grounds. First, these verbs can impose semantic restrictions on their clausal sisters, as we can see by the conflict in time frames in (1–27):

(1–27)   *The water continued [t to spill in an instant].

A clausal complement of *continue* must be a durative proposition. If only predicates could impose semantic restrictions on other items they co-occur with, then (1–27) could be taken as evidence that *continue* is a predicate.

My response has two parts. For one thing, I know of no arguments that only predicates can impose semantic restrictions on the items they co-occur with. In fact, I will argue in section 2.4 that role players can select each other for pragmatic and semantic appropriateness (see the discussion of (1–85)); thus items other than predicates can impose semantic restrictions on their linguistic companions.

For another thing, if *continue* is part of the predicate in (1–27) we have an immediate explanation for the failure of (1–27): the predicate *continue . . . to spill in an instant* is self-contradictory (containing both a durative and a point-time requirement) and, thus, anomalous. Therefore, the analysis with *continue* as part of the predicate accounts for the failure of (1–27) in at least as adequate a way as an analysis with *continue* as a predicate.

The other major objection that one might bring against my claim that all these verbs are not predicates themselves is based on the behavior of *seem*. *Seem* can take a referential nominal in a *to* phrase in addition to a clause, similarly to predicates such as *ridiculous*:

(1–28)   Jack seems to me [t to understand French pretty well].
    That he would even think of firing you is ridiculous to me.

One might claim that the NP in the *to* phrase is a role player of *seem* in the first sentence of (1–28). However, the referent of this NP is not a participant in any event of seeming alone. Instead, the entire event of seeming to understand is viewed from the perspective of the referent of this NP. That is, the judgment that Jack has the property of seeming to understand is anchored on this NP. Thus this NP is attracted into the sphere of role players of the entire predicate. (I will return to a discussion of what this means for the Projection Principle in sec. 4 below.)

I maintain, then, that *seem, appear, happen,* and the aspectual verbs are all parts of predicates but not predicates themselves. This analysis of *seem* is counter to that of most linguists, who claim *seem* is a predicate (a notable exception being Rothstein (1983), who analyzes *seem* as a copula and not as either a predicate or part of a predicate).

I conclude that not every clause need contain a predicate, unanalyzable idioms, identificational clauses, and clauses with verbs such as *seem* and *continue* supplying clear cases of clauses without predicates.

1.4   Multiple predication in a single clause
In all the examples we have seen thus far, the predicate we have singled out has been the only predicate in the sentence and the sentence has consisted of only one clause. It is a highly debated matter as to whether it is possible to have more than one predicate in a single clause. In chapter 2, section 1 I lay out some of the theoretical consequences of allowing

multiple predicates in a single clause, and I compare Chomsky 1981 to Williams 1980, among others. In this book, however, I will not debate this issue. In Napoli 1987a I come down firmly on the side of Williams: there may be multiple predicates in a single clause. And let me point out that even Chomsky (1986b) has abandoned his original position. I therefore here merely assume that there may be multiple predicates in a single clause.

Along with this assumption goes the desire to adhere strictly to the principle that only syntactic data are valid evidence for syntactic structure. (See also the introduction to this book.) Thus the fact that we have the sense of a proposition does not in any way offer evidence that we have the syntactic structure of a clause. The sentence in (1–29), then, is analyzed as consisting of only a single clause, but has two predicates: *painted* and *red*. (That is, I reject a small clause analysis of such sentences; see Williams 1983a.)

(1–29)   We **painted** the barn **red**.

An interesting question arises here: whether there is a distinction to be made between predication and modification. Certainly (1–29) above contrasts with (1–30) below, in which *red* is typically called a modifier of the head N *barn*.

(1–30)   We painted the red barn.

In (1–29) we are painting the barn and the result is that it turns out red. Thus the barn is a role player (the only role player) with respect to the state described by *red*. In other words, *red* predicates of *the barn*. However, in (1–30) (to be read without contrastive stress on *red*) we are picking out a particular barn by calling it red. Yet after painting it might be another color, as in:

(1–31)   We painted the red barn blue for a change.

And before painting it might not have been red, but perhaps we painted it red so it now is. We can even read (1–30) with *the red barn* as the name of the barn (in which case, perhaps we should capitalize: The Red Barn), to indicate the barn that used to be red or that for some reason or other we refer to as "the red barn." But even if the barn is a red barn before we begin and even if we wind up repainting the barn red again, the *red* in (1–30) does not tell us that the barn was painted red. Instead, the red in (1–30) assigns the property to the barn of being that barn that we call red, regardless of our reason for calling it red. We are not asserting in (1–30) that the barn has the property of redness, unlike in (1–29).

In both (1–29) and (1–30) *red* assigns a property to the barn, then, and thus is a theta assigner (and see sec. 4 below). The distinction is whether the redness is being asserted of or being used as a characterization of the barn. One might be led then to propose that in both uses *red* is a predicate, where modification would be a type of predication.

However, there are at least two related reasons for distinguishing the property assignment called modification above from the property assignment called predication. One is that if *red* in (1–30) were a predicate, then its role player would be *barn*, which is an N and not an NP, whereas nominal role players should be phrasal, as already has been argued at the opening of this chapter. That is, NP is the referring level. Thus it makes no sense to speak of an N as being a role player with the notion of role player and predicate that I am developing in this chapter.

Second, the modifier *red* in (1–30) falls within the maximal projection (that is, within the N″) of the N it modifies, so that it is an intrinsic part of defining the reference of the entire NP. In contrast, the reference of the NP predicated of by *red* in (1–29) is independent of the property of redness. This is a major distinction between modification and predication, and one the theory must recognize.

I therefore will treat modification as a separate phenomenon from predication. And I will account for the fact that *red* in (1–30) assigns a property to *barn* by saying that *red* here assigns (or discharges) a theta role to *barn* by way of Theta Identification (see Higginbotham 1985). (I return briefly to the issue of theta identification in sec. 4 below.)

In sum, while the difference between (1–29) and (1–30) is one of difference between what is asserted and what is not asserted, it is also a difference between what is predicated and what is not predicated. My argument that modification should not be identified with predication is in no way dependent upon the fact that redness is asserted of the barn in (1–29) but not in (1–30). In fact, as John Myhill (personal communication) has pointed out to me, if we put the stress peak of the sentence on *red* in (1–30), we can read redness as being asserted of the barn. Thus there is no definitive correlation between nonassertiveness and modification.

Still, the fact that *red* is asserted in (1–29) is worthy of note, since in general asserted information is significant new information, so it can be the focus of a clause and can be understood as a predicate. (See Myhill 1984 for an overview of notions such as assertion, focus, transitivity, semantic complexity, and foregrounding, as well as Chomsky 1972, Erteshik 1973 (who discusses the notion of communicative dynamism of

Firbás 1962), Hopper 1979, and Hopper and Thompson 1980, among others.) In fact, Myhill (1985) demonstrates that in many languages focussed or new information is grammatically marked, sometimes with what could be called the predicate marker. And in English some have argued that the intonation peak marks the focus (see Akmajian 1970, Chomsky 1972, and Higgins 1979, among others). For example, consider sentences such as those below, suggested to me by John Myhill (personal communication).

(1-32)   BILL left town.

(1-33)   Some IDIOT must have suggested that to you.

(The capitals indicate that the stress peak falls on this word.) We can analyze (1-32) with *Bill* as a predicate, assigning the property of being Bill to the one who left town. We can analyze (1-33) with *idiot* (perhaps plus the auxiliary *must*) as a predicate, assigning the property of (obligatory) idiocy to the one who suggested that to you. In fact, we might even allow degree words to be analyzed as predicates when they receive the stress peak (*contra* the discussion in sec. 1.1 above):

(1-34)   I know SOME Spanish.

Here *some* would be a predicate, assigning the property of smallness to the amount of Spanish I know. (And see Bolinger 1972 (pp. 75ff.) for a discussion of predicate degree nouns.)

Of course, if the indicated words above are, indeed, predicates, then we have evidence that non-nominal role players need not be phrasal. And from here on in this book I will assume that non-nominal role players need not be phrasal (see also ch. 6, sec. 7).

If the discussion immediately above of (1-32)–(1-34) is on the right track, we can see that approaches to predication based on syntactic restrictions between the locations of predicates and certain of their role players are hopelessly inadequate. One of my goals in this book is to show precisely that. And while I will be primarily concerned with less controversial instances of predication, the ones discussed here are telling and offer a serious challenge to syntactically based theories of predication.

Let me repeat that one of the most important consequences of my nonsyntactic definition of predicate is that we must allow a grammar in which semantic units do not have to be represented by syntactic units and syntactic units do not have to be mapped into semantic units. This is precisely the point defended on different grounds in Keenan and Faltz

1978. That is, there is no isomorphism between syntax and semantics. (See also Williams 1982.)

1.5 Role players are necessary

Many event words, particularly nominals, can be used without any explicit role players present, as in:

(1–35) I'm saddened by **destruction** of any kind.

Here *destruction* is an event word, and in other sentences it can take explicit role players:

(1–36) I'm saddened by the Venetians' **destruction** of their own city.

The question posed here is whether an event word must have a role player in order to be (the head of) a predicate.

Certainly our discussion of the notion of predicate thus far has repeated continually that a predicate takes one or more role players. And notice that both formal linguistic and philosophical approaches to predication take the stance that a predicate must be an open function which assigns a theta role to (or saturates) some role player (see Higginbotham 1985 and Davidson 1975, among others). Therefore, let us not abandon the idea that a predicate requires a role player unless we are forced to do so.

The problem now is how to analyze *destruction* in (1–35). If *destruction* indeed has no role players in (1–35), then it cannot be a predicate, and we must analyze it as a second nonpredicative use of an event lexical item (where modification is the first we have seen). While the concept of event lexical items having a variety of separate functions does not seem to me to be wrong in any *a priori* sense, it does seem wrong to analyze *destruction* in (1–35) drastically differently from *destruction* in (1–36), given the very strong semantic similarity between the two sentences. Fortunately, we may be able to analyze *destruction* as a predicate in both sentences. There is evidence that while *destruction* in (1–35) has no explicit role player, it does have an implicit one. That is, an implicit role player would be one that appears in the argument structure of an event lexical item in the lexicon, but is not realized as any syntactic entity (although it may be realized as a morpheme – see Roeper 1987). (The significance of implicit arguments for the Projection Principle will be discussed in sec. 4 below.) Thus in (1–37) the infinitival rationale clause requires an agentive controller (see Roeper 1987), which is the implicit role player of *destruction*.

(1–37)   The **destruction** of the city [PRO to prove a point] was deplorable.

One cannot argue that a PRO in specifier of NP is the controller here, since adverbial NPs also can fill this specifier:

(1–38)   Yesterday's **destruction** of the city [PRO to prove a point] was deplorable.

I conclude that an implicit agentive role player of *destruction* is present in (1–35) and it is this implicit role player that controls the PRO of the rationale clause in (1–37) and (1–38). (See Manzini 1983, Williams 1985, and Roeper 1987 for relevant discussion; see also Torrego 1986, who reports on an MIT talk in 1986 by Alessandra Giorgi and Giuseppe Longobardi, in which they give Italian sentences parallel to (1–37).)

Once more we have an instance of predication for which any syntactically based theory of predication is inadequate. The agentive role player of *destruction* in (1–35) not only does not stand in any specified syntactic location with respect to that predicate, it is not even a syntactic entity (although it is a thematic entity).

A similar case is that of impersonal passives (passives of intransitive verbs) in languages such as German, where there is evidence that an implicit agent is present (perhaps even in the passive morpheme on the verb, as proposed in Roeper 1987 for personal passives). The most common types of evidence involve adverbials or AdjP's that can appear in these impersonal passives and that can be licensed only by an agent (see also Hale and Keyser 1986 and 1987, Belletti 1986, and Safir 1987a).

There is at least one other type of serious challenge to the definition of predicate as requiring a role player, and that is nonreferential uses of NPs. For example, consider:

(1–39)   A career girl, which is something my fiancee doesn't happen to be, attracts me most.

(Example (1–39) is from Higgins 1979, p. 253.) Here the NP *a career girl* has a "genus" sense (see Givón 1978, p. 293) rather than a referential sense. Example (1–39) minus the relative clause could be roughly paraphrased as, "The type of female that attracts me most is a career girl." In other words, the semantic representation of a nonreferential NP like *a career girl* should be something like "someone who is a career girl" (or that x, such that CAREER GIRL(x)). With this kind of semantic representation, the nonreferential NP is a predicate and has a role player: that referent which the NP picks out by virtue of its being used predicatively. But now we are talking about nonlinguistic entities that have no linguistic counterparts, and if we were to require our theory of predication to handle the analysis of these NPs, we might have to develop a theory that goes beyond linguistics proper. (And see Chierchia 1985 for a discussion of a range of other difficult problems in this area.)

I will not use NPs like *a career girl* in (1–39) as examples of a predication in any of the rest of this book, since their analysis raises questions I am unable to answer (and some I am unable to even formulate). Let me just point out that no theory of predication that I will be arguing against in chapter 2 can deal any better with this use of an NP than mine.

I will, therefore, set this type of NP aside, and assume that it does not pose a threat to my claim that every predicate requires at least one role player, a claim common to all theories of predication so far as I know, as I said above.

I conclude that in all instances of predication a predicate must find at least one role player.

1.6 Semantic roles and thematic roles

It is a commonplace in the linguistic literature that some lexical items have "argument" structures and assign "thematic" or "theta" roles to their arguments. That is, linguists of various recent theories seem to agree that some lexical items involve the notion of event and call for a range of participants or role players (which are typically dubbed "arguments") in that event. (Exactly at what point in the grammar theta assignment takes place and exactly how argument structure is best represented are much discussed matters. See Stowell 1981, Williams 1984b, and Culicover and Wilkins 1986.) Actually, there is evidence that arguments of an event lexical item can be introduced when that event lexical item appears in a syntactic structure by way of nonlexical principles which allow adjuncts of a lexical head to be interpreted as arguments of that lexical head (see in particular Jackendoff 1987a and b). We will discuss such cases in secs. 2.4 and 4 below.

In this book I do not justify the existence of or investigate deeply the event structure of particular lexical items (although I do discuss nominals and prepositions in secs. 2.3 and 2.4 below in this regard). Much interesting work on this topic is found in Gruber (1965), Jackendoff (1972, 1983, and 1987b), Stowell (1981), Anderson (1983), Pustejovsky (1985), Beth Levin (1985), Croft (1986), Guerssel *et al.* (1986), Talmy (1986), Roeper (1987), and various works issuing from the Lexicon

Project at MIT (including Guerssel 1986, Hale and Keyser 1986 and 1987, Rappaport, Levin, and Laughren 1987), among others. What is essential to my present work is that some lexical items do have event structures, and those that do have arguments (the counterparts to role players for predicates).

Let me point out that in spite of the fact that for the most part event structure is dependent upon meaning, to some extent the particular event structure a lexical item may have is lexically idiosyncratic. That is, words which are close synonyms may have different event structures and subcategorization frames. *Try*, for example, need not take a theme argument, but *attempt* must (*She tries hard* vs.* *She attempts hard*).

Some have argued that all obligatorily subcategorized sisters to a lexical head at DS are arguments of that lexical head. (By "DS" I mean to indicate the first syntactic tree in the derivation.) McGonnell-Ginet (1982), in fact, proposes that all VP internal adverbs are arguments. On the other hand, Dowty (1980) has argued that all "oblique" terms (beneficiaries, locatives, instrumentals, etc.) are not arguments of V. In section 1.1 above I argued that some adverbials and specifiers are not role players of a predicate but, rather, parts of the predicate (although I pointed out that an analysis of certain adverbials as predicates themselves might be justifiable, and we will see in sec. 2.3 below that specifiers of NP can be arguments of the N). For much the same reasons as outlined there, I would argue that these same adverbials are not arguments of a lexical head (*contra* McConnell-Ginet). On the other hand, since beneficiaries of the type found in Indirect Object position are role players in an event, I would argue that they are arguments of a lexical head (*contra* Dowty). And I argue in section 2.4 below that certain instrumental and locative phrases are arguments of a lexical head (see also sec. 3 below). Therefore, at least some adverbials can be arguments with certain lexical items.

As I said above, the traditional approach is to say that lexical heads assign theta roles to their arguments. For example, Vs can take an agent argument and/or a theme argument and/or an experiencer argument and/or a beneficiary argument, etc. Exactly how many and which theta roles exist is something to be established by argumentation based on examination of the data from individual languages. The crucial point for us here and throughout this book is that theta roles exist – not which theta roles exist.

Lexical items which have argument structures, then, are potential heads of predicates. However, a predicate can consist of more than just a lexical item that is an event word (see secs. 1.1 and 1.2 above for predicates that consist of more than one word), and a predicate need not contain any isolable event word at all, but instead may be a phrasal event (as in the case of metaphorical or idiomatic PP and VP predicates, such as in (1–19) above). Still, regardless of a predicate's lexical and syntactic make-up, all predicates take role players and assign properties to those role players.

In this subsection I want to compare the concepts of assignment of a property to role players by a predicate and assignment of theta roles to arguments by lexical heads, for, certainly, there is much in common between the two.

Marantz (1984) uses the term "semantic role" to describe the role a lexical head assigns to its arguments and the role a VP assigns to its syntactic subject when the syntactic subject is an argument of the V. (In sec. 2.6 below I argue against VP as a theta assigner, *contra* Marantz and others.) He points out that semantic roles in his sense are numerous and idiosyncratic, varying according to the lexical item, whereas theta roles are simply features of the more varied semantic roles. Thus, for example, both *eat* and *assassinate* take an agentive argument, but they assign quite different semantic roles to that agentive argument. (The agent of *assassinate* acts maliciously, with aforethought, and with purpose (see Chomsky 1972). The agent of *eat* merely initiates the action, but may even do so unintentionally (as in the situation in which a two-year-old boy eats his chewing gum by accident).)

I here modify Marantz's term of semantic role and apply it to predication: I say that a predicate assigns a semantic role to its role players.

Notice first that the semantic roles a predicate assigns to its role players depend on the entire predicate and not just on the head of the predicate. (Recall that the head of the predicate is the theta assigner for the role players, as in (1–16) above, while the entire predicate includes certain specifiers and modifiers of the head as well.)

(1–40)   Jack **barely passed** the test.

(1–41)   Jack **almost passed** the test.

In (1–40), where the predicate is *barely passed*, Jack passed the test; in (1–41), where the predicate is *almost passed*, he did not. *Jack,* therefore, is assigned a different property by the different predicates (the property of barely passing in (1–40); the property of almost passing in (1–41)). Hence the presence of *barely* and *almost* affects the semantic role assigned to the role players of the predicates in these sentences.

On the other hand, in both (1–40) and (1–41) *Jack* is agentive. That is, the theta role of *Jack* is affected only by the lexical head that *Jack* is an argument of (which is the verb *passed* in both sentences), not by the full predicate that *Jack* is a role player of.

One might object to my claim that adverbials do not affect theta roles, by pointing out much-discussed pairs such as:

(1–42)   Sharon **broke** the window **accidentally (when she fell through it)**.

(1–43)   Sharon **broke** the window **on purpose**.

In (1–43) *Sharon* is agentive. But in (1–42) *Sharon* is not agentive (but perhaps experiencer or instrument, according to the situation). We consider the adverbials *accidentally* and *on purpose* when figuring out what theta role *Sharon* has in these sentences. However, this does not mean that the adverbials are DETERMINING or assigning the theta role. Instead, the sentence without any adverbials is vague with respect to the theta role of *Sharon*:

(1–44)   Sharon **broke** the window.

Broke is an appropriate word to use to describe a range of events, both intentional and unintentional, from the point of view of the person who initiates the action. Part of the lexical structure of this verb is the information that it can be used in such a range of events. We therefore must use context (sometimes linguistic context, sometimes pragmatic context) to figure out which theta role the relevant argument of the verb has in a given utterance (and see Hale and Keyser's 1986 discussion of "constructional" theta roles).

Many lexical heads have a fairly wide range of events that they can be used to describe and are thus vague out of context with respect to the theta role of some of their arguments. Other lexical heads are highly restrictive as to what kinds of events they can be used to describe. Thus *assassinate*, for example, must take an agentive argument in its active form; but *kill* need not (as in *The poison killed John*, where *the poison* is an instrumental, not an agent).

The above discussion points out a flaw in any theta theory that insists that a given lexical item has a fixed set of theta roles to assign to its arguments (and see Jackendoff 1987a for other problems with such a theory). However, the above discussion does not require us to make theta assignment be dependent on context. Instead, we can assume that theta-role assignment applies at DS without regard to context. Then at LF we will check theta-role assignment against context to test for appropriateness. In this way we will be adopting an evaluation procedure similar to that proposed in Farmer (1984) for Japanese particles.

I conclude that theta roles are determined by lexical items and not by predicates. If we consider headed predicates, this amounts to saying that theta roles are determined by the heads of predicates rather than by the full predicates. In this way theta roles contrast sharply with semantic roles, which are determined by predicates (including the head and all the other parts).

If we take a strict and narrow definition of theta role as that role assigned by a lexical head to its arguments, we will reach the conclusion that in a sentence like,

(1–45)   That comment is **off the wall**.

the NP *that comment* has no theta role since it is not an argument of any lexical head, although it does receive a semantic role from the PP predicate *off the wall*. I believe such an approach would miss the generalisation that metaphorical PPs like *off the wall* can take role players which appear to have the same kinds of theta roles that role players of nonphrasal predicates have. I therefore propose that individual words with event structures take arguments, and, furthermore, that any phrasal lexical item that has an event structure takes arguments. The PP *off the wall* is a phrase in the lexicon (that is, it appears in the lexicon as a single lexical item in its nonliteral sense) and it has an event structure. Thus it will take an argument and assign a theta role to that argument (probably the same theta role the adjective *crazy* assigns to its argument).

We can now see that there is a correlation between arguments of lexical items (including phrases as well as single words) and role players of predicates. I sum up this correlation in the following principle:

(1–46)   *Principle of Coincidence*: The arguments of a lexical item are the role players of the predicate headed by that lexical item.

In sum, lexical items – whether single words or phrases – that have event structures take arguments and assign theta roles to their arguments. If such lexical items are single words, they can be the heads of predicates. If such lexical items are strings of words but are not phrasal in the lexicon (such as *take . . . to task*), their syntactic head (that is, the X that heads the minimal XP that contains the entire lexical item – so in *take . . . to task* the syntactic head is the verb *take,* since the VP is the minimal XP that contains *take . . . to task*) can be the head of a predicate. If such lexical items are phrasal (such as *off her rocker*), they are headed predicates (since the whole phrase is the theta assigner). (Notice that all through here we are talking about the potential to head a predicate, since we have seen that event words need not head predicates in the sense developed here, as when they are used as modifiers.)

Theta roles are limited in number and are merely gross semantic features indicating the general nature of the participation of an argument in an event.

Predicates (consisting of a head and perhaps other parts), on the other hand, assign semantic roles to their role players. These semantic roles are unlimited in number and are finely detailed semantic properties, indicating the specific nature of the participation of a role player in the event.

We can sum up the findings of this section in the following chart:

LEXICAL STRUCTURE	PREDICATE STRUCTURE
lexical item = single word, strings of words, or phrase	*predicate* = an event lexical item (the head of the predicate) plus certain specifiers and modifiers of the head
Lexical items take arguments.	Predicates take role players. (All arguments of the head of the predicate are its role players.)
Arguments receive theta roles (which are a few gross semantic features like agent, patient, theme . . .).	Role players receive semantic roles (which are unlimited, detailed semantic properties).

2   Categories that can be predicates

A(djectives), V(erbs), and N(ouns) all can serve as the heads of predicates. I will demonstrate this fact below rather briefly, since much of the material to be covered is not controversial in any way. An exception is the very controversial question of whether N can take a role player in specifier position – to which I answer yes. From that, it follows that an N such as *destruction* can head a predicate.

In the discussion that follows I will call an item an "argument" or a "role player" interchangeably, since arguments of the heads of predicates are always role players of the predicate (see the Principle of Coincidence in (1–46) above). This does not mean that the distinction pointed out between the two in section 1.6 is no longer recognized, but only that that distinction is not relevant to the following discussion.

P(repositions) also can serve as the heads of predicates, but I will argue that in many instances P is not a predicate, but a relational word of a different sort from event lexical items. In particular, in most uses Ps are not the sole theta assigners of other items.

Finally, I will argue that all phrasal categories other than projections of C(omplementizer) can be predicates, but only if they are fixed or idiomatic phrases or if they are headed predicates which just happen to fill the entire maximal projection of the head of the predicate. I argue specifically against the proposal of many that VP (including DO (direct object) and IO (indirect object) arguments) rather than V plus adverbials and auxiliaries is a predicate. Regarding projections of C, I argue in section 2.6 that closed clauses cannot be predicates (where the only open clause is one that contains a variable).

2.1 The lexical head A(djective)

An adjective is always an event word. That is because adjectives denote states (whether stative or active). Accordingly, adjectives always discharge (or assign) theta roles and very often head predicates (see section 1.4 above, where I argue that modification is distinct from predication).

The role players for a predicate headed by A can appear inside the A(djective) P(hrase) or outside the AP. Examples of role players which are inside the AP are given in (1–47), where the relevant role player is italicized and the predicate is in boldface:

(1–47)a. Bill is [_{AP} **fond** of *Jan*].
     b. This fraction is [_{AP} **equal** to *.875*].
     c. Ken is [_{AP} **generous** to *the less talented of us*].

Notice that I have italicized NPs without italicizing the P that introduces each italicized NP in (1–47). In English A does not take NP sisters (see Maling 1982 for relevant discussion). Instead, NP arguments of the lexical head A which appear inside the AP are introduced by prepositions. Those prepositions are either the so-called null preposition *of* (and see M. Anderson 1979, Bouchard 1982, and Chomsky 1986b), as in

(1–47)a; or some preposition lexically chosen by the head A, like the *to* in (1–47)b (something must be "equal to" something else and never "equal at" or "equal on", etc.); or the typical preposition which introduces IOs, like the *to* in (1–47)c (which is also lexically chosen by the head to the extent of the choice between *to* and *for: a gift for NP*, but *a remark to NP; give NP to NP*, but *bake NP for NP*; etc.). (Notice that while a lexical head chooses *to* or *for* to introduce its beneficiary argument, this does not mean that these Ps are contentless. To the contrary, they carry distinct meaning; see Larson 1987.) Sometimes the head A allows a small range of Ps rather than just one. For example, *generous* can introduce a beneficiary argument either with the IO preposition *to* or with *toward* or *with* (as in *generous {toward/with} the less talented of us* but not **generous {of/on} the less talented of us*).

While the italicized arguments in (1–47) are not syntactic sisters to the head A, they appear in PP sisters to the head A, where the P is chosen by the head A (either lexically selected, or merely chosen by the category A – as in the case of the null preposition *of*). In a sense, then, they are "prepositional sisters" to the head A, and I will lump them together with real syntactic sisters, ignoring the configurational effect of the P introducing these arguments.

Of course, not all sisters to A are role players of the A. In (1–48) I have italicized sisters to A that are adverbial, here functioning to tell the extent or degree of the quality denoted by the A.

(1–48)   Debbie was upset *beyond belief.*
Joan is beautiful *to the extreme.*

In accordance with the discussion in section 1.1 above, I analyze these modifying phrases as parts of the predicate. Thus the predicates in (1–48) are *upset beyond belief* and *beautiful to the extreme.* When a PP sister to an A is part of the predicate rather than a phrase containing a role player of the predicate, we find that the P can range lexically, without being chosen by the head A (*upset beyond belief, upset to a small degree, upset in ridiculous ways*). Likewise in a phrase like *generous {for/around} the less talented of us* we do not have an argument of the head A, but, rather, an adverbial PP which is part of the whole predicate (in contrast to (1–47)c).

Another position inside AP where we might expect to find arguments of the lexical head A is specifier position. However, A does not allow arguments in specifier position. Thus if an NP occurs in specifier of A, it is a measure or degree phrase and should be analyzed as part of the predicate (see sec. 1.1 above). In (1–49) the italicized NPs are in specifier position to the A and form part of the predicate headed by that A.

(1–49)   Your remark was *several hours* too late to help.
Margene's *a little bit* happy now.

Every A takes precisely one argument outside the AP, whether the A heads a predicate or a modifier. (We will return to the significance of this fact in sec. 4 below.) Examples of role players which are outside the AP include NPs in GF subject position (such as *Bill, this fraction,* and *Ken* in (1–47) above), as well as NPs in other syntactic relationships to the AP (as discussed in ch. 2), such as the italicized NPs below (where the relevant predicate is in boldface). (By "GF" I mean "grammatical function" as defined in Chomsky 1981.)

(1–50)   I consider *Sally* [$_{AP}$ **fond** of Jan].
With *Sally* [$_{AP}$ **fond** of Jan], you might as well forget about a fair vote in the class treasurer election.

2.2   The lexical head V(erb)

V, unlike A, need not be an event word. We already saw in (1–2) above that the copula *be* can be used as a grammatical word and not as a part of a predicate (although, as we will see in (1–105) of sec. 2.6 below, the copula can head a predicate in some uses). And I argued in section 1.3 above that so-called aspectual verbs like *seem* and *continue* form parts of predicates but are not predicates themselves. Thus not all Vs head predicates. However, V usually heads a predicate.

V, like A, can take sister arguments, typically introduced without a P, but sometimes with the null preposition *of*, sometimes with a P lexically chosen by the V, and sometimes with the IO prepositions *to* and *for*. (As with A, I have lumped together prepositional sister arguments of V with real syntactic sister arguments of V for ease of exposition.)

(1–51)a.   The girl [$_{VP}$ **read** her cousin a book].
   b.   The girl [$_{VP}$ **thought** of *nothing in particular*].
   c.   The girl [$_{VP}$ **depended** on *her cousin*].
   d.   The girl [$_{VP}$ **read** to *her cousin*].

(*Thought*, as in (1–51)b, takes only a PP or clausal argument in most uses, although in casual speech we hear phrases of limited productivity like *She thinks computers day in and day out*.)

V, like A, can take sisters that are not arguments, but that are instead part of the predicate the V heads (that is, V can take sisters that are modifiers):

(1–52)   She's laughing *now*.
          Artisans sleep *in that park*.

And V, like A, cannot take an argument in specifier position (where I am adopting an X-bar theory that is a restrictive version of that in Chomsky 1986a – thus the GF subject slot is not the specifier of V and S (the node I have been calling I) is not a projection of V – see the introduction to this book). In fact, V does not allow any kind of NP in specifier position.

Finally, V, like A, must take precisely one argument which appears outside the VP that the V heads. In (1–51) that argument is *the girl*. Again, the importance of this fact is discussed in section 4 below.

2.3   The lexical head N(oun)

Many nouns are not event words and do not have argument structures; thus they cannot head a predicate. Mona Anderson (1983), in fact, argues that no concrete nouns have argument structures. I differ with her, as will be seen below, but I agree that most concrete nouns in most contexts do not denote events and do not have argument structures. For example, the noun *wallet* can take an NP in specifier position as well as an NP sister, but in both instances that NP is not a role player with respect to the head N:

(1–53)a. I prefer yesterday's wallet.
      b. Sue bought a wallet of leather.
      c. A wallet of true beauty lay on the bureau.

In fact, Mona Anderson (1983, p. 17) calls the *of* in (1–53)b & c the "attributive *of*" and says that its object modifies the head N. Thus the *of* phrase here is part of the object. And I would analyze the NP in specifier position in (1–53)a as part of the object, as well.

Abstract nouns, however, are often event words and, like A and V, they can take NP sisters (with the null P *of*, or prepositions lexically chosen by the head N, or the IO prepositions *to* and *for*) as arguments. Thus these Ns can head predicates. Below only the head of the predicate is in boldface:

(1–54)a. the **death** of *John*
          the **destruction** of *the city*
          the **bounce** of *the ball*

    b. an unhealthy **dependence** on *celery juice*
        the **story** about *the firewoman*
    c. a passing **remark** to *the professor*
        the **gift** for *the landlady*

And, as with A and V, the sisters of N need not be arguments of the N, even if the N is an event word. Instead, they can modify the N – and would then be part of the predicate that the N heads:

(1–55)   destruction of *incredible magnitude*
           a remark *beyond the bounds of decency*
           a look of *anxiety*

Thus far in this section, the items I have identified as arguments of the head A, V, or N are generally accepted in the literature to be precisely that. Now I turn to the much more controversial question of whether NPs in specifier position of N are arguments.

Of course, the question arises seriously only for Ns which have an event structure. Thus in (1–56) *Sharon* is not an argument of the head N, since this N in this context takes no arguments.

(1–56)   Sharon's wallet is embossed with pink letters.

In fact, the relationship of Sharon to the wallet is underdetermined: she could own it, have made it, want to buy it, like it very much, have lost it, drew it, etc. That is, the wallet in (1–56) is characterized by having a relationship to Sharon, but the sentence does not tell us the nature of this relationship. Instead, our ability to imagine contexts is the only clue we have to this relationship when the sentence is used out of context (see Williams 1982 and Higginbotham 1985, among others).

Notice that the situation here is quite distinct from the situation discussed in section 1.6 above regarding (1–42)–(1–44), where I discussed lexical items which can be used to describe a small range of types of events and thus can assign a correspondingly small range of theta roles to their arguments. So while *Sharon* in (1–56) may have an enormous range of possible appropriate relationships to *wallet* out of context, *Sharon* in (1–44), repeated here:

(1–44)   Sharon broke the window.

may not have an enormous range of possible appropriate relationships to *broke,* but, rather, only a few. That is, *Sharon* does receive a theta role in (1–44), from the lexical head *broke,* but out of context we will not be able to determine precisely which of the small set of possible theta roles this

NP might have it actually does have. But *Sharon* does not receive a theta role at all in (1–56).

However, when the head N takes arguments, the question of whether an NP in specifier position can be an argument of the head N arises seriously, as in:

(1–57)   The Huns' destruction of the city upset us.

Chomsky (1970) analyzed the NP *the Huns'* in specifier position of *destruction* in (1–57) as the subject of this head N, and he has maintained that position ever since (as in Chomsky 1986a). And Cinque (1980) has argued for Italian that possessive adjectives, which appear in specifier position of NP, are subjects of NP (but see Ruwet 1972, who points out for French that possessive adjectives have the favored interpretation of possessor over all other possible interpretations, including agent).

Williams (1982), on the other hand, argues that no NP in specifier position of an N is an argument of the N. His reasons are multiple and I will not counter them here. Instead, whenever an argument I am making is relevant to one of Williams' arguments, I will point that out. (See in particular the discussions of (1–58) and of (1–72) through (1–76) below and several points in ch. 2, particularly secs. 3 and 10.) Here let me address just one of his positions. Williams claims that the semantic relationship of the genitive NP to the head N in an NP like that in (1–57) is underdetermined. But Mona Anderson (1983) shows that this relationship is, instead, narrowly defined, in contrast to the relationship between a genitive NP in specifier position and a concrete head N. And Hornstein and Lightfoot (1987) show a variety of ways in which Williams' account of the semantic interpretation of determiners in NPs like that in (1–57) is inadequate.

Notice that this issue is crucial to a theory of predication. For those who require that a predicate take an argument external to the maximal projection of the head of the predicate (as Williams does), *destruction* in (1–57) does not head a predicate. But with my definition of predicate, there is nothing to prevent our analyzing *destruction* in (1–57) as a predicate.

I here follow Chomsky in allowing an NP in specifier position of an event N to be an argument of that head N. In chapter 6, section 2, I argue that anaphors in both Italian and English require that their antecedents bear a theta role. Assuming for the moment that I am correct on this point, let me add here that specifiers of N can bind an anaphor in both Italian and English.

(1–58)   la sua$_i$ finta lettera a se stesso$_i$
        'his fake letter to himself'
        il suo$_i$ libro su se stesso$_i$
        'his book about himself'

(The Italian examples in (1–58) are from Giorgi 1987.) Thus from (1–58) we are led to the conclusion that specifiers of NP can be arguments of the head N.

Before proceeding to a discussion of specifiers of NP, I would like to address Higginbotham's (1985) argument against analyzing specifiers as arguments, an objection based on examples such as (1–59)a.

(1–59)a. John's dog
     b. John is a dog.

Higginbotham asks, if *John* can bear a theta role, why cannot we understand the NP in (1–59)a to mean that John is a dog, parallel to (1–59)b? Higginbotham concludes that NPs in specifier position do not enter into the subject–predicate relationship.

I do not have an answer to Higginbotham's question. However, I would like to argue against a commonly proposed explanation of the lack of a predicational reading in (1–59)a. Some have used the i-within-i constraint to block the missing predicational reading of (1–59)a (see Williams 1982, Hornstein 1984, among others). The i-within-i constraint blocks a phrasal node from being coindexed with another phrasal node that properly contains it. I argue in chapter 2, section 10, that this constraint is incoherent. However, here it is necessary only to show that the i-within-i constraint cannot help us to rule out the missing predicational reading of (1–59)a.

To see this, let us add indices to (1–59)a. The noun *dog* will be coindexed with the overall NP, since heads and maximal projections are coindexed (see Williams 1981b). Then, under a predicational reading, the noun *dog* and the NP *John* would be coindexed by predication coindexing (which will be the topic of chapter 2, and see Williams 1980). The result is:

(1–60)

$$
\begin{array}{c}
\text{NP}_i \\
\diagup\diagdown \\
\text{NP}_i \quad \text{N}' \\
\mid \qquad \mid \\
\text{John's} \quad \text{N}_i \\
\mid \\
\text{dog}
\end{array}
$$

The fact that both NPs in (1–60) have the same index would constitute a violation of the i-within-i constraint.

One problem with this explanation of the lack of a predicational reading for (1–59)a is that the same indexing configuration is found in (1–61), where we understand *John* to have the same semantic role as in (1–62).

(1–61) John's nastiness

$$
\begin{array}{c}
\text{NP}_i \\
\diagup \diagdown \\
\text{NP}_i \quad \text{N}' \\
| \qquad | \\
\text{John's} \quad \text{N}_i \\
| \\
\text{nastiness}
\end{array}
$$

(1–62)   John is nasty.

A proponent of the i-within-i constraint explanation for the failure of a predicational reading in (1–59)a might point out that the NP *John's dog* in (1–60) would have the same referent as the NP *John* under the (ungrammatical) predicational reading, but the NP *John's nastiness* in (1–61) would not have the same referent as the NP *John*. Thus if we were to construe the i-within-i constraint as pertaining only to referential indices (that is, if the i-within-i constraint is a constraint against semantic incoherence, as Williams 1982 presents it to be), then (1–60) would be a violation of the i-within-i constraint but (1–61) would not.

However, there are at least two problems with this account. First, given this account, we would expect both (1–63)a and (1–63)b to be bad on the reading indicated by the indices. But, instead, the second sentence is good, as is the third (suggested to me by Andrew Radford (personal communication)).

(1–63)a. *John$_i$ is [his$_i$ boss]$_i$.
    b. John$_i$ is [his own$_i$ boss]$_i$.
    c. Anyone can see that John$_i$ is [his$_i$ father's son]$_i$.

Hornstein (1984) discusses sentences like (1–63)a as examples of the i-within-i constraint. And he says sentences like (1–63)b and (1–63)c show that the constraint is not a semantic one.

Second, there is empirical evidence that the i-within-i constraint explanation for (1–59)a is wrong. In Italian we find NPs like (1–64)a, which has the structure in (1–64)b (see ch. 3, sec. 2 for justification of this syntactic structure):

(1–64)a. quel matto di Giorgio
        that madman of Giorgio
        'that madman Giorgio'

    b.

```
                NP_i
              /      \
          Spec        N'
           |        /    \
          quel    N_i     PP
                   |     /  \
                 matto  P   NP_i
                        |    |
                       di  Giorgio
```

I argue in chapter 3 that the head N *matto* is a predicate here, taking *Giorgio* as its sole argument. The indices for (1–64)b reflect this analysis. Here whether or not we consider predication indices, we have a violation of the i-within-i constraint. That is, the two NPs with identical indices should constitute a violation of the i-within-i constraint just as much as the coindexed NPs in (1–60) are said to. Yet (1–64) is perfectly grammatical with the reading indicated. Thus the i-within-i constraint does not block (1–64) and should not be assumed to block (1–60), either. (In ch. 4 I analyze English NPs which have a similar syntactic and semantic analysis to the Italian one in (1–64). And I point out in chapter three that a variety of languages have such NPs. Thus (1–64) cannot be considered some aberration of Italian alone.)

I conclude that the failure of (1–59)a to have a reading similar to that of (1–59)b is irrelevant to the question of whether an NP in specifier position can bear a theta role. And I leave open the question of why (1–59)a lacks a predicational reading.

From this point on I will proceed with the assumption that NPs in the specifier position of Ns that have argument structures can be arguments of those Ns. This is a major difference between N and both A and V. And this difference correlates with another major difference, which is that N does not require any arguments to be external to the NP (as in (1–57) and (1–64)), whereas both A and V require precisely one external argument. I will return to these contrasts in section 4 below. Notice that in allowing an argument to appear in specifier position, N is parallel to Chomsky's (1986a) nonlexical category I(nflection).

However, as with NP sisters to N, NPs in specifier position of a head N need not be arguments of that N even when the N is one that does have an argument structure or when the N clearly is being used predicatively.

(1–65)a. yesterday's announcement
     b. Leila is Elena's doctor.

In (1–65)a *yesterday* is not an argument of *announcement*; in (1–65)b, *Elena* is not an argument of *doctor* (in fact, Elena's relationship to the doctor is as underdetermined as the relationship of the specifier to the head N in other concrete NPs, such as *Sharon's wallet*).

There are at least two more interesting facts about event nouns that relate to their argument structure. First, sometimes theme or patient arguments (the so-called objective arguments) that occur as sister arguments to head Ns can also occur in the specifier position:

(1–66)   the city's destruction (cf. the destruction of the city)

Chomsky (1970) proposes that such arguments are generated in sister position and moved to specifier position. I follow Chomsky here (and, in doing so, I am joined by many, including Mona Anderson 1983, Kayne 1984, Aoun *et al.* 1987, Roeper 1987, and Hornstein and Lightfoot 1987; but against this position see Williams 1982, Higginbotham 1983, Rappaport 1983, Grimshaw 1986, Zubizarreta 1986, and Safir 1987a).

The movement rule operative in (1–66) is not limited to just arguments, but can apply to certain adverbial NPs, as Emonds (1976) points out and as we saw above in (1–65)a, which is derived as in (1–67):

(1–67)   the announcement yesterday → yesterday's announcement

The application of NP movement in (1–67) is of special interest in light of the claim commonly found in the literature that arguments and non-arguments of a lexical head bear different syntactic relationships to that head. In particular, some claim that there is a syntactic difference between arguments and non-arguments to the effect of placing arguments of a lexical head H as sisters to the head and non-arguments as sisters to H′ (or, sometimes, even H″). We can see this approach in Jackendoff (1977, 1983), Emonds (1985), and its history is recounted by Speas (1986), who also adopts it (but inconsistently, I believe – see p. 81 versus p. 120). Chomsky (1981, 1982, 1986a, 1986b), however, has never adopted this approach.

As I stated in the introduction to this book, I consider only syntactic data (and not semantic data) as valid evidence for syntactic structure. I know of no convincing syntactic evidence that our X-bar theory need be any more complicated than that first proposed by Chomsky in 1970 and revised in 1986a. Thus for the lexical categories of N, V, A, and P, I take

X" to expand to specifier and X'; and I take X' to expand to X and its phrasal sisters (see more detailed discussion of this in the introduction to this book). Therefore in this chapter (and throughout this work) I have consistently analyzed as sisters to the head all phrases to the right of a lexical head within the phrase. In my analysis, then, the NP movement in (1–67) is the same NP movement that applies in (1–66): movement from sister position of N to specifier position of N. Indeed, the fact that NP movement applies equally to arguments and non-arguments suggests these two semantic functions are indistinguishable syntactically – just as my analysis would demand they be.

The second very interesting fact about the argument structure of event nouns is that arguments of the head N which are not objective are not limited to specifier position, but can also occur as sisters to the head N, always introduced by the null preposition *of*. (For arguments that the object of passive *by* is not the agentive argument, see ch. 2, sec. 8).

(1–68)a. John's {lecture/story} amazed me.
 b. That {lecture/story} of John's amazed me.

(1–69)a. John's {death/arrival} shocked me.
 b. The {death/arrival} of John shocked me.

There is an interesting variation in (1–68)–(1–69) above: some of the sister NPs to the head N have a genitive marker (as in (1–68)b) and some do not (as in (1–69)b). We find that when an N has only one argument in its lexical structure, that argument has no genitive marker in sister position (*the death of John, the happiness of your little sister*). But when an N allows two or more arguments, if one of these arguments is nonprepositional and nonobjective, it appears with a genitive marker. (And see Aoun *et al.* 1987 for an explanation of why the objective reading cannot emerge with the genitive, based on a violation of the E(mpty) C(ategory) P(rinciple) of Chomsky 1981 in logical form.) This is true whether or not any other arguments are syntactically realized (*the lecture of John's (on birth control), the belief of Sam's (in intergalactic communication)*). But if all the arguments are prepositional or objective, none of them is in the genitive (*the betrothal of Judith to Pete*). We can see that if the N takes more than one argument, then the argument typically singled out as the subject in G(overnment) and B(inding) literature is marked with a genitive when it appears as the sister to the head N. (We return to this fact in sec. 4 below.)

Notice that *John('s)* in the (b) examples of (1–68)–(1–69) is the so-called subject argument of the NP; I am taking *John('s)* to be a sister to the head N in these instances. Even linguists who allow a less restrictive version of X-bar theory than the one I adopt in this book should agree that *John('s)* is attached at the sister level in (1–68)b and (1–69)b. This is because, as Speas (1986) has shown, if we trace the method of argumentation often used to advance an X-bar theory in which the X′ level can have sisters (other than conjuncts or the specifier) and in which perhaps even the X″ level can have sisters (other than conjuncts), we find that an overriding principle is that if a theta relationship holds between X and Y, then X and Y are sisters (see Speas 1986, especially p. 81). Thus *John('s)* should be a sister to the head N in (1–68)b and (1–69)b even in theories which allow sisters to N′ and N″.

Cinque (1980) argues that so-called subject arguments of N in Italian are not sisters to N but to N′. However, his argument is based on the claim that the clitic *ne*, when it corresponds to an argument of an N, corresponds only to the subject argument of N. This claim is not accurate, as I show in chapter 3 (see the discussion following (3–97)). Therefore, I maintain that the proper analysis of (1–68)b and (1–69)b has *John('s)* in sister position to the head N. (In chs. 3 and 4 I will give several tests for constituency within NP. By all of these tests *John('s)* is a sister to the head N in (1–68)b and (1–69)b, as the reader can easily confirm.)

In light of the fact that there are good arguments for an NP movement rule that takes a sister of N and places it in specifier position of N (the rule operative in (1–66) and (1–67)), I propose that that same rule is operative in (1–68) and (1–69) and derives the (a) sentences from the (b) sentences. That is, I propose that all arguments of N within NP are sisters of N at DS and that a movement rule can place an argument of N in specifier position of N.

Notice that if we generated all arguments of N that appear within NP as sisters (introduced by *of*) of the head N, the fact that the theta role interpretations of the genitive NPs in specifier position (1–68)a and (1–69)a is the same as that of the genitive NPs that are sisters to the head N in (1–68)b and (1–69)b is accounted for.

Also, we will see in chapter 6, sections 4 and 5.3, that the specifier of NP behaves in the same way sister arguments of N behave with respect to the binding of anaphors. (That is, specifiers behave as though they are within the theta domain of the head N – where the notion of theta domain is defined in ch. 2, sec. 5.) The behavior of specifiers examined in chapter 6, then, would be accounted for with the analysis which generates these specifiers as sisters to N and optionally moves them into specifier position.

Furthermore, as long as we see the advantage of relating the two positions by a movement rule, we should prefer movement from sister position into specifier position rather than vice versa so that the trace will be properly bound.

There is at least one more reason for generating all arguments of N that appear within NP as sisters to N in DS. And that is that if we do so, theta assignment by Ns in Italian observes the same principles that we find for theta assignment by Ns in English (assuming that the subjects of N studied in Cinque 1980 are really sisters to N – see ch. 3). Since this whole book presents a theory of predication that holds for both Italian and English (and that I offer for all configurational languages), and since that theory of predication depends upon theta theory in important ways (as we will see in ch. 2), we should opt for a version of theta theory that will suffice for both languages.

I will hereafter assume the derivation of NPs in specifier position of N as originating in sister position.

If the above analysis of (1–68)a and (1–69)a as coming from (1–68)b and (1–69)b is correct, we would expect this rule to operate on NP sisters of any N, not just on sisters of Ns that have event structures. In fact, it appears that the rule does operate inside all NPs, regardless of whether or not the head N has an event structure:

(1–70)   John's car
          that car of John's
          yesterday's menu
          the menu (of) yesterday

(But see Torrego 1986, who argues that possessives that follow the head N are sisters to N″.) There are, however, restrictions on this movement rule, since not all NP sisters can undergo it (*an idea of great merit*, but not **a great merit's idea*). Those restrictions, however, while puzzling, are tangential to our study, and I will not go into them here.

Let us turn now to a question raised at the opening of section 2 which I said that I would not delve into deeply: how do we know whether a lexical item has an event structure? The question is not acute for A (which always has an event structure), nor for V (which almost always does), but it is critical for N.

At the opening of section 2 I gave a list of references the reader can consult which deal extensively with this very question. Here I want to focus only on one particular related question: whether or not concrete Ns can serve as heads of predicates.

I believe that there is at least one usage in which any N, whether concrete or not, can head a predicate. That context is seen here in (1–71), and we have already come across it in (1–65)b above:

(1–71)   This ratty piece of leather is **a wallet**.
          No one could consider this ratty piece of leather **a wallet**.

In both sentences of (1–71) the concrete N *wallet* is used in its predicative rather than referential sense (and see secs. 1.3 and 1.5 above for a discussion of nonreferential uses of NPs). Thus the property of being a wallet is assigned by the phrase *a wallet* to the NP *this ratty piece of leather*. In fact, it is by virtue of appearing in a predicative position that the N *wallet* must head a predicate and take a role player.

There is at least one other instance in which I would analyze a concrete N as a predicate. Certain concrete Ns appear to have argument structures. Consider

(1–72)   Mary's photograph

Photograph is a concrete N and (1–72) can be used in a wide range of situations, including those in which Mary took or liked or bought or did any other number of actions with respect to the photograph, as well as those in which Mary was in the photograph. In other words, the relationship of *Mary* to *photograph* at first appears to be under-determined, just as the relationship of a genitive NP to other concrete Ns is (as in (1–56) above).

However, if *Mary's* appears in sister position, the theme sense is unavailable:

(1–73)   that photograph of Mary's

And *photograph* can take a nongenitive NP sister that it bears a specific semantic relationship toward:

(1–74)   that photograph of Sue

In (1–74) Sue must be in the photograph, thus *Sue* is a theme argument of *photograph*.

Not all concrete Ns can take theme arguments. The fact that the concrete N *photograph* can stems from the fact that a photograph is always of something – it is inherently transitive. Like *photograph* are *portrait (a portrait of our family), record (a record of the war), story (a story of love),* and many other concrete Ns (including the so-called "picture" nouns, as in Gruber 1967).

When a concrete N has a theme argument present, it will assign the agentive role to a genitive argument. Thus in (1–75) *Mary* can be understood only as performing some action with respect to *photograph* and not as being in the photograph.

(1–75)   Mary's photograph of Sue
        that photograph of Mary's of Sue

Notice that *Mary* does not have the same semantic role in (1–75) as it has in the corresponding clause with the verb *photograph*:

(1–76)   Mary photographed Sue.

In (1–76) Mary was the photographer, but in (1–75) Mary may have performed a range of actions with respect to the photograph. That is, the event denoted by the verb *photograph* is specific in terms of the particular semantic roles assigned to the role players in that event; but we see no such specificity of the agentive role player with the noun *photograph*. It seems that concrete Ns like *photograph* do not really denote events, but, instead, evoke events – and the range of events they can evoke is limited by the referent they denote. Since a photograph can be taken, or bought, or enjoyed, etc., the genitive in (1–75) could bear any of these semantic roles.

Given the remarks above, I conclude that concrete Ns like *photograph* evoke events and have argument structures. As such, they can head predicates.

Looking back at the interpretations of (1–72), then, I would analyze the thematic sense of *Mary's* as being the result of NP movement from sister position of N of a theme argument (as in (1–66)) and the agentive sense of *Mary's* as being the result of NP movement from sister position of N of an agentive argument (as in (1–68) and (1–69) above).

In sum, N may or may not head a predicate, unlike nonmodificational uses of A and unlike most uses of most verbs. And N need not have an argument which appears outside the NP that the N heads, unlike both A and V. We will return to the importance of this last fact in section 4.

2.4   The lexical head P(reposition)

Most have claimed that all lexical heads are theta assigners (following Chomsky 1981), and paid little attention to Ps in particular. Some have considered the potential to be a theta-role assigner to be identical to valency, so that all inherently relational words (words with valency greater than zero) will be theta assigners (as in Croft 1986). Since Ps are generally relational, with a valency approach to theta assignment, we would expect Ps to assign theta roles.

Both of these approaches are inadequate for Ps. I argue here that in some uses P is a theta assigner, but in many others it is not. Thus only in those uses in which P is a theta assigner can P head a predicate.

In this section I discuss only a handful of Ps. My discussion is meant to be representative of the kinds of questions that arise when looking at the semantic structure of strings involving Ps and of the types of analyses I would offer. (The reader interested in discussions of a wide range of Ps might consult Jackendoff 1983, 1987a, 1987b.)

The lexical head P can be an event word and can take arguments. Thus P can head a predicate in examples such as those in (1–77). (This type of example was pointed out to me by Barry Miller (personal communication).)

(1–77)   Pina is into Greek pottery.
Her sister is after my husband.
Those children are on drugs.
I'm onto you.

The sentences in (1–77) are decidedly conversational in style. It is possible that some of these uses of Ps originated as ellipses from longer phrases such as *chase after, dependent on, catch on*, where the V or A head got lost. In fact, these PPs, like certain fixed-phrase PPs, such as *at ease*, and metaphorical PPs, such as *off his rocker*, can undergo AP movement, whereas regular PPs cannot.

(1–78) $\begin{Bmatrix} \text{Happy} \\ \text{Into art} \\ \text{*In bed} \end{Bmatrix}$ though he says he is, he isn't really.

but:

Thus the syntactic behavior of these PPs is like that of APs in some respects.

There are also many uses of P in which P is clearly not an event word and does not assign a theta role to any arguments. We have seen many of

these above, such as uses of the null preposition *of*, or Ps lexically selected
by some other lexical head, or the IO prepositions *to* and *for*:

(1–79)   I'm fond *of* pasta.
         You shouldn't rely *on* translations.
         Jim baked the carrot cake *for* Sally.

Here *pasta* is an argument of *fond*, not *of*; *translations* is an argument of
rely, not *on*; *Sally* is an argument of *baked*, not *for*. We can say that the
prepositions in (1–79) transmit the theta role from the actual theta
assigner to the argument.

The distinction between the usage of the Ps in (1–77) and those in
(1–79) is easy to see, and I expect no reader to balk at my analysis of the Ps
in (1–77) as heading predicates, but the Ps in (1–79) as not heading
predicates. However, in many other instances the functional status of Ps
is not so uncontroversial.

There are instances in which a P interacts with a V to affect which event
a sentence describes. In (1–80)–(1–81) we find a much-studied pair (see
Jespersen 1924, Fillmore 1968, S. Anderson 1971 & 1977, B. Levin and
Rappaport 1986, and Jackendoff 1987b).

(1–80)   Jack sprayed the wall with paint.

(1–81)   Jack sprayed paint on the wall.

In (1–80) we understand the wall to have been painted by way of being
sprayed. *Paint* here is the theme which covers the patient, *the wall*. But in
(1–81) we understand Jack to be doing something to the paint and we
understand the wall to be only the locus of the event. The question now is
how the object of *with* receives the theme role in (1–80).

Let me first point out that *sprayed with* is not a theta assigner, for, if it
were, it would be a lexical item in (1–80). But then we would be missing a
generalization, since *with* can appear with a theme sense for its object
with a variety of other verbs (as in *We loaded the wagon with hay* and
other such examples). Furthermore, another close semantic use of *with*
has an instrumental sense for its object, and again this occurs with a
variety of other verbs:

(1–82)a. Mary broke the piggy bank with a hammer.
     b. Mary opened the door with a key.
     c. Mary paid for the necklace with my dime.

Thus it seems to be either *with* alone or *sprayed* alone that is responsible
for the instrumental sense of the object of the P.

The question now is exactly what the semantic status of *with* is in (1–80) and (1–82). One might posit that *with* is a predicate, taking its object and the entire proposition of the clause minus the *with* phrase as its role players, or, alternatively, its object and the predicate of the clause it appears in as its role players. There is at least one good reason to reject this analysis. Notice that the presence of the *with* phrase affects the appropriateness of the role players of the predicate of the clause. Consider an example with instrumental *with*:

(1–83)a. People/ants/amoebas eat honey.
     b. People eat honey with a spoon.
     c. #Ants/amoebas eat honey with a spoon.

(The symbol # in (1–83)c means semantically or pragmatically ill-formed.) Here the addition of *with a spoon* limits the appropriate agentive role players for the predicate *eat*. However, typically a predicate selects its own role players but does not select the role players inside its own role players. That is, some principle of integrity forces each predicate to treat its role players as semantically unanalyzable wholes, at least with respect to certain kinds of semantic information. If *with* (or even *with a spoon*) were a predicate in (1–83), it could select its own role players, but it should not look down inside those role players; thus it should not participate in the selection of the role players of *eat*. The semantic selection that goes on between the syntactic subject of the sentence in (1–83)b and c, then, and the adverbial *with a spoon*, is evidence that *with a spoon* is a role player in the same event that the syntactic subject is a role player in: the event of eating. That is, the presence of one role player often affects the appropriateness of the choice of other role players of the same predicate:

(1–84)   Mary resembles Pete.
     Certain kinds of anemia resemble diabetes.

(1–85)   #Mary resembles diabetes.

In some respects *with* is a marker (or perhaps a reflex) of the fact that its object is used as a theme or instrument in the event denoted by the predicate of the clause *with* occurs in. It is, then, parallel to the use of special Cases in other languages to mark instrumentals (such as ablative in Latin). I therefore analyze the entire *with* phrase as an argument (an unsubcategorized-for argument) of the verb in (1–80) and (1–82).

Let me point out that Hale and Keyser (1987) argue that *with* is inherently instrumental. They also develop the ideas of central event and central participant. In (1–82)a, for example, the central event is breaking and the central participant is the piggy bank. Mary is less central in that she causes the central event and the hammer is less central in that it is the tool Mary uses to cause the central event. It appears that unsubcategorized-for arguments except subjects of intransitives are noncentral.

Thematic and instrumental *with*, then, are not themselves theta assigners. Instead, their object, with the *with* as a marker on that object, is the argument of some other lexical item, and it bears a theta role assigned by that other lexical item (and see Baker 1987a for this same conclusion regarding instrumentals in PPs in Chichewa). I would analyze other themes and instrumentals introduced by other Ps in the same way (as in pairs such as *Bill cleared the dishes from the table* and *Bill cleared the table of the dishes* where a theme is involved – see Jackendoff 1987b – and idiomatic instrumentals such as *on foot, by hand, in a taxi*, etc.).

Jackendoff (1987b) argues that we interpret the object of theme *with* as an argument of some other lexical item by way of a nonlexical rule that operates once we throw the words together in a syntactic structure. His analysis is consonant with mine here. An immediate question, then, is whether argument structure can be adequately represented in the lexicon. After all, if a nonlexical rule can add an argument, then lexical structure may well not reflect all the argument possibilities of a lexical item. The reverberations of this question affect the Projection Principle, discussed in section 4 below, which requires lexical properties of a lexical item to be reflected at all the syntactic levels. This principle was formulated with the assumption that one of the lexical properties was argument structure. But we are now questioning whether all information about argument structure is truly present in the lexicon, and, depending on our answer, the Projection Principle may well be affected. I think, however, that Jackendoff's nonlexical rule does not necessarily threaten the Projection Principle. All we need do is stipulate that certain lexical items are subject to certain nonlexical rules. This stipulation is part of the lexical information of a lexical item. Thus, the fact that *spray*, for example, can take a theme that appears in a *with* phrase would be encoded in the lexicon by way of the fact that *spray* can undergo the nonlexical rule.

Other Ps which are essentially locative in nature have a strong similarity to thematic and instrumental *with* when they co-occur with a head of a predicate. When these Ps appear in an utterance with a head of a predicate, the P is not lexically selected by the head of the predicate, but rather chosen because of the sense of the proposition the utterance describes (in contrast to the Ps in (1–79) above). The object of a P in a locative PP in such sentences is not an argument of the P itself. Instead, the object of the P is an argument of the head of the predicate of the clause. And the P functions to relate its syntactic object to the head of the predicate. In Rothstein's terms (1983, p. 35), the P indicates the type of thematic relation its object will have to the head of the predicate. For example, consider:

(1–86)a. Mary went inside.
     b. Mary went inside the house.

In (1–86) the P is a locative giving direction or position to the action. It extends one action (*went*) into a new action (*went inside*). As such, the P is part of the predicate (see sec. 1.1 above). The presence of an object of the preposition in (1–86)b but not in (1–86)a specifies the goal of the direction or position of the (newly formed) action, and, thus, introduces another role player, *the house,* onto the scene. That is, in (1–86) the predicate is *went inside*, but in (1–86)a it has only one role player, whereas in (1–86)b it has two. However, in both sentences the theta assigner is *went*, where in (1–86)a it takes one argument, but in (1–86)b it takes two.

In Jackendoff's (1983) sense, we can view these Ps as functions converting things into places. That is, in the lexicon, a verb such as *went* in (1–86) takes an optional place argument, not a thing argument. So in order for a nominal object of a P to be an appropriate argument of such a lexical item, it must be converted into a place via the P. The object of the P, then, is not a location in isolation of context, but becomes a location by virtue of being related to the verb via the locative P. And the exact kind of location the NP becomes is affected by both the P and the V (the head of the predicate). Below we see a variety of contexts and, thus, locative functions of objects of Ps. We find the entirely parallel situation for temporal PPs, where the temporal P converts a thing into a time. And the creativity with which English approaches these PPs is reflected here in some of the more metaphorical examples.

(1–87)   *on*:
         Sue found the jacket on the table.
         I saw my shoes on Mary.
         Jill tapped on Sally's window.
         Mary arrived on time.
         I bought the diamond on Sue's reassurance of a raise.
         I swear it on everything I hold dear.

over:
> Peter drove his car over the manhole.
> Dorothy went over the rainbow.
> Santa drove the reindeers over the rooftops.
> I leaned over Mikey's shoulder.
> You went over his head by talking to the dean.
> He's working over the weekend.
> He'll run for president over my dead body.

Again we have an instance in which the object of a P receives a theta role, but not from the P. Let me stress, however, that unlike with instrumental *with*, the P itself does add more information than just the function of locative. Thus locative *in* adds different information from locative *on*, which adds different information from locative *under*, etc. Therefore, it is not reasonable to analyze the P as being merely a reflex of the thematic role of its object (in contrast to instrumental and theme *with*). Instead, the head of the predicate and the P work together to tell us precisely how the object of the P plays a role in the event. Thus we must analyze the head of the predicate and the P together as a predicate. For example, I analyze *drive . . . over* as a predicate in a sentence such as *Peter drove his car over the manhole* (in (1–87) above).

We see here an important distinction between theta role and semantic role. The verb *went* in (1–86)b, for example, assigns the theta role of locative to the NP *the house*. But the predicate *went inside* in (1–86)b assigns the semantic role to that NP, letting us know that this (now) locative NP is a space that contains, rather than a space that is above or below, etc. (That is, *inside* contributes to the semantic role of its object NP.)

One advantage of analyzing the objects of the Ps in (1–86)–(1–87) above as bearing theta roles and as being role players to the predicate of the clause is that we can capture the similarity in function of NPs which are objects of Ps in locative PPs to NPs which are objects of Vs where the V incorporates a locative sense. And we can capture the same similarity regarding the temporal sense. Thus, as Ken Hale (personal communication) has pointed out to me, the NP object of the V and the NP object of the P have a similar function in each of the pairs below; my analysis captures that fact.

(1–88)a. Our family occupied the house for seven years.
> Our family lived in the house for seven years.
> Heathfern approached the house.
> Heathfern went toward the house.

The panda entered the house.
The panda went into the house.
b. The letter A precedes the letter B.
The letter A comes before the letter B.
The letter B follows the letter A.
The letter B comes after the letter A.

(I am not suggesting that the pairs in (1–88) are synonymous, only that the theta roles of the relevant NPs are identical in each pair. The semantic roles of these NPs, however, vary as the predicates vary.)

In (1–86)–(1–88) the locative and temporal PPs co-occur with a separate head of a predicate. But they certainly need not. I delay the discussion of locative and temporal PPs in the absence of a separate head of a predicate until later in this section.

In all the instances thus far, I have argued that the object of the P in question receives a theta role, but not always from the P. Thus in (1–77) the P is a theta assigner; in (1–79) the P transmits, but does not assign, the theta role from the V to the P's object; in (1–80) the P is merely a reflex of the theme theta role, but the object of the P receives its theta role from the V; and in (1–86)b the object of the P receives its theta role from the head of the predicate of its clause (but it receives its semantic role from the entire predicate, which includes the P). (In this last case the P converts its object into an appropriate argument for the lexical head – that is, from a thing into a place.)

Let me now turn to some instances in which I argue that the object of the P bears no theta role whatsoever.

To begin, consider sentences such as (1–89), where one might be tempted to claim that *Betty* has a theta role.

(1–89)   Beth will eat after Betty.

The most immediate reading we have for (1–89) out of context is that Beth will eat after Betty eats. Thus *Betty* in (1–89) should get the same theta role *Beth* gets – that is, whatever theta role *eat* assigns to this argument.

I contend, however, that despite our first reading of (1–89) out of context, *Betty* in (1–89) is not an argument of any event lexical item and does not receive a theta role. To see this, let us put a sentence like (1–89) in a context. Betty is auditioning for a dancing part in a musical. Beth is the auditioner.

(1–90)   –Hey, Beth! Come on, let's eat.

–Hold on. One more audition. I'll eat after Betty. See, she's on stage already. 5 minutes max.

Here it looks as if *Betty* should get the theta role appropriate for an argument of *dances* (that is, we read (1–90) to mean, "I'll eat after Betty dances"). One might say that since both *eat* and *dance* have an agent-subject argument, there is no difference between the theta assignments for the object of *after* in (1–89) and (1–90), and that thus we have no evidence against allowing *after* to assign the theta role of agent to its object. However, the object of *after* need not be understood as an agent.

(1–91)a. I ate salad after the steak.
     b. I ate a small snack after my bath.
     c. I eat peas only after 4 o'clock.

In (1–91)a our most immediate reading would have *the steak* getting the theta role of theme since it is an appropriate theme argument of the verb *ate*. In (1–91)b we might try to say that *my bath* gets the theta role of theme since it is an appropriate theme argument of some unexpressed verb such as *took*. In (1–91)c we have to admit that the object of *after* is simply a modifying time expression and is not an argument of any lexical head, thus it cannot have a theta role.

The above discussion shows that were we to maintain an analysis of sentences such as (1–89) through (1–91) in which the object of *after* gets a theta role, we would have to allow some abstract verbs at the level relevant for theta-role assignment which assign the appropriate theta roles in order to account for the differences just noted between the roles of the objects of *after* in (1–89) and (1–91)a&b. That is, *after* could not by itself randomly assign agent or theme or no theta roles to its object. Instead, we would need an as yet undefined process of constructing abstract verbs and precisely the right abstract verbs to give the theta role to the object of *after* that is appropriate in the particular sentence in a given situation, or, alternatively and equally as magical and undefined, some process of deleting abstract verbs before the sentences reach phonological form. Furthermore, we still would be in a quandary over (1–91)c, where no theta role is assigned to the object of *after*.

The theoretical and empirical problems raised by this approach are reminiscent of the types of problems that came up with the proposals for deletion rules of Comparative Ellipsis and Conjunction Reduction in the 1960s. And for much the same reasons that we have abandoned the bogus deletion rules of Comparative Ellipsis and Conjunction Reduction (see Napoli 1983), we here abandon this approach to *after* phrases.

We see, then, that (1–89) through (1–91) have objects of *after* which receive no theta role. This is a welcome conclusion, since there is nothing in the conceptual structure of *eat* which would suggest that it takes a temporally sequential argument. That is, we have a very different situation here from that in (1–86). Verbs of motion, like *went* in (1–86), entail a location as part of their conceptual structure – the very idea of space is encoded in the lexical items. Thus it is conceptually appropriate for *went* to take a locative argument. The location is, in an admittedly abstract but no less conceptually real way, a participant or role player in the event. But a verb like *eat* does not encode the very idea of sequential time any more than, say, *cough* or *breathe*. And, accordingly, a phrase like *after NP* (as in (1–91)) can appear in a clause with (almost) any verb.

After in (1–89)–(1–91) relates its object sequentially in time to the proposition expressed by the words preceding *after*. The semantics are skeletal: *after* indicates only temporal sequence. But the context of the utterance allows us to fill out a reasonable interpretation of the utterance, sometimes to the point of letting us imagine a sequence of propositions (as in (1–90) and (1–91)a&b). Prepositional phrases of this sort are strikingly similar in their semantics to so-called comparative ellipsis phrases and are another example of the "efficiency" of language (where I mean the term as developed by Barwise and Perry 1983). The point for us is that we can account for the semantics of sentences like those in (1–89) through (1–91) without claiming that the object of *after* has a theta role; we would have problems of both an empirical and a theoretical nature if we took the opposite stance, that the object of *after* did receive a theta role from *after*.

The above discussion used only one preposition: *after*. One might argue that *after* is unique in not being a theta assigner. However, similar discussions could be made based on other prepositions, such as the concomitant sense of *with* (in contrast to the theme *with* of (1–81) discussed above). I offer the examples in (1–92) and leave the reader to construct the discussion. (Caveat: *With* can also introduce an absolute that can be a clause (with the Accusative-*Ing* construction studied in Reuland 1983: *With Mary crying, how can we just walk out?*) or a simple NP plus sister predicate (as in van Riemsdijk 1978: *With the buses on strike, let's walk*). See Napoli (1987a) for a full discussion. As you test out (1–92) below, be sure not to use the absolutive constructions.)

(1–92)   She left with Barbara.
She ate peas with cream.
She left with no regrets.
She answered with aplomb.
She danced with the music.
She danced with a cheerful smile.

In general, all prepositions which are open to relating an entire proposition to some other point, such as temporal sequence (e.g. *after*), temporal consequence (e.g. *with*), and temporal precedence (e.g. *before*), as well as causal sequence (e.g. *because (of)*) exhibit behavior similar to that discussed above for the *after* sentences. And I argue that in all such uses, the object of the P receives no theta role.

A question unanswered thus far is precisely what semantic function the PPs in (1–89)–(1–91) have. I argued in section 1.1 that adverbials which are not themselves role players are parts of the predicate. Thus these PPs would be part of the predicate: they are modifiers. (With a more abstract approach to predication than mine, of course, the familiar alternative that these PPs are themselves predicates, taking the entire proposition minus the PP as their role player, arises. See the discussion in sec. 1.1.)

In sum, Ps are relational words that connect some other entity to their object. Ps such as *inside, in, over*, etc. in sentences like those in (1–86)–(1–88) are part of the predicate and relate the head of the predicate to their object by indicating the specific nature of the locative role their object plays in the event. On the other hand, Ps such as *after*, concomitant *with, before*, etc. in sentences like those in (1–89)–(1–91) relate the entire proposition of the clause they appear in minus the PP to some point outside that proposition, which is denoted by the object of the P. In the first instance the object of the P receives a theta role from the head of the predicate; in the second instance, it receives no theta role.

Before I leave this subsection, let me point out that I take the object of *by* in a passive sentence not to bear a theta role. Justification of this position is found in chapter 2, section 8.

Let us now turn to propositions in which a PP does not co-occur with a separate head of a predicate. Consider first the locative Ps.

(1–93)   Mary is inside the house.

Here the property of being inside is attributed to Mary. We, as speakers of such a sentence, do not present the concept of inside as being a location or direction which extends some other action or position into a new event.

That is, we do not present *inside* as an extension of some other item, in contrast to how we present it in:

(1–94)   Mary ran inside the house.

Rather, we present the concept of inside in (1–93) as a coherent whole: we view *inside* as denoting an event in itself. Thus *inside* is a predicate in (1–93). And it takes two role players: *Mary* and *the house*. In (1–94), instead, *ran inside* is the predicate, again taking two role players.

We can now see that whether or not a lexical item has an event structure cannot be determined in isolation of context. All Ps have the potential to be viewed as events and to have argument structures. But the crucial question for the analysis of any given utterance is how we view the P in that utterance.

One might object to this contextual approach to the event structure of lexical items and try to get around it by analyzing the copula in (1–93) as the head of the predicate rather than as merely a grammatical word (and see Jackendoff 1983). Then in both (1–93) and (1–94) the P would be part of the predicate but it would not head the predicate. Such an alternative cannot work, however, since the copula plays no semantic role in (1–93) – witness (1–95), where' no copula is present but the same semantic relationship holds between *Mary* and *inside* as in (1–93) (and see the discussion of (1–3) at the opening of this chapter).

(1–95)   I want Mary inside this house by midnight!

Any analysis which treats *is* in (1–93) as the head of the predicate would have to posit some abstract BE function in a sentence like (1–95). (The BE here represents an abstract function that need not have any lexical realization.) Our very nonabstract approach to predication does not allow for such an abstract BE.

Temporal Ps can also occur in such copular sentences, as can many other kinds of Ps:

(1–96)   Mary is before Bill.

Here *before* is viewed as denoting a coherent event, the state of temporally preceding. The predicate, then, is *before*, and it takes two role players: *Mary* and *Bill*.

Thus in both (1–93) and (1–96) the object of the P receives a theta role from the P itself, in contrast to (1–94), where the object of the P receives a theta role from the V, and sentences like (1–89), where the object of the P receives no theta role at all.

We see from everything in this subsection so far that the object of P may or may not receive a theta role, and, if it does, that theta role may or may not be assigned by the P alone. In fact, only in examples like those in (1–77), (1–93), (1–95), and (1–96) is the P alone a theta assigner. Thus, in most uses, P is not a theta assigner.

This conclusion is interesting in several ways. First, others have argued on independent grounds that P is not a theta assigner (Gunnarson 1986, p. 32, Giorgi 1984, among others).

Second, P is a defective lexical category in ways other than just theta assignment. Frequently it has been claimed that P is not a proper governor for binding theory, in contrast to N, A, and V (Kayne 1981b; Chomsky 1981, sec. 5.1; Safir 1985, pp. 51, 88; Aoun 1985, p.68, among others). P is also the only lexical category that is closed (Emonds 1985); for example, there are a limited number of Ps (as opposed to other lexical categories), and new ones are not likely to be coined. And objects of P, unlike objects of V, are not subject to the Definiteness Effect (Safir 1985).

Third, while we cannot call P a grammatical rather than lexical category (since grammatical categories in the sense of Emonds 1985 have no purely semantic feature, whereas Ps generally do, except for the null preposition *of*), monosyllabic Ps are minor categories in prosodic trees, while all other lexical categories are major categories (see Nespor and Vogel 1982). And many Ps have special phonological properties, behaving in ways like syntactic dependents and clitics (see Chomsky and Halle 1968, Kean 1981, among others). Furthermore, Ps have some of the characteristics of functional elements in Abney's (1986) sense.

We would hope that the defectiveness of P in all the above ways would be explained by a single account. Unfortunately, I do not have one to offer, nor do I expect that any such account will be rapidly forthcoming. For example, Ps are theta assigners in certain contexts and in those same contexts Ps behave like proper governors. So we might connect those two facts by claiming that only theta assigners can be proper governors. On the other hand, all Ps are Case assigners, so unless the notion of proper government can be shown to be different for binding theory from that for Case theory, this explanation looks unpromising. (And such fracturization of the notion of proper government would threaten the explanatory value of the notion – thus I hope it would be avoided in any case.) Furthermore, the fact that polysyllabic Ps behave differently phonologically from monosyllabic Ps seems to be an unrelated fact, so far as I can see.

Let me end with an important fact: if it is a theta assigner, P – like A and V but unlike N – must take one argument which appears outside the PP that the P heads.

2.5   Phrasal predicates

As has already been pointed out, there are instances in which whole phrases can be predicates. For example, phrases which form lexical items, such as metaphorical PPs and fixed-phrase VPs, can be predicates. Here the predicate is in boldface:

(1–97)   That analysis **is off the wall**.

(1–98)   John **flew into a rage**.

And, frequently, a predicate just happens to comprise an entire phrase. Thus intransitive VPs are often predicates:

(1–99)   John **ran inside quickly**.

But they need not be:

(1–100)   John **ran inside** the house **quickly**.

Phrases can be predicates in at least two instances, then: either the phrase is a lexical item which denotes an event (as in (1–97)–(1–98)); or the phrase just happens to contain no material other than the predicate (as in (1–99)).

Naturally, if a whole phrase is a predicate, then it must have at least one role player (which is also an argument – see the discussion of (1–45) above in sec. 1.6) which, *per force*, appears outside that phrase, since every predicate must have a role player (see sec. 1.5). Furthermore, phrasal predicates are limited to precisely one role player (see Emonds 1985). This follows from the fact that every category X that we have examined above which can head a predicate can take at most one argument external to XP.

Let us now turn to a closer look at the issue of VP predicates and at whether entire clauses can be predicates.

2.6   Concerning VP and CP as predicates

Many linguists have assumed or argued that all predicates are phrasal (Stowell 1981, Chomsky 1981, Aoun and Sportiche 1983, Marantz 1984, among many others). In particular, Stowell (1981) has argued that VP rather than V is a predicate, and most works within GB follow Stowell on this point.

In this chapter we have seen that predicates can be single words, continuous strings of words that do not form a syntactic constituent, discontinuous strings of words that do not form a syntactic constituent, as well as entire phrases. It is important, then, that I counter the arguments of Marantz for the analysis of VP as a predicate.

Marantz argues that VP is the theta assigner for an argument in G(rammatical) F(unction) subject position, rather than V – thus for us that would mean that the entire VP is the predicate. Marantz's proposal is based partially on an inaccurate claim about the data (and partially on a discussion of idioms, to which Rothstein 1983 responds in a way consistent with my approach). He says that keeping a verb fixed and varying the DO can affect the theta role of an argument in GF subject position, as in (1–101), where I use my own examples rather than his. But no such variability is found in the theta role of the argument found in DO position.

(1–101)a. Mary threw the ball.
     b. Mary threw a party.
     c. Mary threw a fit.
     d. Mary threw up.

In (1–101)a&b *Mary* is agentive; in (1–101)c it is debatable whether *Mary* is agentive or experiencer; in (1–101)d *Mary* is experiencer. Marantz would conclude from (1–101) that it is not the verb *threw* that is assigning a theta role to *Mary* in each of these sentences but the whole VP. However, exactly the same kind of variability is found in the theta role of the argument in DO position if we hold the verb fixed and vary the argument in GF subject position. (The examples in (1–102) were suggested to me by my intermediate syntax class, winter term 1986, University of Michigan.)

(1–102)a. The ball struck Mary.
     b. The idea struck Mary.
     c. Multiple sclerosis (suddenly) struck Mary.

Here *Mary* is a patient in (1–102)a, perhaps a theme in (1–102)b, and an experiencer in (1–102)c.

If we were to conclude from (1–101) that the V plus its DO is a theta-role assigner, we would be led to conclude from (1–102) that the V plus its GF subject is a theta-role assigner, a regrettable conclusion for anyone's theory.

One might argue that sentences like (1–102)b&c are metaphorical, and thus extensions of the "real" use of *struck*, seen in (1–102)a, where the DO gets a patient role. But the same objection would then hold for the sentences of (1–101), where the (b) and (c) examples can be seen as metaphorical. The important point is that (1–101) and (1–102) present entirely parallel questions and problems regarding theta-role assignment. Thus there is no asymmetry between DO and GF subject position with respect to theta-role assignment by a V. Accordingly, Marantz's argument that VP is a predicate, which is based on such a proposed asymmetry, is vitiated.

Notice, of course, that it is also debatable whether there is a single verb *threw* in (1–101) and a single verb *struck* in (1–102), as Bill Croft (personal communication) has pointed out to me. But I will ignore that debate here in the interest of showing that Marantz's argument is inconsistent internally, even if only a single verb is involved in these examples.

In sum, I reject Marantz's position that VP is a theta-role assigner and reiterate that only lexical items can assign theta roles. Other arguments for rejecting VP as a theta assigner are found in Rothstein (1983).

Given that only lexical items assign theta roles, we will say that in (1–101) the lexical head *threw* takes *Mary* as an argument and assigns a theta role to that argument. Likewise in (1–102) the lexical head *struck* takes *Mary* as an argument and assigns a theta role to that argument. However, the theta role that is assigned with these verbs may vary. This is a common situation, as we saw above in section 1.6 with the discussion of (1–42)–(1–44).

A distinct instance of the common claim that VP is a predicate regards the analysis of sentences involving NP movement:

(1–103)   Mary [$_{VP}$ appears [t to have understood]].

Here Williams (1980) argues that the matrix VP is a predicate by virtue of the presence of the trace, which makes the VP an open function, according to him. I have adopted an event-structure approach to the definition of predicate, which has little to do with the notion of an open function except for the fact that predicates require at least one role player. Thus a phrase would be an open function only if one of the role players of the predicate were missing from the phrase. I would therefore not analyze the VP in (1–103) as a single predicate. Instead, the predicate here is the discontinuous string *appears . . . to have understood*, and the trace, being a trace of NP movement, is an anaphor. As an anaphor, this trace is a legitimate role player of the predicate, thus the VP is not an open function in any way relevant to predication: there are no role players missing from this phrase. In chapter 6 I will argue that the principles of coindexing a predicate and its subject role player (which I present in ch. 2, but see sec. 4 below for a definition of subject role player) can be extended to cover the coindexing of an anaphor and its antecedent. Thus my analysis will capture the similarities between the coindexing of trace and *Mary* in (1–103) and the coindexing between a predicate and its subject role player while still maintaining an event-structure notion of predicate.

Williams (1980) is also responsible for the claim that S′ (or, in our terms, CP) can be a predicate. (By S′ Williams intends the phrase consisting of a clause plus its introductory complementizer node. By CP I mean the phrase headed by the complementizer node.) Let me consider that analysis of his which has gained the most following: that instances of obligatory control are predicates. Thus Williams would analyze the embedded clauses here as predicates:

(1–104)   Mary wanted [PRO to leave].

(1–105)   Mary is [PRO to leave by 5].

According to Williams, these clauses can be predicates because they are open by virtue of the presence of PRO. However, while the clauses here have a phonetic hole, so to speak, they are not open in the sense relevant to predication. The PRO in obligatory control clauses is an anaphor (see Hornstein and Lightfoot 1987) – thus these clauses, like the VP in (1–103) above, are closed. These clauses therefore cannot be predicates. However, since the coindexing principles for anaphors and predicates are the same (see ch. 6), the similarities between such sentences and instances of predication are not only unproblematic, but expected (see also ch. 2, sec. 9).

Example (1–105) is important to take a closer look at, however. In all the examples of copular sentences that we have seen thus far, *be* is a grammatical word. However, in (1–105) if *be* were a grammatical word, the GF subject *Mary* would not be licensed in the sense of Chomsky (1986b) (given that I do not analyze the embedded clause as a predicate). Therefore, this use of *be* must not be as a grammatical word. And, in fact, it is not. The *be* here expresses obligation or intention and is not simply a word that carries the tense (see also Safir 1985 and Williams 1983a, who argue that there are two senses of *be*).

There are still at least two other types of open clauses which are candidates for being analyzed as predicates: restrictive relative clauses and appositive relative clauses. But restrictive relative clauses are sisters to the head N they describe (see ch. 3, sec. 2), and thus fall within the NP of the N they describe. This collocation is that of modifiers, not predicates, as was argued in section 1.4 above.

Appositive relative clauses, however, will be argued in chapter 5, section 5 to be outside the NP they are related to at SS – and, in fact, to predicate of that NP. (By SS I intend the level of structure at the output of the syntactic component of the grammar.)

In sum, VPs are predicates only when they consist of phrasal lexical items or when a predicate just happens to comprise an entire VP (as in (1–99) versus (1–100) in sec. 2.5 above). But CPs can be predicates only when they are open (that is, when they contain a variable) and when they are not modifiers. At least one such case arises: the appositive relative clause.

3   Categories that can be role players

Any phrase that can be an argument can be a role player (by virtue of the Principle of Coincidence in (1–46)). Thus far the role players we have looked at are NPs. However, clauses can be arguments.

(1–106)   Jane insisted that we come back.
I'm hopeful that he'll come back.
Jane's insistence that we come back surprised me.

And, as was mentioned earlier, some have argued that all subcategorized-for elements are role players. If this were so, subcategorized-for locative phrases would be role players:

(1–107)   The doctor put notes on Sally's chart.

I have argued (sec. 2.4 above) that, instead of the entire locative PP being a role player, the object of the P is a role player and the P is part of the predicate. Thus the predicate in (1–107) would be *put . . . on*.

We will find in chapter 2 that the principles of coindexing between a subject role player and a predicate are unchanged whether we analyze the object of the P or the whole PP as a role player in (1–107), so long as in either analysis the object of the P receives a theta role (in the analysis with the whole PP as a role player this might be by way of inheritance from the PP to its object NP).

There is another analysis of sentences like (1–107) that I have not yet discussed – that of Simpson (1983b). (I do not have access to this work, but it is referred to in Hale and Keyser 1986. I present here my understanding of the work and I apologize for any unintentional misrepresentation.) Simpson argues that the verb *put* takes the entire locative PP as its argument, but that locative PP is itself a predicate. Simpson uses the term "translative small clause" to describe the type of relationship that holds between the sister arguments of *put* in (1–107) (that is, between *notes* and *on Sally's chart*). I am unsure whether or not in this analysis the NP *Sally's chart* would receive a theta role or not, and, if it did, which item would be its theta assigner. It is quite possible that Simpson would allow *Sally's chart* to be a role player of the predicate even while analyzing the entire PP as the predicate (just as Williams 1980 and Marantz 1984 allow the DO to be a role player even though they analyze the VP that contains the DO as the predicate).

I will maintain my original analysis of sentences like (1–107), in which the NP and not the PP is a role player of the predicate, and I leave open the question of whether or not the alternative analyses I have discussed here would be consistent with my coindexing principles given in chapter 2.

Some theta assigners definitely do take arguments that are themselves predicates, however (and see Chierchia 1985):

(1–108)a. The medication rendered John helpless.
    b. The confirmation of Sarah as a Catholic freaked out Arnie.

In (1–108)a the AP *helpless* is an argument of *rendered* and at the same time it is a predicate (taking *John* as its role player). To see this, notice that *helpless* licenses *John* (**We rendered John*), whereas adjunct (that is, nonargument) predicates must be licensed by their subject role player (and see Emonds 1985, p. 83). Other predicates of other categories can be arguments of *rendered* (*The medication rendered John out of control/a bumbling idiot*). In (1–108)b the PP *as a Catholic* is an argument of the head N *rendered*, where here *a Catholic* is a predicate taking *Sarah* as its role player.

It appears that NP, AP, PP, and clauses can all be arguments of lexical items. So all phrasal nodes can be role players of predicates.

4   Theta assignment

All arguments of an event lexical item receive a theta role. In this chapter we have seen that arguments of a lexical item can appear inside the maximal projection of the syntactic head of the lexical item or outside that maximal projection. (Recall that I allow strings like *take . . . to task* in (1–18) to be a lexical item. Thus it makes sense to talk of the syntactic head of a lexical item, where the X that heads the minimal XP that contains the entire lexical item is the syntactic head of the lexical item.)

When arguments appear inside the relevant maximal projection, they are either (a) sisters to the syntactic head of the lexical item, or (b) objects of a P where the P is part of the lexical item (as in *look after*), or (c) objects of a P where the PP is a sister to the lexical item (as in *depend on*). (Recall that I analyze arguments of N which appear in specifier position as originating in sister position in DS. Thus either these arguments or their trace will be sisters to N at the point of theta assignment.) I will call the (a) case "sister arguments." I will call both the (b) and (c) cases "prepositional arguments."

Two very common principles of theta assignment will account for theta assignment to sister and prepositional arguments.

(1–109)   *Direct Theta Assignment*: A lexical item assigns a theta role to its sister arguments.

(1–110)   *Compositional Theta Assignment*: A lexical item assigns a theta role to its prepositional arguments.

These principles are similar to those commonly assumed in GB (as in Chomsky 1981), as well as in other theories (such as Lexical Functional Grammar, as in Bresnan 1982a&b). Notice that the term "compositional" in (1–110) is, actually, a misnomer, since I am not claiming that the P need have any part in the assignment of the theta role (it might, as in sentences with *look after*; and it might not, as in sentences with *think of*). I adopt this rubric despite the fact that it is a misnomer, since the cases of theta assignment meant to be covered by (1–110) are the same as those meant to be covered by the principle called Compositional Theta Assignment in Chomsky (1981).

There are two very important distinctions, however, between the principles as stated here and those commonly assumed in the literature.

First, theta assignment as stated here applies only to arguments. And arguments are not syntactically identifiable (see sec. 2 above, where I argue that sisters to a lexical head need not be arguments of that head). Thus these principles are semantic in nature. The reference to syntactic structure (to sisters and to prepositional sisters) is needed in order to account for the data we have seen in this chapter, all of which come from

English. The same kinds of data precisely would lead us to the same principles if we had looked at Italian, instead. And I believe that the same kinds of data exist in all configurational languages (in the sense of Chomsky 1981 – that is, languages which exhibit a VP). Thus these principles are syntactic only insofar as the languages they apply to are configurational. That is, the nature of theta assignment is NOT configurational itself – it is semantic, applying to arguments wherever they happen to be located. But in configurational languages the arguments internal to the maximal projection of the head of the lexical item theta assigner will be sisters or prepositional sisters.

Second, Compositional Theta Assignment as stated here is not to be interpreted as a form of syntactic reanalysis. That is, I am not claiming that a lexical head and a P be syntactically restructured into a new constituent (*contra* both the restructuring rule of GB and the verb–preposition incorporation rule of Lexical Functional Grammar (hereafter LFG)). To the contrary, I argue at length against such restructuring in chapter 2, section 3.

Examples of arguments which receive theta roles by Direct Theta Assignment are the italicized items here, where the theta assigners are in boldface:

(1–111) Jack **kicked** *the ball*.
  Your book is **worth** *two cents*.

(See Maling 1982 for the analysis of *worth* as a P.) Direct Theta Assignment may apply to more than one argument of a given lexical item, as in the double object construction (*contra* Emonds 1985, p. 62):

(1–112) I'll **bake** [*you*] [*a cake*].

Examples of arguments which receive theta roles by Compositional Theta Assignment are the italicized items here, where the theta assigner is again in boldface:

(1–113) That **announcement** of *Jack's* shocked everyone.
  I'm **counting** on *you*.
  He isn't **inclined** toward *leniency*.
  Look after *him* for me, won't you?
  Drop the trash into *that can*, please.

Notice that IOs when introduced with a P also receive their theta role by way of Compositional Theta Assignment:

(1–114) I'll **bake** a cake for *you*.

And, like Direct Theta Assignment, Compositional Theta Assignment may apply to more than one argument of a given lexical item:

(1–115) The **lecture** of *Bill's* on *birth control* was an anticlimax, so to speak.

It is commonly claimed that principles of theta assignment hold at DS. However, so long as movement leaves a trace (as in GB) and theta assignment can be to traces, there is no need to specify the level at which these principles hold. I take these principles, then, to account for theta assignment to the italicized arguments here:

(1–116) *Jack's* announcement [t] wrecked havoc.
         What can the children eat [t]?
         What can he be thinking of [t]?

That is, the lexical item assigns a theta role to the trace and, by virtue of being in a chain with that trace, the italicized items in (1–116) are understood to bear a theta role.

Arguments of a lexical item that appear outside the maximal projection of the syntactic head of that lexical item also receive theta roles, but not by the principles in (1–109)–(1–110). As Emonds (1985) has noted, at most one argument may appear outside the relevant maximal projection. I propose the following principle to handle theta assignment to such arguments.

(1–117) *External Theta Assignment*: A lexical item may assign a theta role to at
         most one argument that is external to the maximal projection of (the
         head of) the lexical item.

(Again, recall that I allow lexical items which are strings of words – thus it makes sense to talk about "the head" of a lexical item.)

This principle differs drastically from the generally accepted third principle of theta assignment in GB, which is called Indirect Theta Assignment. With Indirect Theta Assignment a theta role is transmitted from a V via a VP to the GF subject of the clause. Instead, (1–117) makes no mention of anything indirect about this theta assignment: it is directly from the theta assigner to the argument. Furthermore, (1–117) makes no mention of where the external argument may be, only that it must be, in fact, external (that is, outside the phrase).

Let us recapitulate for a moment. In (1–118) all the boldface words are predicates in the sense developed in section 1.

(1–118) Jack **discussed** Bill's **refusal** [PRO **to consider** the best lawyer's **resigna-
         tion** from the firm].

(That *to* in *to consider* is part of the predicate follows from the fact that *to* is an auxiliary. See Pullum 1982 and Napoli 1985.) Predicates can, of course, consist of more than just an event lexical item, as when a specifier or a modifier is part of the predicate (see sec. 1.1 above). But all the arguments of the lexical item that heads the predicate will be role players of the predicate, even if the predicate consists of more than just its head (that is, even if the predicate consists of more than just the event lexical item). We know this from the Principle of Coincidence in (1–46).

We can see, then, that the question of where the external argument covered by principle (1–117) can be is the same question as where the external role player of a predicate can be. This is true even though external role players of a predicate may have originated as internal arguments of the head of the predicate in DS. For example, the GF subject of a passive sentence (derived via movement in GB) is an external role player for its predicate, but it originated as an internal argument (a sister argument).

In section 2 above we saw that A, V, and P, when they are used with an argument structure, must take an external argument. Furthermore, when whole phrases are lexical items that have an argument structure (as in the idiomatic PPs and VPs of sec. 2.5 above), they *per force* take an external argument. If we couple this with the fact that every predicate must have at least one role player, we can see that the external argument is a special argument. Only N does not require an external argument: N can take an external argument (and optional internal ones, as well); or it can take only internal arguments:

(1–119) [*Jack*] is [$_{NP}$ a **failure** (at *tennis*)].

(1–120) [$_{NP}$ *Jack's* **argument** about *Bill*] convinced me.

In (1–119) the N *failure* assigns a theta role to *Jack*, which is external, and to *tennis*, which is internal. In (1–120) the N *argument* assigns a theta role to the genitive NP and to the object of the P, both of which are internal to the NP.

We can now see that predicates headed by N must be singled out from all other predicates, since all other predicates must have an external role player, but predicates headed by N need not. Let me now define one more term:

(1–121) *Subject Role Player*: The external argument of a lexical item at SS is the subject role player of a predicate headed by that lexical item.

(I choose SS as the level of interest in (1–121), since the notion of subject role player relates to the GB notion of subject – as we will see in ch. 2 – and Chomsky (1986b) has argued that his Extended Projection Principle, which requires that V have a subject, holds at SS. In ch. 2, sec. 2 I discuss this further.)

We need a special definition for subject role players of N, however, in precisely those cases where N does not have an external argument at SS. Recall that if N has multiple arguments where all are internal and where one is nonprepositional and nonobjective, then one of its arguments will be a genitive in English, whether it occurs in specifier or in sister position (thus we get *the death of John*, but *that lecture of John's on birth control* – see sec. 2.3 above). And N never has more than one genitive argument (**John's picture of Bill's*). I can now offer the following definition:

(1–122)   *Subject Role Player of N*: If an N takes only one argument in the lexicon, that argument is the subject role player of the predicate headed by the N.

   If an N has no external argument at SS but does have a genitive argument, the genitive argument is the subject role player of the predicate headed by the N.

   Condition: (1–122) holds only if (1–121) does not apply.

Of course, the definition in (1–122) holds only for English and not for Italian, since Italian does not have genitive NPs.

(1–123)   il libro di Moravia sulla guerra
   'the book of Moravia's on the war'

We might be able to modify (1–122) to accommodate Italian by talking about which P can introduce the subject role player of an N (where the P *di* is the most likely counterpart to the English genitive Case). However, there is another serious problem with (1–122): the definition in (1–122) will not help us determine which argument is the subject role player if an N has no external argument and no genitive argument, as in the case of an N with an implicit argument in a sentence such as (1–37), repeated here:

(1–37)   The **destruction** of the city [PRO to prove a point] was deplorable.

Is *the city* or the implicit argument (the argument that controls PRO) the subject role player of *destruction* in (1–37)? Both are arguably internal, so (1–121) does not help us. And neither is observably genitive, so (1–122) does not help us.

There is one thing in common about all subject role players of N which are identified by (1–122) that one might try to use in determining the subject role player of sentences like (1–123) and (1–37). Notice that the internal argument of N that is identified as the subject role player in (1–122) is the argument that would be the external argument of the predicate with a V or A head that most closely corresponds to the sense of the N, if such a V or A exists:

(1–124)a. The death of Jack . . .
  Jack died.
  b. Jack's argument that we should leave . . .
  Jack argued that we should leave.

(1–125) Jack's happiness at the news . . .
  Jack was happy at the news.

One might propose that some comparison of NPs with clauses would help us to determine which argument of an N is its subject role player. However, this approach is fraught with problems. For one, many NPs with head Ns that I have argued do have argument structures do not easily map into any corresponding clause.

(1–126) Jack's book about the war . . .

As we noted in section 2.3 regarding examples like (1–75), repeated here,

(1–75) Mary's photograph of Sue . . .

the genitive NP in such NPs can be understood to have performed a range of activities with respect to the theme argument. Thus there is no one clause to map such NPs into. Furthermore, many Ns that do have morphologically corresponding As do not always have the same relationship to their arguments as the corresponding As do to their arguments.

(1–127) Jack's guilt about the divorce . . .

(1–128) Jack is guilty.

Jack in (1–127) feels guilt, which is a quite different relationship to the concept of guilt from that of *Jack* in (1–128), where Jack actually is guilty.

I believe the above tack raises more problems than it solves and shows that we need an analysis of conceptual structure in order to get at the proper definition of subject role player. This book, however, is not an investigation of conceptual structure – and cannot become one. Thus the best we can hope for here is a definition that is descriptively adequate.

While I realize that the lack of a more conceptual definition of subject role player may leave the reader dissatisfied, the major goal of this work is not really threatened by the absence of such a definition. That is, even if we cannot give a proper definition of subject role player, so long as we can recognize the role players of a predicate, we can go on to develop the principles which govern the domains in which predicates and their role players must appear. And that is the major job of this book.

For now, then, let us keep aiming at a more descriptively adequate definition of subject role players for nominal predicates. A reconsideration of (1–125) and (1–75) can help. In these NPs the genitive NP bears an agentive theta role, regardless of what specific action that NP actually performed. I therefore propose the following definition:

(1–129)   *Subject Role Player of N* – definition two – The agentive argument of an
            N is the subject role player of the predicate headed by the N.
            Condition: (1–129) holds only if (1–121) and (1–122) do not apply.

This definition will now cover both Italian and the instances of NPs in which the N has implicit arguments.

Notice that we need both (1–129) and (1–122), since there are instances in which an N has more than one argument, but none of them is agentive, as in (1–127).

Let me point out that in all the examples we have seen where we posited an implicit argument, that implicit argument was agentive. If all implicit arguments are, in fact, agentive, then all implicit arguments will turn out to be subject role players. This is precisely the result we would expect with Chomsky's (1986b) Extended Projection Principle, in which he holds that subjects need not be syntactically realized, but objects must be (p. 116).

Clearly the fracturization of the definition of subject role player (hereafter srp) is regrettable and surely indicates that further work needs to be done here. Given the fact that N does not require an external argument, I see no possibility for conflating the definitions of srp of N with that of srp of all other types of lexical items except by way of a conceptual definition of srp, a definition that is not readily forthcoming. I therefore leave the issue open, hoping only to have offered definitions that are descriptively accurate.

Let us see now what these three definitions mean for the analysis of different instances of predication. First, the boldface words in all the sentences below are the predicates, where an arrow goes from the head of the predicate to its subject role player. (Some sentences have more than one predicate, but I have marked only one for exemplification.)

(1–130) Mary **wants** potato chips **very much**.

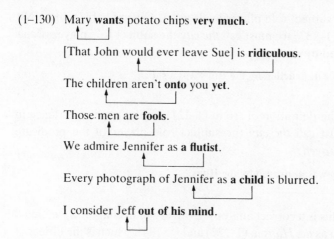

[That John would ever leave Sue] is **ridiculous**.

The children aren't **onto** you **yet**.

Those men are **fools**.

We admire Jennifer as **a flutist**.

Every photograph of Jennifer as **a child** is blurred.

I consider Jeff **out of his mind**.

In (1–130) we have one predicate headed by V, one by A, one by P, and three by N, as well as a PP predicate, all of which have an external argument.

Now let us consider some Ns that have only internal arguments. Here again the predicate we are focusing on is in boldface, and an arrow goes from the head of the predicate to its subject role player.

(1–131) **The death** of John upset us all.

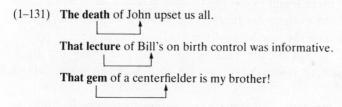

That lecture of Bill's on birth control was informative.

That gem of a centerfielder is my brother!

(For the analysis of the NP in the last sentence of (1–131) as involving predication, see ch. 4.)

In analyzing (1–130) and (1–131), we have used only (1–121) and (1–122). Now let us look at some sentences where we have to use the definition in (1–129).

(1–132) **The destruction** of that city was a shock to all of us.

Here there is an implicit agentive agent of *destruction*. We know that from the fact that we could add a rationale clause to (1–132), and the implicit agentive argument would control the PRO (as in (1–37) repeated above in this section). This implicit agentive agent is the subject role player of the predicate (and it is impossible to draw an arrow to it).

There is at least one more interesting point about the analyses that our definition(s) of subject role player leads us to. Given (1–122), in an NP such as that in (1–133) we must call *the city* the subject role player of the predicate headed by *destruction*:

(1–133)   The city's **destruction by the Huns** was a shock.

In fact, given the definition of srp in (1–121), in the passive sentence in (1–134) we must call *the city* the subject role player of the predicate headed by *destroyed*.

(1–134)   The city was **destroyed by the Huns**.

I believe that this is a correct analysis. I will argue in chapter 2, section 8 that an NP such as *the Huns* in (1–133) and (1–134), which is the object of a passive *by*, is not an argument of any predicate. Rather, these *by* phrases are part of the predicate (they are adverbial modifiers). For now, I merely point out the analyses of (1–133) and (1–134) which follow from my definitions of subject role player.

Returning to the principle of External Theta Assignment in (1–117), given the definitions of subject role player, we can see that whatever requirements there might be on the relative position an external argument can hold to its theta assigner will be subsumed under the requirements that hold on the relative position a subject role player can hold to its predicate. It will be the purpose of chapter 2 to lay out those requirements. I therefore leave (1–117) with no further stipulations added.

There are, however, still some loose strings to tie up. For one, in section 1.4 I adopted the position that there can be more than one instance of predication in a single clause. At this point we can state our Theta Criterion (which is essentially that of Williams 1980, Schein 1982a and b, Rothstein 1983, Chomsky 1986b, Higginbotham 1985, and others).

(1–135)   *Theta Criterion:* Every argument of a lexical item is assigned one and only one theta role by that lexical item.
  Every theta role of a lexical item is assigned to one and only one of its arguments.

This Theta Criterion allows an element to receive a theta role for each argument structure it belongs to.

Emonds (1985, p. 68) notes that whenever an item receives two theta roles, it must be the subject of one of the theta assigners. Let me restate Emonds' observation as a principle:

(1–136) *Functional Criterion*: If an XP receives a theta role from two non-intersecting sources, then it must be the subject role player of at least one of those sources.

(This criterion, of course, raises questions for modification, since modifiers assign theta roles to the items they modify. I address these questions below in this section. Motivation for this criterion is given at the end of ch. 2, sec. 5.)

Another loose string is the issue of what form of the Projection Principle I am adopting. The Projection Principle of Chomsky (1981) ensured that lexical properties would be reflected at all syntactic levels by syntactic entities. For Chomsky (1986b), the phrase-structure component is viewed as a "kind of 'projection' of lexical properties" (p. 81), and we find the explicit claim that whatever element is "understood" in a particular position is actually there in syntactic representation (p. 84). This means that if a V, for example, takes a clausal argument in its lexical structure, then one of its grammatical functions will be filled with a clause (where the GFs are GF subject, DO, IO, object of a P). The obvious question is, where do implicit arguments fit into the grammar given the Projection Principle? Roeper (1987) has argued that implicit arguments have syntactic functions (they can control PRO, for example), but they do not occupy syntactic slots – they do not hold grammatical functions such as subject, DO, IO, object of a preposition). Chomsky himself (1986b, pp. 130–1) raises the question of what to do about implicit arguments, and this is part of the reason that he allows subjects not to be syntactically realized with his Extended Projection Principle.

I propose that we modify the Projection Principle to keep its essence by simply saying that all lexical properties must be reflected at all syntactic levels, but not necessarily by entities that bear GFs. Instead, so long as an entity has syntactic functions (such as being able to control PRO), such an entity will qualify as reflecting lexical properties at the syntactic levels. Thus if a lexical item obligatorily takes an agentive argument in its lexical structure, then when we put this lexical item into a syntactic structure, the agentive argument must appear as an entity that may perform a syntactic function – whether this argument appears explicitly (in some GF position) or implicitly (perhaps in an affix, perhaps not).

In section 2.4 above I discussed Jackendoff's (1987b) nonlexical rule for adding theme *with* arguments to verbs such as *spray*. At that point I raised the question of how such nonlexical rules affected the Projection Principle. But, as I stated there, so long as we encode in the lexical information of a verb the fact that it can undergo the nonlexical rule, then lexical properties of the verb are still reflected in all the syntactic levels. Thus I do not see Jackendoff's nonlexical rules as being a problem for the Projection Principle.

In section 1.3 above I argued that the so-called aspectual verbs are not themselves predicates, but, rather, part of the predicate headed by an item in the clause embedded as a sister to the aspectual verb. But we saw with (1–28) that the object of *to* in a clause with *seem* is a role player for the predicate that *seem* is a part of. Let me repeat (1–28) for convenience:

(1–28)   Jack seems to me [t to understand French pretty well].

The question now is whether such an analysis poses a problem for the Projection Principle since the object of the *to* does not appear in the lexical structure of *understand*, which is the head of the only predicate in this sentence. The question is a tricky one. The Projection Principle says that lexical properties must be encoded in the syntax. But its spirit is to see the syntax as a reflection of lexical properties. So the syntactic presence of the object of *to* but its absence from the lexical argument structure of *understand* is problematic for the spirit, if not the word, of the Projection Principle. And, unlike with our discussion of theme *with* above, we cannot say that the ability to co-occur with *seem* is part of the lexical information of *understand*. Instead, every predicate has the potential of appearing with these aspectual verbs. And since this potential is not lexically idiosyncratic, it should not be built into the lexical structure of individual lexical items. It would seem, then, that our grammar must allow for items in the syntax which do not appear in the lexical structure of a given lexical item, but which can be attracted into the network of role players of the predicate headed by that lexical item.

A final point I would like to address here is where modification fits in. I argued in section 1.4 above that in my approach to predication, there must be a distinction made between modification and predication. And I believe that the fact that a modifier (such as an AP) falls within the maximal projection of the item it modifies (such as an N), so that it is an intrinsic part of the sense of the entire phrase (such as being an intrinsic part of the reference of the NP), is so different from the relationship of a predicate to a role player that this difference demands recognition in the theory.

Others have identified modification with predication. For example, Williams (1980) calls some AP predicates "modifiers" (p. 204), and Higginbotham (1985) calls some AP modifiers "predicates" (p. 564). Yet Williams' coindexing rules for predication will not apply to instances of modification such as

(1–137)   the big butterfly

since his coindexing rules coindex phrases only, but *butterfly* is an N and not a phrasal level – so we cannot coindex the AP *big* with the N *butterfly* in (1–137). Furthermore, Higginbotham is forced to posit a special rule of Theta Identification to allow the AP *big* to discharge its theta role to the N *butterfly* (where other discharge rules apply to phrases, again). Thus, even though these linguists have not made the distinction in terminology that I have made, their theories require special rules to handle the assignment of a theta role from a modifying AP to the head N it modifies.

Certainly, however, there is much in common between predication and modification, and any theory of grammar should capture the similarities, as well as recognize the differences. In the present theory one way a predicate and a modifier are similar is that the head of both assigns a theta role to at least one argument. But I believe the similarity goes beyond that.

The specific proposal I would like to make is that one of the theta assignment principles I have given in this section can handle theta assignment from a modifier to an N: the principle of External Theta Assignment. That is, if we allow "argument" to be loosely understood to include "head of an argument," a theta role can be assigned to an N and not just to NP. That way External Theta Assignment can account for theta assignment by modifiers, since the N receiving a theta role from an A that heads a modifying AP is always external to the AP.

Given this analysis, a modifier will have an external argument. But then it takes only a small relaxation of our definition of subject role player in (1–121) to allow modifiers to have subject role players. That is, we need say only that the external argument of a lexical item is the subject role player of a predicate or a modifier headed by that lexical item. Now we can see that the Functional Criterion in (1–136) can stand unchanged, adequately handling instances in which an item receives a theta role both because it is a role player of a predicate and because its head is being modified (where I am assuming that if N gets a theta role, that theta role will percolate up to N″), as in:

(1–138) I **saw** [the tall kid].

The curved arrows in (1–138) indicate theta assignment. Here *kid* is the subject role player for the modifier *tall*, as predicted by the Functional Criterion.

I suggest further that the coindexing principles that I will develop in chapter 2 for coindexing a subject role player and its predicate will also hold for coindexing an N and its modifier. However, since modification is not the focus of this work, I will not go any further with this suggestion, but leave it for the interested reader to (trivially) confirm.

Let me also point out that modifiers can take more than one argument, as in *anyone talented at the piano*. Here *talented* assigns a theta role both to *anyone,* which it modifies, and to *the piano*. But the arguments of a head of a modifier that appear in addition to the object modified will always be internal to the maximal projection of the head of the predicate. Therefore, Direct and Compositional Theta Assignment will easily handle theta assignment to these arguments.

5   The feasibility and desirability of a formal definition of *predicate*

At this point the reader who is familiar with the literature on predication may still be longing for a formal definition of predicate within the framework here. I will now show that such a formal definition is not possible, and I suggest that it is not desirable, although the real evidence for its undesirability comes from the fact that the present theory is more nearly empirically adequate than the other theories with formal definitions of predicate discussed in this book. That evidence is found in chapters 2 through 5.

We will begin by considering an existing formal definition of predicate. And the examination of this formal statement will allow us to see that formal definitions of predicate that have appeared in the linguistic literature accessible to nonlogicians are not helpful to us.

I have chosen the definition of Culicover and Wilkins (1986) because it is recent, because it is well supported in their work, and because it has points of similarity to most other formal definitions of predicate in the nonphilosophical linguistic literature. It is not, however, useful to us with the framework we are adopting here, for reasons we will see immediately.

(1–139) "A predicate is any non-propositional major category X^{max}, immediately dominated by V^n, which (a) bears no grammatical relation to the verb, or (b) is an infinitival VP."

(From Culicover and Wilkins 1986, p. 121.)

First, we have seen that predicates need not be maximal projections (that is, they need not be X^{max}). In fact, the only predicates that are maximal projections are headed ones that just happen to fill the maximal projection of their head, unheaded predicate PPs and VPs (the idiomatic cases – see sec. 2.5), and appositive relative clauses (see ch. 5, sec. 5).

Second, we are not restricting our predicates to being immediately dominated by a projection of V. For example, to use a variation of a sentence from Emonds (1985, p. 273), in (1–140) the phrase *as Hamlet* predicates of *Meryl*, yet this phrase is immediately under S (or I') (where S is the phrase consisting of a GF subject and the rest of the clause, and where I' is the node dominating Inflection and its sisters):

(1–140) Meryl **as Hamlet** would be a poor choice.

Third, we have made no restriction against our predicates' bearing a grammatical relation to the verb. Culicover and Wilkins are using this restriction to ban predicates (except infinitival VPs) from being assigned theta roles. That is, they take grammatical relations to be what I have been calling GFs (syntactic subject, DO, IO, O(bject of a) P(reposition), but since their predication theory involves a coindexing rule that operates in a structure they call R-structure and since R-structure is formed from DS, the GFs of interest to the definition in (1–139) are what Chomsky (1981) calls GF-theta. We differ, then, from the definition in (1–139) by allowing items such as *helpless* in (1–108)a, repeated here for convenience, to be predicates (where the sole role player of *helpless* is *John*), even though such a predicate is theta-marked by the verb, in this case, *rendered* (see Emonds 1985, p. 83, and sec. 3 above).

(1–108)a. The medication rendered John helpless.

Fourth, we do not allow VP to be a predicate except when it is an idiomatic VP or a headed predicate that just happens to fill the entire VP (see secs. 2.5 and 2.6).

In sum, the theory presented here differs from Culicover and Wilkins' on almost every formal aspect of their definition of predicate. I contend that it would be impossible to write a formal definition of predicate in our sense using syntactic terminology such as categories and projections of categories and domination information. This is trivially so because we are allowing strings which do not form constituents to be predicates (such as *take /. . . to task*).

In chapters 2 through 5 of this book, I hope to make it clear that definitions of predicate and theories of predication which gain their formal properties by relying on syntactic configuration properties are not desirable in/ any case, even if we were to allow only constituents to be predicates. Predication is a semantic relationship and predicates are semantic entities, and there is no one-to-one correlation between semantic entities and syntactic entities. Hence, a useful definition of predicate and a theoretically valid and empirically adequate theory of predication must be built on semantic notions.

In this way definitions of predicate in the philosophical tradition turn out to be more nearly consonant with mine than definitions in the GB literature. Thus, as Bill Croft (personal communication) has pointed out to me, what in natural language counts as a single predicate in first-order logic is anything, with the only condition being that referring expressions cannot be predicates or parts of predicates.

6   Semantic head versus structural head

There is one final distinction that needs to be made. As Abney (1986) has pointed out, a phrase has a structural head and a semantic head. Thus the structural head of a VP is the V and this is also, typically, its semantic head. But Abney argues that the structural head need not be identical to the semantic head, and he analyzes nominals in such a way that the structural and semantic heads are not identical.

I do not follow Abney in his analysis of nominals for reasons extraneous to the present work. However, we will see in chapters 3 and 4 that there are NPs in both Italian and English (and many other languages) whose syntactic head is not identical to their semantic head. Thus I analyze an NP such as (1–64), repeated here for convenience, as having *matto* as its syntactic head, but *Giorgio* as its semantic head:

(1–64)   quel matto di Giorgio
          that madman of Giorgio
          'that madman Giorgio'

Since theta roles are semantic entities, I contend that theta assignment trickles down to the semantic head of a phrase. Of course, this will become an issue only when the semantic and syntactic heads of a phrase are not identical. We will see the ramifications of this contention in chapters 3 and 4.

7   Conclusion

We have defined several terms and offered three principles of theta theory in this chapter. They are listed below for ease of reference as the reader goes on to later chapters. We begin with the definitions and then list the principles.

First, we never set aside a definition of predicate as a numbered example. But we have developed the idea that a predicate is an event lexical item with certain specifiers and modifiers, taking at least one role player. We allow a lexical item to be not just a single word, but a string that may or may not form a constituent and may or may not be continuous (such as *look after* or *take . . . to task* or *off his rocker*):

(1–16)   *Head of a predicate*: The lexical item which assigns a theta role to the role players of a predicate containing that lexical item is the head of that predicate.

(1–121)   *Subject Role Player*: The external argument of a lexical item at SS is the subject role player of the predicate headed by that lexical item.

(1–122)   *Subject Role Player of N*: If an N takes only one argument in the lexicon, that argument is the subject role player of the predicate headed by the N.
If an N has no external argument at SS but does have a genitive argument, the genitive argument is the subject role player of the predicate headed by the N.
Condition: (1–122) holds only if (1–121) does not apply.

(1–129)   *Subject Role Player of N* – definition two – The agentive argument of an N is the subject role player of the predicate headed by the N.
Condition: (1–129) holds only if (1–121) and (1–122) do not apply.

(1–46)   *Principle of Coincidence*: The arguments of a lexical item are the role players of the predicate headed by that lexical item.

(1–109)   *Direct Theta Assignment*: A lexical item assigns a theta role to its sister arguments.

(1–110)   *Compositional Theta Assignment*: A lexical item assigns a theta role to its prepositional arguments.

(1–117)   *External Theta Assignment*: A lexical item may assign a theta role to at most one argument that is external to the maximal projection of (the head of) the lexical item.

(1–135)   *Theta Criterion*: Every argument of a lexical item is assigned one and only one theta role by that lexical item.
Every theta role of a lexical item is assigned to one and only one of its arguments.

(1–136)   *Functional Criterion*: If an XP receives a theta role from two non-intersecting sources, then it must be the subject role player of at least one of those sources.

We did not set aside any formulation of the Projection Principle as a numbered example. However, we took the Projection Principle to require that lexical properties be reflected in the syntactic levels by syntactic entities, where syntactic entities need not fill GFs, but must be able to function syntactically. Thus we see implicit arguments as no problem for the Projection Principle. We noted, however, that the so-called aspectual verbs call for a revision of the Projection Principle to the effect that the grammar must allow role players to be attracted into an event structure via the syntactic mechanism of embedding (where the aspectual verbs take an embedded clause). I leave the exploration of the details of this revision for future research.

The next chapter discusses the restrictions on coindexing a predicate with its subject role player, which is a core part of a predication theory.

2 *The principles of predication coindexing*

In chapter 1 we established that every predicate must have at least one role player, and that for all predicates other than those headed by N, every predicate must have precisely one external role player at SS. We singled out the external role player and labelled it the "subject role player" (where the "subject role player" for predicates headed by N is not necessarily external, however – see (1–122) and (1–129)). It then follows from the definitions of subject role player given in chapter 1 that every predicate must have a subject role player. We noted that all the role players of a predicate receive a theta role, since they are all arguments of the head of the predicate, according to the Principle of Coincidence, repeated here for convenience:

(1–46)   *Principle of Coincidence*: The arguments of a lexical item are the role players of the predicate headed by that lexical item.

We developed the principles for theta assignment (which will be restated below as relevant examples of their application arise).

   In this chapter we will develop the principles for coindexing a predicate with its subject role player (srp). Coindexing principles are common to other theories of predication. In fact, since many other theories of predication treat VPs as predicates (with internal role players being part of the predicate), the coindexing between a subject role player and its predicate is the key relationship to describe. With the definition of predicate in chapter 1, however, all role players of a predicate are semantically on an equal footing. Therefore, if a language were non-configurational, so that all the arguments of a predicate were always external to the maximal projection of the head of the predicate, it is quite possible that there would be no sense in talking about coindexing between a subject role player and its predicate because there might be no special role player which could be identified as the subject role player (and see Miller (1988), who argues that the term "subject" has no grammatical counterpart in Tagalog).

However, English and Italian, the two languages from which the data base for this book is drawn, are configurational. Thus even with my definition of predicate in chapter 1, it makes sense to talk about a subject role player (although, as we saw in ch. 1, a precise definition is elusive when the predicate is headed by an N, since no role player need be external).

In this chapter, therefore, we will develop coindexing principles and examine the types of data used to support competing coindexing principles, showing how the one developed here differs from those.

Unlike many other theories, the present one also involves principles which restrain how multiple predicates in a single clause structure interact. The theory here has been influenced by the notion of thematically governed predication in Williams 1980, by the theory of control in Bresnan 1982a, by the theory of thematic conditions on R-structure in Culicover and Wilkins 1986, and, most of all, by the idea of secondary predication in Rothstein 1983, although certainly other works have helped to shape the principles here.

Most of the examples in this chapter are from English. However, Italian could easily have been used to make precisely the same points. I feel free, therefore, to mix the two languages at will.

Let me remind the reader that throughout this book I assume a restrictive form of X' theory: that in which for $X=N$, V, A, or P, we say that X'' expands only to specifier plus X', and X' expands to X plus all its phrasal sisters (where I do not allow for adjuncts that recursively expand X' into X', and see the introduction to this book). The only exception to this is that every projection of X can have a coordinated like projection (that is, a projection with the same number of bars). (Actually, the restrictions on coordination are not so simple – see Dik 1968, Schachter 1977, Peterson 1981, and Gazdar *et al.* 1982, among others.) C(omplementizer) and I(nflection), however, can have sisters to phrasal projections as well as to the C and I levels. Furthermore, I take the position (defended in Napoli 1987a) that there are no small clauses (but see sec. 12 below), a position which again coincides with a restrictive version of X-bar theory. One of the points I hope to make is that even with such a restrictive version of X-bar theory, the wide range of data on predication can be handled adequately.

The principles for coindexing presented in this chapter are built upon the idea that theta roles exist. However, no attempt is made here to distinguish between different theta roles, thus no attempt is made to define restrictions on predication coindexing which limit the combinations of theta roles that may appear in multiple predicate clauses. Such an endeavor would most certainly merit a separate work of book length (as we can see from the works cited at the outset of ch. 1, sec. 1.6). Still, we will see that even with only the crude idea of whether or not an item bears a theta role, we can recognize important restrictions on the interactions of predicates and theta assigners in multiple predicate clauses.

The goal of this chapter is to present a (largely) nonconfigurational set of predication coindexing principles within the general framework of GB. One of the argument forms used here is: if predication coindexing is allowed between points P_1 and P_2 in a given sentence, then if in another sentence with the same structural analysis predication coindexing between P_1 and P_2 is not allowed, the impossibility of predication coindexing in the second sentence is not due to configurational restrictions on predication coindexing. (Notice that P_1 and P_2 need not be syntactic nodes – or even continuous strings. See secs. 1.1 and 1.2 of ch. 1 for arguments that predicates are semantic units that can be realized by a variety of syntactic strings. See ch. 1, sec. 1.4 and the analysis of (2–159) in sec. 14 below for evidence that non-nominal role players are, likewise, semantic units that can be realized by a variety of syntactic strings.) The result of using this argument, as the reader will see, is that all configurational restrictions in the linguistic literature previously claimed to hold on predication coindexing do not hold. However, there are still many sentences in which predication coindexing is disallowed. My theory correctly rules out many of them, but not all.

The next question, then, is what rules out the instances of predication that my theory cannot handle. I address this question in section 11.

1   Brief overview of theories of predication within GB

The prevailing interest in recent work on predication within GB has centered on the configurational restrictions on the coindexing rule that applies between a predicate and its srp. There are two major approaches to consider here.

One approach takes subject role players and their predicates to stand in the relationship of sister nodes which form a constituent together (perhaps with adjuncts or adverbials as additional sisters within that constituent) at SS. This is the approach of Chomsky (1981), among others. With this analysis the subject and predicate mutually c-command each other and they form a clause (one type of which lacks a verb and is called a small clause). Furthermore, the VP of a sentence is taken to be the predicate (rather than just the head V and its specifiers and modifiers, as in my theory). One of the debates with this approach centers on what category this constituent is (S, AP, PP . . .) in a given small clause construction (see, for example Kitagawa 1985). This approach would analyze (2–1) as having two clauses, one being a small clause, where I have labelled the small clause node SC for expository purposes. (The trees here are simplified, since they are intended only to show the relevant branching relationships.)

(2–1)

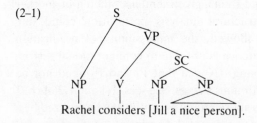

Rachel considers [Jill a nice person].

With this approach, the subject of many predicates is taken to be PRO, as in the small clause of (2–2). (That is, while *consider* in (2–1) is analyzed as having a clausal argument, *paint* in (2–2) is analyzed as having a simple NP argument with an adjunct proposition.)

(2–2)

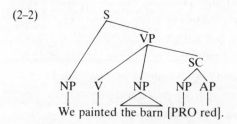

We painted the barn [PRO red].

This approach to predication assumes that the lexical head of every predicate assigns a theta role to all the arguments of that lexical head (via the maximal projection of the predicate, if the argument is external), and it takes the category P to be a theta assigner. Therefore, this approach is consistent with the Projection Principle of Chomsky (1981), which requires all lexical properties of a word to be present at DS, SS, and L(ogical) F(orm). It is also consistent with Chomsky's (1981) Theta

Criterion, whereby an item may receive at most one theta role and each theta role can be assigned to at most one argument, and, thus, no item can be a member of more than one argument structure.

A second approach takes subject role players to c-command and to be external to the maximal projection of their predicates with the subjects c-subjacent to their predicates but with no stipulation that the subject and the predicate form a constituent, all of these conditions holding at SS (see Williams 1980, among others). (B is c-subjacent to A iff A is dominated by at most one branching node which does not dominate B.) This approach explicitly denies the existence of any notion of subject role player independent from external argument. Also, in this approach the presence of the external argument–predicate relationship does not necessarily indicate the presence of a clause.

A variation on this general approach takes subject role players and their predicates to be sister nodes, that is, to mutually c-command each other, but again not necessarily to form a constituent (see Schein 1982a).

Again in Williams' and Schein's approach, the lexical head of a predicate is taken to assign a theta role to all its arguments and the category P is taken to be a theta role assigner. However, obligatory control is taken to be an instance of predication (unlike with Chomsky 1981), thus this theory will somehow have to incorporate a way for the infinitival clausal predicate to give a theta role to its external argument, perhaps by way of a coindexing involving PRO. I lump these two approaches together since both take the theta criterion as limiting any given item (such as an NP) to receiving at most one theta role from a single predicate, but they allow an item to have more than one theta role if it is an argument of more than one predicate. With this approach we do not posit a small clause in a sentence like (2–1), but rather a single clause, as in (2–3).

(2–3)

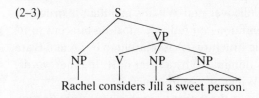

And with this approach we do not need a small clause with a PRO subject in the analysis of a sentence like (2–2), but rather a single clause, as in (2–4).

(2–4)

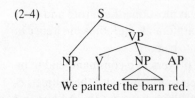

We painted the barn red.

This approach requires alteration of the original Theta Criterion of Chomsky (1981) and of the Projection Principle along the lines suggested in Schein (1982b). The Theta Criterion proposed in chapter 1 is consistent with this approach, as is the discussion of the Projection Principle in section 4 of chapter 1. I repeat that Theta Criterion here for convenience:

(1–135)   *Theta Criterion*: Every argument of a lexical item is assigned one and only one theta role by that lexical item.
Every theta role of a lexical item is assigned to one and only one of its arguments.

More recently attention has been drawn away from the structural restrictions on predication coindexing to thematic restrictions. Culicover and Wilkins (1986) offer a coindexing rule which coordinates restrictions on the theta roles of predicates and their subject role players in a grammatical level called R-structure, which is read off of DS. (That is, if the predicates themselves receive thematic roles from some other source, the coindexing rule is sensitive to the choice of theta roles, and, if the predicates do not receive theta roles, the coindexing rule is sensitive to the very fact that the predicates lack a theta role.) Like Williams and Schein, Culicover and Wilkins do not require that there be a clause structure every time we encounter the subject role player–predicate relationship and, since their predicate is a maximal projection, the subject role player is external to the predicate. Unlike Williams and Schein, they do not require the subject role player to c-command its predicate (although such a requirement would not be contrary to any of their findings). Still, even Culicover and Wilkins maintain a structural restriction: under certain conditions a predicate must be bijacent to its subject role player in syntactic structure. (A is bijacent to B if A and B are sisters or if A is immediately dominated by a sister of B. In other words, bijacency is the converse of Williams' c-subjacency.)

We will make comparisons to these three approaches to predication and to others in the material which follows. But before we leave them, let me point out something that all of these approaches have in common. They all see the semantic relationship between a predicate and its subject role player as a unified phenomenon. However, as we will see in this chapter, predication is not a unified phenomenon, it splits between primary predication and secondary predication.

A fourth work on predication, Rothstein 1983, is the one that I believe is most nearly on the right track. Rothstein makes a division between primary predication, defined configurationally, and secondary predication, and argues that all secondary predicates must find a subject role player that is theta marked by some lexical head other than the secondary predicate. She finds a middle ground between Chomsky (1981) and Williams, by employing small clauses in structures where a predicate's subject role player does not get a theta role from some other source (thus she would adopt the analysis in (2–1) over that in (2–3)), but not in structures where a predicate's subject role player does get a theta role from some other source (thus she would adopt the analysis in (2–4) over that in (2–2)). (Chomsky 1986b follows Rothstein here.) While I differ from Rothstein both in my definition of the distinction between primary and secondary predicates and in the restrictions I put on secondary predication, I agree with her that all of the predicates she called secondary predicates should fall under my Proviso One in sec. 5 below. The present work, then, owes much to the insights of Rothstein.

Below I define primary and secondary predication and I offer a coindexing principle for primary predication based on the claim that clauses are the domain for primary predication. Then I look at the kinds of evidence that led other linguists to propose configurationally based coindexing principles and I show how they are empirically inadequate. I offer a new set of coindexing principles for secondary predication based on the notions of barriers, lexical structures, and primary predication domains. Thus no structural relationship that is independent from the semantic notions relevant to predication are employed in these principles.

2   Primary versus secondary predication and primary predication coindexing

In chapter 1 I assumed the position (defended explicitly in Napoli 1987a) that there can be multiple predicates in a single clause. This position is shared by many linguists who propose varying predication theories (Williams 1980, Schein 1982a, Bresnan 1982a, Rothstein 1983, Culicover and Wilkins 1986, Chomsky 1986b, among others), and it forms the cornerstone for my theory of predication by allowing us to distinguish between two types of predication: primary and secondary.

Rothstein (1983) first pointed out a difference between primary and secondary predication (where her secondary predicates were not arguments of any lexical head, but, rather, adjuncts). What follows is a variation on Rothstein's position that is close in spirit, although distinct in form.

In the definitions that follow I use the X-bar theory of Chomsky (1986a), in which I(nflection) is a head, taking the GF subject as its specifier and taking the main VP (or AP or NP or PP or CP) as its right sister. The definitions that follow hold at Predicate Structure, a structure formed from SS, which is the relevant level for predication coindexing (as will be argued below).

(2–5)   *A primary predicate* is a predicate
(a) whose head is the syntactic head of the first XP right sister to I, or
(b) which is itself the first XP right sister to I.

The definition of head of a predicate was given in chapter 1; I repeat it here for convenience:

(1–16)   *Head of a predicate*: The lexical item which assigns a theta role to the role players of a predicate containing that lexical item is the head of that predicate.

I assume that when *be* is used as a grammatical word (as in (1–2) of chapter 1: *The man who marries young is happy*) the first right sister to *be* will qualify as the XP in (2–5).

It is easy to see that a primary predicate is the "ideal" predicate, in some sense; it is our canonical idea of a predicate. If there is only one predicate in a clause, it will, by definition, be the primary predicate. And, as we all know, the subject role player of that primary predicate will be its GF subject. We can now state this fact as the coindexing principle for primary predicates:

(2–6)   *Primary Predication Coindexing*: Coindex a primary predicate with its GF subject.

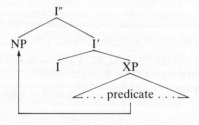

It is now a trivial matter to define secondary predicates:

(2–7)   *A secondary predicate* is any predicate other than a primary predicate.

That is, secondary predicates can appear in a wide range of syntactic positions, as can their subject role players. The real job of this chapter, then, will be to discover the principles of coindexing for secondary predication.

We can see two facts from (2–5)–(2–7) that will be used below. First, the relevant configurational domain of a primary predicate is its clause. Second, every secondary predicate belongs to a clause that has a unique primary predicate, but a primary predicate may have more than one secondary predicate within its domain.

Rothstein (1983) proposed that primary predication could be determined by a structural relationship only or by a structural and semantic relationship. I differ from her here in limiting all predication coindexing to elements bearing only the semantic relationship of subject role player–predicate. I thus exclude from discussion any purely structural relationship. (And I know of no convincing arguments that structurally based coindexing between a V and its GF subject (if it should be shown to be needed), for example, is the same kind of grammatical phenomenon as predication coindexing.)

In (2–8)–(2–9) we see examples of primary predication in both Italian and English in which the GF subject of the clause is the subject role player of a predicate. In (2–8)–(2–9) the entire predicate is in boldface, with the head of the predicate italicized. An arrow goes from the head of the predicate to its srp.

(2–8)   Maria **ha** *innaffiato* i fiori.

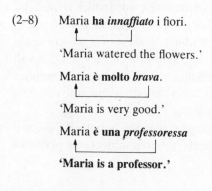

'Maria watered the flowers.'

Maria è **molto** *brava*.

'Maria is very good.'

Maria è **una** *professoressa*

'Maria is a professor.'

(2–9)a. Maria è **appena** *arrivata*.

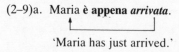

'Maria has just arrived.'

b. Maria è **stata** *ignorata*.

     ┎─────────────┚

'Maria has been ignored.'

c. Maria **was run over by the truck**.

     ┎─────────┚

In the examples in (2–8) the lexical head of the predicate assigns a theta role to the NP *Maria* at DS by way of External Theta Assignment, restated here for convenience.

(1–117) *External Theta Assignment*: A lexical item may assign a theta role to at most one argument that is external to the maximal projection of (the head of) the lexical item.

In (2–9)a&b the head of the predicate assigns a theta role to *Maria* by way of Direct Theta Assignment, restated here for convenience.

(1–109) *Direct Theta Assignment*: A lexical item assigns a theta role to its sister arguments.

In (2–9)c the head of the predicate assigns a theta role to *Maria* by way of Compositional Theta Assignment, restated here for convenience.

(1–110) *Compositional Theta Assignment*: A lexical item assigns a theta role to its prepositional arguments.

In (2–8) we have active sentences in which *Maria* is an argument of the single word which is the head of the predicate and is external to the maximal projection of the predicate at all syntactic levels. In (2–9)a we have an ergative structure (Burzio 1986) and in (2–9)b a passive structure, in both of which *Maria* is an argument of the single word which is the head of the predicate and is a sister (the DO of the V) to that lexical head at DS. In (2–9)c we have a passive structure in which *Maria* is an argument again of the verb which heads the predicate, but is the object of a P at DS. In all of these examples the predicate (consisting of a lexical head, sometimes with the addition of specifiers and modifiers) assigns a semantic role (see ch. 1, sec. 1.6) to its subject role player.

In (2–10) we see examples of primary predication in both Italian and English in which the GF subject of the clause is the subject role player of the XP.

(2–10) Maria è **senza** {**pietà/cuore**}.

     ┎─────┚

'Maria is without {pity/heart}.'

In (2–10) the GF subject is an argument of the entire PP, which is a single lexical item. Thus we have a phrasal predicate here. (The copula in (2–10), as in two of the examples of (2–8) above, is a purely grammatical word. See the discussion following (1–2) in ch. 1.)

As was argued in chapter 1, the relevant level for the determination of what functions as a predicate cannot be the lexicon. Instead, it is not until the level of DS that we have modifiers and specifiers present, which can be parts of the predicate. Therefore, coindexing cannot apply before DS. Furthermore, since movement can result in an argument being external to the maximal projection of (the head of) its predicate (as in passive sentences, such as in (2–9)b&c), and since if there is an external argument at SS it must be the srp of the predicate, coindexing cannot apply before movement. Therefore, coindexing cannot apply before SS.

I contend that coindexing applies at SS to build up a level called Predicate Structure (PS), and I will proceed on that assumption in this chapter. (The term "Predicate Structure" is borrowed from Williams 1980, who has PS derive from SS.) However, in chapter 5 we will see evidence that PS must be built from a level of representation in which certain reconstruction rules have applied. Thus it would appear that PS is built from an even later level than SS: from some point in LF after the application of the relevant reconstruction rules. For now I will set aside this refinement, noting only that PS cannot be formed at any point prior to SS.

As noted in chapter 1, not all clauses involve a predication relationship between their GF subject and some other element. In (2–11)–(2–13) we see such examples:

(2–11)   Mia zia è la Signorina Prothero.
         'My aunt is Miss Prothero.'

(2–12)   Mum's the word.

(2–13)   It seems that Bertha isn't into art anymore.

In (2–11) the GF subject is identified rather than predicated by the NP *la Signorina Prothero* (see ch. 1, sec. 1.3). In (2–12) the GF subject is part of a semantically unanalyzable idiom and as such bears no theta role (again see ch. 1, sec. 1.3). In (2–13) the *it* is a dummy that bears no theta role (see Napoli 1987a) and the matrix V *seems* is not the head of a predicate (again see ch. 1, sec. 1.3). None of these is an example of predication (although the discontinuous string *seems . . . isn't into . . . anymore* in (2–13) is a predicate, whose srp is *Bertha* and which has an additional role player, *art*). However, so far as I can see, if there were coindexing between an identifying referential phrase (such as *la Signorina Prothero* in (2–11)) and the referential phrase it identifies (*Mia zia*), this coindexing would occur under the same conditions as primary predication coindexing (given in (2–6) above). (See Jackendoff 1983 for more similarities between the relationships of identification and predication.)

Secondary predication is all instances of predication other than primary predication. The srp for a secondary predicate may be in GF subject position (of a primary predicate) or not.

(2–14)   Maria ha invitato Giulia **come amica**.

'Maria invited Giulia as a friend.'

(2–15)   Maria ha mangiato la carne **nuda**.

'Maria ate the meat nude.'

In (2–14) the predicate *come amica* finds its subject role player, *Giulia*, in DO of the matrix V. (Of course, (2–14) is, irrelevantly for us, ambiguous: *come amica* could also predicate of *Maria*.) In (2–15) the predicate *nuda* finds its subject role player, *Maria*, in GF subject position of the matrix V. In both sentences the secondary predicate is not the (head of the) first XP right sister to I. Both *come amica* and *nuda* are secondary predicates, then. (A discussion of the fact that I am assuming a single clause analysis for sentences like those in (2–14)–(2–15) is found in ch. 1, sec. 1.4. A defense of this position is given in Napoli 1987a.)

We will see in chapters 3, 4 and 5 that the examples in (2–16)–(2–23) are also instances of secondary predication.

(2–16)   Hai visto quel **matto** di Giorgio?

'Have you seen that madman George?'

(2–17)   I love to watch a **gem** of a centerfielder like Jake.

(2–18)   We all expected some **asshole** officer to make the welcoming address.

(2–19)   Hai visitato il **paesino** di Framura?

'Have you visited the little town of Framura?'

(2–20)   Soffra del **fatto** [che non insegna più la sintassi].

'She suffers from the fact that she doesn't teach syntax anymore.'

(2–21)   Ha scolpito **una statua** di marmo di Cappella.

'She sculpted a statue from the marble of Cappella.'

(2–22)   Those **first-grade** pictures of Bill's are great.

(2–23)   Sassari, **una città della Sardegna**, è bella.

'Sassari, a city of Sardegna, is pretty.'

In (2–16) the predicate *matto* finds it subject role player in its PP sister and the whole NP *quel matto di Giorgio* is the DO of the matrix V (see ch. 3). In (2–17) the predicate *gem* finds its subject role player in its PP sister and the whole NP *a gem of a centerfielder* is the DO of the matrix V (see ch. 4, sec. 1). In (2–18) the predicate *asshole* finds its subject role player in its sister N *officer* inside the complex nominal *asshole officer* (see ch. 4, sec. 2). The NP *some asshole officer* is the GF subject of the embedded clause. In (2–19) the predicate *paesino* finds its subject role player in its PP sister and the whole *il paesino di Framura* is the DO of the matrix V (see ch. 5, sec. 1). In (2–20) the predicate *fatto* finds its subject role player in the clausal sister to the head N *fatto* (see ch. 5, sec. 2). The whole NP headed by *fatto* is object of the inflected preposition *del*. In (2–21) the predicate *una statua* finds its subject role player as the object of the preposition *di*, where the PP is a daughter of V′ (see ch. 5, sec. 3). In (2–22) the predicate *first grade* finds its subject role player in the object of its PP sister, *Bill's* (see ch. 5, sec. 4). And in (2–23) the predicate *una città della Sardegna* is in apposition to the GF subject of the primary predicate, *Sassari*, and takes that NP as its subject role player (see ch. 5, sec. 5).

   In this chapter I will concentrate on the analysis of primary predication structures (as in (2–9)–(2–10)) and on the analysis of secondary predication structures such as those in (2–14)–(2–15). I take up the discussion of examples such as those in (2–16)–(2–23) in later chapters.

3   C-command and objects of prepositions

One of the most pervasive claims (or, sometimes, basic assumptions) in configurational approaches to predication is that the srp must c-command its predicate. I will here show that the notion of c-command is irrelevant to the coindexing of a predicate with its srp. We will start by evaluating the data and arguments that led other linguists to propose that a subject role player c-command its predicate.

From a look at the literature, it seems clear that the unavailability of many objects of prepositions to be subject role players to secondary predicates outside their PP is the source of the proposal that subject role players must c-command their predicates. In fact, Schein (1982a) points out sentences with oblique objects in Russian, Finnish, and Icelandic in which the oblique NP cannot be the subject role player of a predicate and argues that oblique Case and prepositions should both be represented in the same way. Thus in his opinion even these examples fall under the rubric of objects of prepositions that are unavailable as subject role players for secondary predicates.

In what follows, I show that some objects of prepositions can be subject role players to secondary predicates outside their PP, using examples that linguists typically agree involve predication. Then I will argue that the NP objects of P examined here which are available to be subject role players of such secondary predicates receive a theta role (via Compositional Theta Assignment) from the lexical item that the secondary predicate is a sister to. But NP objects of P examined here which are not available to be subject role players of any secondary predicate outside their PP do not bear any theta role at all. This fact will lead us directly to a new set of principles for secondary predication coindexing. And our new principles will allow us to account for the types of data that Schein (1982a) noticed without having to resort to the claim that oblique Case NPs are somehow syntactically the equivalent of PPs in languages such as Russian, Finnish, and Icelandic. Instead, these NPs will be unavailable as subject role players to secondary predicates, just as certain objects of Ps in languages like English and Italian are, because they, like the objects of Ps, do not receive a theta role. (Given Schein's presentation, I would analyze the relevant NPs as being modifiers, not arguments.) Our new coindexing principles, then, allow an explanation for Schein's data that is true to the semantics of the sentences and need not pose any abstract (and unlikely, in my opinion) syntactic nodes. However, since I do not collect data on

Russian, Finnish, or Icelandic myself, I leave my remarks here as a mere suggestion for others who do work on them.

Let us begin with an example in the literature. First, some NPs which are objects of prepositions can be subject role players for secondary predicates outside the PP. Example (2–24) is due to Williams 1980.

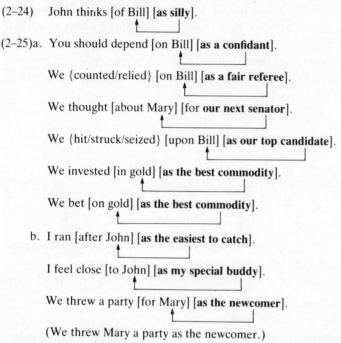

(2–24)   John thinks [of Bill] [as silly].

(2–25)a. You should depend [on Bill] [as a confidant].

We {counted/relied} [on Bill] [as a fair referee].

We thought [about Mary] [for our next senator].

We {hit/struck/seized} [upon Bill] [as our top candidate].

We invested [in gold] [as the best commodity].

We bet [on gold] [as the best commodity].

b. I ran [after John] [as the easiest to catch].

I feel close [to John] [as my special buddy].

We threw a party [for Mary] [as the newcomer].

(We threw Mary a party as the newcomer.)

That the secondary predicate in (2–24) is outside the PP is assumed by Williams. However, it is easy to verify that the secondary predicates in (2–24) and (2–25) are outside the PP by way of standard tests for constituency. For example, consider the clefting possibilities for the first sentence of (2–25)a.

(2–26)a.   It's Bill that you should depend on as a confidant.
      b.   It's on Bill that you should depend as a confidant.
      c.   *It's on Bill as a confidant that you should depend.

(2–26)a is a perfectly natural pseudo-cleft sentence. (2–26)b, with the P separated from the V that lexically selects it, is a stilted sentence, but my informants judge it acceptable. But (2–26)c, which is to be read without pauses around the secondary predicate, was not accepted by any of the speakers I asked. These data are as expected if the secondary predicate, *as a confidant*, is outside the PP (see Higgins 1979). Thus the bracketing in (2–24) and (2–25) is justified.

It is important here and throughout this chapter that sentences with secondary predicates be read without pauses around the secondary predicates. With pauses, we have a type of predication that is similar to appositives. I postpone the discussion of this other type of predication until chapter 5, section 5, where I will propose that a rule in LF places the secondary predicate inside the PP in a sentence such as (2–26)c in the reading with pauses around the secondary predicate (the only grammatical reading).

Williams argues that *think of* in (2–24) has been reanalyzed syntactically as a complex verb; thus *Bill* does, in fact, c-command the predicate *as silly*. His analysis is:

(2–27)

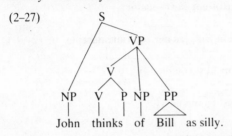

Williams, however, is inconsistent in his argument. He attributes the fact that *John* can be the subject of *as stupid* in (2–28)a but not in (2–28)b to the claim that *John* c-commands *as stupid* in (2–28)a but not in (2–28)b.

(2–28)a.   John struck Bill as stupid.
     b.   *Bill was struck by John as stupid.

However, Williams accepts the movability of an object of a P as evidence for reanalysis, following Hornstein and Weinberg (1981). Hornstein and Weinberg argue that any PP inside a VP can undergo reanalysis so that the P becomes part of a complex V. If this happens, the NP which used to be the object of the P is no longer an object of a P and is free to move, leaving behind an empty category that is governed by the new complex V and gets objective Case. On the other hand, a PP that is outside the VP cannot undergo reanalysis. Therefore the object of such a P cannot move, since the empty category left behind would get oblique Case (from the P that governs it); Hornstein and Weinberg propose that there is a filter blocking empty NPs with oblique Case. Movability, then, is a test for reanalysis, according to Hornstein and Weinberg. And in (2–29) we see that the object of the P in a string like *struck by* in (2–28)b is movable.

(2–29)   I was struck by his ingenuity.
        What were you struck by?

Thus if reanalysis were the proper explanation for the acceptability of (2–24), then reanalysis should also allow (2–28)b, since *struck by* would be a complex verb and *John* would c-command *as stupid*. Williams has no explanation, then, for the failure of (2–28)b. Therefore, Williams' reanalysis explanation for (2–24) is faulty.

Reanalysis fares no better as an explanation for (2–25). While in general the NP objects of P in (2–25) are movable by wh-movement, as expected with Williams' theory, those in (2–25)b seem only marginally movable when the predicate is present.

(2–30)   Who did you run after (??**as the easiest to catch**)?
         Who do you feel close to (?**as your special buddy**)?
         Who did you throw a party for (??**as the newcomer**)?

The fact that the presence of the predicates in parentheses in (2–30) renders the sentences marginal casts doubt on the reanalysis explanation for these examples.

Furthermore, if reanalysis were the full story about (2–24)–(2–25), we would expect that any time we have reanalysis, the NP that used to be the object of the preposition would be available as the subject role player to some predicate outside the (now defunct) PP. This is not the case. In (2–31)–(2–32) Williams would have to say reanalysis has taken place (witness the movability of the relevant NP), yet the object of the (defunct) P is not a possible subject role player for a secondary predicate.

(2–31)   I ate after someone.
         Who did you eat after?
         *I ate after Bill **as my date**.

(2–32)   I arrived before Bill.
         Who did you arrive before?
         *I arrived before Bill **as the latecomer**.

Thus the connection Williams makes between reanalysis (which would, according to him, take place in (2–31)–(2–32)) and the availability of an object of a P to be the subject role player for a secondary predicate (which does not occur in (2–31)–(2–32)) is a spurious one.

One might argue that the crucial difference between (2–24)–(2–25) and (2–31)–(2–32) is the notion of natural predicate or possible semantic word, a notion developed by many linguists, some of them cited by Hornstein and Weinberg (including Baltin 1978 and van Riemsdijk 1978, but others are also important here, such as Davison 1980). The point with this hypothesis is that while all PPs within the VP can undergo reanalysis, only certain resulting complex Vs are natural predicates or possible semantic words. (This brings to mind the related ideas of others that only Ps which are semantically related to the verb somehow are to be analyzed as part of a complex V, as in Thomason and Stalnaker 1973, Miller and Johnson-Laird 1976, and similarly to verb–preposition incorporation in Bresnan 1982b and Baker 1987b. See also George 1980, who analyzes many Ps as Case markers.) Proponents of this approach would say that those combinations of V plus P which are possible semantic words can themselves be taken as predicates in LF and those which are not possible semantic words cannot. Thus NP movement in passive sentences is possible with the object of a P only if the P has been reanalyzed as part of a complex V which then qualifies as a possible semantic word and thus can serve as a predicate to the new subject in PS. One might propose that only when the P has been reanalyzed into part of a complex V where the complex V is also a natural predicate, is the object of the now defunct P available as a subject role player for a secondary predicate. We can use NP movement to see that the putative complex Vs in (2–24)–(2–25), with this theory, are possible semantic words, whereas the putative complex Vs in (2–31)–(2–32) are not.

(2–33)a.   Bill was thought of as silly.
    b.   Bill was depended on as a confidant.
        Bill was {counted/relied} on as a fair referee.
        Mary was thought about for the next senator.
        Bill was {hit/struck/seized} upon as our top candidate.
        Gold was invested in as the best commodity.
        Gold was bet on as the best commodity.
    c.   *Bill was eaten after (as my date).
        *Bill was arrived before (as the latecomer).

However, the examples in (2–25)b, which were resistant to wh-movement in (2–30), are also resistant to NP movement.

(2– 34)a.   *Bill was run after (as the easiest to catch).
    b.   *John was felt close to (as my special buddy).
    c.   *Mary was thrown a party for (as the newcomer).

Notice that the sentences in (2–34) are bad with or without the secondary predicate in parentheses present, in contrast to (2–30). That is, NP movement simply cannot apply here even though the putative rule of reanalysis can apply in (2–30). Yet it is difficult to conclude that the string *run after* in (2–34)a is not a possible semantic word in light of the fact that *pursue* and *chase* are lexical items of English.

(2–35)   We chased Bill as the easiest to catch.
Bill was chased as the easiest to catch.
Who did you chase (??as the easiest to catch)?
(cf. Who do you think of as the easiest to catch?)

And I, for one, certainly can imagine a language in which *feel close to*, as in (2–34)b, could correspond to a lexical item, as well as *throw a party for* (which is not that far from the English verb *fete*), as in (2–34)c. Thus the possible-semantic-word-hypothesis is not convincing.

Another argument against a reanalysis explanation for (2–24)–(2–25) comes from the fact that linguistic material can intervene between the V and the P, as Andrew Radford (personal communication) has pointed out to me with the following example:

(2–36)   We counted entirely on Bill as a fair referee.

Here *entirely* would prevent *counted . . . on* from being syntactically reanalyzed as a complex V, yet the secondary predicate is still acceptable. So *Bill* does not c-command its secondary predicate.

Let me deal one final deadly blow to reanalysis. Italian, like English, allows the object of a P to be the subject role player of a secondary predicate outside the P, but only when the P is selected lexically by the lexical head that the PP is a sister to. Thus we find secondary predicates like those in (2–37)a, but none like those in (2–37)b.

(2–37)a.   Dipendo da Claudio **come prete**.

'I depend on Claudio as a priest.'
b.*Tullio mangia dopo Claudio **come padrone**.

'Tullio eats after Claudio as master.'
(where Claudio is the master)

In (2–37a) the verb *dipendo* selects the P *da*. But in (2–37)b the verb *mangia* does not select the P *dopo*. We cannot possibly appeal to reanalysis to account for the contrast between (2–37)a & b, since Italian shows no evidence of a syntactic or lexical rule of reanalysis: Ps can never be stranded (and see Kayne 1981c for evidence that there is no reanalysis rule in French).

(2–38)   *Chi dipendi da (come prete)?
'Who do you depend on (as a priest)?'

> Da chi dipendi (come prete)?
> 'On whom do you depend (as a priest)?'
> *Giorgio è stato dipeso da.
> 'Giorgio was depended on.'

(I do not take examples such as *Mi apparve davanti* – 'It appeared before me' – as examples of stranded Ps. The lexical item *davanti* here is of the category Adverb, not P (see Napoli 1978). And even if one could argue that *davanti* was a P, the fact still remains that the P *da* in (2–38) shows no evidence of participating in the putative rule of reanalysis.)

I conclude that reanalysis cannot account for (2–37) in Italian, and, accordingly, it should not be appealed to in the explanation of (2–24)–(2–25) in English.

In sum, we have no good argument that the subject role player of the secondary predicate in each example of (2–24) and (2–25) c-commands this predicate. Rather, the subject role player of the secondary predicate looks as if it is structurally the object of a preposition and the secondary predicate is located outside the PP.

Notice that I am not denying that some prepositions bear a closer semantic relationship to their sister verb than others. On the contrary, this fact is crucial to the theta-theory principle of Compositional Theta Assignment. Thus once more I am claiming that semantic units do not necessarily correspond to syntactic units. And with this realization, we can proceed, having dispensed with a syntactic or lexical rule of reanalysis, which is empirically inadequate.

4   The importance of theta assignment for secondary predication coindexing

At this point we must take a second look at the examples in (2–24), (2–25), and (2–37)a, where a secondary predicate outside a PP can take the object of the P as its subject role player. An immediate generalization that emerges is that the object of the P in all these sentences is assigned a theta role by the theta assigner to which both the PP and the secondary predicate are sisters.

On the other hand, if we look at the examples in (2–27)b, (2–31), (2–32), and (2–37)b, where a secondary predicate outside a PP cannot take the object of the P as its srp, we see that here the object of the P bears no theta role at all.

Let me go through this in detail.

The objects of the Ps in (2–24), (2–25), and (2–37)a are arguments of the lexical item of which the PP and the secondary predicate are both sisters. For example, in (2–24) the verb *think* is not a Case assigner; thus it structurally selects *of* to introduce its theme argument. And in (2–25) the verbs *count/rely* lexically select *on* to introduce their theme argument; *think* lexically selects *about*; *hit/strike/seize* in the sense used here lexically select *upon*; *invest* lexically selects *in*; *bet* lexically selects *on*; *run* lexically selects *after* in the sense of "chase" found here; the adjective *close* lexically selects *to*; the sequence *throw an X* lexically selects *for* to introduce the IO (rather than *to*). Finally, in the Italian example (2–37)a, the verb *dipendo* lexically selects *da*. Therefore, in all these examples the lexical item I have indicated takes the object of the P as an argument. (Note that I am not claiming that lexical selection of a P by the head V is necessary in order for the P to introduce an argument of the V. Instead, for example, verbs of motion often take their arguments in locative PPs, where the V does not select the P. See ch. 1, sec. 2.4 for a full discussion.)

The Ps in (2–27)b, (2–31), (2–32), and (2–37)b, however, do not introduce arguments of any lexical item. I discuss the evidence that passive *by* (as in (2–27)b) does not introduce an argument in section 8 below. However, the evidence that the Ps in these other examples do not introduce arguments already has been given in chapter 1, section 2.4: in general, all Ps that relate an entire proposition to some outside point (in time or space) do not introduce arguments.

I propose that the description of the facts in section 3 above is not accidental. In fact, I claim that **only if an object of P is the argument of a lexical item H can a secondary predicate which is outside the PP and which is a sister to H take that object of the P as its srp.** Since we came to this claim by way of looking at examples in which the relevant lexical item was always a V, we will now test this claim on new data where the relevant lexical item is of categories other than V.

Here I will take up data that parallel the data in chapter 2, section 2. So we will begin by looking at PPs that are sisters of a lexical item of the category A(djective). We predict that if the object of the P is an argument of the A, the object of the P will be available as a srp for a secondary predicate found outside the PP and which is a sister to the A. Otherwise, the object of the P should not be a possible srp for a secondary predicate found outside the PP that is a sister to the A. This is so.

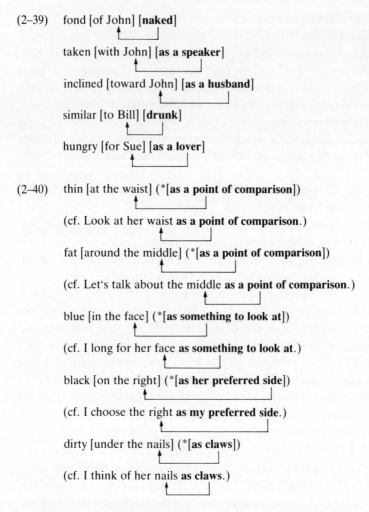

(2–39)   fond [of John] [**naked**]

taken [with John] [**as a speaker**]

inclined [toward John] [**as a husband**]

similar [to Bill] [**drunk**]

hungry [for Sue] [**as a lover**]

(2–40)   thin [at the waist] (*[**as a point of comparison**])

(cf. Look at her waist **as a point of comparison**.)

fat [around the middle] (*[**as a point of comparison**])

(cf. Let's talk about the middle **as a point of comparison**.)

blue [in the face] (*[**as something to look at**])

(cf. I long for her face **as something to look at**.)

black [on the right] (*[**as her preferred side**])

(cf. I choose the right **as my preferred side**.)

dirty [under the nails] (*[**as claws**])

(cf. I think of her nails **as claws**.)

In (2–39) the object of the P is an argument of the A and a secondary predicate is allowed. (The Ps in (2–39) are either the null P *of*, or Ps lexically selected by the head A (such as in *taken with*).) In (2–40) the object of the P is not an argument of the A. (And the Ps here are not restricted in any way; see ch. 1, sec. 2.1.) Instead, here the PP modifies the A. And a secondary predicate is not allowed.

Of course, the claim that (2–39) and (2–40) are examples of the same phenomenon we saw in section 3 above holds only if the secondary predicates in (2–39)–(2–40) are truly outside the PP, as indicated by the brackets. Unfortunately, standard tests for constituency are not of much help here, since separating these Ps from the As sounds less than lovely, regardless of the presence of a secondary predicate. Still, I believe that the (b) example below is distinctly better than the (c) example, where I have taken the first AP of (2–39) to analyze:

(2–41)a.   Who are you fond of naked?
    b.   Of whom are you fond naked?
    c.   *Of whom naked are you fond?

There are also semantic reasons for analyzing the secondary predicates in (2–39)–(2–40) as outside the PP, as Barry Miller (personal communication) has pointed out to me. Notice that if the material following *of* in an AP such as the first one in (2–39) were all inside the PP, then we would have the equivalent of a "small clause" here (see ch. 1, sec. 1.4, and sec. 2 above). (Notice that with this analysis we would have to have a small clause rather than an absolutive, since absolutives are always adjuncts.) Thus this material should correspond to a proposition. That is, a sentence such as:

(2–42)   I'm fond of John naked.

should mean something like:

(2–43)   I'm fond of the {fact/idea/thought/. . .} that John is naked.

But (2–42) does not mean that. Rather, (2–42) means that I am fond of John when he is naked. In fact, the propositional sense is disallowed in these constructions:

(2–44)   *I'm fond of John intelligent.

(2–44) is bad because it makes no sense to talk of John as sometimes being intelligent and sometimes not being intelligent. However, we can certainly express our fondness of this proposition with a different construction:

(2–45)   I'm fond of the fact that John is intelligent.

I conclude that in (2–42) *of* is not introducing a small clause (and, as I have said repeatedly, I do not accept small clauses in syntactic analysis, anyway, for reasons independent of those found here – see Napoli 1987a). Thus the secondary predicate falls outside the PP.

Notice further that (2–39)–(2–40) cannot be accounted for by reanalysis (which we have already rebutted in sec. 3 above on other grounds), since the head here is an A and not a V, whereas the putative rule of reanalysis was proposed to apply to form complex verbs only.

Given that (2–39) and (2–40) have the same syntactic structure, it is an undeniable fact, and one that we will see illustrated again and again below, that we cannot look simply at the syntactic profile of a phrase in order to predict the possibilities for predication coindexing. Instead, we must consider the argument structure. That is, predication coindexing is a semantic phenomenon and it is not predictable from syntactic structure.

I conclude that secondary predicates inside AP behave just like the secondary predicates inside the VPs studied in section 3.

Now consider Ns with sister PPs and secondary predicates. We predict that when the object of the P is an argument of the sister N, the secondary predicate outside the PP can take the N as its srp. Otherwise it cannot. The facts, once more, go as predicted.

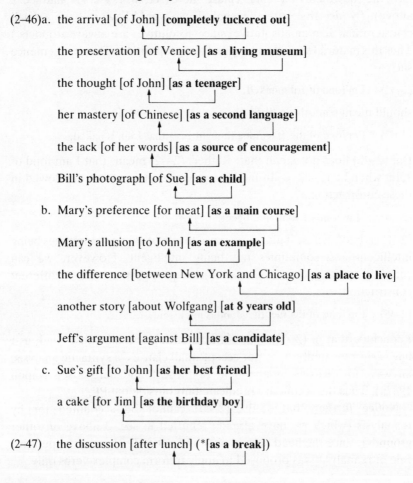

(2–46)a. the arrival [of John] [**completely tuckered out**]

the preservation [of Venice] [**as a living museum**]

the thought [of John] [**as a teenager**]

her mastery [of Chinese] [**as a second language**]

the lack [of her words] [**as a source of encouragement**]

Bill's photograph [of Sue] [**as a child**]

b. Mary's preference [for meat] [**as a main course**]

Mary's allusion [to John] [**as an example**]

the difference [between New York and Chicago] [**as a place to live**]

another story [about Wolfgang] [**at 8 years old**]

Jeff's argument [against Bill] [**as a candidate**]

c. Sue's gift [to John] [**as her best friend**]

a cake [for Jim] [**as the birthday boy**]

(2–47)   the discussion [after lunch] (*[**as a break**])

(note: the reading with the asterisk is with lunch as a break, not the discussion)

(cf. Let's treat lunch **as a break**.)

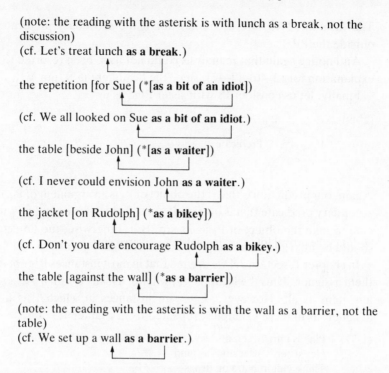

the repetition [for Sue] (*[**as a bit of an idiot**])

(cf. We all looked on Sue **as a bit of an idiot**.)

the table [beside John] (*[**as a waiter**])

(cf. I never could envision John **as a waiter**.)

the jacket [on Rudolph] (***as a bikey**])

(cf. Don't you dare encourage Rudolph **as a bikey**.)

the table [against the wall] (***as a barrier**])

(note: the reading with the asterisk is with the wall as a barrier, not the table)

(cf. We set up a wall **as a barrier**.)

In (2–46) the object of the P is an argument of the N and a secondary predicate is allowed. (In (2–46)a we find the null P *of*; in (2–46)b, a P lexically selected by the head N; in (2–46)c, the IO P *to* or *for*.) In (2–47) the object of the P is not an argument of the N. (And the range of Ps here is not restricted in any way.) Instead, the PPs here modify the head N. And a secondary predicate is not allowed.

Notice that the fact that *Bill's photograph of Sue as a child* in (2–46)a is acceptable is consistent with the analysis we gave of Ns such as *photograph* in chapter 1, section 2.4 as having an event structure.

Again, the claim that (2–46)–(2–47) exemplify the same phenomenon seen in section 3 above depends upon the analysis of these secondary predicates as falling outside the PP. And standard tests for constituency support this analysis. Thus, NP movement can move a sister argument of N introduced by *of* into specifier position (see ch. 1, sec. 2.3). But the secondary predicate cannot move with the argument:

(2–48)   the preservation of Venice as a living museum
          Venice's preservation as a living museum
         *Venice as a living museum's preservation

The facts in (2–48) are accounted for if the secondary predicate falls outside the PP.

And notice again that reanalysis could not have been resorted to as an explanation for (2–46)–(2–47), since the head here is N, not V.

Finally, let us consider Ps with sister PPs, as in:

(2–49)

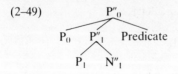

Again, our prediction is that if the object of P_1 is an argument of P_0, then a secondary predicate that is outside P''_1 and that is a sister to the P_0 will be able to take the object of P_1 as its srp. But, otherwise, the object of P_1 should be unavailable as a srp to such a secondary predicate.

In chapter 1, section 2.4 we argued that in most instances P is not itself a theta assigner. Thus the P_0 of (2–49) will not usually assign a theta role to any item at all. However, there are instances in which P is a theta assigner, as in these examples, repeated from chapter 1:

(1–77)   Pina is into Greek pottery.
          Her sister is after my husband.
          Those children are on drugs.
          I'm onto you.

Unfortunately, in none of these special colloquial uses does the P take a PP sister instead of an NP sister, so we cannot test our hypothesis here. (However, as expected, the P can take both an NP argument and a secondary predicate adjunct that takes that NP argument as its srp: *Pina is into brown as a background for her paintings.*)

Another type of usage in which P is a theta assigner is seen here (again with examples repeated from chapter 1):

(1–93)   Mary is inside the house.

(1–95)   I want Mary inside this house by midnight!

(1–96)   Mary is before Bill.

That is, any P has the potential to be used as an event word (and, therefore, as the head of a predicate), and, in isolation of any other potential predicate, P must be read predicatively. Now we can try to test our hypothesis. And, as expected by now, the results suggest we are right.

(2–50)   Mary is up [in the loft] [**as a hiding spot**].

Here *the loft* is an argument of *up* (where *in* functions to convert a thing into a place, thus allowing its object to be an appropriate argument for *up* – see Jackendoff 1983 and the discussion in ch. 1, sec. 2.4), and it is available as the srp to the secondary predicate.

The only complication with (2–50) (and a serious complication it is for our claim) is that we have no evidence that *as a hiding spot* is inside P''_0; it might well be a sister to P''_0. We will return to this issue in section 5 below.

We have thus far discussed only half of our claim by looking at (2–50). The other half is that if N''_1 in (2–49) does not bear a theta role, then it is unavailable as a srp to the secondary predicate. I cannot think of a way to test this hypothesis since I am unable to find any secondary predicates that are arguably sisters to P_0, where P_0 does not assign a theta role to N''_1 in (2–49). This is because in all instances where P_0 does not assign a theta role to NP_1, P''_0 is a modifier of some other item and the analysis is always available that the secondary predicate is a sister to that other item rather than to P_0.

There are other ways to test our hypothesis regarding Ps that take PP sisters, however. We argued in chapter 1, section 2.4 that many Ps transmit a theta role from some theta assigner to their object. Now, while we did not consider such cases in chapter 1, it is clear that a theta assigner outside P''_0 in (2–49) could assign a theta role to NP_1 if both P_0 and P_1 were functioning merely to transmit theta assignment. Such instances do arise:

(2–51)   Mary **climbed up into** the tree

Here *climbed* is a motion verb which optionally takes a place argument (as argued in ch. 1, sec. 2.4). Both *up* and *into* are working together to convert the thing *the tree* into the place *the tree*. That is, we view *the tree* as a role player, a participant of sorts, in the activity. Thus the event is one of climbing-up-into and there are two role players in the event: *Mary* and *the tree*, both of which receive a theta role from the head of the predicate, *climbed*.

In contrast, in (2–52) *the tree* is simply the site of eating: it is not a role player but a modifier. Accordingly, I analyze *up in the tree* here as part of the predicate, and *the tree* receives no theta role.

(2–52)   Mary **ate** potato chips **up in the tree**.

Now given our claim (which is in boldface earlier in this section), we would predict that a secondary predicate which is a sister to the V in (2–51) or (2–52) could take the object of a P as its srp only if the object of that P received a theta role from the V. While the judgments are delicate for some speakers, everyone I have asked agrees that (2–53) is superior to (2–54):

(2–53)   Mary climbed up [into the tree] [**as a hiding place**].

(2–54)   Mary ate potato chips up [in the tree] (?? [**as a relaxing spot**]).

In general, a secondary predicate in a structure such as that in (2–53)– (2–54) can take the object of the lower P as its srp only if we view that prepositional object as a role player of the verb. Thus we find some interesting and subtle contrasts. For example, everyone I have asked accepts (2–55):

(2–55)   He went up [into the loft] [**as the best hideout**].

But most people reject the secondary predicate in (2–56):

(2–56)   We went out [through the gate] (*[**as a passageway**]).

That is, we do not view *the gate* as a place role player for the motion here, but only as an object, a thing. Instead, the whole PP *through the gate* is the place or direction that can be viewed as fulfilling the optional place-argument slot of this motion verb. Accordingly, if a secondary predicate takes the entire PP as its srp, the sentence is good, as in this example pointed out to me by Ken Hale (personal communication):

(2–57)   We went out [through the gate] [**as the best route to the creek**].

Here the whole PP *through the gate* is the route. Thus the whole PP is the srp of the secondary predicate.

I conclude that the claim in boldface near the beginning of this section is correct. That is, contrasts such as those in (2–39) versus (2–40), and (2–46) versus (2–47), and (2–53) versus (2–54), and (2–55) versus (2–56) demand an account of secondary predication coindexing in which we look not simply at the syntactic profile of a phrase, but at the argument structure of the phrase.

5 Secondary predication coindexing

At this point we should try to formalize the claim of section 4 above. Notice first that every secondary predicate, just like every primary predicate, must find its srp in the minimal clause that contains the secondary predicate. Thus, for example, in (2–58) *penniless* can predicate of *Mary*, but in (2–59) it cannot.

(2–58) **Penniless** Mary left John.

(2–59) *__Penniless__ I knew that Mary left John.

(There is an irrelevant and good reading of (2–59) with *penniless* predicating of *I*.) This restriction is certainly built into every predication theory I have read in the literature; thus I expect no disputes over it. I therefore state this restriction as part of the coindexing principle, making use of the term domain of a primary predicate (which is simply making use of the fact that every secondary predicate belongs to a clause with a primary predicate – see the remarks following (2–5) above).

(2–60) *Secondary Predication Coindexing*: Coindex a secondary predicate SP with a phrase that will be called its subject role player that is within the domain of the SP's primary predicate.

Now we must formulate the provisos on (2–60) that follow from the data we have looked at in sections 3 and 4. Before we can do that, we need to define some terms.

Let me use the term "theta domain" to mean all the sisters of a theta assigner. We can see, then, that our claim in section 4 was about secondary predicates that fall within a theta domain. We can also see that any item which receives a theta role via Direct Theta Assignment is within the theta domain of the theta assigner at the point of theta assignment. I will also allow any item which receives a theta role via Compositional Theta Assignment to be said to be within the theta domain of the theta assigner at the point of theta assignment. That is, the configurational contribution of the P in these instances will be ignored. External Theta Assignment, then, is the only principle of theta assignment that obtains outside a theta domain.

Second, we will need to make use of the concepts of L-marking and barrier developed in Chomsky (1986a), as follows.

Any element that undergoes Direct Theta Assignment is L-marked by its theta assigner. (Notice that since I have not included I(nflection) as a direct theta assigner, there is no need to qualify this definition further.) Any element that undergoes Compositional Theta Assignment is also L-marked by the theta assigner (which, in essence, has the same effect as Chomsky's assigning a theta role to the PP itself). In other words, all theta assignment that takes place within a theta domain will be called L-marking.

Any maximal projection @ is a blocking category for # iff @ is not L-marked and @ dominates #.

Any maximal projection @ is a barrier for # if @ is a blocking category for # and @ is not IP (Inflectional Phrase), or if @ is the first maximal projection dominating $, where $ is a blocking category for #.

The tree structure for a sentence will be:

(2–61)

```
            C″
          /    \
        X″      C′
              /    \
            C        I″
                  /     \
                X″       I′
                       /    \
                      I      X″
```

Here C is the familiar Complementizer node, which is taken to head a phrase of its own with IP as its sister. And I is the familiar Inflection node, which is taken to head a phrase with the GF subject in its specifier position (the X″ sister to I′) and with a sister that most typically is V″, but could be P″, N″, or A″ (as in those instances in English in which *be* is a grammatical word only – see ch. 1, sec. 1).

Given these definitions, if Compositional Theta Assignment takes place, strictly speaking the object of the P is L-marked, but the P″ is not. This result is counter to the spirit of the concept of L-marking, however, since the P acts to introduce an argument of the theta assigner and should not be a barrier between its object and the theta assigner. I will therefore call such PPs L-marked. The welcome result, then, is that the PP is not a barrier for its object when the object is the argument of some theta assigner outside the PP.

Before going on, let me point out that in Chomsky (1986a) there is another definition for barrier which is part of the Minimality Condition. This definition, however, does not concern itself with theta marking; thus there is no reason, given our section 4 above, to suspect that this definition of barrier will be relevant to secondary predication coindexing. Furthermore, if the interested reader admits this second definition of barrier into the discussion below, that reader will find that none of the claims below is affected. The only change would be that my demonstrations would be longer and more involved. But no new insights about the nature of predication coindexing would emerge. Therefore, I will ignore the Minimality Condition and use the term barrier to mean only the first definition given above.

We can now formulate the claim of section 4 above as a proviso to the coindexing principle in (2–60). There are at least three possibilities. One is that the notion of theta domain is the only relevant notion. If that were so, we would be led to the following proviso:

(2–62)   *Proviso One* (a first approximation): If a secondary predicate is within the theta domain of a lexical item H, its subject role player must receive a theta role from H.

(I will revise Proviso One later in this section – this is a first version of the proviso.) This proviso is simply a restatement and generalization of the claim in boldface near the beginning of section 4. Let me repeat that claim. I said that only if an object of P is the argument of a lexical item H can a secondary predicate which is outside the PP and which is a sister to H take that object of the P as its srp. The restatement part of (2–62) is that I have used the term theta domain instead of talking about sisters. The generalization part of (2–62) is that I have not limited the claim to only instances in which the srp is the object of a P.

The generalization of my original claim is, actually, trivial. That is, if an item is not the object of a P, then it is either in GF subject, DO, or IO (as in the double object construction in: *I gave Mary the book*) position. Of these, DO and IO are the only two that fall in a theta domain, since they are the only two that are sisters to lexical items. And, typically, both DO and IO receive a theta role. (I will return to the question of whether or not DOs need receive a theta role below in the discussion immediately preceding (2–77).)

Let me point out that Proviso One is equivalent to saying that if a secondary predicate falls within the theta domain of H, its subject role player must be T-governed by H, in the sense of T-government introduced in Chomsky 1986b. I do not use the term "T-government" in my predication theory, however, because the term "government" is a configurational one, involving notions of hierarchical syntactic structure.

But the relevant restriction on predication coindexing has to do primarily with argument structures; it has to do with configurational structures only in so far as the notion of theta domain is configurationally based in languages like English and Italian (which are configurational languages). This is obvious from the sets of data in section 4 above, where sentences with the same structural profile but contrasting argument profiles have contrasting predication coindexing possibilities. The use of a term such as "T-government" obfuscates the basically nonconfigurational nature of the concept it denotes. Therefore, to avoid any possibility of a misinterpretation of my theory of predication as a configurational one, I will continue to talk about theta assignment and lexical structures.

An alternative to Proviso One does not explicitly mention theta domains. Consider (2–50) again:

(2–50)   Mary is up [in the loft] [**as a hiding spot**].

As I said above, the possibility arises that the secondary predicate here is not inside the higher PP, but, instead, is a sister to that PP. In fact, secondary predicates do not generally appear as sisters to P unless the P introduces an absolutive construction, as discussed below in section 7. An analysis of (2–50), then, in which the secondary predicate is outside the higher PP, would be:

(2–63)   Mary is [up in the loft] [**as a hiding spot**].

(See Williams 1984a, p. 138, for arguments that the XP right sister to I in (2–61) above can take an optional PP sister, and, thus, that the bracketing in (2–63) is possible.) Proviso One would not pertain to (2–63), since the secondary predicate would not be in a theta domain. Therefore, if we wanted a single proviso to pertain to all the data of sections 3 and 4 including (2–50) with the analysis in (2–63), we might be led to the proposal that only the notion of barrier is relevant to secondary predication coindexing. We would then come up with the following proviso.

(2–64)   *Proviso Two*: A subject role player must not be separated by any of its barriers from the head of its predicate.

Proviso Two is to be interpreted in the following way. We locate the minimal node that dominates both the head of a predicate and its srp. If that node or any node dominated by it contains a barrier for the subject, the predication coindexing is disallowed (see the notion of path in Kayne 1984).

We can easily see that in all the good examples in sections 3 and 4, the secondary predicate was not separated from its srp by any of the barriers of its srp. But in the bad examples, it was. For example, consider the first examples of (2–40) and (2–47) in contrast to the first examples of (2–39) and (2–46):

(2–39)   fond [of John] [**naked**]

(2–40)   thin [at the waist] (*[**as a point of comparison**])

(2–46)   the arrival [of John] [**completely tuckered out**]

(2–47)   the discussion [after lunch] (*[**as a break**])

In (2–39) and (2–46) the object of *of* is an argument of the head A or N and the PP is therefore not a barrier for the object of the P. But in (2–40) and (2–46) the object of the P is not an argument of the head A or N (in fact, the PP is a modifier of that head A or N), and the PP is therefore a barrier for the object of the P. Thus Proviso Two correctly predicts the grammaticality of (2–39) and (2–46), but the ungrammaticality of (2–40) and (2–47) with the secondary predicate.

At this point, we have not had much evidence to choose between Proviso One and Proviso Two. The third alternative, then, is that they both apply. And, in fact, it turns out that we do need them both. Thus, while both of them will account for the contrast between (2–65) and (2–66):

(2–65)   his thoughts [about beauty] [**as an ideal**]

(2–66)   a moment [of beauty] (*[**as an ideal**])

there are other instances in which only one of the provisos applies. For example, in (2–67) the secondary predicate *as a Catholic* is within the theta domain of the N *confirmation*. And Proviso One correctly rules out coindexing between this secondary predicate and the GF subject. But since no barrier of the GF subject intervenes here, Proviso Two will not rule out this coindexing.

(2–67)   *I described [the confirmation of Mary **as a Catholic**] to Arnie

Berkowitz.

(Of course, (2–67) has the irrelevant good reading with coindexing between the secondary predicate and *Mary*.) Thus we need Proviso One independently of Proviso Two.

But we also need Proviso Two. For example, in (2–68)a the secondary predicate is not within a theta domain, yet coindexing with *Mary* is disallowed. Proviso Two correctly rules out the coindexing here, whereas Proviso One would not apply.

(2–68)a. ***Penniless**, John left Mary.

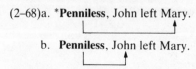

    b. **Penniless**, John left Mary.

In (2–68)a the VP is a barrier for *Mary* and its intervention blocks the coindexing. But the GF subject *John* has no barrier between it and the secondary predicate. Let me go step by step through the argument that *John* can have no barrier between itself and *penniless*. First, there are only two maximal projections that might intervene between *John* and *penniless*: IP and CP. Now IP cannot be a barrier except by inheritance. However, IP is a blocking category for *John* in (2–68). That means that CP will be a barrier (by inheritance). However, if *penniless* is a sister to CP (which I argue immediately below that it is), it is also a daughter to CP; that is, *penniless* is Chomsky-adjoined to CP (*per force*, since there is no node higher than CP in the sentence):

(2–69)

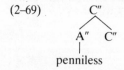

But then *penniless* is not excluded from CP (in the sense of Chomsky 1986a – see the discussion on pp. 9 ff., in particular), so the sister CP to *penniless* is not a barrier – only the highest CP is a barrier, but that CP dominates the A″.

One might argue that some sort of "closeness" condition is operating in (2–68), rather than Proviso Two. That is, *John* is linearly closer to the secondary predicate than *Mary* is, so the srp must be the closer of the two. However, such an alternative fails dismally. When the secondary predicate is in S-final position, both *John* and *Mary* are possible srp's, even though one is closer than the other.

(2–70)   John married Sue **penniless**.

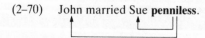

Of course, the burden now falls on me to argue that *penniless* in (2–70) is inside the VP, for if it were outside the VP, the VP would be a barrier for *Sue* and Proviso Two would (incorrectly) rule out one of the good coindexings in (2–70).

I contend that secondary predicates which can appear in initial or final position, like that in (2–68) and (2–70), attach at the same place that adverbials that can appear in either of these linear positions attach. Consider sentential adverbials, such as the *when* clauses here:

(2–71)a. When John arrives, he will tell Bill everything.
    b. John will tell Bill everything when he arrives.
    c. He will tell Bill everything when John arrives.
    d. John will tell him everything when Bill arrives.

In (2–71)a we can understand *John* and *he* as coindexed. Therefore, by the Binding Theory, we know that *he* does not c-command *John*. Thus the sentential adverbial in initial position is attached outside I′ (which is equivalent to S in standard theory). In fact, these initial adverbial clauses can precede a matrix clause that begins with a lexically filled Comp and even with a filled specifier of Comp, as Andrew Radford (personal communication) has pointed out to me. But when the following clause is an embedded clause, the adverbial clause must follow the Comp.

(2–72)a. When John arrives, WILL he get you!
       When John arrives, who will you talk to?
    b. I know that when John arrives, Mary will be happy.

(Here the capitals indicate stress peak.) Thus the structure for a sentence with an initial sentential adverbial like that in (2–72)a is as in (2–73)a. And the structure for a sentence with an initial adverbial like that in (2–72)b is as in (2–73)b. (I have simplified the matrix clause in (2–73)b, since its structure is not relevant to the point under discussion here.)

So I propose that all initial adjuncts to a matrix clause are sisters to C″, and all initial adjuncts to an embedded clause are sisters to I″. In particular, *penniless* is a sister to C″ in (2–68). And there is direct evidence

(2–73)a.

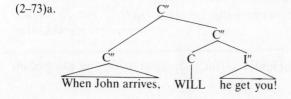

b.
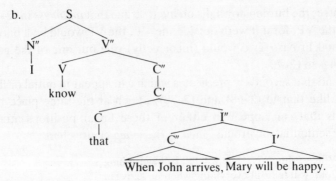

When John arrives, Mary will be happy.

for this analysis, as well, since *penniless* can be followed by a filled specifier of Comp:

(2-74)   **Penniless**, who can we trust?

Turning now to S-final adverbial clauses, in (2–71)b we can coindex *he* with either *John* or *Bill*. However, in (2–71)c, we cannot coindex *He* and *John*. Thus we know that *He* c-commands *John*; therefore the S-final sentential adverbial must be attached as a daughter to I′ or lower. In (2–71)d we cannot coindex *him* with *Bill*. Thus we know that *him* c-commands *Bill*, and the sentential adverbial must therefore be attached as a daughter to V′. The structure for sentences with S-final sentential adverbials like that in (2–71)d is:

(2-75)
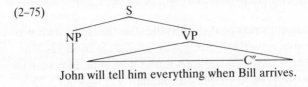

John will tell him everything when Bill arrives.

Let me point out that for some speakers, (2–71)d is good with the reading of *him* and *Bill* as coreferential. But, as Ray Jackendoff (personal communication) has pointed out to me, this reading emerges when there is a pause preceding the sentential adverbial. I contend that sentential adverbials in S-final position preceded by a pause are attached as daughters to I′ or some higher level, just as are other kinds of S-final adjuncts that are preceded by a pause (as argued in ch. 5, sec. 5). Under that analysis, *him* would not c-command *Bill*, so the coreference would be admitted.

In sum, we can see that initial and final adverbial clauses are attached at different levels: the initial ones are attached as sisters to C″; the final ones are attached as daughters to V′ (see also Haegeman 1984, who notes similar data). When there is no evidence to the contrary, I will assume that all initial and final adjuncts are attached at these same levels. Thus the secondary predicate in (2–70) would be inside VP.

There is also direct evidence that S-final secondary predicates are inside VP: they pass the standard tests for VP constituency, as Andrew Radford (personal communication) has pointed out to me:

(2–76)   John might leave nude, and so might Bill.
          John might leave nude, and Bill might, too.
          John says he'll leave nude, and by God LEAVE NUDE he will.

And, finally, Culicover and Rochemont (1986) argue that extraposed elements (which they base generate in place) are inside VP (although they have multiple levels within VP, unlike the phrase structure we are assuming here). So they offer one more piece of evidence that S-final clauses and secondary predicates are inside VP.

I conclude that *penniless* in (2–70) is inside the VP and, thus, that (2–70) is correctly predicted to be good by both provisos.

Let me point out in passing that our analysis of *penniless* in (2–68)b places it outside the I′. This means that the subject role player of this predicate does not c-command it. Hence we have another type of predication that falls outside the theory of predication offered in Williams (1980).

There is still one more issue that the analysis of S-initial and S-final adjuncts brings up, and that is the nature of X-bar theory. As I said in the introductions to both this book and this chapter and at various points in chapter 1, I am adopting an X-bar theory for X=N, A, V, or P, in which the only sisters to X″ at DS are coordinated X″, and in which the only sisters to X′ at DS are coordinated X′ and/or specifier. Thus all modifiers, arguments, and secondary predicates must be sisters to X at DS (but see ch. 5, sec. 5).

The various projections of C(omplementizer) and I(nflection), however, may well allow sisters. Perhaps (2–69) and (2–73) are examples of base-generated sisters to C″ and I″. But if we were to assume for a moment that C″ and I″ could not have base-generated sisters, the S-initial adverbial clauses (such as that in (2–73)) and S-initial secondary predicates (such as that in (2–69)) must be analyzed as having been moved into their SS position from some position where they were sisters to an X. The obvious position, of course, is sister to V, since I have shown already that these same items when they occur in S-final position are sisters to V. While I see no evidence to choose between these two analyses, let me point out that the movement analysis in no way affects any of the above remarks on secondary predication coindexing, since it is SS and not DS that Predicate Structure is formed from. Furthermore, I take the stance that only referential items leave traces (and see the ninth point of sec. 14 below). Thus it is the SS position of a predicate, without any information about its DS position, that we see when Predicate Structure is formed.

Let me return briefly now to an issue I raised above. Notice that in generalizing the claim of section 4 above to cover cases other than objects of Ps, I raised the question of whether phrases in GF subject, DO and IO (in the double-object construction) positions need receive a theta role. This question is relevant to the correct formulation of Proviso One. For example, consider a secondary predicate that falls within the domain of a V. Given Proviso One we would then require that its srp be an argument of that V. The question I am asking now is whether a GF subject, DO, or IO of that V which does not receive a theta role can serve as the srp for the secondary predicate. If it can, Proviso One must be modified.

First, we can dismiss the IO case, since it will not arise. Every IO has the theta role of beneficiary. (This is an unusual and interesting fact which calls for explanation, since there is no other GF that I know of that requires a certain theta role to be associated with it. However, the explanation of this fact would go far beyond the limits of this book.)

Second, we can dismiss the GF subject case, since it will not arise. That is, any V which is a theta assigner takes an external role player in SS. Thus if a theta assigner V has no argument in GF subject position in DS, a movement rule will put one there, as in (2–9)a&b, repeated here for convenience:

(2–9)a. Maria è appena arrivata.
        'Maria has just arrived.'
     b. Maria è stata ignorata.
        'Maria has been ignored.'

In (2–9)a NP movement in an ergative sentence has applied to move *Maria* from DO to GF subject position (see Burzio 1986). In (2–9)b NP movement in a passive sentence has applied, again from DO to GF subject position.

The real question for us, then, is that of the DO. And some have argued that DOs need not receive a theta role from their V. For example,

Williams (1982) argues that in a sentence such as (2–3), *Jill* receives no theta role from the V, but only from the secondary predicate, where the structure would be:

(2–3)

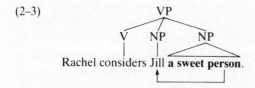

Likewise, Emonds (1985, p. 83) claims that *John* in (1–108)a receives no theta role from the V but only from the secondary predicate in:

(1–108)a.

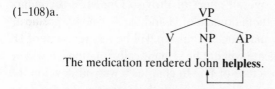

The claim in both cases is that the V takes not a referential role player, but an event role player. (And notice that the fact that *John* in (1–108)a gets Case from *rendered* does not entail that *John* gets a theta role from *rendered*; see Davis 1986.) While it is difficult to find arguments for Williams' and Emonds' position, I believe they are correct. In (2–3) we are not considering Jill directly; we are judging that a certain property should be assigned to Jill. In (1–108)a the medication is not rendering John; it is rendering an event (the state of helplessness) which takes John as its role player.

Therefore, I see Proviso One as being in need of an addendum to the effect that a srp in the theta domain of a lexical head H must be an argument of or bear a GF toward H. If we were to assume that the lexical structure for every H includes not only an argument structure, but also the information as to what GFs H takes (that is, its subcategorization information), then we could revise the original Proviso One to read:

(2–77)   *Proviso One*: If a secondary predicate is within the theta domain of a lexical item H, its srp must appear in the lexical structure of H.

There is still one instance of predication not handled properly by Proviso One as stated in (2–77). To see that, consider the secondary predicate whose head is an N and for which every argument is internal to the NP, as in:

(2–78)   I hate [the Huns' **destruction** of the city].

In chapter 1, section 2.3 we argued that *the Huns'* here is the srp of the predicate *destruction*. And *destruction* is a secondary predicate. Now by Proviso One, we would expect that the srp of *destruction* would have to be either an argument of *hate* (whose theta domain the NP headed by *destruction* is within) or bear a GF toward *hate*. But the srp, *the Huns'*, does neither.

It appears that Proviso One as stated in (2–77) applies only when a secondary predicate takes an external srp. This fact is, actually, not surprising. Consider the overall effect of Proviso One. If a secondary predicate falls within the theta domain of H and the secondary predicate is an adjunct (that is, a nonargument), its srp will be an argument of H. Thus the secondary predicate will not be semantically floating – it will be tied into the thematic structure of H. (In chapter 6 we will develop the notions of argument rungs and ladders. With these notions we could say that the secondary predicate will be tied into the argument rung defined by H.)

If, on the other hand, a secondary predicate falls within the theta domain of H and the secondary predicate is an argument of H, as in (2–3) and (2–108)a above, its srp need not be an argument of H. Why not? Because the secondary predicate is already tied into the thematic structure of H. (That is, the secondary predicate is already on the argument rung defined by H.) In fact, the secondary predicate ties its srp into the thematic structure of H.

Now in (2–78) the secondary predicate *destruction* does, in fact, bear a theta role (by percolation from the NP it heads, since that NP is an argument of *hate*). So *destruction* is tied in to the thematic structure of the theta assigner whose domain it falls within. And *destruction*, in turn, ties its srp into that thematic structure.

In other words, the motivation for Proviso One is licensing, as in Chomsky 1986b. Every element in a sentence must be properly licensed, and one way for an element to be licensed is for it to tie in to the thematic structure of some lexical head in the sentence. Therefore, secondary predicates either tie in to thematic structure directly (by bearing theta roles) or indirectly (via their srp, which must, then, bear a theta role assigned by the relevant lexical head). The only exception is absolutives, which I return to in section 7 below.

We therefore need a less powerful alternative to Proviso One for predicates that fall within the theta domain of Ns.

(2–79) *Alternative to Proviso One for H=N*: If a secondary predicate is within the theta domain of a lexical item H, either the secondary predicate or its srp must receive a theta role from H.

The question now is whether we need both (2–77) and (2–79), or whether (2–79) should replace (2–77) (that is, whether (2–79) will suffice for H of any category and not just for H=N).

First, in almost every example in section 4 above the secondary predicate was an adjunct. Let me repeat the first example of (2–25)a:

(2–25)   We depended on Bill **as a confidant**.

Here *as a confidant* does not receive a theta role from *depended,* whose theta domain it falls within. But its srp, *Bill*, does. So both (2–77) and (2–79) correctly allow this coindexing. And both (2–77) and (2–79) likewise correctly allow the good sentences of section 4 and disallow the bad sentences.

Second, whenever a secondary predicate is the head of an argument, the secondary predicate receives a theta role via percolation. Examples include:

(2–3)   Rachel considers Jill **a sweet person**.

(2–78)   I hate the Huns' **destruction** of the city.

Here the predicate in boldface receives a theta role from the V whose theta domain the maximal projection of the head of the predicate falls within. But its srp does not have to receive a theta role from that V – and I have argued that that srp does not receive a theta role from that V in either (2–3) or (1–108)a. Both (2–77) and (2–79) will allow (2–3), but only (2–79) will allow (2–78).

And, in general, both (2–77) and (2–79) can handle the data discussed thus far, except for the data involving secondary predicates that fall within the theta domain of an N, where only (2–79) suffices. Therefore, we might be led to adopt (2–79) in place of (2–77). However, there is an important difference between (2–79) and (2–77): (2–79) does not require that a srp which does not receive a theta role from H hold a GF toward H, while (2–77) does. We might expect problems to arise by dropping this requirement. For example, consider:

(2–80)

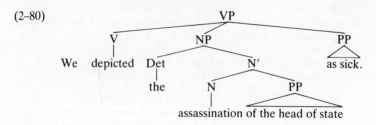

We might ask what keeps *sick* from taking *the head of state* as its srp in (2–80). Example (2–79) will not help here, since *sick* is an argument of *depicted* (it is, for example, subcategorized for: *We depicted the assassination of the head of state*), so its srp has no restrictions on it. Now if the NP *the assassination of the head of state* is not an argument of the V, then this NP is a barrier for the contained NP *the head of state*, so Proviso Two will block the reading in which *sick* predicates of the *head of state*. And it could be that Proviso Two will always "cooperate" with (2–79) in this way, to block all those cases that would have been covered by (2–77).

However, I believe that it is arguable that *the assassination of the head of state* is an argument of *depicted* in (2–80), since we understand this to mean not that I am depicting a situation, but that I am depicting the assassination in a particular way. With this analysis, the NP *the assassination of the head of state* is not a barrier for elements contained inside it. And with this analysis, we need Proviso One as stated in (2–77) in order to account for the failure of the indicated predication.

For now I will proceed with the assumption that we need both Proviso One as stated in (2–77) and the alternate for H=N as stated in (2–79). This fracturization of the proviso, however, should not be seen as a flaw in the theory. In chapter 6, (2–77) and (2–79) will conflate as we develop a set of coindexing principles that apply to anaphor binding as well as predication.

Given that we have offered a semantic motivation for Proviso One, that of proper licensing, we would hope that such a motivation would exist also for Proviso Two, as well. I believe one does.

A barrier for an item K is any maximal projection that contains K and that is not L-marked and is not IP. IP can be a barrier for K, also, by way of inheritance, if IP is the minimal maximal projection containing a barrier for K. The crucial point here is that maximal projections that are not L-marked do not participate directly in the argument structure of material outside them. They therefore cut off the material dominated by them from this kind of participation. In other words, no subpart of that maximal projection may be an argument of some lexical head outside the maximal projection. Now the srp of a predicate is an argument of the head of the predicate. Therefore, it is natural that a predicate cannot be separated from its subject role player by any barriers of the subject role player. We have, thus, motivated Proviso Two from the very definition of barrier.

Finally, we are now in a position to motivate one of the principles stated in chapter 1 and repeated here:

(1–136) *Functional Criterion*: If an XP receives a theta role from two nonintersecting sources, then it must be the srp of at least one of these sources.

We have already argued that both Provisos One and Two follow from general principles of the grammar: both are needed in order to have all elements properly licensed and in order to preserve the argument structure of the lexical items in a given sentence. Both of them function to tie in the secondary predicate to the argument structure of the primary predicate whose domain the secondary predicate falls within. In general, every secondary predicate needs to be thematically tied in somehow. And the only requirement on all predicates is that they have srp's. Therefore, it is natural that a secondary predicate should have to be tied in via its only required part: its srp. We now have a motivation for the Functional Criterion. If an item receives two theta roles, it must be the srp of a secondary predicate (or of a modifier – see ch. 1, sec. 4), since the item receiving two theta roles is the link between the secondary predicate and the argument structure of the primary predicate.

At this point we have developed motivations for all our coindexing principles. In the remainder of this chapter I deal with potentially problematic issues for these principles and with some of the predictions these principles make.

6   A simpler theory

The reader might well have noticed by this point that every time we found a secondary predicate that was not within a theta domain in the examples above, that secondary predicate found its srp in GF subject position. Thus the reader might be thinking that instead of Proviso Two, all we need is:

(2–81)   *Alternative*: If a secondary predicate does not fall within a theta domain, coindex it with the GF subject of its clause.

I have not chosen this alternative to Proviso Two, however, because it is inadequate to deal with secondary predicates of the types found in chapters 3, 4, and 5. Let me give just one example (which by this time the reader is familiar with):

(2–82)   Ci sono andata [con [quel [**matto** di Giorgio]]].

there I have gone with that madman of Giorgio
'I went there with that madman Giorgio.'

In chapter 3 I argue that *matto* is a predicate taking *Giorgio* as its subject role player. Since *matto* is a secondary predicate here and since neither it nor its maximal projection is the sister of a lexical head theta assigner (see ch. 1, sec. 2.4 for arguments that Ps such as *con*, 'with', are not theta assigners in most uses), then with the simpler proviso in (2–81), we would require the subject role player of *matto* to be the GF subject of the clause. But *Giorgio* is not the GF subject of the clause in (2–82). For this and similar reasons, I adopt the original Proviso Two as stated in (2–64) above.

7   Absolutives and other examples not covered by our provisos

Our theory says that secondary predicates which do not fall under Proviso One (that is, which do not fall in a theta domain) need find their subject role players within their clause only so long as they are not separated from that role player by one of its barriers. Let us look at such cases.

There are only two positions for secondary predicates that are not covered by Proviso One: sister to no lexical head, or sister to a non-theta-assigner lexical head.

Let us first consider secondary predicates which are not sisters to any lexical head. We already saw such an example with the S-initial predicate *penniless* in (2–68). Many others can be found.

(2–83)   I announced that the ambassador, **completely nude,** had finally arrived.

Here *completely nude* is a secondary predicate which is not the sister of any lexical head. It is, instead, a sister to an NP on its left and a VP on its right. This predicate can be understood to take *the ambassador* as its subject role player, but not *I*. Neither Proviso One nor Proviso Two blocks the coindexing of *I* with *completely nude*. However, only *the ambassador* and not *I* belongs to the domain of the relevant primary predicate. Thus the fact that (2–83) has only one interpretation is explained by our principle of secondary predication coindexing in (2–60). And in general we find that all secondary predicates which are not sisters to any lexical item are adequately handled by the coindexing principle plus the provisos of section 5 above.

Now let us consider predicates which are sisters to a non-theta-assigner lexical item. We find that P in many uses is not a theta assigner (see ch. 1, sec. 2.4). And there is at least one instance in which a non-theta-assigner P can take a secondary predicate as a sister: when P is used to introduce an absolutive. In Napoli 1987a I argue that the absolutive *with* takes two kinds of complement structures. One has a clause and employs the Accusative-ING construction (see Reuland 1983), as in (2–84).

(2–84)   [[With] [Elena **playing** the flute **so well**]], we better look for one with

open holes soon.

The other takes two (or more) complements, where the first is an NP which is predicated by the second, as in (2–85) (from McCawley 1983) (see also van Riemsdijk 1978 and Ruwet 1982).

(2–85)   [[With] [the bus drivers] [**on strike**]], we'll have to ride our bicycles.

The structure of (2–85) is as follows (see Napoli 1987a).

(2–86)

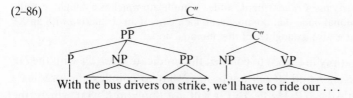

With the bus drivers on strike, we'll have to ride our . . .

That the initial absolutive before a matrix clause occurs as a sister to C″ follows from the fact that a filled specifier of C″ can follow this absolutive, as pointed out to me by Andrew Radford (personal communication). And parallel to the data we found on S-initial adverbial clauses in (2–72) above, we find that initial absolutives before an embedded clause are sisters to I″ (they follow Comp):

(2–87)a. With the bus drivers on strike, how will we get to work?
   b. I know that with the bus drivers on strike, everyone will walk.

The absolutive in (2–86) contains a secondary predicate (here *on strike*) which is a sister to a P (here *with*). The reading of this sentence is that the bus drivers are on strike, not that we are on strike. The question now is what blocks coindexing between *on strike* and *we*.

Proviso One does not apply here since the secondary predicate does not fall within a theta domain. Proviso Two also does not apply, since although the top C″ in (2–86) is a barrier to the GF subject *we*, the sister C″ to the absolutive PP is not a barrier (since C″ does not exclude this PP – see the discussion immediately following (2–68) above).

This same problem arises for all absolutives, whether they are introduced by a P or not. Thus Belletti (1981) analyzes absolutives not introduced by a P in Italian such as that in (2–88):

(2–88)   Arrivata Maria, la riunione ebbe inizio.
         'Maria having arrived, the reunion began.'

Here again the secondary predicate *arrivata* cannot be understood to predicate of the NP *la riunione* in GF subject position, but only of the NP *Maria*.

In general, secondary predicates inside absolutives must find their srp's within the absolutive (and see Stump 1981 for a detailed and comprehensive study of many types of absolutives). In fact, elements inside absolutives do not interact either syntactically or semantically with elements of the clause to which the absolutives are attached. Absolutives are insular in this way. I therefore propose the following coindexing principle for absolutives:

(2–89)   *Absolutive Coindexing*: Coindex a predicate which is a daughter of the minimal node that dominates all members of an absolutive with an XP that is also a daughter of that minimal node.

(2–89) will apply in (2–85) to coindex the predicate *on strike* with the NP *the bus drivers*. And it will apply in (2–88) to coindex the predicate *arrivata* with the NP *Maria*. But it will not apply in (2–84), where the absolutive *with* introduces a clause. That is because the secondary predicate is not a daughter of the minimal node (the PP) that dominates all members of the absolutive. Instead, Primary Predicate Coindexing, stated in (2–6), applies in (2–84).

We can see that coindexing in an absolutive is similar in essential ways to primary predication coindexing. This is no surprise, given the autonomous nature of an absolutive, both from a syntactic and a semantic viewpoint.

I know of no instances of secondary predicates being sisters to non-theta-assigner Ps except in absolutives. This observation correlates with the demonstration in chapter 6, section 5.3 that when Ps introduce a nonargument, the PP sets off the material inside it as being semantically an integral unit with respect to the material outside the PP. Thus no proper part of such a PP can be semantically related to linguistic material outside the PP by a rule of grammar, such as predication coindexing.

Before leaving absolutives, notice that once more we have an instance in which C″ or I″ has a sister node, as in (2–86). One question that arises is whether the absolutive is base generated as a sister to C″ or I″, or is, instead, moved to this position from some position in which it is a sister to a lexical head. If these absolutives were generated as sisters to a lexical head, that lexical head would be V, as in:

(2–90)   We'll have to ride our bicycles with the bus drivers on strike.

This source requires a particular intonation if it is to be acceptable without a pause before the absolutive. And with this particular intonation the binding facts here parallel those we saw above for S-initial and S-final adverbial clauses in (2–71)–(2–73).

(2–91)a. With John always sick, I can't visit him anymore.
    b. I can't visit him anymore with John always sick.

In (2–91)a *John* and *him* may be understood as coreferential. But in (2–91)b, with the same intonation pattern that renders (2–90) acceptable without a pause, we find that *John* and *him* cannot be understood as coreferential unless *John* has already been brought up in the discourse, so that we do not have sentential binding here, but, rather, a discourse determined referent for the pronoun. These facts are as expected if the absolutive in (2–90) is within the VP.

However, the fact remains that there is another way to read (2–90), and that is with a pause before *with*. On this reading, which is the more common one, (2–91) is acceptable with coindexing between *him* and *John*. We must conclude that on this reading the absolutive in (2–90) is outside the VP.

Once again we may have evidence here that the phrasal projections of C(omplementizer) and I(nflection) can have base-generated sisters, in contrast to the projections of N, A, V, and P (and see the introduction to this book).

There is another lexical category besides P which can be a non-theta-assigner: N. I argued in chapter 1 that some concrete nouns do not have argument structures. We therefore predict that if a secondary predicate finds itself as a sister to such an N, it will be able to look anywhere in the clause for its subject role player so long as it does not violate Proviso Two. In (2–92), however, we see that no secondary predicates can occur as sisters to such Ns.

(2–92)a. *Jeff's wallet **as a bigshot** lay open on the table.

     b. *Jeff's wallet **broke** lay empty on the table.

     c. *I gave [Jeff's wallet **broke**] to Mary.

In (2–92)a&b the secondary predicates cannot be understood to predicate of *Jeff's*. In (2–92)c the secondary predicate cannot be understood to predicate of *I* or *Mary* or *Jeff's*. Yet in none of these sentences is the relevant NP separated by one of its barriers from the secondary predicate.

The fact is that concrete Ns that have no argument structure head NPs that must relate to their external context as a unit: no subpart of them may undergo a grammatical rule with respect to any position outside the NP. In this way these NPs display an insularity similar to that noted just above for absolutes. I will also argue in chapter 6, section 5.3 that PPs that function as modifiers display the same grammatical insularity.

This insularity accounts for the failure of the secondary predicate in (2–92)c to take *I* or *Mary* as its subject role player.

We still need to account for why *Jeff's* in (2–92) cannot be the subject role player for the secondary predicate, since *Jeff's* is inside the NP. I propose that this predication coindexing is disallowed because the secondary predicate would not be properly licensed. Let me explain.

Typically an adjunct (that is, a non-theta-marked) secondary predicate is licensed by way of coindexing with a subject role player that is independently licensed by appearing in the argument structure of some other lexical head (see the discussion from (2–77) to (2–79) in sec. 5 above). Now concrete Ns like *wallet* have no argument structure. Thus *Jeff's* is not an argument. We see then that both *Jeff's* and the secondary predicates in (2–92) are non-arguments. But adjunct secondary predicates cannot be licensed by non-arguments (and see the remarks on licensing in various parts of ch. 6). Thus the failure of examples like (2–92) is entirely expected, with no need to revise our coindexing principles.

A final lexical category that can be a non-theta-assigner is V, as with the so-called aspectual verbs (see ch. 1, sec. 1.3) and the purely grammatical word use of *be* (see ch. 1, sec. 1.1). Certainly such Vs can take sister predicates. With *be* one might argue that these predicates are primary predicates (taking the *be* to be under I(nflection)), as in:

(1–2)   The man who marries young is **happy**.

But if we have a sentence with *seems*, for example, the issue is much more complicated, since surely *seems* is not under I(nflection).

(2–93)   John **seems happy** to me.

Here the predicate is not *happy* alone, but *seems happy* (see ch. 1, sec. 1.3). Technically, however, the predicate is not a primary predicate (since *happy* is not the syntactic head of the first XP right sister to I, nor is *seems happy* the first XP right sister to I). If we classify *seems happy* as a secondary predicate, we still have problems. That is, the principle of secondary predication coindexing in (2–60) becomes unintelligible with this analysis, since there is no primary predicate here whose domain the secondary predicate falls within. I believe we must extend the definition of primary predicate in such a way that *seems happy* in a sentence like (2–93) qualifies as a primary predicate. In support of this extension, note that in (2–93) the srp can be only *John* and not *me*. This follows if *seems happy* is a primary predicate, since all primary predicates must find their srp in GF subject position.

I conclude that the coindexing principles given in section 5 above, augmented by the principle of Absolute Coindexing in (2–89), are empirically adequate with respect to all the data so far.

8   Passive *by*

In chapter 1, section 2.4 we argued that prepositions, with a very few exceptions, do not assign theta roles themselves (although objects of P may receive theta roles from sources other than the P by way of Compositional Theta Assignment). We did not at that time pay particular attention to the passive *by* phrase. Now we must do so, for in section 3 above we came across a passive example, (2–28), repeated here:

(2–28)   *Bill was struck by John as stupid.

This example was inexplicable for Williams (1980), given that the putative rule of reanalysis should apply here (as shown in (2–29)); thus the NP *John* would c-command the predicate *as stupid*. Example (2–28) can easily be ruled out by the theory presented here if it violates Proviso One or Proviso Two. Thus I shall now argue that the object of *by* does not receive a theta role and that the coindexing of *John* with *as stupid* in (2–28) would violate both Proviso One and Proviso Two.

Certainly the prevalent idea in the literature is that *by* introduces the agentive argument of the passivized verb. Some have argued, instead, that the object of *by* has the same interpretation (whether agentive or something else) as the external argument of the verb in lexical structure (see Zubizarreta 1985, p. 254, and Marantz 1984, p. 247, where he has the object of *by* receive a theta role by way of the VP just as he has the GF subject in an active sentence get a theta role via the VP). One would conclude in either case that the object of *by* has a theta role. Zubizarreta, in fact, argues against this, claiming that the *by* phrase is adverbial, an opinion I concur with. (For a discussion of the use of the term "adverbial" as a functional term, see ch. 1, sec. 1.1.) Marantz, on the other hand, argues that the *by* phrase is adverbial, but the object of the *by* still gets a theta role.

However, there is evidence that the object of *by* does not receive a theta role. The object of *by* in a passive sentence can be an NP which is not a possible argument of the corresponding active verb.

(2–94)a. The new president was chosen by general acclamation of the common folk.
          *General acclamation of the common folk chose the new president.
      b. Margaret was appointed by executive fiat of the king.
          *Executive fiat of the king appointed Margaret.

(No American speakers I have asked accept the sentences with asterisks in (2–94). But the only British speaker who has seen these examples (Andrew Radford) accepts them. It may well be that the argument I am about to make holds only for American speech, although nothing I know of in British speech concerning these sentences goes against my claim that the object of the *by* does not get a theta role.)

One might protest that the *by* phrases in (2–94) are not passive *by* phrases. However, these particular *by* phrases do not occur in active sentences.

(2–95)   *Someone chose the new president by general acclamation of the common folk.

(cf. The common folk chose the new president by general acclamation.)
*Someone appointed Margaret by executive fiat of the king.
(cf. The king appointed Margaret by executive fiat.)

Furthermore, these particular *by* phrases do not co-occur with so-called agentive *by* phrases in passive sentences:

(2–96)   *The new president was chosen by general acclamation of the common folk by all of us.
          *Margaret was appointed by executive fiat of the king by someone important.

Thus I see no evidence whatsoever against the analysis of the *by* phrases in (2–94) as passive *by* phrases. And (2–94), then, supplies evidence that the object of passive *by* need not be an argument of the verb.

Another argument against the object of a passive *by* having a theta role is based on rationale clauses. Rationale clauses require an agentive controller (see Lasnik 1984, among others), as in:

(2–97)   I ran the vacuum cleaner [PRO to upset Dad].
          *I understood French [PRO to upset Dad].

But rationale clauses cannot be controlled by the object of a passive *by*. Example (2–98) is from Roeper (1987, p. 302):

(2–98)   *a symphony by Mozart [PRO to win a prize]

Here *Mozart* cannot control the PRO of the rationale clause. Roeper (1987) concludes from these and other facts that the object of *by* does not itself carry the agentive theta role in a passive sentence; instead the passive morpheme (the *-en/-ed* suffix) on a passive participle "carries the Agent role" (p. 269) (see also Zubizaretta 1985, Jaeggli 1986, and Larson 1987, for the same claim). This analysis accounts for the fact that a rationale clause can appear in (2–99), where we have a *by* phrase – just as in (2–98) – but where we also have the passive affix, which we do not have in (2–98).

(2–99)   That symphony was written by Mozart [PRO to win a prize].

Roeper is inexplicit about whether the object of a *by* actually receives a theta role, but he points out that the object of *by* can have a variety of interpretations, including agent, instrument, locative, or general manner. But this is precisely what we would expect if the object of *by* received no theta role at all (see the discussion of *after* phrases in ch. 1, sec. 2.4).

I conclude that the object of *by* in a passive sentence is not the agentive argument of the passivized verb, nor does it receive a theta role from the *by* itself: the object of *by* does not receive a theta role at all. Instead, as with the other prepositions we saw in chapter one, *by* is a relational term that signals that its object stands in an underdetermined relationship of source or cause with respect to the proposition that the *by* phrase modifies. With this analysis, we might expect the use of the *by* phrase in (2–94) not to be restricted to only passive sentences. And in (2–100) we have active sentences plus one lexical passive, all with *by* phrases.

(2–100) Laura got to be boss by lots of hard work.
We recognized her by her tie.
We understand what a proposition is by definition.
She turned on the t.v. by remote control.
I'll come home by 5 o'clock.
This area of the country has been uninhabited by mammals since the nuclear accident.

Clearly, calling all the *by*'s in (2–100) one kind of *by* goes counter to the assumptions of most linguists today. Yet the different ranges of situation types that a *by* phrase can cover are no more vast than the different ranges of situation types that an *after* phrase can cover in examples (1–89)–(1–91) of chapter 1, section 2.4. Thus I invite the reader to consider my contention seriously.

Still, whether or not I am correct in identifying the *by* in (2–100) with the *by* in passive sentences, the fact remains that the object of a passive *by* does not receive a theta role.

Accordingly, we predict that the object of a passive *by* cannot be coindexed with a secondary predicate. And it cannot. The contrasting examples in (2–101) were offered to me by John Myhill (personal communication):

(2–101) *the destruction by the army as a hostile force
the destruction of the army as a hostile force
*the argument by Bill as a candidate
the argument against Bill as a candidate

Another argument that the object of passive *by* does not receive a theta role comes from facts about anaphor binding in Italian. In chapter 6, section 2, I argue that the antecedent of an anaphor must bear a theta role. But notice that the object of a passive *by* phrase cannot serve as the antecedent of an anaphor.

(2–102) Osvaldo$_i$ è stato convinto da Gianni$_j$ del fatto che la propria$_{i/*j}$ casa è la
più bella del paese.
'Osvaldo has been convinced by Gianni that self's house is the nicest in
the village.'

(Example (2–102) is from Giorgi 1984, in which see arguments that
proprio is an anaphor; and ch. 6, sec. 6 below for arguments that the
regular principles of anaphor binding obtain with *proprio*.) This fact
follows if the object of passive *by* does not receive a theta role.

A final argument against the object of passive *by*'s being an argument
of any lexical head can be made on the basis of extraposition. As Guéron
1980 shows, PP extraposition from NP cannot apply to arguments of the
head N. However, *by* phrases can be extraposed.

(2–103) John read a book by Chomsky over the summer.
John read a book over the summer by Chomsky.
(cf. John analyzed the destruction of the city over the summer.
*John analyzed the destruction over the summer of the city.)

I conclude that the *by* does not introduce an argument of the head N.

In sum, passive *by*, like most other Ps, is not a theta assigner, and the
object of a passive *by* does not receive a theta role from any source.

We can now see that coindexing of the object of the *by* phrase and the
secondary predicate in (2–28) is a violation of both Proviso One and
Proviso Two. That is, *as stupid* in (2–28) falls within the theta domain of
the V, but *John* is not an argument of that V (thus Proviso One is
violated). Furthermore, the *by* phrase is a modifier of the V in my
analysis, so the PP is not L-marked, hence it is a barrier to the object of
the P (thus Proviso Two is violated).

An interesting question arises now: if the passive suffix can behave like
an agentive argument and control a rationale clause (as in (2–99) above),
why cannot this same suffix behave like an agentive argument and serve
as the srp of the secondary predicate in a sentence such as (2–28), and thus
rescue this sentence from ungrammaticality? I have no answer to this
question. It is particularly baffling in light of the fact that implicit
arguments can serve as the srp of secondary predicates inside NPs (for a
discussion of implicit arguments see ch. 1, sec. 1.5). Example (2–104)a is
from Safir (1987a), who attributes it to Tom Roeper; (2–104)b is from
Safir (1987a), who attributes it to Jay Keyser; (2–104)c is added just to
show that not just depictives, but also *as* secondary predicates can take
implicit arguments as their srp's.

(2–104)a. A trip **sick** is no fun.
     b. An entrance **smashed** can embarrass one's host.
     c. A plane trip **as an invalid** isn't much fun.

In sum, I see no reason why the passive suffix in (2–28) cannot serve as the srp to the secondary predicate. As a result, I suspect that something else is responsible for the failure of (2–28). There may be some restriction on the coindexing here that goes beyond the types of concerns we have considered thus far (and see sec. 12 below for more discussion). If that is true, we would expect to find that some passive sentences with secondary predicates can have coindexing with the passive suffix and others cannot. In fact, we find precisely this variability.

Thus the examples in (2–105) are unacceptable (where the last example is from Bresnan 1982a) to everyone I asked.

(2–105) *I was shocked by Bill {**nude/as a nudist**}.

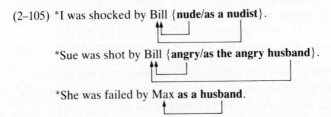

*Sue was shot by Bill {**angry/as the angry husband**}.

*She was failed by Max **as a husband**.

However, Bresnan (1982a) offers (2–106) as a good sentence (although I, personally, reject it, as do many of the people I have asked):

(2–106)   John said he was passed by Mary in the hall yesterday **drunk**.

And Andrew Radford (personal communication) has offered me a range of examples, all of which the people I have asked find acceptable:

(2–107)   I wasn't impressed by him **as a singer,** but I was impressed by him **as a comedian.**

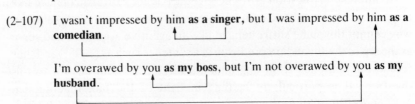

I'm overawed by you **as my boss,** but I'm not overawed by you **as my husband**.

Thus it appears that the passive suffix can serve as the srp to a secondary predicate under certain as yet unclear conditions. What is clear, however, is that these conditions are not structural, since both the good and bad examples in the discussion above have identical syntactic structures.

It is interesting to note that the Italian counterparts to (2–106) and (2–107) were accepted by everyone I asked, but a wide range of other passive sentences with secondary predicates was rejected. And Demonte (1986) argues that in Spanish, secondary predicates cannot be understood to be coindexed with the agentive argument of the passivized verb. Furthermore, Zubizarreta (1985) argues that generally in French secondary predicates cannot be understood to be coindexed with the agentive argument of the passivized verb, but she does find one good example:

(2–108)   Ces vers ont été récités par Marie **complètement soule**.

'Those verses were recited by Marie completely drunk'

Example (2–108), however, is open to an analysis in which *complètement soule* is an adverbial phrase, modifying the verb. Zubizarreta, in fact, raises and immediately dismisses the possibility that the phrase *complètement soule* is not a predicate here but an adverbial. Her objection to the adverbial analysis of *complètement soule* is based on the fact that *soule* here is inflected for gender and number agreement, whereas she says adverbs in French are not inflected for gender and number. However, the distinction between adverbs and non-adverbs based on inflection in Romance may not be totally secure. I argue elsewhere (Napoli 1975) that certain adverbs in Italian undergo gender/number agreement as though they were secondary predicates. And we will see clearly in chapter 6, section 2.1 that quantifier phrases which serve as adverbials can undergo gender agreement (as with *ciascuno*, 'each') and sometimes also number agreement (as with *tutti*, 'all'). Also, Hook and Chauhan (1987) show that adverbs in Bhitrauti can undergo agreement just as adjectives can. (See also O'Grady 1982 for a discussion of the differences between predicates and adverbials.)

It seems, then, that such secondary predicates are rare in passive sentences in Romance (at least in Italian, Spanish, and French), and they are certainly not common in English.

To conclude, secondary predicates in passive sentences may not take the object of a *by* (or its counterpart in Romance) as their srp's. But under certain (as yet not studied) conditions they may take the passive suffix as their srp's. This is because the object of a passive *by* is not the argument of any lexical item, but the passive suffix is an argument of the passivized verb.

9   **Objects of Ps and obligatory control**

Williams (1980) argues that instances of obligatory control are instances of predication. I differ from him on this point, taking PRO in obligatory control structures to be an anaphor, where the coindexing with the antecedent of PRO is a binding coindexing and not a predication coindexing (and see Hornstein and Lightfoot 1987). However, I will argue in chapter 6 that the coindexing between an anaphor and its antecedent obeys the same principles that govern coindexing between a predicate and its srp. Therefore, my theory predicts that an object of a P can serve as the controller for PRO (where the infinitival clause falls outside the PP) in instances of obligatory control only if that object of P is assigned a theta role. This prediction turns out to hold true.

Solan (1977) has observed that objects of P cannot control PRO unless the verb and the P form a verbal complex (which, in our terms, would mean that the verb would assign a theta role to the object of the P by Compositional Theta Assignment). Solan's observation calls for revision; it should be restricted to structures of obligatory control. With such a restriction, we have now explained Solan's observation.

Rouveret and Vergnaud (1980) offer essentially the same explanation for Solan's observation, since they find that only arguments can be controllers. Again, we would improve on Rouveret and Vergnaud's solution by restricting their conclusion to obligatory control structures. The theory of predication offered here goes a step further in recognizing that not just objects of P that are in PP sisters to V, but objects of P that are in PP sisters to any theta assigner, are potential controllers in obligatory PRO structures, depending upon whether or not they receive theta roles.

In (2–109) we see an instance of obligatory control by an object of a P that bears a theta role, where the relevant lexical head here is an N, rather than a V. (The material in parentheses after the example shows that this is an instance of obligatory control. Thus in obligatory control structures the PRO never alternates with a full NP. And in obligatory control structures the controller must be linguistically present. For diagnostics distinguishing between obligatory and nonobligatory control, see Williams 1980.)

(2–109) our reliance on Watson [PRO to find where the last monkey in Yorktown is hidden]

(cf. *our reliance on Watson for Mary to find where the last monkey in
Yorktown is hidden
cf. *our reliance [PRO to find where . . .])

(Note that (2–109) is a counterexample to Williams (see 1980, p. 219, in
particular), since here we have obligatory control in an NP and reanalysis
cannot apply, being limited to V plus P. Therefore the subject role player
does not c-command its predicate in (2–109).)

On the other hand, nonobligatory control, which does not involve the
anaphor PRO, can easily have an object of a P as the controller, even
when that object of the P receives no theta role.

(2–110)   the decision by John [PRO to shoot himself]
(cf. the decision for Sue to leave)

The data on obligatory control, then, offer nice support for the theory
of predication offered here, given the argument in chapter 6 that the
binding of anaphors obeys the same principles that hold on the coindexing of predicates and their srp's.

10   External argument versus subject role player

In chapter 1, sections 2.3 and 4 and in this chapter thus far we have seen
examples in which the subject role player of a predicate was not external
to the maximal projection of the head of the predicate, such as in:

(1–57)   The Huns' **destruction** of the city upset us.

And chapters 3 through 5 will analyze more such examples, another of
which has by now become familiar (see also ch. 3):

(1–64)   quel **matto** di Giorgio

'that madman Giorgio'

In chapter 1, section 4 we observed that srp's can be internal only when
the head of the predicate is an N.

We see, then, that a requirement of externality on a srp is empirically
wrong. However, the externality of a subject role player to its predicate is
a given in virtually every theory of predication in the recent GB linguistic
literature. Therefore, it is useful here to examine some of the theoretical
reasons for its proposal.

There seems to be two theory based reasons for the externality requirement. One involves the claim that predicates must be maximal projections (as in Williams 1977, 1979, 1980, Culicover and Wilkins 1986, among others). However, this claim is inaccurate. Lexical heads alone may be predicates. Lexical heads plus certain modifiers and specifiers may be predicates. And, certainly, in the Italian examples like (1–64) above, it is impossible to claim that the predicate *matto* is a maximal projection.

The other theory based reason is put forth by Williams (1983). He argues that a head and its maximal projection are coindexed and a predicate and its srp (in our terms) are coindexed. Thus if a srp were internal to the maximal projection of its predicate, and if the predicate were simply the head, then the srp would be coindexed with the head, but the head would be coindexed with its maximal projection, so we would wind up with an NP (the srp) coindexed with an XP (the maximal projection of the predicate) that contains the NP, as in (2–111).

(2–111) XP_i

$$\ldots X_i \ldots NP_i \ldots$$

Such a structure would violate the i-within-i constraint (see also ch. 1, sec. 2.3, where I point out problems for this constraint).

But I am not sure that Williams himself is consistent about how to apply the i-within-i constraint. Thus in Williams (1984b) we find (2–112):

(2–112)   John wants $Mary_i$ to [like $herself_i]_{VP_i}$.

Here we have again an i-within-i structure. Yet Williams makes no mention of any i-within-i violation. And Williams (1980) argues that the matrix VP in (2–113) is a predicate (*contra* my analysis in ch. 1, sec. 1.3), so, as Barry Miller (personal communication) has pointed out to me, the indexing would be as shown here:

(2–113)

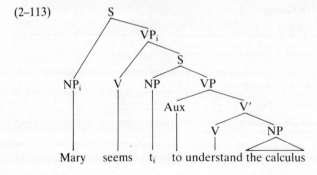

Again we have an i-within-i configuration (that is, the trace has the same index as the matrix VP). Certainly in (2–111) the relevant indices are assigned by predication and head-maximal projection coindexing rules (as proposed in Williams 1981b), while in (2–112) the relevant indices are assigned by binding and predication coindexing rules, and in (2–113) the relevant indices are assigned by virtue of movement and by predication coindexing. Obviously for Williams only certain combinations of indices and not others violate the i-within-i constraint. And Williams presents (1982) the i-within-i constraint as a constraint against referential incoherence, thus only referential indices should count for this constraint according to him. Yet in (2–111) he has counted the index assigned by predication as though it were a referential index, and he has counted the index assigned by the head-maximal projection coindexing rule as a referential index. So why does he not count the other indices in (2–112) and (2–113)? Furthermore, if Safir's (1985) Unity of Indexing Hypothesis is correct, all the indices here should count for the putative i-within-i constraint. And notice that the i-within-i constraint was first brought up to handle binding theory problems, I believe. Therefore, examples such a (1–63)b and c must count for the constraint:

(1–63)b. John is [his own boss].
    c. Anyone can see that John is [his father's son].

Let me point out further that the violation in (2–111) depends crucially on the existence of coindexing between a head and its maximal projection (as in Williams 1981b), a proposed coindexing which demands extensive support.

I contend that the i-within-i constraint is not a coherent constraint in the literature, anyway. I refer the reader to Aoun (1985) for a general discussion and I ask the reader to contrast, for example, Hornstein (1984, p. 93) and Williams (1984b, p. 648). And, finally, the reader might look at Huang (1982), who argues that the i-within-i constraint does not hold for pronominals. But, surely, pronominals are referential. Hence the very motivation for the constraint is called into question.

I conclude that there is no good *a priori* reason why a subject role player need be external to the maximal projection of the head of its predicate. And, as I said above, we have seen above and will see more examples in later chapters of constructions in which the subject role player is internal to the maximal projection of its predicate.

Finally, let me point out that Williams (1983, p. 297) argues on empirical grounds that a predicate must be a maximal projection (from which it would follow that its srp must be external). He points out examples such as:

(2–114)   John considers Bill Bob's best friend.

Here *Bob's* is the specifier of the predicative N *friend*. Williams concludes that since *Bob's* starts the predicate and *Bob's* is a specifier, the predicate is a maximal projection. However, even though I agree that the entire NP *Bob's best friend* is the secondary predicate in (2–114), this example shows only that predicates can be maximal projections, not that they must be. (See also Stuurman 1985, pp. 245 ff., where he addresses Williams' position and shows that given his q-interpretation and theory of PS rules, a specifier does not necessarily indicate the beginning of a maximal projection.)

The issue of externality as regards predication is, I conclude, a bogus one.

Notice that srp's are always arguments of the head of their predicate (by virtue of the Principle of Coincidence in (1–46)). Thus I am saying that a predicate need not have an external argument. I would like to go a step further and suggest that externality of an argument may never be relevant to grammatical processes (except, of course, those that are sensitive to constituency, regardless of argumenthood).

Some have argued that whether an argument is internal or external to the maximal projection of the lexical item that it is an argument of is relevant to various rules of grammar. (Note that this argument is distinct from the question of whether arguments which wind up as subject role players, in particular, must be external arguments.) Some of these arguments involve the claim that lexical rules make crucial distinctions between internal and external arguments. One example is found in Williams (1981a). Another is in Poser (1982), who argues that morphological rules can switch around internal arguments only. I will not here address the arguments in either of these works.

Another place where externality has been claimed to be important is with respect to resultative adjectives. Simpson (1983a) argues that these adjectives may be predicated only of a lexical internal argument. But Rothstein (1983) argues that resultatives can be predicated only of a theme, with no reference to externality versus internality of the argument.

Zubizarreta (1985) argues that internal arguments must be syntactically realized but external ones need not be, even though they are lexically realized. That is, an external argument may be lexically present but syntactically absent (which is, essentially, consistent with Chomsky's position in 1986b). In support of this she claims that derived nominals must have all their internal arguments realized. But this is false. Thus, beside Zubizarreta's ungrammatical example in (2–115)a (where the judgment of ungrammaticality in (2–115)a is reported by Zubizarreta, but the speakers I have asked do not share this judgment, nor do I – still, I will allow her judgment of grammaticality for the purposes of this argument), we find the perfectly grammatical (2–115)b.

(2–115)a. *The destruction by the Romans took place last year.
   b. Destruction by earthquakes is common.

Destruction takes a theme argument in lexical structure, yet no theme appears syntactically in (2–115)b. In order to shore up Zubizzareta's analysis, one might try to argue that *destruction* in (2–115)b is monadic in lexical structure, whereas *destruction* in (2–116) is diadic.

(2–116)   Destruction of Columbian cities is common.

Such an argument would be similar to the argument that there are two lexical structures for verbs such as *eat,* thereby accounting for the fact that no object appears in the surface in sentences like (2–117).

(2–117)   We eat at night.

(Zubizarreta 1985 makes such an argument for *eat,* following Gruber 1965.) But then Zubizarreta could not explain why (2–115)a is bad for her informants (although, as I said above, I accept (2–115)a, as do the speakers I have asked – I am working with Zubizarreta's reported judgment here only to show that her argument is internally inconsistent). And if we try to say that the monadic *destruction* occurs only with a generic sense, thus accounting for the contrast between (2–115)a and (2–115)b, we are at a loss to explain the grammaticality of (2–118).

(2–118)   The savage destruction by the earthquake in 1985 led to permanent evacuation of the area.

Thus derived nominals do not, after all, support Zubizarreta's contention that internal arguments must be syntactically realized.

   Zubizarreta briefly mentions another argument for the claim that internal arguments must be syntactically realized. This argument is based on the claim that if a lexical item is a member of a compound, all of its obligatory internal arguments must be syntactically realized. Zubizarreta refers us to Roeper and Siegel (1978), Selkirk (1982), and Lieber (1983). Then Zubizarreta claims (p. 258, n. 6) that compounds like that in (2–119) are bad because the external argument cannot appear, whereas internal arguments must.

(2–119) *children swimming

But Zubizarreta, as most GB linguists today, accepts the ergative analysis of Burzio 1986 for verbs like *arrive*. (I do not accept the ergative analysis for English, however – see Napoli (1988), although I do accept it for Romance.) She therefore has no explanation for the failure of (2–120).

(2–120) *soldier arriving

In (2–120) *arriving*, by Zubizarreta's own assumptions, should take only internal arguments in lexical structure. Therefore, according to the works cited in this paragraph, *soldier* obligatorily should be syntactically realized. But it cannot be. Thus externality cannot be the relevant criterion for whether or not an argument cannot or must syntactically surface in these compounds.

Zubizarreta uses the claim that internal arguments must syntactically surface in order to explain why in French in the complement of causatives with *par* and in perception verb complements, we do not find examples like (2–121).

(2–121) *On a vu partir.
'One saw leave.'

She analyzes the complement in (2–121) as a VP, not an S. Now since *partir* is an ergative verb, it takes an obligatory internal argument in lexical structure. However, that internal argument must be realized in external position in SS (as with all ergative verbs). But in (2–121), since there is only a VP after *vu* and not an S with her analysis, there is nowhere for the internal lexical argument to be realized, according to Zubizarreta. Thus (2–121) fails. However, in Italian (2–122) is also bad.

(2–122) *Abbiamo visto dormire.
'We saw (people) sleep.'

But *dormire* is not an ergative verb. Thus Zubizarreta's explanation for (2–121) (whose Italian counterpart is also bad) cannot be extended to account for (2–122). If (2–121) and (2–122) are out for the same reason, that reason cannot be the reason Zubizarreta gives. Thus the internal/external distinction may well not be relevant here.

Furthermore, Ruwet (1987) gives a long list of examples in French that he shows should be ungrammatical given Zubizarreta's analysis, but that are, instead, just fine, such as:

(2–123) Cette drogue fait mourir lentement mais surement.
'That drug makes (people) die slowly but surely.'

Barry Miller (personal communication) has offered me another argument against the claim that internal arguments must be syntactically realized. If we assume that the verb for "go" in Tagalog is ergative (following Burzio 1986, as Zubizarreta does), all of its arguments are internal. Therefore, if Zubizarreta were correct, all of its arguments should have to be syntactically realized. But the subject argument is not realized in:

(2–124) Nakikita ko   ang   pumupunta sa tindahan.
         see   1-sg focus go   to store
         'I see the one who goes to the store.'

Miller (1988) argues that we cannot posit a phonetically empty but syntactically present subject argument of *pumupunta*. His argument is based on quantification facts and is, I believe, decisive. Thus, once more we see that not all internal arguments need be syntactically realized.

Zubizarreta gives other arguments for her claim. And, as I mentioned above, there are other arguments in the literature for the necessity of distinguishing between internal and external arguments. It is not my purpose here to go through these arguments in detail. I merely want to suggest that closer scrutiny may reveal that some other distinction rather than the internal/external one is the crucial one. And I reiterate that there are no valid arguments I know of for the claim that arguments which wind up as subject role players, in particular, must be realized as external to the maximal projection of the head of their predicate.

In conclusion, the notion subject role player is an independent one in linguistic theory and cannot be defined by configurational properties. Other linguists have also argued that reference to the formal notion of subject is necessary (as in Rouveret and Vergnaud 1980, for example).

We have, then, completely abandoned the externality requirement, with the nice result that we can now face the Italian and English data in later chapters with a single theory that can handle them both adequately.

There are other advantages to abandoning the requirement that a subject role player be external to the maximal projection of its predicate. For example, Safir (1985) claims that NP adjoined to VP (as in subject-inversion sentences in Italian) can be the subject argument of the VP. Such an NP would not be excluded from the VP in the sense of Chomsky (1986a), and could be seen as a violation of the externality restriction on subjects. For Safir this positioning of the subject, therefore, was a special situation. But in the present theory, this is handled with the ordinary rules of predication.

11   Multiple factors affecting acceptability – mediation, pragmatics, GF hierarchies

Let us turn our attention once more to Proviso One. We have now arrived at one of the most interesting points of our theory of predication. Proviso One stipulates that when a secondary predicate is a sister to a theta role assigner, either its subject role player or the secondary predicate itself must appear in the argument structure of that theta role assigner. What this proviso is doing is saying that a predicate which is located in the theta domain of a lexical head must connect up to the thematic structure of that lexical head, either directly or via its srp (and see the discussion at the end of sec. 5 above).

What this means is that the interpretation of the subject role player of the secondary predicate in its lexical relation to the theta-role assigner will be mediated by the secondary predication. The term "mediation" is due to Barry Miller (personal communication), who develops it fully through the analysis of the syntax and semantics of Tagalog with comparisons to English. Consider (2–125)–(2–126), both of which fall under Proviso One:

(2–125) I like Pepsi **cold**.

(2–126) You make me **crazy**.

In (2–125) the secondary predicate *cold* is an adjunct which is not L-marked by *like*. *Pepsi* is L-marked by *like* and it is the DO of *like*. We understand (2–125) to mean that I like Pepsi when it has the property of being cold. That is, coldness mediates the relationship between *Pepsi* and *like*. On the other hand, in (2–126), the secondary predicate *crazy* is L-marked by *like*. *Pepsi* is L-marked by *like* and it is the DO of *like*. We and its subject role player *me* is the DO of *make*. Again we have a mediated reading: we understand (2–126) to mean that you do an action to me resulting in my being crazy. So the appearance of *me* in DO position is justified only by the fact that I was acted upon by the verb *make* to wind up in the state of the predicate *crazy*. That is, craziness mediates the relationship between *me* and *make*.

Another motivation for Proviso One (in addition to the motivation of licensing, discussed at the close of sec. 5 above), then, is found in the concept of mediation. We find that a secondary predicate that falls within the theta domain of the lexical head H mediates the relationship between H and the srp of the secondary predicate. The result is that we can have a simple syntactic construction which maps into a complex semantic relationship.

The present theory of predication calls for mediation whenever a secondary predicate falls within a theta domain, but it does not call for any particular theta role to be assigned to any particular secondary predicate or to any particular subject role player. Instead, it revolves only around the question of whether or not some item gets a theta role (not which theta role the item gets) and from where. In this way the present theory is similar to Rothstein's (1983), although it differs from hers in allowing unmediated secondary predication (which can occur whenever a secondary predicate falls outside a theta domain). (Rothstein defined secondary predicates in such a way that they fall only within theta domains, and thus they are always mediated.)

Other linguists have tied in theta roles to their rules involving secondary predicates by requiring that certain theta roles be given to certain items. For example, in Williams (1980) we find the claim that a secondary predicate that finds itself in the VP must take the theme of the V as its subject role player. Williams is right to see that secondary predicates within the theta domain of a verb must be connected to the lexical structure of that verb somehow. But pinning down the theta role of the subject role player to just theme does not work. In the last sentence of (2–25)b above, repeated here, we see that a beneficiary can be the subject role player of such a secondary predicate.

(2–25)b. We threw a party for Mary **as the newcomer**.

(We threw Mary a party **as the newcomer**.)

Culicover and Wilkins (1986) offer the most developed theory of predication with respect to restrictions on theta roles of a predicate and its subject role player. They offer thematic conditions on predication such that if a secondary predicate has a certain theta property, then that predicate can take only a subject role player with a certain other theta property. For example, they say that if the secondary predicate bears no thematic role, its subject role player must be a theme. Again the examples from (2–25)b immediately above can be used as evidence against this claim.

Still, it is clear that while in some sentences a mediated secondary predicate can take either of two arguments of the lexical head H whose theta domain it falls within as its subject role player (as in (2–127)), it is also clear that in other sentences only one argument is possible.

(2–127)   Mary kissed John **nude**.

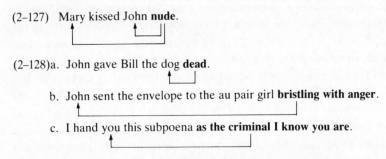

(2–128)a. John gave Bill the dog **dead**.

     b. John sent the envelope to the au pair girl **bristling with anger**.

     c. I hand you this subpoena **as the criminal I know you are**.

In (2–128)a (which is from Williams 1980, p. 207) the subject role player of the secondary predicate *dead* is the theme argument of the verb *gave*. In (2–128)b the subject role player of the secondary predicate *bristling with anger* is the agent argument of the verb *sent*. In (2–128)c the subject role player of the secondary predicate *as the criminal I know you are* is the beneficiary argument of the verb *hand*.

It is my contention that it is pragmatics as well as lexical structure that determine whether or not the secondary predicate has a choice of subject role player among the arguments of the lexical head within whose theta domain it falls. Thus, beside (2–128)a through (2–128)c, we find:

(2–129)a. John gave Bill the dog **angrier than hell**.

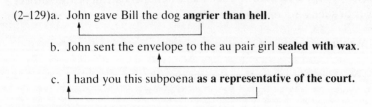

     b. John sent the envelope to the au pair girl **sealed with wax**.

     c. I hand you this subpoena **as a representative of the court**.

Now all the subject role players of the secondary predicates have shifted, and this shift is due to knowledge we have of the world. (For example, people are not the kind of thing we typically seal with wax, but envelopes are.)

In (2–129) I am analyzing all the secondary predicates as being within the VP, just as in (2–128). Their placement inside the VP is necessary with my theory in order to account for their mediated interpretation. Independent support for this analysis is found in section 5 above. Notice that the problems (2–128)–(2–129) present for other theories of predication hold regardless of the syntactic analysis of (2–128)–(2–129).

In (2–129) we see just one example of the possibility that pragmatic factors are relevant to secondary-predication coindexing. Let me offer another. There are multiple restrictions on secondary predicates which begin with *as* (none of which has been pointed out in the literature, so far as I know). An anonymous reader of an earlier version of this manuscript pointed out to me the following sentences with this reader's acceptability judgments:

(2–130)   I looked upon Bill {as my protector/as my enemy}.
I mouthed off at Bill {*as my protector/?as my enemy}.
I wanted Bill {as my protector/as my enemy}.
I shot Bill {*as my protector/as an enemy}.

These examples of secondary predicates introduced by *as* show that theta assignment to the srp of an adjunct secondary predicate in a theta domain from an outside source is a necessary but not sufficient condition for coindexing. One might then object that the examples with asterisks in (2–130) (and those with asterisks and with *as* secondary predicates in secs. 3 and 4 above) cannot be used as support for my Proviso One, after all.

I believe such a dismissal of the evidence I have brought to bear on the issue would be hasty. Notice that in (2–130) there may well be pragmatic interference in the sentences with asterisks (for example, we shoot enemies, not our protectors). But in none of the examples with asterisks of sections 3 or 4 is the predication that fails either pragmatically implausible or inappropriate. Thus I maintain the claim that these examples support my predication coindexing principles. And in general I believe that data such as those in (2–130) are not destructive of the principles I have developed in this chapter. Rather, they show a need for attention to the additional restrictions on particular types of secondary predications that go beyond the restrictions common to all secondary predications.

Now that I have put forth pragmatics (and maybe other factors) as an explanation for (2–128), the reader might expect me to reject entirely any proposal that particular theta roles matter to secondary-predication coindexing. However, in fact I suspect that there are semantic restrictions on predication coindexing that involve the choice of theta roles on the items involved in the coindexing. While others have proposed this in detail (see Williams 1980, Bresnan 1982a, Rothstein 1983, Culicover and Wilkins 1986, the remarks on the determination of the controller of PRO in Jackendoff 1987a, the proposal of semantic tiers in Talmy 1985, among others), I find problems (some of which are indicated above in this chapter) with all the proposals thus far, but I believe the line of research is promising.

I will not go further into this particular question in this book. Yet I recognize that there probably are restrictions on combinations of thematic roles other than purely pragmatic or lexical ones. In fact, slight lexical variations on the sentences given here sometimes result in different grammaticality judgments. And this is true, as well, of the examples in all the recent literature on predication cited in this book. This fact is probably the strongest piece of evidence that configurational restrictions on predication must be wrong. **The unacceptability of a predication coindexing between points P_1 and P_2 in a given structure cannot be due to configurational constraints if in another sentence with the same syntactic structure predication coindexing between points P_1 and P_2 is acceptable.** I return to this point in the final section of this chapter. Thus, while I reject the idea that such restrictions will involve configurational properties, I leave open the possibility that there may be thematic conditions on secondary predication (not precisely those that have been proposed in the literature thus far, but perhaps similar ones). And I stress once more that the theory here is based not on which theta role an item receives, but simply on whether or not an item receives a theta role at all.

At this point it is appropriate to discuss the one major theory of predication outside a GB framework that has great similarities to mine, but is conceptually distinctly different. That is the theory presented by Bresnan (1982a).

Bresnan organizes secondary predicates that are sisters to lexical heads into two groups: XCOMP and XADJ. The XCOMP ones are subcategorized for by the lexical heads. The XADJ ones are not. She has the Lexical Rule of Functional Control which will allow an XCOMP secondary predicate to find a subject role player in the positions of GF subject, DO, or the second object of a double-object construction (what I still would call the DO). She has the Constructional Rule of Functional Control to allow an XADJ secondary predicate to find a subject role player in a variety of positions, including for English object of a preposition, so long as the object of the P bears a theta role.

In my terms Bresnan would be saying that for secondary predicates that fall within a theta domain, an L-marked secondary predicate must find its subject role player in GF subject or DO position of the theta assigner, while a non-L-marked secondary predicate can find its subject role player in any GF position of the theta assigner so long as the srp is an argument of the theta assigner.

My organization of secondary predicates that fall within theta domains is almost identical to Bresnan's. A crucial difference, however, is that I analyze the objects of many Ps as not receiving theta roles, whereas Bresnan takes the objects of most Ps to bear theta roles. Consider the sentences below ((2–131)a&b are from Bresnan 1982a).

(2–131)a. I presented it to John **dead**.

     b. *I presented John with it **dead**.

     c. The dean presented us with the new program **already approved**.

        (cf. the nonpredicative counterpart:
        The dean presented us with the new, already approved, program.)

Bresnan claims that *dead* in (2–131)a is an XCOMP, so its subject role player must be a GF subject or DO. Therefore (2–131)b fails since *it* is the object of a P.

However, (2–131)c is good, despite the fact that it has the same structure as (2–131)b. Bresnan could get around (2–131)c by claiming that the secondary predicate in (2–131)c is an XADJ, and that thus it can take the object of a P as its subject role player. But we are left then with the question of why (2–131)b cannot also be analyzed as having an XADJ. Bresnan's theory offers no answer.

A much worse problem for Bresnan's theory, though, is that by being able to analyze these secondary predicates as XADJ, she actually could get around any potential counterexample to her restrictions on the subject role player of XCOMP merely by analyzing a secondary predicate as an XADJ, instead.

The only situation in which Bresnan could not get around a potential counterexample in this manner would be that in which the secondary predicate is obligatorily subcategorized for by the head V. Then if the subject role player of the secondary predicate were the object of a P, we would have a counterexample to Bresnan's theory.

However, Bresnan could get around this kind of potential counterexample with another tack. She has an operation on lexical form called verb-preposition incorporation (Bresnan 1982b, p. 51) which allows us to analyze the object of a P as a DO. So she could claim simply that the object of a P in the kind of example described above was, after all, a DO, by virtue of verb-preposition incorporation.

As far as I know, then, Bresnan's theory is untestable. I see this as a serious flaw of her theory.

Since I allow no rule comparable to verb-preposition incorporation, neither in the lexicon nor in the syntax (see my arguments against reanalysis in sec. 3 above), and since I make explicit the circumstances under which an object of a preposition can have a theta role (see ch. 1, sec. 2.4), my theory is testable.

A second claim of Bresnan's is that S-initial XADJ secondary predicates must take the GF subject as their subject role player. This follows from no independently supported principles: it is an *ad hoc* restriction. But this restriction, exemplified in my (2–68)b above, repeated here:

(2–68)b.   **Penniless**, John left Mary.

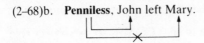

follows from Proviso Two – the proviso that a barrier of the subject role player may not intervene between it and its predicate (and see ch. 6, sec. 3 for further evidence that barriers block coindexing).

Thus, while Bresnan's and my theories at first look quite similar, they are conceptually and empirically distinct. In particular, mine is sensitive to theta-role assignment whereas hers is not. And mine is testable whereas I do not believe hers is.

I must add, however, that Bresnan's work in nonconfigurational approaches to predication has paved the way for my work and the debt my work has toward hers is significant.

Before we leave this section let me point out that I have no explanation for the failure of (2–131)b, but it is clear that that failure is not due to configurational factors, given the acceptability of (2–131)c.

And, just as I was unwilling to dismiss the possibility that the choice of particular theta roles is relevant to predication coindexing, I am unwilling to dismiss the possibility that a hierarchy of GFs is involved in the choice of a subject role player for a predicate, as in the Lexical Rule of Functional Control of Bresnan (1982a), and as claimed for different kinds of depictive predicates by Jackendoff (1987b).

Let me also point out that there are some simply baffling differences between primary and secondary predications, as pointed out by Stuurman (1985, p. 244), who offers the examples:

(2–132)a. She preferred her meat to be veal.
   b. *She preferred her meat veal.

The only difference between (2–132)a and (2–132)b is that the (a) example has a primary predication and the (b) example has a secondary predication. Yet the acceptability difference is strong.

It is clear to me that an investigation of these questions calls for an investigation of the distinctions between different theta roles and of event structures (as in the works cited in ch. 1) as well as a range of other issues that I cannot even begin to guess at here; this is a matter beyond the scope of this book. I thus leave these questions unanswered, noting only that the evidence thus far suggests that their answers will not jeopardize the principles of predication developed in this chapter, but only enrich the overall understanding we have of the nature of predication.

12 Honorary NPs

Many have noted that secondary predicates which are not set off by pauses (and hence do not come under those studied in ch. 5, sec. 5) can accompany an NP srp in such a way that the secondary predicate together with its srp behaves like an NP, as in:

(2–133) Moses Malone **an invalid** is the last thing the Bullets need (especially

     since he's their star player).

Example (2–133) is from Safir (1983), who calls the string *Moses Malone an invalid* an honorary NP. He analyzes these strings as small clauses which behave like NPs. For example, they can undergo NP movement,

(2–134) Workers angry about the pay does indeed seem [t] to be just the sort of situation that the ad campaign was designed to avoid.

Safir also points out that subject–verb agreement behaves as though these honorary NPs are clauses and not singular or plural regular NPs:

(2–135) Workers angry about the pay {is/*are} just the sort of situation that the ad campaign was designed to avoid.

As Safir points out, these honorary NPs are restricted to GF subject position of copular sentences at DS.

Thus far in this book I have not considered this type of secondary predication and I do not intend to go into it here in depth. The analysis of these honorary NPs requires a thorough discussion of small clauses and an examination of the structure of a wide range of other constructions that go far beyond the bounds of this book (see Napoli 1987a for relevant discussion).

However, let me point out that while the agreement facts in (2–135) are nicely handled by Safir's analysis and are hard to account for unless the material in GF subject position is somehow propositional, the data in (2–134) need not call for an analysis in which the string *workers angry about the pay* is a constituent. We will see in chapter 5, section 5, that appositives, like the string *angry about the pay* in (2–134), give the appearance of moving with the element they stand in apposition to. Yet there we will see an explanation for this fact which is consistent with an analysis in which appositives do not form a constituent with the element they stand in apposition to at either DS or SS (and see Emonds 1979).

In any case, these honorary NPs do not present any problem for my secondary predication coindexing principles. First, they only occur in subject position of copular sentences, so no NP other than the correct one will be eligible as the srp since a barrier will block off all other NPs, by Proviso Two. Second, they do not fall within a theta domain, so Proviso One is not applicable.

13   Barriers and movement

I argue in chapter 6 that the predication coindexing principles developed in this chapter apply also (with some modifications made in ch. 6) to the coindexing between an anaphor and its antecedent. Given that the trace of NP movement is an anaphor, whereas the trace of wh-movement is not (see Kayne 1981a, Chomsky 1981, and elsewhere), we predict that the coindexing between the trace of NP movement and its antecedent will be constrained in the same way that the coindexing between a predicate and its srp is, but the coindexing between the trace of wh-movement and its antecedent will not be so constrained.

In chapter 6 I argue that the parallel is between predicates and anaphors on the one hand, and srp's and antecedents on the other. We therefore expect that a trace of NP movement that is not theta marked and that is the object of a P cannot find its antecedent outside its PP, since such a trace is an anaphor (and should obey whatever restrictions predicates obey). But a trace of wh-movement in the same position can, since such a trace is a variable. This expectation arises from the fact we noted in section 7 above, that secondary predicates inside such PPs cannot be coindexed with any srp outside the PP. The expectation is met:

(2–136)a. *Betty was eaten after [t].
     b. Who did Ralph eat after [t]?

Certainly, any proponent of Chomsky's (1986a) theory of grammar will recognize the data in (2–136) as following from otherwise needed principles in that theory. Thus Chomsky would argue that movement in (2–136)a should be blocked by his minimality condition (we have here a violation of the ECP). And Chomsky would allow (2–136)b by first admitting a rule to extrapose the PP *after NP* and right adjoin it to the VP, so that movement out of this PP will not cross any barriers.

Independent motivation for the PP extraposition rule is, however, lacking (and see Bach's 1977 comments on Chomsky 1977), and questions arise – such as why the putative PP extraposition rule cannot also apply to salvage (2–136)a.

I therefore offer my alternative account of (2–136) with the hopes that it will supplant certain stipulated restrictions in Chomsky (1986a), while complementing others.

Since movement is not central to the present work and since a detailed examination of the restrictions on movement could not be brief, I will go no further with this discussion here. Let us just note that, from this quick look, it appears that the behavior of the trace of NP movement supports my contention in chapter 6 that a theory of indexing (which covers predication coindexing and anaphor binding) exists and is comprised of the principles I have been developing in this chapter.

14 Explanatory power of the theory

At this point I would like to show the reader some additional benefits we reap from the principles of predication coindexing offered in this chapter.

First, we predict a semantic difference between minimally different sets of sentences like the following.

(2–137)a. The ambassador, nude, arrived.
           Nude, the ambassador arrived.
        b. The ambassador arrived nude.

In (2–137)a the secondary predicate, *nude*, is not within a theta domain.
Therefore we understand these sentences to mean that the ambassador
arrived and that he was nude. But the nudeness does not characterize his
arrival. Instead, it is an additional fact we know about the ambassador. In
(2–137)b, however, *nude* is inside the VP and it is within the theta domain
of the verb *arrived*. Therefore we understand this sentence to mean that
the ambassador was nude when he arrived. Nudeness characterizes the
arrival. This is a mediated predication. And this kind of semantic contrast
is found generally in such pairs (*Poverty-stricken, Mary died* versus *Mary
died poverty-stricken*, etc.) (see also relevant remarks in Stump 1981).

We can certainly get mediated predication in structures other than
those in which a secondary predicate finds itself in a theta domain.
Sometimes this mediated interpretation is due to pragmatics. That is, we
cannot think of any interpretation other than a mediated one in the given
situation that the sentence describes. Another way to have mediation is
by using *as*. If we say Mary did something "as" something else, we have
explicitly set up a mediated interpretation. This is the case with the
sentences in (2–138), where speakers find no semantic contrast between
the sentences in each pair to parallel that between (2–137)a and (2–137)b.

(2–138) Cooked with rosemary, rabbit is out of sight.
         Rabbit is out of sight, cooked with rosemary.
         As a musician, Maria is off her rocker.
         Maria is off her rocker, as a musician.

The point of (2–137)b, however, is that the mediation here is not told to
us by any explicit lexical word such as *as*. Nor is it the result of pragmatics
(since the sentences in (2–137)a have unmediated readings). Instead, the
mediation in (2–137)b is a result of the structure. And the lack of
mediation in (2–137)a is, in the absence of any explicit information in the
context to the contrary, also a result of the structure.

Second, as Barry Miller (personal communication) has pointed out to
me, we expect minimal pairs such as the following.

(2–139) *Mary dared to swim the Channel nude before anyone else topless.

(2–140) Mary dared to swim the Channel nude before anyone else did topless.

(For an analysis of pseudogapping sentences like that in (2–140), see

Levin 1978.) In (2–139) the NP *anyone else* is the object of a P where the PP is not L-marked. Thus the PP is a barrier for this NP and this NP cannot be the subject role player of the secondary predicate *topless*, because of Proviso Two. On the other hand, in (2–140) the NP *anyone else* is the GF subject of the clause introduced by *before*. The secondary predicate *topless*, which is inside the VP, can therefore take this NP as its subject role player.

Third, many have noticed that NPs in specifier position of NPs are often not available as subject role players for secondary predicates. And some have argued that this is because the specifier is not an argument position (Williams 1982, Rothstein 1983, among others). Thus we find examples such as (2–141) with asterisks in the literature.

(2–141)   *John's arrival nude

In the present theory a secondary predicate that is a sister to the head N *arrival* will not be L-marked by that head. Therefore, by Proviso One, this secondary predicate must find a subject role player that receives a theta role from *arrival*. This would be an instance of mediated predication. I take the position that genitive NPs in specifier position can bear theta roles (see ch. 1, sec. 2.3). The question then becomes, why cannot *nude* mediate John's relation to *arrival* in (2–141)? The answer here may well be in the time frames, as Barry Miller (personal communication) suggests. An arrival is an action at a point in time, but nudeness is a state that endures. An NP, unlike a clause, can be devoid of a time frame. But if we add a time adverbial to pin down the nudeness so that it coincides with the arrival, we find an acceptable secondary predication.

(2–142)   John's arrival at precisely 8:15 buck naked threw the party into chaos.

It is only the idea of mediation that can account for the difference of acceptability between (2–141) and (2–142). (And some speakers are flexible enough to imagine a context for (2–141) without the need for an added time adverbial. Thus Andrew Radford (personal communication), for example, accepts (2–141) as is.)

Other examples of acceptable secondary predication inside NP include those in (2–143) (where some of these were suggested to me by Andrew Radford and Jacqueline Guéron (personal communication)):

(2–143)   I sought Mary's advice **as a disinterested friend**.
          I sought the advice of Mary **as a disinterested friend**.
          Mary's insistence **as a friend** that we should leave finally prevailed.

My advice to you **as your best friend** is to quit.
My advice to you **as my little sister** is to stay in school and not get married till you're twenty-one.
This dictionary is an award to you **as our Top Sophomore Girl**.
This dictionary is your award **as our Top Sophomore Girl**.
Mary's first photograph **as an amateur photographer** won her a lot of money.

Notice that these examples support my contention in chapter 1, section 2.3 that not only abstract but also certain concrete Ns can have an argument structure (as in the last example above).

Fourth, we find contrasts like the following:

(2–144)   *The woman in a blanket **as a skirt** is Beth.

(2–145)   The woman wrapped herself in a blanket **as a skirt**.

In (2–144) *a blanket* cannot serve as the subject role player for *as a skirt*. Both Proviso One and Proviso Two will rule out (2–144), since the PP *in a blanket* is not L-marked, thus it serves as a barrier for the NP *a blanket,* and since *a blanket* is not an argument of *woman*. The question is not why (2–144) is out, then, but why (2–145) is good.

As a skirt is an adjunct secondary predicate within the theta domain of the V *wrapped*, but it is not L-marked by the head V *wrapped* in (2–145). Therefore, by Proviso One, we require that *a blanket* be an argument of the verb *wrapped*. The interesting thing here is that *a blanket* is in a PP. Thus we need to argue that *a blanket* here gets its theta role by Compositional Theta Assignment from the head V. But, surely, this must be the case. We find that *wrap* can occur in two structures: beside (2–145) we find (2–146).

(2–146)   The woman wrapped a blanket around herself as a skirt.

Thus the lexical structure for *wrap* allows the theme argument to appear either as a DO (as in (2–146)) or as the object of a P (as in (2–145)), and allows the goal argument to appear either as the object of a P (as in (2–146)) or as a DO (as in (2–145)).

Our theory predicts the grammaticality of pairs such as (2–145) and (2–146). Similar pairs are discussed in Bresnan (1982a, p. 377), where she explicitly denies that both sentences of this kind of pair can be grammatical unless the verb does not subcategorize for the secondary predicate. Of course, the verb in (2–145)–(2–146) does not subcategorize for the secondary predicate. So Bresnan would admit the possibility of both these sentences being grammatical, as, in fact, they are. Still, with my theory, even if a secondary predicate were subcategorized for (or L-marked), we would allow pairs such as (2–145)–(2–146), since the only requirement would be that *a blanket* satisfy a position in the lexical structure of *wrapped*, as it does. This is a point on which Bresnan and I differ, and we have already seen above, in the examples in (2–131), that Bresnan's claim cannot be maintained (where Bresnan analyzes the secondary predicate in (2–131) as an argument – that is, an XCOMP in her terms).

Fifth, we can account for the ambiguity of (2–147), noted by Safir 1983.

(2–147) I believed John sober.

We can understand (2–147) to mean that I believed John when he was in a sober state, or I believed John to have the property of being sober. (Of course, (2–147) can also mean that I believed John while I was sober, but that reading is irrelevant to the discussion here.) Notice that *believe* can take in its lexical structure a propositional argument or a simple referential argument, as in (2–148) through (2–150).

(2–148) I believed that John was sober.

(2–149) I believed John to be sober.

(2–150) I believed John.

That means that we have two ways to analyze (2–147). We can analyze *John* as being L-marked by the head V *believed*, in which case the secondary predicate is a non-L-marked adjunct. This accounts for the reading in which we believed John while he was sober. That is, the secondary predicate *sober* mediates the argument status of *John* with respect to *believed*. Or we can analyze the secondary predicate *sober* as being L-marked by the head V *believed*, in which case *John* is a DO of *believed* but not an argument of it. This accounts for the propositional reading of (2–147). That is, the secondary predicate *sober* mediates the GF status of *John* with respect to *believed*. (This second analysis, in which *John* gets no theta role from *believe*, is similar to that of Williams 1980 for sentences with *consider*.)

We have thus accounted for the two readings of (2–147) and similar such sentences without resorting to claiming a dual syntactic analysis and without the need of any new mechanisms in our predication theory.

Sixth, we find that speakers greatly prefer (2–151) over (2–152).

(2–151)   I led Mary into the study as a quiet place to talk.

(2–152)   *I write my letters in the top floor study as a quiet place to work.

The verb *led* in (2–151) takes a locative argument and the P *into* here maps the thing designated by the NP *the study* into a place (in Jackendoff's 1983 terms – and see ch. 1, sec. 2.4). Thus the secondary predicate in (2–151) can take the object of the P as its subject role player since that NP bears a theta role assigned by the verb. However, *write* in (2–152) does not take a locative argument. Thus (2–152) is a violation of both Proviso One and Proviso Two.

Seventh, with the approach we are taking here, both arguments and modifiers of a lexical head can be sisters to it. Some other theories of predication, instead, have assumed a phrase structure that allows multiple levels within VP, for example (as in Emonds 1985, Culicover and Wilkins 1986, among others). At times linguists have appealed to multiple levels within VP to account for the failure of secondary-predication coindexing. For example, Culicover and Wilkins (1986) claim that (2–153) fails because the secondary predicate *full* is not bijacent to the NP *the wagon*. They give the structure in (2–154).

(2–153) *John loaded the wagon with the hay full.

(2–154)

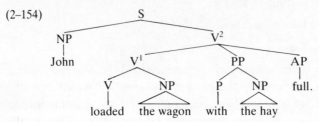

I, on the other hand, would analyze (2–153) as in (2–155).

(2–155)

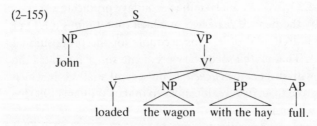

I therefore must account for why (2–153) fails. First, let me point out that if the AP is a bit heftier, the sentence sounds fine.

(2–156)   John loaded the wagon with hay full to the brim.
       John loaded the wagon with hay as full as he could.

Since it is a well-known fact that heftier items can appear extraposed out of their base-generated position (as with heavy NP shift), I propose that in (2–156) a movement rule has applied, taking a hefty secondary predicate and extraposing it to the end. With this analysis (2–156) would come from (2–157).

(2–157) John loaded the wagon full to the brim with hay.
John loaded the wagon as full as he could with hay.

We do not, therefore, generate (2–153), since *full* is not hefty enough to undergo the shift rule. We do, however, generate the source for (2–153):

(2–158) John loaded the wagon full with the hay.

Culicover and Wilkins, on the other hand, cannot account for the difference between (2–153) and (2–156). Their rules of predication take place at a level they call R-structure, which is read off of DS, before all movement. Thus no appeal to a shift rule can account for the difference. Example (2–156) should be ungrammatical in Culicover and Wilkins' theory. Instead, it is fine.

Eighth, Williams (1984a) argues that an XP immediately dominated by S can have a right sister PP (in our terms, that would mean that I(nflection) can take two right sisters: XP and a following PP). Thus far we have not had to appeal to this adjunct position in the analysis of our multiple predicate sentences. But if we had a secondary predicate in clause-final position that was attached at I' rather than inside XP, we predict that such a secondary predicate could take anything for its subject role player so long as that anything was within the clause set up by the primary predicate. In fact, we find that such secondary predicates do occur and that they can take the entire clause minus themselves (and, in (2–159), minus the negative) as their subject role player.

(2–159) I don't walk my children home from school as a responsibility, but as a treat.

Examples like (2–159) are anathema to a theory of predication that calls for the semantic units of predication to have syntactic units as counterparts. In (2–159) the semantic notion of subject role player with respect to the secondary predicate has no syntactic constituent that corresponds to it.

Notice that in chapter 1, section 1 I maintained the idea that srp's must be phrasal if they are nominal, since reference is determined at the phrasal level. But we have seen repeatedly that srp's need not be phrasal if they are non-nominal. Example (2–159) is one more such example.

Ninth, so long as we allow our theory of predication to permit traces of NP to undergo predication coindexing, nothing need be said about variables. Thus examples like (2–160) are no problem, assuming a trace in the position marked [t].

(2–160) Who did you think [t] saw Bill?
          What did Bill eat [t] raw?

The primary predicate of the embedded clause in the first sentence finds its subject role player in GF subject position, so its srp is the trace. The secondary predicate in the second sentence finds its subject role player in the trace in DO position of the verb *eat*, where it receives a theta role from *eat*. No violations of our predication theory are encountered.

On the other hand, there is scarce evidence that any item other than a referential one leaves a trace when it moves. Thus I have built up my predication coindexing principles on the assumption that it is the SS position of a predicate that matters for coindexing. In support of this position, notice that secondary predicates which are arguments cannot front, in contrast to secondary predicates which are adjuncts:

(2–161) *Sick the medication rendered John.
          (cf. The medication rendered John sick.)

(2–68)b. Penniless, John left Mary.
          (cf. John left Mary penniless.)

(See the discussion in sec. 5 above of the possible analysis of (2–68)b as involving movement.)

Tenth, Bresnan 1978 first noticed pairs like:

(2–162) They make good cooks.

(2–163) *Good cooks are made by them.

Williams (1980) accounted for the ungrammaticality of (2–163) by noting that the subject role player does not c-command its predicate. In my theory, however, c-command has no part. But (2–163) will be ruled out by Proviso Two, since the PP node of *by them* is a barrier for the NP *them* (see sec. 8 above). And I would argue that the passive affix is, likewise, unavailable as a srp for the moved secondary predicate *good cooks*, since the VP is a barrier for this affix. Thus (2–163) fails because the secondary predicate can find no srp.

Eleventh, Bresnan (1982a) noticed the unacceptability of:

(2–164) *Tom will serve you the fish tasty.

Her analysis is the following. *Tasty* is a subcategorized for complement of *serve*. (I am not completely convinced by this claim, but I lay aside this question for the sake of the argument.) *Tasty* is also a state predicate. Subcategorized for state predicates must describe an objective state of the verb's theme argument. The problem with (2–164), then, is that *tasty* is not objective, but evaluative. Bresnan contrasts (2–164) to:

(2–165) Tom will serve you the fish raw.

I offer an alternative analysis. The secondary predicates in (2–164) and (2–165) fall within the theta domain of the matrix verb. They must therefore mediate the relationship between their subject role player and the verb *serve*. The problem with (2–164) is that the temporal nature of *tasty* is open (being a state that typically endures) whereas the matrix verb pulls us into a particular point time frame (being an action predicate). If we add a temporal modifier to *tasty*, the resulting sentence is fine:

(2–166) By the time you got here the fish was rotten. But I ate the fish still tasty and fragrant. Ha ha!

The contrast between (2–164) and (2–165), is, then, explained in the same way that the contrast between (2–141) and (2–142) above is explained. We have no need to prohibit these state predicates from being non-objective, and such a prohibition would incorrectly block (2–166). (See Rothstein 1983 for further comments on (2–164) that are compatible with mine here.)

Twelfth, Chomsky (1986b) notes the ungrammaticality of:

(2–167) *John seems [that it is raining] angry.

His explanation involves the notion of T-government and I hesitate to represent that explanation here since either I do not understand it or it is incoherent.

My theory offers a simple explanation for (2–167). I argued in chapter 1, section 1.3 that *seem* is not itself the head of a predicate, but it is part of a predicate headed by some other element. I argued in section 7 above that the definition of primary predicate must be extended to allow the predicate that *seem* is part of to qualify as a primary predicate in some instances (for example, when it is the only predicate in a clause). Given these positions, we can see that in (2–167) either the discontinuous string *seem . . . is raining* is the primary predicate, or the discontinuous string *seem . . . angry* is the primary predicate.

But if *seem . . . is raining* is the primary predicate, *John* is not an

appropriate srp for this predicate. Instead, *it* is the srp (see Napoli 1987a).
It then follows that *John* is not licensed. *Angry* cannot license *John* since
adjuncts cannot license other material (see secs. 5 and 7 above). And
since *John* is not in the lexical structure of *seems* or *raining, John* is
unlicensed.

On the other hand, if *seem . . . angry* is the primary predicate, then its
srp is *John*. But now the clause *that it is raining* is not licensed: it is
semantically untied to the rest of the utterance. That is, it is not a role
player of the primary predicate; it is not a modifier; it cannot be an
adjunct secondary predicate since it is a closed clause (see ch. 1, sec. 2.6).
It simply has no function in (2–167). And its intrusion into the utterance
renders the sentence ungrammatical.

Thus with either analysis of what the primary predicate is in (2–167),
we have a straightforward explanation for the failure of (2–167).

Thirteenth, in chapter 1, section 2.5 I argued that fixed phrases can be
phrasal predicates, where any item that is part of the fixed phrase is not
semantically separated from the rest of the fixed phrase. We have such an
example here:

(2–168) Mary threw a fit.

Mary gets a theta role from the fixed phrase (which I analyze as a lexical
item) *threw a fit*, but *a fit*, being an inseparable part of the phrase *threw a
fit*, does not. We predict, then, that an adjunct secondary predicate within
or outside of the VP of such a sentence can take an NP outside of the fixed
phrase as its subject role player, but never an NP that is part of the fixed
phrase. This is so.

(2–169)   Mary threw a fit **on heroin**.

(2–170)   *Mary threw a fit **frightening**.

Fourteenth, in chapter 1 I argued (as many have – see, for example,
Higginbotham 1985) that the head of a modifier phrase gives a theta role
to the element modified. We predict, then, that an adjunct secondary
predicate that is in the theta domain of the head of a modifier can take the
element modified as its subject role player. And it can.

(2–171)   the girl sitting on the bench **nude** is Joan.

Here we understand the girl to be nude.

We could go on like this. But the reader by this point has a good feel for what the theory can do, and that was the point of this section.

15   Conclusion

We have seen that the principles for predication coindexing of this chapter are empirically adequate and theoretically valid. Let me repeat these coindexing principles here along with the definitions we have developed, for future reference as the reader goes on to other chapters.

(2–5)   *A primary predicate* is a predicate
        (a)   whose head is the syntactic head of the first XP right sister to I, or
        (b)   which is itself the first XP right sister to I.

(2–6)   *Primary Predication Coindexing*: Coindex a primary predicate with its GF subject.

(2–7)   *A secondary predicate* is any predicate other than a primary predicate.

(2–60)   *Secondary Predication Coindexing*: Coindex a secondary predicate SP with a phrase that will be called its subject role player that is within the domain of the SP's primary predicate.

(2–77)   *Proviso One*: If a secondary predicate is within the theta domain of a lexical item H, its srp must appear in the lexical structure of H.

(2–79)   *Alternate to Proviso One for H=N*: If a secondary predicate is within the theta domain of a lexical item H, either the secondary predicate or its srp must receive a theta role from H.

(2–64)   *Proviso Two*: A subject role player must not be separated by any of its barriers from the head of its predicate.

(2–89)   *Absolute Coindexing*: Coindex a predicate which is a daughter of the minimal node that dominates all members of an absolutive with an XP that is also a daughter of that minimal node.

This theory makes use of no configurational relationships other than those that are intrinsic to theta theory (the relevant concepts here being theta domains and barriers) and to the definition of primary predicate (the relevant relationship here being a clause).

With the theory here, a secondary predicate that falls within a theta domain generally finds its subject role player in the lexical structure of the theta assigner whose domain it falls in (the only exception being secondary predicates that fall within the theta domain of N). That is, either the srp will be an argument of the theta assigner whose domain the secondary predicate falls within or the srp will bear a GF toward that theta assigner.

Typically this means that the subject role player will, in fact, c-command its predicate and be external to its maximal projection and the predicate will be bijacent to its subject role player. However, when the subject role player is the object of a P, it does not c-command its predicate nor is its predicate bijacent to it. Furthermore, when a secondary predicate falls outside a theta domain, its subject role player often does not c-command it (as in examples such as (2–68)b) and the predicate often is not bijacent to it. As for externality, it also is not a necessity (as we saw in sec. 10 above). Thus configurational approaches to predication must be abandoned. This, of course, is one of the conclusions of Bresnan (1982a). However, I have shown that we can throw away configurational restrictions on predication while still working within the GB framework.

The reader who has struggled with all the examples here has undoubtedly realized that sometimes minor lexical changes in a sentence change the acceptability of a secondary predicate. What is crucial for me is not those changes that render a previously grammatical sentence ungrammatical, but those changes that render a previously ungrammatical sentence grammatical. That is, if a sentence is good with a given structure, our theory must allow the predication coindexings in that structure. So any lexical changes which affect the grammaticality prove nothing about structural restrictions on predication. Instead, such changes only underscore how inadequate a configurational approach to predication is. Lexical, pragmatic, and probably some sort of thematic interdependence factors (as discussed in sec. 11 above) affect predication in ways that go beyond the theory offered here. And it is my hope that the theory offered here will pave the way for future investigations of those factors with more promise of success now.

On the other hand, whenever I have given an example above of an ungrammatical sentence whose ungrammaticality my theory attributes to structure, if the reader can find a good example with the same structure, such an example would threaten my theory. For example, I have claimed that subject role players cannot be separated by any of their barriers from their predicates. If someone finds a good sentence in which a subject role player and its predicate are, indeed, separated by one of the subject's barriers, then my Proviso Two above must be wrong.

One last thing I would like to emphasize is that throughout this chapter we never needed to appeal to multiple phrasal levels within the major categories of N, A, V, or P in order to account for predication facts.

Instead, a restrictive X-bar theory for X=N, A, V, or P in which X″ branches only to a specifier and X′, and in which X′ branches only to X and its sisters (whether arguments or modifiers or anything else) is adequate for handling the data on predication.

In the present chapter we have reexamined much of the traditional data considered in works on predication, and we have seen how the coindexing principles offered here help in the analysis of these sentences. In the next three chapters we will look at new data that, so far as I know, have not been studied at any great length from the point of view of predication theory. We will see that our coindexing principles can handle the new data, whereas other approaches to coindexing cannot.

3 Predication coindexing within NP in Italian

In this chapter we examine phrases in Italian like *quel matto di Giorgio* ('that madman Giorgio'). I argue that these phrases are externally NPs. Their internal analysis is the typical one of NPs: *quel* is the specifier, *matto* is the head N, and *di Giorgio* is a PP sister to the head N. I further argue that *matto* is a predicate taking *Giorgio* as its subject role player.

With the above analysis these phrases are an example of secondary predication, and they are adequately handled with the theory of predication offered in chapter 2.

Let me point out that the type of NP discussed in this chapter subdivides into two groups. In one group the NP following *di* is definite. In the other group, it is indefinite. These two groups, however, are syntactically identical. Thus I treat them interchangeably in sections 1 and 2 (which deal with syntax). Their differences are semantic and I discuss those differences in section 3.

Let me also point out that a typical use for these NPs is as insults (see also Milner 1978, Ruwet 1982). Many of the examples here, most of which are attested, are, therefore, obscene. In the glosses of these examples I sometimes opt for a more mild rendition than the literal in an attempt not to offend the non-Italian reader. To the Italian reader I can only say that since I am not a native speaker, I have not attempted to modify the examples offered by my informants.

1   The external structure of phrases like *quel matto di Giorgio*

I argue here that the external structure of these phrases is NP. In doing this I discuss semantic properties these phrases have as well as syntactic properties.

First, they occur in all and only those positions that NPs can occur in.

Here we have examples with these NPs in the positions of GF subject, DO, IO, OP, and appositive.

(3–1)   Quel matto di Giorgio mise il libro nell'armadio.
        'That madman George put the book in the wardrobe.'

(3–2)   Avvicinai quel matto di Giorgio alla finestra.
        'I brought that madman George to the window.'

(3–3)   Hanno mandato la lettera a quel matto di Giorgio.
        'They sent the letter to that madman George.'

(3–4)   Oreste ha organizzato con quel matto di Giorgio di andare al cinema.
        'Oreste arranged with that madman George to go to the movies.'

(3–5)   Tuo fratello, quel matto di Giorgio, rassomiglia ad un grillo.
        'Your brother, that madman George, resembles a cricket.'

Second, they can undergo NP movement, as in raising, passive, ergative constructions (Burzio 1986), *si* constructions (Napoli 1973), and inversion (Rizzi 1982).

(3–6)   Quel fesso di Paolo sembra [t] lamentarsene.
        'That dumbo Paul seems to be complaining about it.'

(3–7)   Quel fesso di Paolo è sprezzato [t] da tutti.
        'The dumbo Paul is discounted by everyone.'

(3–8)   Quel fesso di Paolo è arrivato [t].
        'That dumbo Paul has arrived.'

(3–9)   Quel fesso di Paolo non si vede più [t].
        'That dumbo Paul isn't seen anymore.'

(3–10) [t] L'ha fatto quel fesso di Paolo.
        'That dumbo Paul did it.'

Third, they trigger subject–verb agreement.

(3–11) Quei coglioni dei suoi fratelli non ci vengono/*viene.
        pl.   pl.   sg.
        'Those jerks of her brothers aren't coming.'

Fourth, they are non-propositional. Thus, they cannot bear a propositional sense when they are complements of verbs.

(3–12) Trovo quell'imbrogliona di Marta.
        only 'I find that cheater Marta.'
        not 'I find Marta a cheater.'
        (cf. Trovo Marta un'imbrogliona.
              'I find Marta a cheater.')

Fifth, they behave like R-expressions with respect to the Binding Conditions. Thus they can bind an anaphor or a pronoun, but they must themselves be free.

(3–13)a.   Quel matto di Giorgio parla fra sè e sè.
'That madman George talks to himself.'
  b.   [Quel matto di Giorgio]$_i$ vuole che io lo$_i$ inviti.
'That madman George wants me to invite him.
  c.   *Ho detto a lui$_i$ che [quel matto di Giorgio]$_i$ non poteva venire.
'I told him that that madman George couldn't come.'

I conclude that phrases like *quel matto di Giorgio* are NPs.

2   Internal structure

I will now argue that phrases like *quel matto di Giorgio* break down into a specifier, a noun, and a prepositional phrase. Then I will show that the proper analysis for this type of phrase is that shown in (3–14).

(3–14)

This is precisely the structure we would expect with X-bar theory.

For the sake of simplicity of argumentation, I will begin with the issue of the specifier, then pass to the prepositional phrase, and end with the issue of the noun, the argumentation for which will depend upon the analyses of the specifier and PP.

2.1   The specifier

Specifiers of NP in Italian can be demonstratives, determiners, the partitive marker, and quantifiers. In contrast to English, Italian does not allow NP in specifier position of NP unless it is a degree phrase (such as *un po' di zucchero* ('a little sugar') but not *Moravia (di) libro* ('Moravia's book')).

Turning to our phrases of interest, we find that the initial item is typically the demonstratives *quel* ('that') and *questo* ('this') (which inflect for number and gender) or the indefinite determiner *un* (which inflects for gender, but as a determiner is used only in the singular).

(3–15)   quei fessi dei tuoi fratelli
'those dumbos of your brothers/those dumbo brothers of yours'
questo straccio di gonna
'this rag of a skirt'
una peste di bambino
'a wretch of a boy'

The partitive, while only infrequently used in these constructions, is acceptable. The examples in (3–16) were offered to me by Raffaella Zanuttini (personal communication):

(3–16)   delle pesti di bambini
'some wretches of boys'
dei pezzi di ragazzi
'some bits of boys'
degli stracci di vestiti
'some rags of dresses'
della meraviglie di fanciulle
'some marvels of young girls'

But the definite determiner was not accepted by any of my informants except when accompanied by a possessive:

(3–17)   *il matto di Giorgio
'the madman Giorgio'
but: il tuo cretino di marito
'your cretin of a husband'

Marta Lujàn and Osvaldo Jaeggli (personal communication) have pointed out to me that in Spanish the parallel phrases can begin with *muy* ('very'), a specifier that does not typically occur in NPs. However, *muy* can occur as the specifier of a head N that is used as a predicate (just as *molto* ('very') can so occur in Italian: *Carlo è molto uomo* ('Carlo is very much a man')). Since I am going to argue that the head N in these phrases is, precisely, a predicate, the Spanish data suggest that these phrases in Spanish are open to the same type of analysis as the Italian data. My Italian informants, however, reject the use of *molto* in these phrases.

(3–18)   *molta carogna di dottore
'very much a scoundrel of a doctor'

None of my informants accepted even marginally any other lexical item as the initial item in these phrases. And nowhere in my readings have I come across any other items in this initial slot. We can see that the permissible initial items, therefore, form a proper subset of those items that can be specifiers of NPs in Italian. I conclude that the initial item in these NPs is a specifier.

2.2   The PP

Here I argue that in a phrase such as *quel matto di Giorgio* the words *di Giorgio* form a PP.

First, Italian has a *di* that is undeniably a preposition and that occurs in a variety of constructions (see Napoli and Nespor 1986). Simply on the basis of phonological identity and in the spirit of avoiding proliferation of homophonous items, in the absence of evidence to the contrary I would want to propose that the *di* of our phrases is a P. Since the P *di* is obligatorily transitive, I argue that *di Giorgio* is a PP.

Second, as we do with other instances of the P *di*, we find complementary distribution with the corresponding inflected P *del/dell'/dello/dei/ degli/della/delle* (see Napoli and Nevis (1987) for an analysis of inflected Ps in Italian), where the form of the inflected P depends upon the gender and number of the noun that is the head of the object of the P. In (3–19) *dei* is the inflected (masculine plural) P, and this form is in accord with the noun *ragazzi* (which is masculine plural).

(3–19)   Quei cretini dei ragazzi non ci sono.
           m.p. m.p.
         'Those cretin boys aren't here.'

This complementary distribution would follow if our *di* were a P and if it formed a PP with the material following it.

Third, the material following *di* or its inflected counterpart in our construction exhibits the full range of expansion possibilities that other NPs have (with certain semantic restrictions that will be discussed in sec. 3 below). For example, (1) it can have a possessive with the N; (2) it can be an NP of the very type under consideration in this chapter – in fact, the recursion can go on and on; (3) it can be a complex nominal. We see these three possibilities in (3–20).

(3–20)a. quella carogna del tuo dottore
          'that scoundrel of your doctor'
     b. cet imbécile de salaud de tyran de Staline
          'this imbecile of a slut of a shrew of Staline'
          cette vacherie d'ordure de camelot de saloperie de voiture
          'this cowhouse of a filth of a cheap stuff of a slovenliness of a car'
     c. quella bruttura di vagone ristorante
          'that filth of a (train) dining car'

Examples (3–20)b indicate the comparable French construction taken from Ruwet (1982, p. 260). Recursion of this sort apparently is just fine in French, while it is rather comical in Italian (although grammatical – see the remark following (3–42) below), and it is out, I believe, in English. Thus the phrases here have the full range of expansion possibilities that other *di* PPs have. This is predicted if these phrases are normal *di* PPs.

Fourth, like other Ps, our *di* governs oblique Case. To see this we must use a phrase containing a pronoun after the *di*, since Italian, like English, does not show audibly distinguishable Case on nonpronominal NPs. However, not all Italians find these phrases perfectly acceptable with a pronoun following the *di*. Still, all agree that if a pronoun is present, it must be oblique and never nominative.

(3–21)   Quel cretino di {te/*tu}!
                    {obl/nom}
         'That cretin you!'

Assuming that Case is assigned under government, the fact illustrated in (3–21) follows if *di* is a P and if it forms a PP with the material following it.

I conclude that *di Giorgio* in a phrase such as (3–14) is a PP.

Before I leave this issue, however, I would like to consider the most likely alternative to a PP analysis of the *di* phrase in these NPs, and that is one in which the *di* is a Case marker and not a true preposition (see Stowell 1981 for one side of this argument with respect to English *of*, but others, such as Zubizarreta 1985, for the other side). This alternative is interesting with respect to the issues handled in this book only insofar as one could argue with the Case-marker analysis of *di* that the external analysis of the *di* phrase is NP, instead of PP. In that instance the NP which is the maximal projection headed by *Giorgio* would be *di Giorgio* and, thus, the maximal projection of *Giorgio* would c-command the head N *matto*. As we noted in chapter 2, some theories of predication have claimed that a subject role player must c-command its predicate. So if *di Giorgio* were an NP and if it were the subject role player of *matto*, then the subject role player here would c-command its predicate and this construction would not present a problem for the c-command restriction in those theories. (Still, the subject role player would not be external to the maximal projection of the predicate, as we will see in sec. 2.4 below; thus this type of phrase is problematic for many theories regardless of the Case-marker-versus-P issue.)

The Case-marker analysis is not viable, however. As we noted above with respect to (3–19), the *di* of our phrases appears in complementary distribution with the corresponding inflected P, just as the true preposition *di* does. Now since the inflected P is a true preposition and not a Case-marked article (see Napoli and Nevis (1987) for arguments to this effect), we need to admit a PP as the proper analysis for the *dei ragazzi* in (3–19). But given that a PP can follow the head N of our NPs in some instances (such as (3–19) and many others below), we gain nothing from a theoretical point of view by arguing that *di* in other examples is a Case marker and not a true P.

I propose that *di*, like *of* in English (see M. Anderson 1979, Bouchard 1982, and Chomsky 1986b, as well as the discussion in ch. 1, sec. 2), is the P most commonly used to give Case when no sense of a preposition is needed. Thus, semantically, *di* may be a formative in some of its uses and may appear for the sole purpose of assigning Case to the NP that follows it. However, a *di phrase* is syntactically a PP and not an NP. Thus *di* is a true P.

In sum, the *di* phrase found within our NPs is a PP.

2.3   The N and its AP sisters

Evidence that the material between the initial specifier and the PP in a phrase such as *quel matto di Giorgio* is an N is offered by three facts.

First, the types of specifiers that occur before this material are those that Ns typically take, as we saw above in section 2.1. Furthermore, heads of other categories do not take these same specifiers. Thus no head of any category other than N can take determiners or demonstratives as their specifier. This is a strong indication that the specifier in our phrases introduces an N.

Second, the lexical items that can appear in this slot are only those that can appear as the head of regular NPs (see also Milner 1978, p. 175, for a similar observation about the corresponding construction in French). Thus, adjectives that can appear in regular NPs in the absence of an N only with an elliptical sense (where such a reading is not necessarily the result of any deletion rule – see Napoli 1985, pp, 309ff.) cannot appear in this slot, nor can Vs or Ps.

(3–22)   Preferisco il verde.
       'I prefer the green (one/color/thing/. . .).'
    *una verde di frutta
    'a green of a fruit'

And multiple word strings that are single nouns in the lexicon can appear in this slot:

(3–23)   quel [figlio di puttana] di Giorgio
           'that [son of a whore] Giorgio'
           (cf. *quel fesso di professore di Giorgio
               'that jerk of a professor of Giorgio')

Here *figlio di puttana* qualifies as a single lexical item, but *fesso di professore* does not.

Third, the material in this slot can be filled by more than just an N, in which case we always get a word that can appear as the head of regular NPs plus an adjective phrase. In (3–24) (which is from Lepschy and Lepschy 1979) *ripulito* is an adjective phrase.

(3–24)   quel cafone ripulito di Giorgio
           'that polished-up bumpkin Giorgio'

In Italian adjective phrases occur in three positions: on one side of the copula, in positions that secondary predicates can occur in (see ch. 2), or as sisters to the lexical head N.

(3–25)   Letizia è energica.
           'Letizia is energetic.'

(3–26)   Considero Letizia energica.
           'I consider Letizia energetic.'

(3–27)   La vecchia signora energica brandiva un ombrello.
           'The energetic old lady brandished an umbrella.'

Thus in (3–24) the appearance of *ripulito* is strong evidence that *cafone* is an N.

With regard to my claim that *ripulito* is a sister to *cafone* in (3–24), let me remind the reader that I am adopting an X-bar theory in which both modifiers and arguments of X are sisters to X (see the introductions to the book and to ch. 2 and various parts of ch. 1). We will see empirical evidence for this claim below (see the discussion of examples like (3–54)).

I conclude that the material between the initial specifier and the PP in our construction is an N or an N plus its AP sisters.

2.4   Internal configuration

I must now argue that the specifier, the N (and its optional AP sisters), and the PP in our construction connect together as in (3–14).

It is instructive at this point to consider alternative analyses in comparison to (3–14). I repeat (3–14) here and list three alternatives.

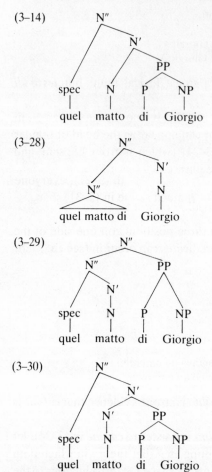

(3–14)

(3–28)

(3–29)

(3–30)

I list these three alternatives because all of these internal breakdowns for NPs have appeared in the literature.

The structure in (3–28) is the pseudopartitive proposed in Selkirk (1977), who labels the top node N′′′ instead of N″. This is also one of the two possible structures proposed in Janda (1980) for the NPs studied there, including the English construction corresponding to our Italian construction (which I analyze in ch. 4). This structure fails immediately, since we have already seen in section 2.2 above that the *di* forms a PP with the material following it.

A second argument against (3–28) is based on the fact that in (3–28) the head N of the entire construction would be *Giorgio*. Since Case is manifested on the head N of an NP, we would predict with (3–28) that the N following *di* would bear the appropriate Case for the entire construction. However, as we saw above in (3–21), this N never gets nominative Case even if the overall NP is in GF subject position of a tensed S, the position typically assigned nominative.

(3–31)   Quel cretino di {te/*tu} ha rovinato tutto di nuovo.
          {obl/nom}
          'That cretin you ruined everything again.'

(Again, as with (3–21), some speakers reject (3–31) since they reject all pronouns from these constructions. However, as with (3–21), everyone agrees that the nominative pronoun *tu* is much worse in (3–31) than the oblique pronoun *te*.)

A third argument is that (3–28) places an NP that does not have a degree sense in specifier position, which is a syntactic option that Italian lacks (in contrast to English), as was mentioned at the outset of section 2.1 above. Thus the structure in (3–28) is inconsistent with the limited range of possible specifiers that N in Italian exhibits.

I conclude that (3–28) cannot be correct.

The structure in (3–29) is the structure given in Jackendoff (1977) for appositives (and earlier, in Stockwell, Schachter, and Partee 1973), where Jackendoff labels the entire construction an N''' instead of an N''. So far as I know, the only proposals in the linguistic literature for sisters to N'' within an overall noun phrase are appositive sisters (whether the appositives be sentential or not). In section 5 of chapter 5 I will present a different structure for appositives (following Emonds 1979). However, here I will argue simply that the construction of interest to us is not an NP plus an appositive.

My first argument against an appositive analysis is that (*di*) *Giorgio* simply is not understood as an appositive. That is, (3–32) means 'that Giorgio who is a madman' and not 'that madman, who we call Giorgio'. The true appositive, seen in (3–33), on the other hand, does mean 'that madman, who we call Giorgio'.

(3–32)   quel matto di Giorgio

(3–33)   quel matto, Giorgio

That is, the referent of (3–32) is the Giorgio who has a certain property.

So *Giorgio* is not simply an alternative or additional label for the madman, as it is in the appositive in (3–33).

Second, (3–32) does not have the characteristic intonation pattern of an appositive, which is set off by pauses, like parentheticals (see also Safir 1985, p. 319). Instead, it has a single NP intonation contour like that of the simple NP in (3–34). In fact, (3–34)b is a completely ambiguous NP out of context.

(3–34)a. quell'amico di Giorgio
'that friend of Giorgio's'
   b. quel cane di Giorgio
'that dog Giorgio' or 'that dog of Giorgio's'

Third, it is a well-known fact that appositives can never be stacked, but only coordinated, as illustrated in (3–35) (see Jackendoff 1977, Emonds 1979, among many others).

(3–35)   *Giorgio, il tuo fratellino, il mio nemico, sputa nelle sue tasche.
*'Giorgio, your little brother, my enemy, spits in his pockets.'
Giorgio, il tuo fratellino e il mio nemico, sputa nelle sue tasche.
'Giorgio, your little brother and my enemy, spits in his pockets.'

However, our construction can be followed by an appositive NP.

(3–36)   quel matto del tuo fratellino, il mio nemico
   – 'that madman of your little brother, my enemy'

And our construction cannot have a conjoined appositive NP tacked on.

(3–37)   *quel matto del tuo fratellino e il mio nemico
'that madman of your little brother and my enemy'

Thus our *di Giorgio* in (3–32) is not an appositive.

Fourth, restrictive relative clauses may not follow an appositive NP (again, a well-known fact), as illustrated in (3–38).

(3–38)   *Quel ragazzo, il tuo vicino, che ho conosciuto ieri sera dipinge sulle mura.
*'That boy, your neighbor, who I met last night paints on the city walls.'

However, restrictive relative clauses may follow our construction.

(3–39)   Quel matto di pittore che ho conosciuto ieri sera dipinge sulle mura.
'That madman artist that I met last night paints on the city walls.'

In defense of the analysis in (3–29), one might try to argue that the restrictive relative in (3–39) is a sister to *pittore* only, and does not modify the entire nominal. However, such an analysis is contrary to the interpretation of (3–39).

Fifth, with (3–29) we would expect that the head N *matto* could have a modifying restrictive relative immediately following it, just as we can in regular appositive constructions, as in (3–40).

(3–40) Quel matto che ho incontrato ieri sera, il pittore, dipinge sulle mura.
'That madman that I met last night, the artist, paints on the city walls.'

However, a restrictive relative after the head N in our construction is impossible.

(3–41) *Quel matto che ho incontrato ieri sera di pittore dipinge sulle mura.
'That madman that I met last night of an artist paints on the city walls.'

I conclude that our construction is not an appositive construction.

My sixth argument is that the material preceding the *di* phrase cannot be a full NP, for if it were, we would expect that it could be an NP of the type under consideration in this chapter. But it cannot be.

(3–42) *quel matto del vicino del dottore
*'that madman neighbor doctor'

(Of course, (3–42) is (predictably) good with the reading in which *matto* is predicated of the *vicino del dottore*, as pointed out to me by Raffaella Zanuttini (personal communication); compare (3–42) and (3–20)c above. But it fails with the relevant reading, that in which *matto del vicino* is predicated of the *dottore*.) Thus the material preceding the *di* phrase is some string other than an NP.

From the above six arguments, I conclude that (3–29) is not the correct analysis of our construction.

Before completely dismissing (3–29), however, let me discuss an alternative interpretation for this structure. Andrew Radford (personal communication) has raised the possibility that the structure in (3–29) is an NP with an adjunct PP (not an appositive PP) similar to the initial NP in:

(3–43) You in the blue shirt – what are you up to?

My arguments against an appositive interpretation of (3–29) will not hold against this alternative adjunct interpretation. In particular, notice that we do not have a pause in (3–43), unlike in appositives. Also, we can get stacking in (3–43) (*you over there in the blue shirt*). And restrictive relatives are permissible after the whole NP in (3–43) (*you over there who I talked to yesterday*). And, finally, restrictive relatives are not permissible after the head N in (3–43) (*you who I talked to yesterday in the blue shirt*).

On the other hand, the adjunct interpretation of the analysis in (3–29) meets the serious objection that the *di* phrase inside our NP does not introduce an adjunct, but, rather, an argument (the only argument) of the head N *matto* (as we will see in sec. 3.1.2 below). And, as will be discussed below, linguists who work in GB seem to agree that theta assignment would require that the PP be a sister to the head N, rather than a sister to N‴ (as in (3–29)). Thus I believe the structure in (3–29) with the adjunct interpretation is not helpful in analyzing our NPs. Furthermore, I am not convinced that this structural analysis is helpful for analyzing NPs like that in (3–43), either. I see no evidence against analyzing *in the blue shirt* in (3–43) as a sister to the head N. In fact, this analysis is the null hypothesis. That is, so long as N takes sister modifying phrases anyway (which we will see that it must in (3–54) below), we should analyze all modifying phrases that are adjacent to N as sisters unless we have evidence to the contrary. Thus, in the absence of evidence to the contrary, I do not take (3–43) as an instance of an N‴ with an adjunct PP, but rather as an N with a sister PP. And the very fact that a restrictive relative can follow the PP inside the NP in (3–43) is evidence that this PP cannot be a sister to N‴, as we will see directly below.

In sum, we have seen no evidence in favor of the structure in (3–29) and much evidence against it. I therefore reject (3–29) as the analysis for our NPs.

Now we turn to (3–30), which is the structure given by Jackendoff (1977) (and earlier, in Stockwell, Schachter, and Partee 1973) for restrictive modifiers of a head N in English. In the introduction to this book I take the stance that for the lexical categories N, V, A, and P, all modifiers of a head within the maximal projection of that head are sisters to the head in DS on the grounds of trying to maintain as strict an interpretation of X-bar theory as possible. (See also van Gestel 1986 and Spooren 1981, who argue that restrictive and nonrestrictive relative clauses in Dutch have the same structure.) Given my X-bar theory, then, (3–30) is to be rejected.

One may object to this argument against (3–30) by saying that before such a restrictive X-bar theory can be taken seriously, I must first meet every empirically based argument that has been put forth in the past fifteen years or so for a more complex X-bar theory. For example, consider the NP:

(3–44)   the man and the woman in the corner who you know well

On the reading in which you know both the man and the woman and they are both in the corner, it is impossible to defend an analysis in which the PP and the clause following the N *woman* are sisters to that N. However, this NP would force me to abandon my restrictive X-bar theory only if there were no analysis of it that was consistent with my X-bar theory. But there is such an analysis. If Right Node Raising (as in Maling 1972) is taken to have applied in (3–44), then at SS the conjoined NPs have a sister PP and a sister relative clause that was moved there by Right Node Raising. But at DS the conjoined NPs have no sisters; only the Ns have sisters. I contend (without further argumentation here – since such argumentation could fill a separate book) that all evidence for a more complex X-bar theory can be refuted in a similar way.

However, there is no doubt that Jackendoff's analysis has influenced many (such as Emonds 1985, Culicover and Wilkins 1986, and other works that I cite repeatedly in this book) and has, perhaps, become the standard way of analyzing restrictive modifiers in the literature today. Therefore, I will now argue against (3–30) on grounds independent of the X-bar theory I have adopted.

First, the semantic relationship of *(di) Giorgio* to *matto* in (3–32) is not one of restrictive modifier to head: a proper name is not a modifier. Thus the proponents of an X-bar theory that allows sisters to X' other than the specifier when these sisters are restrictive modifiers would never propose (3–30) as an analysis for the NP *quel matto di Giorgio* anyway.

Second, the people who propose structures like (3–30) also take the position that a lexical head N cannot assign a theta role to a sister of N', but only to a daughter of N' (and, for some linguists, to the specifier of the NP – but *(di) Giorgio*, as we saw in secs. 2.1 and 2.2 above, is not the specifier of the overall phrase; see Speas 1986 for a history of this issue). However, I will show in section 3.1 below that *Giorgio* is the subject role player of the predicate *matto* in (3–32). In the terms of the linguists who propose (3–30), then, *Giorgio* would be getting a theta role from *matto*, and hence *di Giorgio* must be a sister to X and not to X'.

Third, restrictive modifiers of a head N that are of the category PP can be followed or preceded by other restrictive modifiers of that head also of the category PP. Furthermore, these modifiers are typically coordinated. (See d'Addio 1974 for a fuller discussion of AP collocation inside NP.)

(3–45)   una famiglia di grande distinzione (e) di grandi richezze
'a family of great distinction (and) of great wealth'

(3–46)   una famiglia di grandi richezze (e) di grande distinzione
'a family of great wealth (and) of great distinction'

However, restrictive modifiers of a head N that are of the category PP follow arguments of the head N and are never conjoined to the argument. (Below I mark acceptability judgments on the English translations through example (3–57), although I do not always do this, since I will be making use of these translations in ch. 4.)

(3–47)a.   La discussione del problema di maggior interesse è state quella del Professor Biaggi.
            'The discussion of the problem of greatest interest was that of Prof. Biaggi.'
       b.   *La discussione di maggior interesse del problema è stata quella del Professor Biaggi.
       ??   'The discussion of greatest interest of the problem was that of Prof. Biaggi.'
       c.   *La discussione del problema e di maggior interesse è stata quella del Professor Biaggi.
            *'The discussion of the problem and of greatest interest was that of Prof. Biaggi.'

In our construction, restrictive modifiers of the head N that are of the category PP follow the *di* phrase and are never conjoined to that *di* phrase.

(3–48)a.   una carogna di dottore di grande infamia
            'a scoundrel of a doctor of great infamy'
       b.   *una carogna di grande infamia di dottore
            *'a scoundrel of great infamy of a doctor'
       c.   *una carogna di dottore e di grande infamia
            *'a scoundrel of a doctor and of great infamy'

Thus when we consider the presence of restrictive modifiers of the head N that are of the category PP, we can see that our *di* phrase behaves like an argument of the head rather than as a restrictive modifier with respect to collocation.

Fourth, as Raffaella Zanuttini (personal communication) has pointed out to me, when two restrictive modifiers of a head N follow the N where one is an AP and the other is a PP, the AP can come first and an optional (but preferred) conjunction may come between the two modifiers.

(3–49)   una famiglia numerosa (e) di grande distinzione
         *'a family large (and) of great distinction'

But if the PP comes first, we must have a conjunction between the two modifiers:

(3–50)   una famiglia di grande distinzione e numerosa
          *una famiglia di grande distinzione numerosa
          *'a family of great distinction (and) large'

This ordering holds regardless of whether the NP is definite or indefinite:

(3–51)   la famiglia numerosa (e) di grande distinzione
          *'the family large (and) of great distinction'
          la famiglia di grande distinzione e numerosa
          *la famiglia di grande distinzione numerosa
          *'the family of great distinction (and) large'

However, when an N is followed by a restrictive modifier and an argument of the N, we find that the modifier and the argument can never be conjoined, regardless of their order:

(3–52)   *una distruzione brutale e di Troia
          *'a destruction brutal and of Troia'
          *una distruzione di Troia e brutale
          *'a destruction of Troia and brutal'

Furthermore, if the NP is definite, the restrictive modifier must precede the argument:

(3–53)   la distruzione brutale di Troia
          *la distruzione di Troia brutale

But if the NP is indefinite, the restrictive modifier may precede or follow the argument:

(3–54)   una lettura superficiale del testo
          una lettura del testo superficiale
          'a superficial reading of the text'

In the NPs of interest in this chapter, we find that the PP behaves like an argument of the head N with respect to its ordering when a restrictive modifier of the head N is also present. Thus we never find conjunction, regardless of order of the modifier and the PP:

(3–55)   *una carogna terribile e di dottore
          *'a scoundrel terrible and of a doctor'
          *una carogna di dottore e terribile
          *'a scoundrel of a doctor and terrible'

And when the overall NP is definite, the restrictive modifier must precede the PP:

(3–56)   quella carogna terribile di dottore
*quella carogna di dottore terribile
*'that scoundrel terrible of a doctor'

But when the overall NP is indefinite, the restrictive modifier can precede or follow the PP:

(3–57)   una carogna terribile di dottore
una carogna di dottore terribile
'a terrible scoundrel of a doctor'

The facts in (3–55) through (3–57) parallel those in (3–52) through (3–54) precisely.

I conclude that our *di* phrase behaves like an argument rather than like a restrictive modifier with respect to these new collocation facts.

In sum, there is no syntactic motivation for (3–30) and much evidence against it.

All of the data here, however, are easily accounted for if (3–14) is the structure of our NPs. That is, *di Giorgio* in (3–32) has all the syntactic and semantic properties (with respect to those studied in this section) of an argument of the head N and should, therefore, be placed in the typical spot that arguments which follow a head N are placed in in Italian: sister to the head N.

Let me point out, by the way, that examples such as (3–54) and (3–57) offer strong evidence that the difference between modifiers and arguments is not built into the syntax. In particular, both modifiers and arguments are sisters to X. Thus this distinction in function is a semantic distinction unparalleled by any syntactic distinction. Once more in this book we find that syntax and semantics are orthogonal, rather than parallel or isomorphic, components of the grammar.

There are other facts that are consistent with (3–14) but call for explanation with any other analyses we have discussed. One such fact regards the choice of P in the PP inside our NPs. The arguments of a head N in Italian are introduced either by the null P *di* (parallel to English *of*), as with DO arguments, or with the IO prepositions *a* ('to') or *per* ('for'), or with a range of prepositions that are lexically selected by the head N.

(3–58)a. la costruzione di un nuovo magazzino
'the construction of a new store'
b. un annuncio agli studenti
'an announcement to the students'
un regalo per Umberto
'a gift for Umberto'

c. un patto col diavolo
'a pact with the devil'
una dipendenza dalle sigarette
'a dependence on cigarettes'

When an argument can be understood as a subject argument (see the discussion of the comparable constructions in English in ch. 1, sec. 2.3), it is introduced with the null P *di* (and see Cinque 1980).

(3–59)   una fotografia di Marina
'a photograph of Marina/Marina's'

Example (3–59) can be interpreted with Marina having taken the photograph or being in the photograph.

On the other hand, PP sisters of a head N that are not arguments of the head can be introduced by a wide range of Ps which are not lexically selected by the head. In some instances the choice of the P depends totally upon the relationship it is to express between the head N and its object NP. In other instances the P is part of a fixed phrase that serves as a modifier.

(3–60)   la sua partenza in fretta e furia
'his departure in haste and fury'
l'avvenimento di maggior interesse'
'the happening of greatest interest'
la sua partenza senza la moglie
'his departure without his wife'

In our construction the PP is always a *di* phrase, regardless of the lexical choice of head N and regardless of the lexical choice of the NP that follows the *di*. Given (3–14) we expect the null P *di*, since this is the P that normally introduces subject and DO arguments (that is, this is the P that normally introduces the so-called nonprepositional arguments of N). But with any of the other analyses we have discussed in this section, there is no reason to expect only *di* to occur here. In particular, if our PP were a modifier (as in the most common interpretations of the analyses in (3–29) and (3–30)), we would never expect a fixed P at all, since modifiers of the head can be introduced by a variety of Ps.

Let me point out that consistent with our configurational analysis in (3–14) is at least one other syntactic fact: the *di* phrase cannot extrapose, just as other PP arguments of N cannot extrapose (see Cinque 1980).

(3–61)   *Quel ficcanaso non si vede più di Stefano.
'That busybody isn't seen anymore (of) Stefano.'

(3–62)   *Quei libri non si vedono più di quello scrittore.
'Those books aren't seen anymore by that author.'

At this point the reader who is familiar with Italian may have noticed that the *di* phrase of our construction is immovable and may be expecting me to address this fact. I postpone the relevant discussion, however, until section 3.1.2 below, since we need to have an understanding of the semantics of these NPs before we can discuss movability.

I conclude from the evidence of this section that (3–14) is the correct structure for our NPs.

3   Semantics

The semantic properties of these NPs are complex. I will first discuss those properties in common among all NPs of this type. Then I will discuss properties that only some NPs of this type have.

3.1   Semantic properties in common

The head N of the overall NP in (3–14) acts as a predicate to the NP introduced by *di*, which acts as its subject role player, and the initial specifier, as expected, specifies the entire NP.

3.1.1   The specifier

The claim about the specifier is simpler to justify, so I will begin with it. When the specifier of these NPs is definite, the entire NP is interpreted as definite. To see this, consider (3–63):

(3–63)   Per quanto la ragazza sembri onesta, non lo è.
'Honest though the girl may seem, she isn't.'

In the construction illustrated in (3–63), if the GF subject of the subordinate clause is specific, it must be definite when it is understood as coreferential with the GF subject of the matrix clause. In our NPs the initial specifier satisfies this requirement, whether the NP following *di* is definite, as in (3–64)a, or indefinite, as in (3–64)b.

(3–64)a.   Per quanto quel cretino del dottore sembri onesto, non lo è.
'Honest though that cretin doctor may seem, he isn't.'
    b.   Per quanto quella carogna di dottore sembri intelligente, non lo è.
'Intelligent though that scoundrel of a doctor may seem, he isn't.'

Indefinite NPs can also occur in the GF subject position of the embedded clause in the construction in (3–63): if the NP is nonspecific, it can appear in this construction only as an indefinite with a genus interpretation (see Givón 1978, p. 293, and ch. 1, sec. 1.5 above). This is true whether we have a regular NP, as in (3–65)a, or our special NP, as in (3–65)b.

(3–65)a. Per quanto una ragazza giovane sembri onesta, non lo è necessaria-
mente.
'Honest though a young girl may seem, she isn't necessarily.'
b. Per quanto una carogna di mafioso sembri onesto, non lo è.
'Honest though a scoundrel mafioso may seem, he isn't.'
Per quanto un cretino di burocrate possa sembrare competente, di fatto non lo è.
'Competent though a cretin of a bureaucrat may be able to seem, he isn't.'

In (3–65)b we find only indefinite NPs in the PP. This is because when the overall NP is indefinite, the NP and the PP must be indefinite (as will be explained below in the discussion of (3–123) through (3–126)). So I cannot use (3–65) to bolster my argument. I point these data out only so that the reader can see the full range of possibilities in this construction and that these possibilities pose no problem for my analysis.

I conclude from (3–63)–(3–64) that it is the initial specifier of our NP that specifies the entire NP.

Likewise, when the initial specifier of these NPs is indefinite, the entire NP is indefinite. In the construction illustrated in (3–66), if the position following *Antonio* is filled by an NP, it must be a predicative NP. In general indefinite NPs are potential predicates whereas some uses of definite NPs are not, with context being one of the relevant factors for potential interpretation of definite NPs as predicates (see ch. 1, sec. 1.3). The initial specifier on our NPs satisfies this requirement. Thus (3–66)a, with *una*, the indefinite article, is good, whereas (3–66)b, with *quella*, the definite demonstrative, is not.

(3–66)a. Considero Antonio una meraviglia di marito.
'I consider Antonio a marvel of a husband.'
b. *Considero Antonio quella meraviglia di marito.
'I consider Antonio that marvel of a husband.'

Notice that in both sentences of (3–66) the NP following *di* is indefinite. Thus the indefiniteness of the overall NP is due to the initial specifier, not to the specifier of the NP following *di*.

I conclude that the initial specifier specifies the entire NP.

3.1.2   The predicate and its subject role player

I will now argue that the head N of our NPs, as analyzed in (3–14), functions as a predicate taking the NP following *di* as its subject role player.

Before I focus on arguments specific to our NP, let me point out that in Italian the subject role player of a lexical head N is typically in a *di* phrase that is a sister to the N (see Cinque 1980, who, however, assumes a more complex X-bar theory than I do, but whose discussion could as well be framed in my more restrictive version of X-bar theory). Given that the head N in our NP is of the type that takes only one argument and given that every predicate must have a subject role player, it is natural that the only argument of our N should appear in a *di* phrase that is a sister to the N. Our NPs, then, are not special at all. As Swanson (1969) shows in detail, the single syntactic structure of $[_{NP} \text{ spec } [_{N'} \text{ N } [_{PP} \text{ di NP}]]]$ in Italian can be mapped into a wide range of semantic relationships. Thus our NP is not problematic, and, instead, just ordinary. What makes them seem so special at first is that they present insurmountable problems for other theories of predication. But, as we will see, they are easily accounted for with the predication coindexing principles given in chapter 2.

Let me now proceed with the arguments specific to our NPs.

My first three arguments all have the same form: I show that the N I am calling a predicate and the NP I am calling its subject role player exhibit properties that typically occur only between predicates and their subject role players.

First, as Alinei (1971) has pointed out, there must be a matching of selectional restrictions between the N predicate and the NP subject which is identical to the matching of selectional restrictions we would find in the corresponding sentences with the copula. (It is this matching property that led Giurescu 1972 to derive these NPs from copular Ss.)

(3–67)a.   *quella lagna di monumento
        'that complainer of a monument'
        (cf. quella lagna di tua sorella
          'that complainer of your sister')
    b.   *Il monumento è una lagna.
        'The monument is a complainer.'
        (cf. Tua sorella è una lagna.
          'Your sister is a complainer.')

(3–68)a.   *quel polpettone di motore
        'that confused mess of a motor'

(cf. quel polpettone di articolo
'that confused mess of an article')

b. *Il motore è un polpettone.
'The motor is a confused mess.'
(cf. L'articolo è un polpettone.
'The article is a confused mess.')

(3–69)a. *quella bruttura di organizzazione
'that filth of an organization'
(cf. quella bruttura di mobile
'that filth of a piece of furniture')

b. *L'organizzazione è una bruttura.
'The organization is a filthy thing.'
(cf. Il mobile è una bruttura.
'The piece of furniture is a filthy thing.')

Not all copular sentences involve semantic predication (as we saw in ch. 1, sec. 1.3). However, if we take our construction of $Spec_1-N_1-di-(Spec_2)$ N_2, and consider the corresponding copular sentences which consist of $(Spec_2)-N_2-$copula$-$(indefinite determiner)$-N_1$, all these sentences do, in fact, involve semantic predication.

(3–70)   quell'angelo di tua moglie
'that angel of your wife'

(3–71)   Tua moglie è un angelo.
'Your wife is an angel.'

If we assume that selectional restrictions in copular sentences with semantic predication are a reflex of the predication relationship, then the fact that these same restrictions hold internally in our NP is evidence that our NP involves the predication relationship.

Notice that it is common in the linguistic literature to assume that selectional restrictions are evidence of argumenthood. One might, therefore, object to my argument above on the grounds that the selectional restrictions show that *moglie* in (3–70) is an argument of the lexical head N *angelo*, but not that *moglie* is necessarily the subject role player for the predicate *angelo*. However, the kind of N that can be the head N in our NPs is always a one-place function. That is, it never takes arguments at all except when it is used as a predicate or modifier and then its only argument is, in fact, its subject role player or the element modified. Thus selectional restrictions are evidence that the NP following *di* is the subject role player, after all. (Of course, modifiers, which discharge theta roles (see ch. 1, sec. 4), also impose selectional restrictions on what they modify. I argue against the possibility of our head N being a modifier below.)

Second, if the predicate is one that may vary for gender and/or number, it must agree with the NP for those features, just as it would in a copular construction, as Milner (1978, p. 192) has pointed out for French.

(3–72)a. quello stronzo di Mario
           m.s.   m.s.
           'that slime Mario'
           (cf. Mario è uno stronzo.
              'Mario is a slime.')
     b. quella stronza di Giuliana
           f.s.   f.s.
           'that slime Giuliana'
           (cf. Giuliana è una stronza.
              'Giuliana is a slime.')

(3–73)a. quel coglione di suo fratello
           m.s.   m.s.
           'that jerk of his brother'
           (cf. Suo fratello è un coglione.
              'His brother is a jerk.')
     b. quei coglioni dei suoi fratelli
           m.p.   m.p.
           'those jerks of his brothers'
           (cf. I suoi fratelli sono coglioni.
              'His brothers are jerks.')

But if gender and/or number of the head N is invariable in a copular construction, it is also invariable in our NPs. (Here I give examples of invariance for gender only, since I have been unable to come up with any natural examples exhibiting number invariance.)

(3–74)   quell'angelo di tua moglie
           m.s.   f.s.
           'that angel of your wife'
           (cf. Tua moglie è un angelo.
               'Your wife is an angel.')

(3–75)   una peste di bambino
           f.s.   m.s.
           'a pest of a boy'
           (cf. Il bambino è una peste.
               'The boy is a pest.')

Certainly, gender–number agreement also occurs in modification relationships, as in (3–76).

(3–76)   la bella ragazza/il bel ragazzo
          f.s.   f.s.   m.s. m.s.
          'the pretty girl'/'the handsome boy'

However, some of the Ns that can be the head N in our construction cannot be used as modifiers, but only as predicates.

(3–77)   *la meraviglia moglie
          *la moglie meraviglia
          'the marvel wife'

(Contrast (3–77) to (3–66) above and (3–94) below.) Thus the gender – number agreement in our constructions is evidence of the predication relationship, not the modification relationship.

Third, the head N in our construction is understood to bear the same semantic relation to the NP following *di* that the corresponding predicate bears towards its subject role player in indisputable cases of predication constructions. (See ch. 1, for the development of the notion of semantic relation, particularly sec. 1.6.) Milner (1978) says of the comparable French construction that the NP following the P "apparait en quelque sorte comme le sujet logique de l'ensemble" ("appears in some ways as the logical subject of the whole [phrase]") (pp. 174–5). Ruwet (1982) also recognizes that there is a predication relationship inside these NPs in French. Thus in (3–78) we understand that the dress in question is shabby and in (3–79) we understand that the doorman in question is rude, just as we do in the indisputable predication structures in (3–80) through (3–83).

(3–78)   questo straccio di vestito
          'this rag of a dress'

(3–79)   quello sgarbato del portiere
          'that rude person doorman'

(3–80)   Questo vestito è uno straccio.
          'This dress is a rag.'

(3–81)   Questo portiere è sgarbato.
          'This doorman is rude.'

(3–82)   Considero questo vestito uno straccio.
          'I consider this dress a rag.'

(3–83)   Considero questo portiere sgarbato.
          'I consider this doorman rude.'

Given that the role player of the predicate in our construction is internal to the maximal projection of the predicate, someone with a different theory of predication from mine might argue that the NP following *di* is a role player for the predicate but not a subject role player (as has been argued, for example, for the ergative verb constructions in Burzio 1986). But with such an analysis we would have no explanation for why the same semantic relation is assigned to the NP following *di* as that assigned to the subject role player of these same predicates in copular constructions (like (3–80) and (3–81)) or elsewhere (like (3–82) and (3–83)). Furthermore, once we admit that the head N of our construction is a predicate, then we need to analyze the NP following *di* as its subject role player, since every predicate must have a subject role player by the time we reach the level of PS (see Williams 1980, 1984b, Rothstein 1983, among many others, including ch. 1, secs. 1.5 and 4).

Fourth, as Rothstein notes (1983, p. 104), the more evaluative an N (or N′) is, the easier it is to interpret it as a predicate. In our construction the head N always gives an evaluative judgment of the NP following *di*. That is, the head N is precisely the type of N that can be a predicate. (See also Milner 1978, p. 175, who notes that only Ns which can function as predicates can occur as the head N in the corresponding construction in French.) This is the reason why proper names and pronouns cannot occur as the head N in our construction: they cannot be used as evaluative predicates.

(3–84)a. *quello Carlo d'uomo
　　　　*'that Carlo of a man'
　　b. *un tu/te di persona
　　　　　　nom/acc
　　　　*'a you of a person'

The only exceptions I know of are proper names that by connotation have become evaluative, as Greg Carlson (personal communication) has pointed out to me:

(3–85)　un Hitler d'uomo
　　　　'a Hitler of a man'

One might object to my explanation of (3–84) on the grounds that proper names and pronouns do not occur with specifiers (except in special contexts, as outlined in Lepschy and Lepschy (1979, pp. 163 ff.) and in Napoli and Nevis (1987)); thus (3–84) will be rejected on grounds independent of predication considerations. There are other classes of nouns, however, that easily co-occur with specifiers and that do not lend themselves to being interpreted as predicates in our construction. For example, the names of inanimate objects which are typically used for specific purposes are not generally employed as predicates with the sense of an evaluative judgment. Therefore, these classes of nouns are also barred from head N position in our NPs.

(3–86) *una chiave di attrezzo
    *'a wrench of a tool'
    *una lampada di mobile
    *'a lamp of a piece of furniture'
    *un quadro d'opera d'arte
    *'a picture of a work of art'

As expected, those inanimate objects which are colloquially used with the sense of an evaluative judgment can appear in head N position in our NPs.

(3–87) un fiore di ragazza
    'a flower of a girl'
    (cf. *un tulipano di ragazza
        *'a tulip of a girl')
    un gioiello di marito
    'a jewel of a husband'
    (cf. *un rubino di marito
        'a ruby of a husband')

The same selection of head N occurs in the English counterpart to this construction (which is analyzed in ch. 4, sec. 1). Example (3–88) was suggested to me by Josh Ard (personal communication).

(3–88) a pistol of a lecturer
    (cf. *a revolver of a lecturer)

On the other hand, Ns which easily lend themselves to being interpreted as predicates of the appropriate type easily appear as the head N in our NPs. Any of the good examples in this chapter can attest to this point.

Typically the judgment expressed by our head N is negative, but it can be positive (see Alinei 1971). If the overall NP is definite, the most likely reading is of negative judgment, so that (3–89), for example, out of context would favor an ironic reading (see Lepschy and Lepschy 1979).

(3–89) quel tesoro di Giorgio
    'that treasure George'

If the overall NP is indefinite, the tendency for a negative judgment disappears, so that (3–90) and (3–91) have no ironic flavor.

(3–90)   un gigante d'uomo
          'a giant of a man' (with a positive evaluation)

(3–91)   un gioiello d'amico
          'a jewel of a friend'

At this point the reader may be convinced that the head N of our construction assigns a theta role to the NP following *di*, but may well still consider viable an alternative analysis in which the head N modifies rather than predicates. (In Higginbotham's 1985 terms that would amount to the question of whether or not we have theta identification here; ch. 1, sec. 4.) There are several arguments against analyzing the head N of our construction as a modifier.

First, as we just saw, this N must be evaluative. Predicates fall naturally into an evaluative class and a nonevaluative class with respect to their distribution and other properties, as others have noted (see Bresnan 1982a, Maling 1982 – who uses the term "gradable" – and Safir 1987b, among others), but no parallel classification of modifiers is needed.

Second, modifiers modify proper Ns only under special circumstances. For example, in (3–92) the presence of the modifier *sgarbata* suggests that there is more than one Maria relevant to the discourse and *sgarbata* picks out the Maria of interest:

(3–92)   la sgarbata Maria
          'the rude Maria'

But in (3–93) there is no sense of multiple Marias in the frame of the discourse:

(3–93)   quella sgarbata di Maria
          'that rude person Maria'

Instead, in (3–93) there is only one Maria and she is rude.

Likewise, modifiers do not typically modify pronouns. But some speakers accept a pronoun in the *di* phrase, as noted above with regard to (3–21) and (3–31).

Third, as we saw above in (3–77), Ns that cannot be modifiers can occur as our head N:

(3–77)   *la meraviglia moglie
          *la moglie meraviglia
          'the marvel wife'

but:

(3–94)   una meraviglia di moglie
          'a marvel of a wife'
          (cf. La moglie è una meraviglia.
             'The wife is a marvel.')

Thus if we were to analyze our head N as a modifier in (3–94), we would have to make the *ad hoc* claim that *meraviglia* acquires the possibility of being a modifier by virtue of appearing in this construction. But if our head N is a predicate, then the fact that all evaluative Ns that can occur as predicate nominals in copular sentences can also occur as our head N follows naturally.

I thus dismiss the possibility that our head N is a modifier and continue with the contention that it is a predicate.

Let us now turn to a different kind of argument for the claim that our NP consists of a predicate and its subject role player. I will show that with the analysis here, certain expectations arise about reference and agreement phenomena and, indeed, these expectations are realized.

First, if the NP following *di* is the subject role player of the head N, then the reference of the overall NP (if the NP is used referentially) should be that of the NP following *di* as predicated of by the head N (see sec. 3.2 below). That is, we should expect the referent of the overall NP to be more closely related to the sense of the NP following *di* than to the sense of the head N. This is the case. In (3–95) we understand the subject of the sentence to want to marry a special kind of girl (one who is as fine as a flower) rather than to want to marry a special kind of flower.

(3 – 95)   Vorrei sposare un fiore di ragazza.
            'I'd like to marry a flower of a girl.'

Example (3–95) is even more telling: we see that the NP following *di* rather than the head N is the one to meet the selectional restrictions that the larger context imposes on the whole NP in sentences of the type in (3–95), as Milner (1978) points out for French. In other words, the NP following *di* is semantically crucial to the determination of the reference of the entire NP.

Let me now return to a notion I mentioned in chapter 1, section 6. Abney (1986) distinguishes between the notions of syntactic head of a phrase and semantic head of a phrase. While he looks at phrases whose heads are functional elements (such as Inflection and Determiner) to make such a distinction, and while he claims that for thematic categories the semantic and structural head of the phrase are always the same, his distinction turns out to be helpful to us here. In our NP the syntactic head is the N that functions as a predicate. But the NP following *di* is the element that determines the reference of the overall NP. I propose, then, that the NP following *di* is the semantic head of our overall NP.

We would expect, then, that despite the fact that the syntax of our NPs (as given in (3–14) above) will not automatically block movement of the *di* phrase, such movement would be disallowed since the semantic head of an NP (under anybody's account) is not movable.

In fact, the NP following *di* is immovable and has to be, because Ps cannot be stranded in Italian. However, the *di* phrase is also immovable. Thus it cannot be questioned.

(3–96)   Vorresti sposare un fiore di ragazza.
          'You would like to marry a flower of a girl.'
          *Di chi vorresti sposare un fiore?
          'Of whom would you like to marry a flower?'
          (cf. Di chi è quel libro?
          'By whom is that book?')

Marcel Danesi (personal communication) has pointed out to me that (3–96) does have a good, though decidedly perverse reading: that in which the *di* phrase is possessive (i.e., 'Whose flower would you like to marry?'). That is, the movement in (3–96) is not blocked for structural reasons; it is blocked because the semantic head of a phrase cannot be removed.

Our PP also cannot correspond to a clitic *ne*.

(3–97)   *Ne ho visto quel matto.
          'I saw that madman him.'
          (cf. Ne ho visto la foto.
          'I saw that photograph of him.' – only with the sense of his being in the photograph)

If the formation of *ne* involves movement (see Rizzi 1982), (3–97) is once more expected so long as the NP following *di* is the semantic head of our overall NP. (Notice that Cinque's 1980 claim that only subject arguments of N inside NP can correspond to the clitic *ne* is empirically inaccurate, as the example in parentheses in (3–97), which was offered to me by Giulio Lepschy (personal communication), shows. Thus the fact that the *di* phrase in our construction cannot correspond to the clitic *ne* (as in (3–97)) is not to be taken as evidence against the analysis of the object of *di* as the subject role player. See also Belletti and Rizzi 1981.) If the formation of *ne* does not involve movement, then the failure of (3–97) is still expected, since we should be unable to interpret an item outside an NP as the semantic head of that NP.

Our PP also cannot prepose.

(3–98) *Di Giorgio non si vede più quel matto.
        'George one doesn't see anymore that madman.'
        (cf. Di quello scrittore non si vedono più i libri.
        'By that writer one doesn't see books anymore.')

In its immovability, the *di* phrase of our construction is similar to the *di* phrase in NPs such as *la città di Sassari* ('the city of Sassari').

(3–99) *Di cosa hai visto la città?
        'Of what did you see the city?'
        *Ne ho visto la città.
        'I saw the city of it.'
        *Di Sassari mi piace la città.
        'Of Sassari I like the city.'

It is significant that the *di* phrase in *quel matto di Giorgio* and the *di* phrase in *la città di Sassari* are syntactically inflexible in the same ways since I argue in chapter 5, section 1 that NPs like *la città di Sassari* also involve predication, where *Sassari* is the semantic head of the overall NP. Thus I would offer the same explanation for their syntactic inflexibility. Furthermore, the English counterparts to both of these types of NPs in Italian are also syntactically inflexible, as noted in Janda (1980, p. 332).

(3–100) *Who did Mary invite that fool of?
         (cf. Mary invited that fool of a doctor.)
         but: Who did Mary invite the sister of?
         *What did Mary see the city of?
         (cf. Mary saw the city of Taormina.)
         but: What did Mary see the destruction of?

And, finally, Milner (1978) observes the syntactic inflexibility of the comparable French construction and partly because of it he argues that in *Nominal₁ de Nominal₂* the *de Nominal₂* is not a PP, and that the N_2 is an N′ and not an N″. The structure he offers is given in (3–101) (see his p. 190), where Nominal₁ is under the specifier slot and Nominal₂ is under N′.

(3–101)

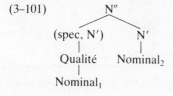

For Italian it is clear that the *di* phrase is a PP with the full range of syntactic possibilities for the object of the P (see sec. 2.2 above and, particularly, examples such as (3–20) and many others of this sort). However, Milner gives no French examples comparable to (3–20). It may be that Italian and French differ on the crucial data here. (See also Milner's ungrammatical example 6.23 on his p. 235, whose Italian counterpart is perfectly grammatical.) Still, if the French construction turns out to be open to the same analysis that the Italian construction is open to (that given in (3–14)), we have an explanation for the syntactic inflexibility of the French construction.

Thus, the semantic analysis given to our construction offers an unexpected account of the syntactic inflexibility demonstrated in (3–96) through (3–100) of constructions in Italian, English, and French. That is, data like those in (3–96)–(3–98), which in the absence of a semantic analysis of our NPs appear problematical and inexplicable in light of the overwhelming evidence for the syntactic analysis in (3–14) above, turn out to be entirely consistent with this analysis, after all.

There are other data we expect if the head N is truly a predicate taking the NP following *di* as its subject role player. For example, we expect that the *di* phrase cannot appear across the copula from the head N plus the specifier (or plus an indefinite article), in contrast to other PP complements of N, since the semantic head of a phrase cannot appear separated from the rest of the phrase. This is so.

(3–102)   *Quello/Uno stupido è di Franco.
          'That/A stupid person is of Franco.'
          (cf. Quel libro è di Franco.
          'That book is by Franco.')

(I exclude from consideration the irrelevant and grammatical reading of (3–102) in which the *di* phrase is a possessive, parallel to the good reading of the interrogative example in (3–96) above.) Instead, like other one-place predicates, there would be no *di* to the right of the copula.

(3–103)   Quello/Uno stupido è Franco.
          'That/A stupid person is Franco.'
          (cf. Felice sono io.
             'Happy am I.'
             Una gioia è Maria!
             'A joy is Maria!')

Similar facts are found, not surprisingly, for the relevant other constructions that I argue to involve predication in chapters 4 and 5. I give just one example here.

(3–104) *La città è di Sassari.
     'The city is of Sassari.'
     (cf. La città è Sassari.)

Third, if the NP following *di* is the semantic head of our phrase, and if the predicative N is the syntactic head of our phrase, we might expect grammatical processes that are sensitive to semantics to apply relative to the NP following *di* rather than to the syntactic head N.

In order to test this prediction, we need to find some grammatical processes which are sensitive to semantics. Agreement rules in Italian are sensitive to the features of person, number, and gender – all features which correlate in varying degrees with semantic properties of the referent of the nominals triggering the agreement. Let us look, then, at agreement processes. I will argue first that Subject–Verb Agreement is a grammatical process that displays an overriding sensitivity to syntax, and I will show that when our construction is in GF subject position, Subject–Verb Agreement makes agreement with the syntactic head. I will then argue that gender agreement shows more of a sensitivity to semantics, and I will show that when our construction undergoes gender agreement, it can be with the semantic or the syntactic head.

Subject–Verb Agreement in Italian makes agreement for person between a tensed verb and its GF subject. In Italian morphological person on the verb is correlated with semantic person of the referent of the verb's GF subject except in formal speech (where a semantic second person correlates to a morphological third person) and in the indefinite subject *si* construction (where various semantic persons can correlate with a morphological third person; see Napoli 1973). However, Subject–Verb Agreement takes place between all syntactic subjects and their tensed verbs, whether the syntactic subject is an argument of that verb or not (witness passives involving idiom chunks). Thus Subject–Verb Agreement, while usually paralleled by the semantic relationship of predication, is not definitionally founded on such a semantic relationship. Instead, it is a structurally sensitive process involving features (person and number) which irrelevantly (with respect to Subject–Verb Agreement) have semantic correlates. Therefore, I predict that Subject–Verb Agreement will take person strictly off the syntactic head N of our NPs.

To test this we must find an NP of the type in (3–14) in which the two contained Ns have different person, and see whether this overall NP when it occurs in GF subject position calls for person agreement with the head N or with the NP that follows the *di*. Since NPs in Italian are all third-person except for pronouns, we must use a pronoun either as the head N or as the NP following *di* in order to allow for a contrast in person. However, pronouns cannot appear in head N position, as explained above with regard to (3–84). And, as we saw above with (3–21), pronouns are rejected by many Italians in the position following *di* in these NPs. Thus, unfortunately, we must test with sentences which are not acceptable to all speakers. Still, all speakers agree that the morphological marking on the verb in these cases must be third-person. (That is, the morphological marking on the verb must match the person of the head N.) We can use (3–31), repeated here as (3–105), to see this.

(3–105)   Quel cretino di te {ha/*hai} rovinato tutto di nuovo.
  3   2   3   2
'That cretin you ruined everything again.'

Subject–Verb Agreement, as predicted, picks out the syntactic head of our NPs, regardless of a contrast in person between head N and the NP following *di*.

There is another feature that figures in Subject–Verb Agreement in Italian: number. The analysis here predicts that if we find NPs in which the head N and the NP following *di* have different number, number agreement will be strictly with the syntactic head N. This prediction holds, as John Swales (personal communication) has pointed out to me. In (3–106) the NPs have two readings, and in the predicative reading the semantic head is singular but the syntactic head is plural. On both readings, however, Subject–Verb Agreement is with the syntactic head, as in (3–107).

(3–106)   i cretini della Mafia
      'the cretins of the Mafia'
      nonpredicational reading: the cretins who are part of the Mafia
      predicational reading: the Mafiosi, all of whom are cretins
      quei fessi della Società
      'those dumbos of the Society'
      nonpredicational reading: those dumbos who are members of the Society
      predicational reading: those members of the Society, all of whom are dumbos

(3–107)   I cretini della Mafia non {capiscono/*capisce} l'onore.
      pl.   sg.   pl.   sg.
      'Those cretin Mafiosi don't understand honor.'

Quei fessi della Società {oppongono/*oppone} ancora il divorzio.
    pl.   sg.   pl.   sg.
'Those dumbo members of the Society still oppose divorce.'

On the whole, then, Subject–Verb Agreement treats our NPs as we would expect it to: it is a syntactically sensitive process and it picks out the syntactic head of our NPs.

There is yet another feature for which agreement can be made, and that is gender. This concord is not realized on a tensed verb, but rather on certain participles and almost all adjectives and sometimes Ns, as we saw above with examples (3–72) through (3–75). Certainly with respect to adjectives, the fact that they agree with an N or NP is related to the fact that they modify or, in the case of predicate adjectives, predicate of, the N or NP. The same is true for concord on Ns: it occurs only in a predication relationship.

(3–108)   Considero Maria {una buona amica/*un buon amico}.
                    f.s.   f.s.   m.s.
           'I consider Maria a good friend.'

Thus this agreement process is truly semantically based (the basis being one of the relationship of modification or predication), unlike Subject–Verb Agreement. We predict, therefore, that speakers might make gender agreement with the NP following *di* rather than with the head N̄ in our NPs when it is predicated of by some adjective or NP outside the overall NP. If we could find an NP of the type in (3–14) in which the head N and the NP following *di* contrasted in gender, we could test whether an element outside the NP which is to agree in gender with that NP takes the head N or the NP following *di* to agree with. We have, in fact, already seen such contrasts in gender:

(3–74)   quell'angelo di tua moglie
          m.   f.
       'that angel of your wife'

(3–75)   una peste di bambino
          f.   m.
       'a pest of a boy'

When such NPs are used in sentences where gender agreement with some adjective or NP outside the NP is called for, speakers are not happy. They typically hesitate in giving a judgment on a prepared sentence or in producing the required sentence on their own. Then more often than not they choose agreement with the NP following *di*. Milner (1978, p. 193) likewise reports for French that agreement is with the NP following *de* in these instances.

(3–109)a. Un gioiello di moglie non sarebbe {incinta/??incinto} continuamente.
'A jewel (m.) of a wife (f.) wouldn't be pregnant (f./??m.) continually.'

b. Questo straccio di gonna è troppo {?lungo/lunga}.
'This rag (m.) of a skirt (f.) is too long (?m./f.).'

c. Voglio quel fiore di ragazza come {un'amica/*un amico}.
'I want that flower (m.) of a girl (f.) as a friend (f./*m.).'

And this hesitation is even felt on perfect participles of the verb (although perfect participles agree here for gender with the GF subject regardless of whether there is a semantic relationship of predication between the V and the GF subject).

(3–110)   Una bestia di avvocato è {arrivato/??arrivata}.
'A fool (f.) of a lawyer (m.) has arrived (m./??f.).'
Quel diavolo di Maria è ?arrivato/?arrivata.
'That devil (m.) of Maria (f.) has arrived (?m./?f.).'

The only time when a speaker absolutely chooses gender agreement with the head N over the NP object of *di* is when the opposite agreement choice would lead to a number clash with a tensed verb or when a conflict of number agreement is also involved.

(3–111)   Quei cretini della Mafia sono {difficili/*difficile}.
   p.   s.   p.   p.   s.
'Those cretins of the Mafia are difficult.'

Quei cretini della Mafia sono {arrivati/*arrivata}.
   p.   s.   p.   p.   s.
'Those cretins of the Mafia have arrived.'

(3–112)   Considero quei cretini della Mafia {pericolosi/*pericolosa}.
             m.p.   f.s.   m.p.   f.s.
'I consider those cretins of the Mafia dangerous.'

One might object that the oddity of *incinto* ('pregnant') in the masculine adds to the problem in (3–109)a. Such an objection does not hold, however, since sentences such as (3–113) are perfectly acceptable.

(3–113)   Il donnone è incinto per la quinta volta.
          m.s.   m.s.
'The big woman is pregnant for the fifth time.'

The problem in (3–109)–(3–110), then, is due to the contrast between genders of the two Ns within the NP, where the overall NP's referent is determined more by the referent of the NP that follows *di* than by the syntactic head N. While not all speakers may give precisely the acceptability judgments I have indicated in (3–109)–(3–110), no speakers feel completely at ease with whatever choice of agreement they make in these examples (except, perhaps, in (3–109)c where we have agreement not of an adjective or participle, but of a nominal – the judgment is particularly strong here). And all speakers say they would avoid using such sentences. Their discomfort, I contend, is due to the conflict set up by the fact that in this construction the semantic head and the syntactic head are not the same. Yet, unlike in the cases Abney (1986) cites, both the syntactic and the semantic heads have descriptive content: neither is a functional element. Thus speakers feel insecure about ignoring the semantic contribution of the predicative N when picking out the semantic head of the construction. The confusion speakers feel at sentences like (3–109)–(3–110) is expected, given the analysis here.

Notice further that the confusion reflected in the judgments of (3–109)–(3–110) is particular to our NPs. Thus other NPs in which a syntactic head N has a modifying phrase and in which we find a gender conflict do not cause the same confusion. Speakers invariably make gender agreement with the syntactic head.

(3–114) Quella schifezza mascherata da gentiluomo non è affatto {simpatica/*simpatico}.
'That filth (f.) dressed up as a gentleman (m.) isn't at all likable (f./*m.).'

Contrasts such as (3–114) versus (3–109) give strong evidence for analyzing our NPs as having a syntactic head that is distinct from its semantic head.

I conclude that in our construction in (3–14) the head N is a predicate which takes the NP following *di* as its subject role player.

We can now explain an otherwise peculiar fact about our construction: some speakers can have a complement on the head N which semantically belongs to the NP following *di*. All such speakers that I found are also speakers of English, and since English does this rampantly (see Hall 1973), I do not know for sure if there may not be interference here. However, Milner (1978) gives many examples which display the same phenomenon in the comparable French construction, so I do not attribute this to any influence of English on my informants.

(3–115) Italian: il tuo cretino di fratello
'your cretin of a brother'

English: your jerk of a sister
French: mon crétin de mari
'my cretin of a husband'

The phenomenon in (3–115) may be taken as one more indication of the strength of the NP following *di/of* with respect to the determination of the referent of the overall NP. That is, despite the fact that there are two Ns in this construction, there is only one referent, so any modifier of the semantic head (which is the nominal following *di*) is, actually, a modifier of the overall NP.

3.2   Other semantic properties

This section describes differences in semantics between different kinds of NPs, all of which are examples of our construction of interest.

First, when the NP following *di* is indefinite and lacks the indefinite specifier (as in many of the examples thus far), that NP is understood as having a referent picked out by the fact that it bears the property which it itself describes by definition (that is, by the sense of the N), and it is in the capacity of having this property that it is assigned the additional property of the sense of the syntactic head N of the overall NP. (Thus an indefinite NP lacking the indefinite specifier and following *di* in our NPs has only the genus sense – as discussed in Givón 1978 and ch. 1, sec. 1.5). The overall NP, therefore, can be used as a predicate assigning a property to some argument, as well as being used referentially.

(3–116)a. Maria è un fiore di moglie.
            'Maria is a flower of a wife.'
        b. Quel fiore di moglie è una meraviglia.
            'That flower of a wife is a marvel.'

In either use in (3–116), it is in the property of being a wife that the NP following *di* is assigned the added property of being flowerlike. The NP following *di*, then, does not have a specifier of its own, just as it would not in the corresponding sentence with a copula (see Gunnarson 1986, p. 35, for French).

Thus, as Lepschy and Lepschy (1979, p. 161) point out, the difference between a predicative nominal with an indefinite specifier and one without is that in the first instance the subject role player is distinguished as belonging to the category of people who comprise the set denoted by the nominal, whereas in the second instance the subject role player is distinguished as having the property inherent in the sense of the nominal (see also Renzi and Vanelli 1975).

(3–117)a. Ada è una pianista.
'Ada belongs to the class of people we call pianists.'
   b. Ada è pianista.
'Ada is a pianist (by profession).'

It is the property sense, the genus sense, of the predicate nominal in (3–117)b (where we have the predicate nominal without an indefinite determiner) that we find in our NPs with an indefinite NP that lacks a specifier after *di* (see also the discussion in Ruwet 1982 of the French construction).

However, it is also possible to have an indefinite determiner on the NP following *di* if that NP is used not in the genus sense, but, instead, to pick out a particular person who has the property signified by the N of the NP following *di*. For example, consider the context here, suggested to me by Raffaella Zanuttini (personal communication):

(3–118)Q. Chi è stato?
'Who was that?'
   A. Quel fesso di un vicino.
'That jerk of a neighbor.'

Here the questioner does not know that the person is a neighbor, so the answerer gives that information by using the indefinite article on the NP following *di*. Another context in which an indefinite article can appear is when the NP following *di* contains a restrictive relative clause. Example (3–119) is due to Raffaella Zanuttini (personal communication):

(3–119) Quel cretino di uno zio che mi ritrovo!
'That cretin of an uncle that I find myself!'

Returning to the more common of our NPs (those with no determiner or only a definite determiner on the NP following *di*), let me show how the genus sense comes out in the interpretation of these NPs with an indefinite NP lacking a specifier in the *di* phrase. Consider (3–120), suggested to me by Giulio Lepschy (personal communication).

(3–120)a. quell'ignorante di dottore
'that ignoramus of a doctor'
   b. quell'ignorante del dottore
'that ignoramus doctor'

The referent of (3–120)a is that person who in the property of being a doctor is ignorant. In other words, he does not know his job, but perhaps as a musician he is a cultured person. Example (3–120)a contrasts with (3–120)b. Here the NP following the inflected P *del* is definite and the whole NP is understood as having as its referent someone who is a doctor, the property of being a doctor is accidental to the assignment of the additional property of being an ignoramus. It may well be that he is a very fine doctor, but he is culturally ignorant. In (3–120)a, then, the property of being a doctor is crucial to the assignment of the property of being an ignoramus. But in (3–120)b the property of being a doctor is accidental to the overall NP and is merely one way of identifying the person who happens to be an ignoramus. (This distinction holds for the Italian construction, but not for its English counterparts, as seen in the glosses of (3–120) and discussed in ch. 4.)

We expect, then, that if the sense of the indefinite NP following *di* is not an appropriate property to be assigned the additional property of the predicate N preceding *di*, the overall NP will be rejected. This is the case, as pointed out to me by Peter Hook (personal communication).

(3–121)a.   *un fesso di neonato
             *'a dumbo of a newborn'
             un fesso di ragazzino
             'a dumbo of a little boy'
             un fesso d'uomo
             'a dumbo of a man'
         b. ??quel fesso del neonato
             *'that dumbo newborn'

(3–122)a.   ?*quel donnaiuolo di dottore
             ?*'that woman-chaser of a doctor'
         b. quel donnaiuolo del dottore
             'that woman-chaser doctor'

In (3–121)a we see that in someone's property of being a newborn it is absurd to assign the property of being a dumbo. That is, we do not typically characterize the behavior of newborns as being like that of dumbos or not. But the absurdity disappears as the person's age and ability to be a dumbo at that stage of life increases. Thus characterizing little boys as being dumbos is not silly at all and characterizing grown men as being dumbos is utterly normal. The NP following *di* in (3–121)b, however, is definite, and while (3–121)b is certainly odd, it is not absurd in the same way as the first sentence of (3–121)a. With the definite following *di* we are picking out that newborn that happens to be a dumbo. The oddness is in the judgment: how on earth might someone come to the conclusion that a given newborn is a dumbo? But the possibility arises that this newborn may have done something which is stupid, even for a newborn. Such a situation is odd but not definitionally absurd, in contrast to the idea of setting up classifications for newborns into dumbos and non-dumbos.

In (3–122)a, with an indefinite following *di*, we see that the property of being a doctor is most probably unrelated to the property of being a woman-chaser. That is, it is hard for us to imagine a context in which in the capacity of being a doctor a certain person is a woman-chaser. But (3–122)b (in which the *del* tells us that the doctor is male) shows us that a doctor can happen to be a woman-chaser, just probably not as a result of his capacity as a doctor.

We are now in a position to explain the following array of data. Our NPs can be definite or indefinite overall and the NP following *di* can be definite or indefinite (see the discussion of (3–63) through (3–66)). There are four logically possible combinations of definiteness on the specifiers in these NPs, then. But only three of them occur.

(3–123)   quell'egoista del direttore
          'that egotist director'

(3–124)   quell'egoista di direttore
          'that egotist of a director'

(3–125)   *un egoista del direttore
          'an egotist director'

(3–126)   un egoista di direttore
          'an egotist of a director'

Given that when the NP following *di* is a definite NP it is understood as a referential NP, and given that the referent of the overall NP is determined more by the referent of the NP following *di* than by the head N, we can see that if the NP following *di* is definite, the entire NP must be definite or we will be assigning contradictory features to the referent of the overall NP. Thus (3–125) is unacceptable because we know we are talking about the referent of *del direttore* as though it is old to the discourse but at the same time the indefinite specifier *un* tells us we are talking about the referent of the overall NP as though it is new to the discourse. Therefore, when the NP following *di* is definite, the entire NP must be definite. We have now offered a new explanation for the matching of specifiers, traditionally accounted for with Bembo's rule of corresponding articles.

When the NP following *di* is indefinite, however, we have a different type of situation because the NP following *di* now functions to pick out a referent in its capacity of having a certain property rather than as just happening to be identifiable by that property. Since it is a property assignment we are dealing with, there is no information given us by this NP as to its oldness or newness within the discourse. And, as noted above, we typically have no specifier on the NP following *di* at all. Thus the specifier of the overall NP is the only specifier, or, at least, the only specifier which indicates the feature of discourse oldness/newness. Therefore, if the overall NP is new to the discourse, an indefinite specifier in initial position is appropriate, and if the overall NP is old to the discourse, a definite specifier in initial position is appropriate. No potential for contradiction internal to the overall NP arises.

4   Implications for predication theory

Phrases like *quel matto di Giorgio* are NPs with the internal breakdown given in (3–14) and in which *matto* functions as a predicate whose subject role player is *Giorgio*.

In these constructions the subject role player does not c-command its predicate, nor is it external to the maximal projection of its predicate. Furthermore, the predicate is not bijacent to its subject role player. And, finally, the maximal projection of the predicate does not form a clause (small or otherwise) with its subject role player. We have here a single construction that is a counterexample to every theory of predication within a GB framework discussed in chapter 2, section 1.

On the other hand, this construction presents no problem for the predication coindexing principles offered in chapter 2, section 5. Let us go through that in detail.

First, this construction is an instance of secondary predication. Coindexing is always within the domain of the primary predicate, since coindexing is within the maximal projection of the secondary predicate (that is, within the NP). No barrier of the subject role player intervenes between the predicate and that subject, so Proviso Two (in (2–64)) is satisfied. We must now check to make sure Proviso One (in (2–79) is satisfied.

Proviso One contends that if a secondary predicate falls within the theta domain of H, either it or its srp must be theta marked by H (according to (2–79)), and, if H is not N, then the srp must appear in the lexical structure of H (according to (2–77)). Let us now consider examples in which our construction falls within a theta domain and in which our construction is used referentially.

(3–127)   Ieri ho incontrato un gigante d'uomo.
'Yesterday I met a giant of a man.'

(3–128)   Non intendo parlare mai più a quel donnaiuolo del dottore.
'I don't intend to ever speak again to that woman-chaser doctor.'

(3–129)   Anche se non voglio, dipendo da quel matto di Giorgio.
'Even if I don't want to, I depend on that madman Giorgio.'

(3–130)   Sono molto affezionata a quel fesso di Pasquale.
'I'm very fond of that dumbo Pasquale.'

(3–131)   Ho una fotografia di quel matto di Giorgio.
'I have a photograph of that madman Giorgio.'

In (3–127) through (3–129) our construction falls within the theta domain of a V; in (3–130), of an A; and in (3–131), of an N. In all these we could choose appropriate examples to show that it is not the syntactic head N that meets the selectional restrictions of the theta assigner, but the NP of the *di* phrase (see the discussion of (3–95) in sec. 3.1.2 above). Thus the actual secondary predicate, the syntactic head N of our construction, is arguably not L-marked by the theta assigner in whose domain it falls. But its subject role player definitely is. This is precisely the situation we expect, given Proviso One.

Now we turn to examples in which our construction falls within a theta domain and is used predicatively.

(3–132)   Considero Maria un fiore di moglie.
'I consider Maria a flower of a wife.'

(3–133)   La discussione di Guglielmo come una carogna di dottore ha stupito la moglie.
'The discussion of Guglielmo as a scoundrel of a doctor stupified his wife.'

Consider first (3–132). What is at issue is the semantic status of the N *fiore*. In chapter 2 I assumed the position that lexical items alone or with modifiers and specifiers can be predicates. The question, then, is whether the head N *fiore* alone is the predicate that takes *Maria* as its subject role player in (3–132). To answer this we need only look at the meaning of (3–132). With this sentence the speaker is expressing an evaluation of Maria as a wife of the best quality. The speaker is not expressing an evaluation of Maria as a flower. (3–132) is similar semantically, then, to (3–134).

(3–134)   Considero Maria una moglie buona come un fiore.
'I consider Maria a wife good like a flower.'

What we have in (3–132) is a predicate (*moglie*) which is itself predicated of (by *fiore*), to yield the complex predicate *un fiore di moglie*. This complex predicate is L-marked by the verb *considero* (see Williams 1982 and the discussion in ch. 2, sec. 5 preceding (2–79)) and takes *Maria* as its subject role player.

The N *fiore* in (3–132), then, is not L-marked by the verb *considero*. At this point we might want to ask whether *fiore* is consistent with Proviso One. However, such a question would be misguided. *Fiore* is part of a complex predicate, thus it does not take a subject role player in the usual sense. Instead, *fiore* contributes information that restricts the interpretation of the predicate *moglie*, so that the complex is not semantically divisible. That is, in Predicate Structure, the complex predicate is a unit that takes only one subject role player: *Maria*. Thus it makes no sense to ask about the subject role player of just *fiore* in isolation. And since the entire complex predicate in (3–132) is L-marked, this type of example is consistent with Proviso One.

Furthermore, like referential uses of our NP, predicative uses also display a syntactic inflexibility:

(3–135)   *Di chi/che cosa consideri Maria un fiore?
          *'Of who/what do you consider Maria a flower?'
          *Ne considero Maria un fiore.
          'I consider Maria a flower of it.'
          *Di moglie considero Maria un fiore.
          *'Of a wife I consider Maria a flower.'

The reason for the syntactic inflexibility, of course, is that the sentences in (3–135) cannot be interpreted as involving the complex predicate *un fiore di moglie*. This is because if *di moglie* is questioned or rendered by a clitic or preposed, as in (3–135), it will be interpreted at LF as a whole unit. But *di moglie* cannot be interpreted as a whole unit and at the same time be interpreted as part of the semantically indivisible unit that a complex predicate forms.

Let us now turn to (3–133). The situation is similar. *Una carogna di dottore* is a complex predicate with a subject role player: *Guglielmo*. Here the complex secondary predicate is not L-marked but its srp, *Guglielmo*, is L-marked by the N *discussione*. Thus (3–133) is perfectly consistent with Proviso One. (Again, it makes no sense to talk about *carogna* as a predicate in isolation.)

Our construction, then, will never present a problem for Proviso One.

In sum, our construction is consistent with the principles of predication coindexing put forth in chapter 2.

4 *Predication coindexing within NP in English*

American English has two structures which are comparable semantically to the Italian NPs studied in chapter 3. One is syntactically similar in the surface, with some restrictions not found in the Italian NPs. This one is the topic of section 1. The other, discussed in section 2, is syntactically quite different in the surface, but I argue that it comes from the same structure in DS by way of a restructuring rule which maps morphological form into phonological form.

British English has constructions similar to the American ones, but I have not analyzed the British constructions here since the data often differ on crucial examples. Below I indicate where the British data differ if I have the facts. My information on British English here, unless otherwise noted, is due to Andrew Radford (personal communication).

1   NPs like *that crook of a chairman*

English has NPs which are very similar syntactically and semantically to the NPs of Italian discussed in chapter 2. In (4–1) we see an example.

(4–1)   that crook of a chairman

I propose that their syntactic analysis is identical to that of the corresponding Italian construction:

(4–2)

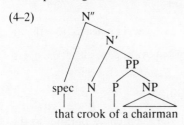

The types of evidence one can bring to bear in support of (4–2) are parallel to the types of evidence one can bring to bear in support of the same analysis for the comparable Italian construction (given in (3–14) of

209

ch. 3). Rendering each argument in full, then, would be highly repetitive. Still, the English glosses of chapter 3 do not always use the construction exemplified in (4–1) because of differences between the two languages. And these differences are interesting because they often shed further light on the analysis of the constructions. Thus simple reference to chapter three does not suffice in our analysis of (4–1). I will, therefore, handle each argument, but only briefly. And I will list the relevant English data with the number of the corresponding Italian example in chapter 3 and refer the reader to the appropriate sections of chapter 3 for more extensive arguments and, particularly, for reference to other relevant works (whereas in this chapter I do not generally repeat references). My longer remarks, then, will be limited to points upon which the Italian and English constructions differ.

Just as with the Italian NPs of chapter 3, I will show here that the English NP is syntactically and semantically an ordinary NP.

1.1   The external structure is NP [parallel to ch. 3, sec. 1]
I argue here that the external structure of phrases like that in (4–1) is NP.

First, they occur in all and only those positions that NPs can occur in.

(4–3)   Even a fool of a chairman wouldn't be nasty to his most prolific professor. [(3–1)]

(4–4)   I'd never trust that fool of a professor. [(3–2)]

(4–5)   It's stupid to confess to that rogue of a doctor. [(3–3)]

(4–6)   I organized the block picnic with that gem of a neighbor, Bob Hatfield. [(3–4)]

(4–7)   Your brother, that gem of a centerfielder, is gonna be on my team. [(3–5)]

Second, they can undergo NP movement.

(4–8)   That gem of a centerfielder seems to have caught it again. [(3–6)]

(4–9)   No crook of a chairman should be trusted by the department members. [(3–7)]

(4–10)   That gem of a neighbor arrived. [(3–8)]

English does not have rules which would yield sentences parallel to the Italian examples in (3–9) and (3–10).

Third, they trigger Subject–Verb Agreement.

(4–11)   A gem of a centerfielder {is/*are} always welcome. [(3–11)]
     s.   s. pl.

Fourth, they are non-propositional.

(4–12)   I found that dumbo of a neighbor. [(3–12)]

Fifth, they behave like R-expressions with respect to the Binding Conditions.

(4–13)a.   That dumbo of a neighbor talks to himself.
     b.   [That dumbo of a neighbor]$_i$ wishes I'd invite him$_i$.
     c.   *I told him$_i$ that [that dumbo of a neighbor]$_i$ couldn't come. [3–13]

I conclude that phrases like (4–1) are NPs.

1.2   **Internal structure [parallel to ch. 3, sec. 2]**
I will now argue that phrases like *that crook of a chairman* break down into a specifier, a noun, and a PP. Then I will show that the proper analysis is that given above in (4–2), where the PP is a sister to the head N.

1.2.1   The specifier [parallel to ch. 3, sec. 2.1]
Specifiers of NP in English include demonstratives, determiners, quantifiers, numerals, measure phrases, and genitives (including possessive adjectives).

In our phrases the most common initial elements are the demonstratives *that* and *this* and the indefinite determiners *a* and *one*.

(4–14)   that gem of a centerfielder [(3–15)]
        this rag of a dress
        a wretch of a boy
        (He's) one prince of a friend.

The definite determiner is not common in this construction, but it is possible. Examples like (4–15) were offered to me by Andrew Radford (personal communication).

(4–15)   He lied to us, the crook of a chairman! [contrast to (3–17)]

Quantifiers that fill specifier are possible, but only singular ones, since this construction occurs only in the singular. (An explanation for this fact is found in sec. 2, where I discuss complex nominals.) Thus plural quantifiers are rejected, as are numerals (other than the determiner use of *one* seen in (4–14) above).

(4–16)   Every wretch of a date that I've ever picked up in a singles' bar has had herpes.
    but: *some wretches of boys [contrast to (3–16)]
    *many/most/all/four wretches of boys

(British English accepts NPs like *many wretches of boys*, and one American speaker I have found (Stuart Davis) finds these marginal.) Greg Carlson (personal communication) has pointed out to me that the restriction here brings to mind the restriction against plurals in the adjectival construction *How thick (of) a book did you read?/*How thick (of) books did you read?* I will not go into the analysis of the adjectival construction in this book, but it looks to be fertile ground for comparison.

Returning to our NPs, we find that the parallel to (3–18), which is ungrammatical in Italian (a fact for which I have no explanation, but which is not a problem for the claim that the initial element of our construction is a specifier), is fine in English.

(4–17)   very much a scoundrel of a doctor [(3–18)]

Possessives can occur in English under precisely the same conditions that license them in Italian: when they belong semantically to the NP of the PP.

(4–18)   your jerk of a brother [(3–17) and (3–115)]

I conclude that the initial element in (4–1) is a specifier.

1.2.2   The PP [parallel to ch. 3, sec. 2.2]

Here I argue that *of a chairman* in (4–1) forms a PP, where *of* is the P and *a chairman* is its NP object.

First, English has a preposition *of* which is obligatorily transitive:

(4–19)   We talked of John.

In the interest of non-proliferation of homophonous items that have similar distributions (see the first argument of ch. 3, sec. 2.2), I propose that *of* in (4–1) is this P. Since this P is obligatorily transitive, I conclude *of a chairman* in (4–1) is a PP.

In chapter 3 another argument for the existence of a PP inside our construction was based on data involving inflected prepositions (see (3–19) and the discussion there). The same argument cannot be made for English because English does not have inflected Ps. However, for the reader interested in the British English construction a parallel argument can be made considering the morphosyntactic properties of the P *of*, as

Andrew Radford (personal communication) has pointed out to me. *Of* in British English allows for vowel reduction to schwa and final consonant deletion before a word beginning with a consonant. And the *of* of our construction does the same (where, of course, (4–20)b is accepted in British speech but not in American speech, since the NP here is plural):

(4–20)a. a pound o' [schwa] plums, please, darlin'
     b. those wretches o' [schwa] boys

Second, the English construction in (4–1) is more restricted than its Italian counterpart in requiring that the NP following *of* be indefinite.

(4–21) that fool of {a/*the} student
        quel fesso {di/dello} studente

(British speech allows the definite article on an N that habitually co-occurs with a definite article: *that fool of the chairman*.) English also requires that the indefinite determiner appear on the material following *of*, whereas this determiner is unusual in Italian (see the discussion of (3–118)–(3–119) in ch. 3). We therefore find the contrast in (4–22)–(4–23):

(4–22) that fool of a neighbor
       *that fool of neighbor

(4–23) only in special contexts: quel fesso di un vicino
       in most contexts: quel fesso di vicino

This contrast is mirrored by the fact that in English the indefinite determiner may not be omitted on a singular predicative NP (as seen in (4–24)a), whereas in Italian it may in special circumstances (and is, with the reading typical to our construction – contrast the readings of (4–24)b and (4–24)c and see ch. 3, sec. 3.2 for relevant discussion):

(4–24)a. Ada is a pianist.
       *Ada is pianist.
     b. Ada è una pianista.
       'Ada belongs to the class of people we call pianists.'
     c. Ada è pianista.
       'Ada is a pianist (by profession).'

Note that (4–25) is not a counterexample to my claim that English does not allow omission of the indefinite article in copular constructions such as that in (4–24)a, since in (4–25) the missing determiner would be definite, not indefinite (see Higgins 1979, p. 256).

(4–25) Ada is boss.
      (similar to: Ada is the boss.
      contrast to: Ada is a boss.)

The fact that the indefinite determiner appears in (4–22) is evidence that the material following *of* is an NP, since indefinite determiners in English introduce only NPs.

Third, the English construction contrasts with the Italian one in resisting an AP sister of the N inside the PP. In fact, it resists all kinds of sisters to varying degrees.

(4–26)   *that creep of your doctor [contrast to (3–20)a]
*that creep of a professor with tenure
??that creep of a teacher of physics

(British English speakers accept the last example of (4–26).)

Still, there is other evidence that the material following *of* is an NP. That is that we can get complex nominals here. Andrew Radford (personal communication) offered me the examples in (4–27):

(4–27)   that jerk of a physics professor [(3–20)c]
that bitch of a two-bit hooker

We can learn one more thing about the English construction from considering (4–18), (4–21), and the first sentence of (4–26) together, so I will repeat them here for convenience:

(4–18)   your jerk of a brother

(4–21)   that fool of {a/*the} student

(4–26)   *that creep of your doctor

The requirement that the NP following *of* be indefinite accounts for the asterisks in (4–21) and (4–26). However, the sense of (4–18) is with the brother being yours. On this basis one might want to argue that the requirement that the NP following *of* be indefinite is not a semantic requirement but some sort of morphosyntactic requirement. In support of this, notice that (4–18) can be used in two senses. First, (4–18) can mean that you have a brother and he has the quality of being a jerk in his capacity of being a brother. That is, your brother falls into the class of jerk brothers, not just into the class of jerks. In this reading the possessive in (4–18) goes with the overall NP and not with the NP following *of*. On that reading one could maintain the position that the requirement that the NP following *of* be indefinite is semantic in nature. However, (4–18) can also be used to mean that you have a brother who is a jerk in some other capacity. For example, as Andrew Radford (personal communication) has pointed out to me, in a sentence like (4–28), your brother is a jerk in his capacity of being a lover, not a brother:

(4-28)   Your jerk of a brother left me high and dry.

So here the possessive adjective goes only with the NP following *of*.

Likewise, there is reason to believe that the requirement that the N of the NP following *of* have no sisters of any type is morphosyntactic rather than semantic in nature: contrast the third sentence of (4-26) to the first of (4-27), again repeated for convenience:

(4-26)   ??that creep of a teacher of physics

(4-27)   that jerk of a physics professor

The complex nominal is better than the analytic construction that corresponds to it semantically.

I will return to these morphosyntactic restrictions at the very end of section 1.3.2 below.

In chapter 3 another argument was made for the PP status of the Italian phrases parallel to *of a chairman* in (4-1), and that argument was based on the fact that when a pronoun appears following *di*, it gets the oblique Case that we would expect if it were, in fact, the object of the P (see (3-21) of ch. 3). No parallel argument can be made for English, since pronouns are definite, and only indefinite NPs are allowed to follow *of* in the English construction in (4-1).

While the evidence is not copious, it is indicative, and there is no evidence I know of to the contrary, thus I conclude that in (4-1) *of* is a P and that it forms a PP with the NP following it.

Before leaving this section, there is an alternative to consider. As with the Italian *di* (see the discussion in ch. 3 at the end of sec. 2.2), the most likely alternative to *of*'s being a P is that it might be a Case marker, so that the string *of a chairman* in (4-1) would be a Case marked NP rather than a PP (see Stowell 1981 versus Zubizarreta 1985, among others). If one could defend the analysis of *of a chairman* as an NP rather than a PP, then we could say that the subject role player of the predicative N *crook* c-commands it and that *crook* is bijacent to the Case marked NP *of a chairman*. With this structural analysis, (4-1) is no problem for the c-command restriction and the bijacency restriction on predication common to some theories of predication (see ch. 2, sec. 1). Still, (4-1) is a problem for the externality requirement on predication, since *of a chairman* is within the maximal projection of *crook*, and (4-1) is a problem for the requirement of some theories that a predicate be a maximal projection. Therefore, we do not gain a great deal with respect to the theories discussed in chapter 2, section 1 by analyzing *of a chairman* in (4–1) as a Case-marked NP. Furthermore, as we saw at the end of chapter 3, section 2.2, the Case-marked NP analysis is not viable for Italian. Therefore, since the two constructions in the two languages have so much else in common, I opt for a common syntactic analysis, as in (4–2). At no point, however, is the analysis of *of* as a P rather than a Case marker of crucial import to anything in this chapter. Furthermore, I have presented no evidence here that *of* must be present at DS, rather only that in (4–1) *of* is followed by an NP that it forms a constituent with. We will see in section 2 below (in the discussion of (4–88)–(4–90)) that an analysis of these constructions which allows *of* to be inserted in the P(honological) F(orm) may be justified. For now I will continue talking about this construction as though the *of* is present in SS, but nothing will hinge upon this assumption.

1.2.3   The head N and its AP sisters [parallel to ch. 3, sec. 2.3]
First, the specifiers of the overall phrase are those that Ns typically take, as we saw in section 1.2.1. Furthermore, heads of other categories do not take these same specifiers. Thus no head of any category other than N can take the singular indefinite determiner as its specifier (although, unlike in Italian, in English adjectives can take a demonstrative as specifier: *No one is that pretty!*). This is a strong indication that the specifier in our phrases introduces an N.

Second, in English there are not many lexical items that can double as adjectives or nouns, in contrast to Italian. One of the few possibilities is *fun*. Color terms are another, as Greg Carlson (personal communication) has pointed out to me.

(4–29)a. She's so fun. (like: She's so nice.
                     cf. *She's so woman.)
      b. Let's have some fun. (like: Let's have some tea.)
                     cf. *She's some nice.)

It is a simple matter, then, to determine that the lexical items that occur in the slot between the initial specifier and the PP are only those that can appear as the head of regular NPs.

Third, the material in this slot can be filled by more than one word, in which case we get a word that can appear as the head of regular NPs plus an AP.

(4–30)a. What a rowdy jerk of a professor! [(3–24)]
      b. "Prut!" says that wicked witch of a Step-mother.

Example (4–30)b is from Pyle (1915, p. 156). (British English also allows complex nominals here: *that baby-batterer of a chairman.*)

Fourth, the lexical item in this slot can have morphemes that only Ns have, such as the agentive *er* (affixed to a V to yield an N; see Selkirk 1982, Sproat 1985, among others):

(4–31)   What a stinker of a letter she wrote me!

(No parallel argument can be made for Italian, I think, since there are no affixes that apply to Ns but not As (see Lepschy and Lepschy 1979).)

I conclude that the material between the initial specifier and the PP is an N or an N plus its AP sisters.

1.2.4   Internal configuration [parallel to ch. 3, sec. 2.4]

I will now argue that the specifier, the N (and its optional sisters), and the PP in our construction connect together as in (4–2).

In chapter 3 when making this argument, I contrasted our analysis to three other analyses of NPs in the literature. I will do that here, as well, but very briefly. Please consult the more detailed arguments of chapter 3 for elaboration.

The analyses to compare are our (4–2), repeated here, plus the additional three:

(4–2)

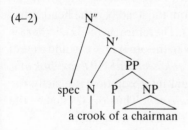

(4–32)

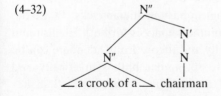

(4–33)

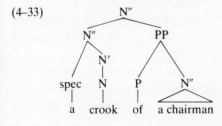

(4–34)

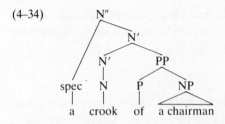

A first argument against (4–32) is that we have already seen that the *of* forms a PP with the material following it, but (4–32) does not reflect this fact.

No argument parallel to that for Italian based on (3–31) can be made, since the relevant sentences in English are all ungrammatical, given that personal pronouns may not appear in the PP (since they are definite and the NP object of *of* must be indefinite).

There is at least one other argument that can be made against (4–32), based on the interpretation of these NPs. We will see below in section 1.3 that these NPs are interpreted with *crook* being a predicate that takes *a chairman* as its subject role player. Now in English (unlike in Italian), NPs can appear in specifier position of NP whether they have a degree sense or not (whereas in Italian they must have a degree sense). When they do, they may receive a theta role from the head N if the head N has an argument structure (see ch. 1, sec. 2.3). Therefore, in (4–32), if there is any assignment of a theta role from one N to the other N, we would expect the N *chairman* to assign a theta role to *crook*, since the NP *that crook of* is in specifier position. However, the actual interpretation is exactly the opposite: *crook* gives a theta role to *chairman*. Thus (4–32) makes the wrong prediction about the direction of theta role assignment.

Finally, note that (4–32) allows a non-degree NP in specifier position, which is a syntactic option that English has but Italian lacks. I take the position that we should prefer a common analysis for both English and Italian if one that is both empirically and theoretically adequate can be found, since the constructions are so similar both syntactically and semantically, as a comparison of this chapter with chapter 3 makes obvious. But (4–32) is impossible for Italian because of the NP in specifier position. Thus (4–32) should be avoided for English, as well, so long as an alternative that will hold for both languages and that is of equal or superior explanatory adequacy is available.

I therefore reject (4–32).

Moving on to (4–33) we see that this structure is that of appositives (in many works, including Jackendoff 1977 – although I will present a different analysis in ch. 5, sec. 5, following Emonds 1979). There are several arguments against an appositive analysis of our construction.

First, (4–1) does not mean the same thing as an appositive. Thus, (4–35) contrasts with (4–1):

(4–35)   that crook, our chairman [(3–33)]

Second, (4–1) does not have the characteristic pauses we find with appositives (see also Safir 1985, p. 319). (On the other hand, unlike in Italian, it does not have the same intonation contour of an NP like *a friend of John's*. I will return to this point in sec. 1.3 below in the discussion of (4–56) through (4–60).)

Third, appositives can never be stacked, but only coordinated (see the English glosses of (3–35) of chapter 3). But our NP can be followed by an appositive NP:

(4–36)   that crook of a chairman, our department's leader [(3–36)]

And it cannot have a conjoined appositive NP tacked on:

(4–37)   *that crook of a chairman and our department's leader [(3–37)]

Fourth, restrictive relative clauses may not follow an appositive NP (see the English glosses of (3–38) of ch. 3). However, restrictive relative clauses may follow our construction.

(4–38)   That crook of a chairman that just got appointed will ruin us all. [(3–39)]

Notice that the interpretation has the relative modifying the entire NP, not just *a chairman*.

Fifth, if (4–33) were the correct structure, we would predict that the head N could have a restrictive relative clause immediately following it, just as we can in regular appositive constructions (see the English gloss of (3–40) of ch. 3). But such a relative is rejected.

(4–39)   *That crook that I met yesterday of a chairman isn't coming. [(3–41)]

For the above reasons, I reject (4–33).

The last alternative is (4–34), the structure offered in Jackendoff (1977) for restrictive modifiers of a head N in English. In the introduction to this book I adopt an X-bar theory that disallows sisters to N' other than the specifier. Thus (4–34) is not a structure that I believe a grammar should base generate. However, since this structure is so prevalent in recent linguistic literature, I will argue against (4–34) on other grounds. And there turn out to be several reasons to reject (4–34).

First, as I pointed out above in the discussion of the contexts for (4–18), an NP such as *your jerk of a brother* can be used either to indicate your jerk brother or your brother who is a jerk (in some other capacity) (as in the context in (4–28)). Thus the semantics of NPs like that in (4–1) does not suggest that the NP following *of* should be in a position reserved for restrictive modifiers.

Second, proponents of structures like (4–34) argue that only sisters of N can get theta roles from N (see Speas 1986, among others). But *a chairman* (as we will see in sec. 1.3 below) is the subject role player of *crook*, so in these linguists' terms, it would get a theta role from the head N. But, then, it should be structurally a sister to the N. So (4–34) is unable to account for the facts on theta assignment.

Third, in regular NPs restrictive modifiers of a head N of the category PP can be preceded or followed by other restrictive modifiers of that head N of the category PP, usually conjoined (see the English glosses of (3–45) and (3–46) of ch. 3). However, restrictive modifiers of a head N that are of the category PP most typically follow arguments of the head N and are never conjoined to the argument (see the English glosses of (3–47)). But in our construction restrictive modifiers of the head N that are of the category PP follow the *of* phrase and are never conjoined to the *of* phrase.

(4–40)a.   a crook of a chairman of unspeakable stupidity [cf. (3–48)a]
    b.   *a crook of unspeakable stupidity of a chairman [cf. (3–48)b]
    c.   *a crook of a chairman and of unspeakable stupidity [cf. (3–48)c]

The only exceptions I know of where it looks as if a PP can intervene between the head N and the *of* phrases are instances in which the head N and the intervening PP are so frequently found together that they are open to an analysis as a single lexical item:

(4–41)   that *stick in the mud* of a date
        that *son of a gun* of a chairman
        (cf. a stick-in-the-mud attitude)

And for the speaker interested in this construction in British English, let me point out that this restriction does not seem to hold at all. The examples in (4–42) are good in British English but rejected by every American I have asked (as the asterisks reflect):

(4–42)   *that [purveyor of rubbish] of a chairman

      *that [persecutor of the poor] of a lawyer
      *that [poor excuse for an thinker] of a professor

In any case, the American data strongly support my argument against the analysis in (4–34).

No argument parallel to that of chapter 3 involving (3–49) through (3–57) can be made, since English does not place APs that consist of a lone A to the right of a head N.

On the basis of the above arguments, I conclude that (4–34) is not the correct analysis of (4–1).

All of the data given above and all the rest below with regard to NPs like that in (4–1) are easily accounted for with the structure in (4–2).

Furthermore, consistent with (4–2), we can note that *of*, the null P, is the common introducer for non-prepositional arguments of a head N. And prepositional arguments of a head N have prepositions lexically selected by the head N. On the other hand, PP sisters of a head N that are not arguments of that head N can exhibit a wide range of Ps. Thus the fact that it is always *of* that appears in our NPs and never any other P follows from the analysis in (4–2), in which this *of* introduces an argument of the head N. However, with any of the other analyses considered above, we have no reason to expect an *of* as our P rather than any other P.

In chapter 3 another argument for the structure in (4–2) (which is given there as (3–14)) was based on the fact that PP extraposition from NP is impossible in Italian (see the discussion in ch. 3 of (3–61) and (3–62)). However, English allows PP extraposition from NP – thus a parallel argument cannot be made. Still, we can point out facts about PP extraposition in English that are consistent with (4–2). First, note that PP extraposition in English does not apply to arguments of an N head (for reasons why, see Guéron 1980, from whom the examples in parentheses after (4–43) are taken).

(4–43)   John analyzed the destruction of the city over the summer.
         *John analyzed the destruction over the summer of the city.
         (cf. John read a book by Chomsky over the summer.
         John read a book over the summer by Chomsky.)

(Recall from ch. 2, sec. 8 that the object of passive *by* is not an argument.) PP extraposition also does not apply to our NPs.

(4–44)   I read that atrocity of an article over the summer.
         *I read that atrocity over the summer of an article.

Example (4–44) is predicted by (4–2) plus the semantic analysis I give below in section 1.3, in which I argue that *an article* in (4–44) is the subject role player of *atrocity*, and therefore an argument of *atrocity*. Other factors may block PP extraposition from NP besides argument status of the object of the P, and therefore the data in (4–44) may be taken only as consistent with my analysis, rather than as supplying a strong argument for it. Still, only (4–2) of the four analyses considered here can account for the data in (4–44) with the same explanation used to account for (4–43). Given the strong similarity between (4–43) and (4–44), I believe these data should be considered, then, more than merely consistent with my analysis, but supportive of it.

I conclude that (4–2) is the correct structure.

1.3   Semantics
The head N of the overall NP in (4–2) acts as a predicate to the NP introduced by *of*, which acts as its subject role player, and the initial specifier, as expected, specifies the entire NP. I will now support this claim.

1.3.1   *The specifier*
The specifier of the NP following *of* is always *a*. However, the specifier of the overall NP can vary. When the initial specifier is definite, the entire NP is interpreted as definite. In the construction in (4–45)–(4–46) the GF subject of the embedded clause must be definite when it is understood as coreferential with the GF subject of the matrix clause. We can see that the definiteness of the overall NP is determined by the initial specifier only.

(4–45)   Honest though that idiot of a neighbor may seem, he isn't. [(3–64)]

(4–46)   *Honest though an idiot of a neighbor may seem, he isn't.

(In ch. 3 we saw that the comparable Italian construction to that in (4–45) and (4–46) could admit an indefinite NP on the genus reading. Many speakers of English also allow this reading, as well, as Greg Carlson (personal communication) has pointed out to me. Thus the glosses of (3–65) are good for many English speakers, as is (4–46) with a genus reading.)

Likewise, when the initial specifier is indefinite, the overall NP is understood to be indefinite. As we have noted before (in ch. 1, sec. 1.3 and again in ch. 3, sec. 3.1), indefinite NPs are readily interpreted as predicates, whereas some uses of definite ones are not (context being a relevant factor; and see the discussion of (4–85) below). In (4–47) and

(4–48) the position following *GB* must be filled by a predicate. And we see that it is the initial specifier on our NP that determines whether or not it is easily interpreted as a predicate.

(4–47)   Some people consider GB a mess of a theory. [(3–66)a]

(4–48)   *Some people consider GB that mess of a theory. [cf. (3–66)b]

I conclude that the initial specifier serves as the specifier for the entire NP.

1.3.2   The predicate and its subject role player [parallel to ch. 3, sec. 3.1.2]

I will here argue that the head N of our NP functions as a predicate taking the NP following *of* as its subject role player.

First, there must be a matching of selectional restrictions between the two that mirrors the restrictions in copular sentences (see the English glosses of (3–67) through (3–69) of ch. 3). If selectional restrictions are a reflex of the predication relationship, then our NP involves the predication relationship. And since these head Ns as predicates take only one role player, the NP following *of* must be their subject role player.

Second, the head N and the NP following *of* must match each other for semantic gender and/or number, just as they must in copular sentences involving predication.

(4–49)a.   a prince of a man
    b.   *a prince of a woman
    c.   *a prince of people

Example (4–49)c does, of course, have the good reading in which *people* is who the prince lords over. Thus the matching for gender and/or number in (4–49) is not a necessity of the structure but, instead, of the semantics. The data here would follow if our NPs involve predication. (This argument is similar to that based on (3–72)–(3–73) for Italian, although sometimes the gender of the predicative head N in Italian is invariable (and, hence, not semantic in nature) – in which case no agreement takes place.)

Third, the head N of our construction is understood to bear the same semantic relationship to the NP following *of* that the corresponding predicate bears towards its subject role player in indisputable cases of predication constructions. (See the English glosses of (3–78)–(3–83) and the discussion there.) This is explained if our NP involves predication.

Fourth, the more evaluative an N is, the easier it is to interpret it as a predicate. In our construction only head Ns that give an evaluative judgment of the NP following *of* can appear (see the English glosses of (3–84)–(3–89) and the English example (3–88) in ch. 3).

Sometimes the evaluative judgment is inherent in the word for all speakers, as in (4–50)a (from Pyle 1915, p. 300). But sometimes speakers will vary on whether they consider a word to be inherently evaluative. Thus for me (4–50)b is good, although for many speakers the word *sexist* is not (yet) inherently evaluative. And, as expected, given my analysis of predicates as including modifiers (see ch. 1, sec. 1.1), if the head N is not itself evaluative but if this N forms an evaluative predicate when it has an appropriate modifier with it, it can appear in our construction. Thus Andrew Radford (personal communication) has offered me (4–50)c.

(4–50)a. "See mother," said the princess, "that rogue of a drummer answered my question without winking over it."
   b. a sexist of a director
   c. a lame duck of a president (cf. *a duck of a president)

Other words that by metaphorical extension or association are evaluative in nature can appear here.

(4–51)   one hell of a story
         a whale of a story

And head Ns that by connotation have become evaluative can appear here. Thus Greg Carlson (personal communication) offers the following example repeated from chapter 3:

(3–85)   a Hitler of a man

This semantic restriction on the head N is explained if our NPs involve predication, since it is a well-known fact that predicates break down into an evaluative class and a non-evaluative class.

Fifth, if the NP following *of* is the subject role player of the head N, we expect the reference of the overall NP, if it is used referentially, to be that of the NP following *of* as predicated of by the head N. Thus the NP following *of* is the crucial one in determining the referent of the overall NP. And in chapter 3 I called this NP the semantic head of the construction. With this analysis, we expect the NP following *of* to be the one that satisfies selectional restrictions put on the overall NP from external context. This is true.

(4–52)   I'd like to marry a flower of a girl. [(3–95)]

This is not to say that the head N is semantically void. In fact, the head N contributes greatly to the semantics of the overall NP and we are claiming in (4–52) that the girl is, metaphorically, a flower. Thus these NPs can appear easily in contexts that extend that metaphor, as in (4–53)a. Yet the head N *flower* need not be present in order to get this metaphor, as (4–53)b shows:

(4–53)a. Such a flower of a girl will blossom in this castle.
  b. A girl like that will blossom in this castle.

Now, given the analysis in which the NP following *of* is the semantic head of the construction, we expect this NP to be inseparable from the rest of the construction, since the head of a phrase cannot appear separated from the rest of the phrase. This is exactly what we find.

(4–54) *Who/What did he marry a flower of? [(3–96)–(3–100)]

Sixth, if the head N is a predicate taking the NP following *of* as its subject role player, we expect that the *of* phrase cannot appear across the copula from the head N, in contrast to other PP sisters of N. Instead, as with other one-place predicates, there would be no *of* on the other side of the copula. This is so.

(4–55) *That fool is of a doctor. [(3–102)]
    (cf. The most brutal destruction was of the small town.)
    That fool is a doctor. [(3–103)]

For the corresponding Italian construction, additional arguments were made for the distinction between a semantic head and a syntactic head in our construction based on agreement rules. We saw in chapter 3 that when the syntactic head and the semantic head differed on gender, the semantically sensitive process of gender/number agreement of adjectival and nominal (and even participle) predicates takes the semantic head rather than the syntactic head of our overall NP to make agreement with (see the discussion of (3–109) through (3–114)). No comparable argument can be made for English, since Ns are not morphologically marked for gender in English.

We can, however, make another argument for our semantic analysis based on prosodic facts in English that have no parallel in Italian. Consider (4–56) and (4–57).

(4–56) Have you met her prince of a husband?
    She used to have a prince of a husband.

(4–57) Jack certainly is a prince of a husband.

Whether our NP is used referentially (as in (4–56)) or predicatively (as in 4–57)), we are pointing out that a person who has the quality of being a husband has, in the very capacity of being a husband, the quality of being a prince (which is a metaphor for saying he is very fine at being a husband). The information in the head N, then, is always new and asserted. That is, in (4–58) the listener may or may not be assumed to know Jane is a lecturer, but the speaker is clearly asserting as new information that Jane is terrific as a lecturer.

(4–58)   Jane is a whiz of a lecturer.
          Jane is a hell of a lecturer.

The stress pattern of these NPs supports this semantic analysis: the head N receives the stress peak (see Bolinger 1958, Donegan and Stampe 1983, and many others in between). Compare the non-contrastive and non-emphatic intonation contour of the NP containing predication in (4–59) to that of the regular NPs in (4–60).

(4–59)   a foól of a doctor

(4–60)   a friend of the dóctor's
          an enemy of my síster's

Finally, just as with the Italian construction, the English construction can be used referentially or predicatively, and in either case the property denoted by the NP following *of* is assigned the additional property denoted by the syntactic head N. We find, then, that there must be an appropriate combination of head N and NP following *of* in order for the construction to make sense (see the English glosses of (3–121)–(3–122)).

We can now explain an interesting point about our construction, illustrated by the contrast we noted above in the first example of (4–27) versus the third example of (4–26), repeated here for convenience.

(4–26)   ??that creep of a teacher of physics

(4–27)   that jerk of a physics professor

There is a requirement that the NP following *of* have the form *a N*, where the N can be a complex nominal but it resists having sisters. This resistance against sisters is clearly morphosyntactic rather than semantic, since (4–27) shows that the NP following *of* can be understood semantically as having arguments (the complex nominal *physics professor* is equivalent semantically to the analytical form *professor of physics*).

Before attempting to account for the above fact, let us look at another fact we saw above in (4–40)a versus (4–40)b, repeated here for convenience.

(4–40)a.   a crook of a chairman of unspeakable stupidity
    b.   *a crook of unspeakable stupidity of a chairman

In (4–40)a we see that a PP restrictive modifier of the head N of our construction (the PP *of unspeakable stupidity*) must follow the PP that contains the subject role player. However, in regular NPs we have a strong preference for such PP modifiers to follow arguments of the head N, but if they do precede those arguments, the result is marginal rather than ungrammatical.

(4–61)   the destruction of Troy of great distinction [(3–47)a]

(4–62)   ??the destruction of great distinction of Troy [(3–47)b]

That is, the preference to place post-head modifiers after arguments in regular NPs becomes a requirement in our construction.

We can account for the above facts with one explanation. Notice that the effect of the above is to place the head N of our construction adjacent to the head N of the NP following *of* with only the minimal intervenors *of a*. I call these intervenors minimal, since *of* is the null P and *a* is the indefinite specifier used purely as a grammatical word when the nominal it introduces is predicative (as contrasted to its semantic role with referential NPs). Thus both intervenors here are grammatical formative intervenors and not semantic intervenors. The effect is that we keep the head N and the N of the NP following *of* as close to each other as possible. I contend that we do this so that their intricate semantic relationship is not disturbed by semantic intervenors. As with the Italian construction, the English construction has a syntax that is iconistic to the semantics.

I conclude that in our construction the syntactic head N is a predicate taking the NP following *of* as its subject role player.

1.3.3   Implications for predication theory [parallel to ch. 3, sec. 4]
With the analysis in (4–2) our construction presents a problem for every theory of predication discussed in chapter 2, section 1. The subject role player is not external to the maximal projection of its predicate. If the *of* is present as a true P (one that heads a PP) at SS, the subject role player does not c-command the predicate and the predicate is not bijacent to its subject role player. The predicate itself is not a maximal projection. And the subject role player and the maximal projection of its predicate do not form a clause.

On the other hand, this construction is no problem for the theory of predication put forth in chapter 2. Let us go through the relevant points.

First, this construction is an instance of secondary predication. Coindexing is always within the domain of the primary predicate, since coindexing is within the maximal projection of the secondary predicate (that is, within the overall NP). No barrier of the subject role player intervenes between the predicate and that subject, so Proviso Two (in (2–64)) is satisfied. We must now check to make sure Proviso One (in (2–79)) is satisfied.

Proviso One says that if our secondary predicate falls within the theta domain of H, either it or its srp must receive a theta role from H, and, if H is not N, then the srp must appear in the lexical structure of H (see (2–77) and (2–79)).

To start, let us look at examples in which our construction falls within a theta domain and in which our construction is used referentially.

(4–63)   I met a giant of a man. [(3–127)]

(4–64)   I never intend to speak again to that jerk of a neighbor. [(3–128)]

(4–65)   Even if I don't want to, I depend on my prince of a husband. [(3–129)]

(4–66)   I'm very fond of that dumbo of a grad student. [(3–130)]

(4–67)   I have a photograph of that madman of a mailman. [(3–131)]

(4–68)   I'm really into this puzzle of a construction.

In (4–63) through (4–65) our construction falls within the theta domain of a V; in (4–66), of an A; in (4–67), of an N; and in (4–68), of one of the few uses of Ps in English where P is a theta assigner (see ch. 1, sec. 2.4). In all these different configurations, we could choose appropriate examples to show that it is not the syntactic head N that meets the selectional restrictions of the theta assigner, but the NP following *of* (see the discussion in 1.3.2 above). Thus the actual secondary predicate, the syntactic head N of our construction, is arguably not L-marked by the theta assigner in whose domain it falls, but its subject role player definitely is. This is precisely the situation we expect, given Proviso One.

Now we turn to examples in which our construction falls within a theta domain and is used predicatively.

(4–69)   I consider Maria a pearl of a sister. [(3–132)]

(4–70)   The discussion of Bill as a charlatan of a historian stupified his wife. [(3–133)]

Consider first (4–69). What is at issue is the semantic status of *pearl*. In chapter 1, section 1.1 I argued that predicates can be multiple word strings. The question, then, is whether the head N *pearl* alone is the predicate that takes *Maria* as its subject role player in (4–69). To answer this we need look only at the meaning. With this sentence the speaker is expressing an evaluation of Maria as a sister of lovely or valued qualities. The speaker is not expressing an evaluation of Maria as a pearl. (4–69) is similar semantically to (4–71).

(4–71) I consider Maria a sister as lovely as a pearl. [(3–134)]

In (4–69), then, the predicate *sister* is itself predicated of by the predicate *pearl*, to yield the complex predicate *a pearl of a sister*. This complex predicate is L-marked by the V *consider* and takes *Maria* as its subject role player.

The N *pearl* in (4–69), then, is not L-marked by the verb *consider*. At this point we might want to ask whether *pearl* is consistent with Proviso One. However, such a question would be misguided. *Pearl* is part of a complex predicate; thus it does not take a subject role player in the usual sense. Instead, *pearl* contributes information that restricts the interpretation of *sister*, so that the complex predicate is a unit that takes only one subject role player: *Maria*. Thus it makes no sense to ask about the subject role player of *pearl* in isolation. And, just as with the Italian complex predicate (see the discussion of (3–134) in ch. 3), the English complex predicate is syntactically inflexible. In (4–69), then, the secondary predicate is the complex predicate *a pearl of a sister* and it is L-marked (by *consider*); thus it presents no problem for Proviso One.

The situation in (4–70) is similar. *A charlatan of a historian* is a complex predicate with a subject role player, *Bill*. Here the complex predicate is not L-marked, but its srp is L-marked by the N *discussion* – thus, this example is perfectly consistent with Proviso One. (Again, it makes no sense to talk about *charlatan* as a predicate in isolation.)

Our construction, then, will never present a problem for Proviso One.

In sum, our construction is consistent with the theory of predication put forth in chapter 2.

1.4   Our NP is a normal NP

In chapter 1, section 2.3 we argued that the specifier of an NP can bear a theta role assigned to it by the head N. In Chomsky's (1986a) terms, such a specifier must be the subject argument of the head N (since subject is defined as the X″ immediately dominated by X″). Certain questions now face us.

First, one might try to revive the structure given in (4–33) above – the appositive structure – for our construction, on the grounds that if *of* is a Case marker which is not a P, then the structure of (4–72) would allow us to predict that the NP Case marked by *of* is the subject of the overall NP, since this N″ would be immediately dominated by N″.

(4–72)

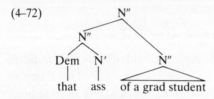

However, the revival of this analysis will lead only to new problems. For example, in (4–73) both *John* and *a brother* would qualify as a subject argument for *ass*.

(4–73)   John's ass of a brother

Also, in (4–72), since the overall NP has two daughters both of which are N″, we have no way of determining which should be the subject of the other. Thus, I maintain the conclusion reached in section 1.2 above: that (4–2) is the proper analysis of our construction.

Another question that now faces us is why (4–74) cannot be understood as semantically similar to (4–75).

(4–74)   my brother's fool

(4–75)   that fool of my brother

Example (4–74) means that fool that my brother knows or leads around or has many other possible relationships to, except the relationship of identity: (4–74) does not mean that my brother is a fool. This question is, of course, the same as that posed by Higginbotham (1985), and which we already have raised twice before in this book (see ch. 1, sec. 2.3 and ch. 2, sec. 10). As I stated earlier, the subject role player of a predicative N may not appear in specifier position in our special NPs. I do not know whether this has to do with restrictions on indices or something else.

What we can see, however, is that our NP is just a regular NP. The head N takes its subject argument (which in this case is also its subject role player) as a sister in an *of* phrase, just as other Ns do:

(4–76)   that photo of John's
         the death of John
         that lecture of John's

So no special rules of the grammar are needed to account for our NPs.

2   Complex nominals

One of the most striking differences between the English construction discussed in section 1 above and its Italian counterpart discussed in chapter 3 is that the English construction is limited to having indefinite NPs in the *of* phrase and is limited to only singular NPs, at least in American speech. I contend that the reason for this is that the base-generated English construction with a definite NP in the *of* phrase and the base-generated plural English construction are obligatorily mapped into complex nominals in Phonological Form. I will now argue for this position.

We can start by noting that the Italian construction with a definite NP following *di* does, in fact, have an English counterpart in certain complex nominals. We have seen many of these already in the English glosses of the Italian examples of chapter 3. In all of these the first element of the complex nominal is an N that describes a quality or property that can be assigned only by way of an evaluative judgment. And in American speech the second element of the complex nominal is a proper name, and its referent is understood to have the property described by the first element. Thus the second element is predicated of by the first element.

(4–77)   that madman George
         that dumbo Paul
         that cheater Marta

The second element need not be a simple one-word name; it can be a multiple word name.

(4–78)   that madman Henry the Fourth
         that fool Big Bill

And the second element can have a specifier on it if the specifier is considered part of the title. Example (4–79) was suggested to me by Andrew Radford (personal communication); examples like (4–80), by Dick Hudson (personal communication).

(4–79)   that madman the King

(4–80)   that villain our Prime Minister

In British speech, the second element need not be a proper name. Thus both Dick Hudson and Andrew Radford accept (4–81).

(4–81)   that fool the doctor

While Americans I have asked accept (4–79) and (4–80), none accepts (4–81). (Notice that (4–81) should be read with the intonation of a complex nominal, that is, without a pause after *fool*.) I will restrict my analysis below to the American complex nominal, for which the analysis will work rather neatly. The British construction differs from the American one in ways crucial to the analysis I am proposing here, and it may well be that a quite different analysis must be posed for the British construction. Below (as I did in section 1 above) I indicate the data differences I have come across between British and American English regarding these constructions.

The American complex nominal under consideration here, then, requires that if the second element of the complex nominal is definite, it be a proper name.

Just as with the Italian, these definite complex nominals tend to be used most with negative evaluative judgment Ns as the first N of the complex nominal:

(4–82)   ??that gem Bill

(British speakers do not seem to have this restriction; they find (4–82) perfectly natural.) Thus these complex nominals tend to be used as insults.

The English complex nominal, however, need not be limited to only an overall definite NP. Thus if the second item of the complex nominal is definite, the overall complex nominal is definite. But if the second item of the complex nominal is indefinite, the overall complex nominal can be definite or indefinite.

(4–83)   *a madman George
          that madman George

(4–84)   {a/my} busybody neighbor
          {a/that} busybody neighbor
          {some/that} jerk lawyer
          {an/that} ignoramus doctor
          {What an/That} idiot mailman!
          {a/that} sneak office mate
          {a/that} bumpkin director
          {a/that} scoundrel dean

{a/that} fool brother of mine
{a/that} complainer brother of mine
{a/that} crook chairman

The data in (4–83) and (4–84) reflect precisely the same restriction we saw in the Italian data, (3–123) through (3–126) of chapter 3: when the NP following *di* is definite, the overall NP must be definite; but when the NP following *di* is indefinite, the overall NP can be definite or indefinite. And the same explanation offered for the Italian data will suffice here: the second item of the complex nominal is the crucial one for determining the reference of the overall complex nominal. That is, the second item is the semantic head of the complex nominal. In this way complex nominals are like compounds (see Selkirk (1982, p. 20) and Zwicky (1985, p. 18), who looks at both English and German). Let us take a closer look at how the explanation runs for our complex nominals.

First, let us consider the complex nominals in which the second element is definite. These complex nominals can be used only referentially. And it is the second element that is most important in determining the referent. Thus in (4–83) *that madman George* is the person George who has the property of being a madman. Since it is the person George, the overall NP must be definite. Therefore the initial specifier (in American English, the only specifier) must be definite.

Now let us look at complex nominals in which the second item is indefinite, as in (4–84): {*a/that*} *crook chairman*. These complex nominals can be used predicatively or referentially. We have seen above already that when determining whether an NP is used predicatively or not, we are influenced by the specifier: an indefinite NP is more likely to be interpreted as a predicate than a definite determiner. However, a definite determiner is possible, too, particularly in superlatives (see ch. 1, sec. 1.3 and the references given there).

(4–85) Gus is a fool doctor.
        Gus is the worst fool doctor I know.

Thus the predicative use allows the NP to be definite or, more typically, indefinite.

We can now consider the referential use of a complex nominal like that in (4–84), in which the second element is indefinite. These complex nominals refer to a person who has the property indicated by the sense of the second element of the complex nominal and who in having this property is assigned the additional property of the sense of the first item of the complex nominal. That is, when the second element is indefinite, these complex nominals have the same interpretation that the NPs studied in section 1 above have. Therefore, the whole complex nominal. can be definite or indefinite, depending on its use in the context external to the complex nominal.

The data in (4–83) and (4–84) are, therefore, explained by considerations already quite familiar to the reader.

The English complex nominal also has another semantic possibility: when the second item of the complex nominal is indefinite, the complex nominal can be plural.

(4–86)   some jerk students
          those fool doctors
          most scoundrel lawyers
          those cretin boys

(4–87)a. *those jerk Bill and Paul
     b.   those jerks Bill and Paul

In (4–87)a we see that the definite complex nominal is not allowed in the plural. Example (4–87)a contrasts with (4–87)b; that is, given that the first element of a complex nominal is always singular (see the discussion of (4–96)–(4–97) below), (4–87)b must not be a complex nominal (but an appositive instead).

Recall now that the English NP studied in section 1 above differed from the Italian one of chapter 3 in two major ways: first, the NP following *of* could not be definite; second, the overall NP could not be plural. We can see from (4–77) through (4–87) above that the English complex nominal has all the semantic possibilities of the NP of section 1, plus it has all the semantic possibilities of the Italian NP of chapter 3, including the ability to have a definite NP as the second element and the ability to be plural.

I propose that the English complex nominal under examination here is derived from an underlying NP in which we have a head N with a right sister NP, where the head N is a predicate taking the sister NP as its subject role player. In other words, I propose that the complex nominal of this section be derived from the same source as the NP studied in section 1 above. With this analysis the English NP studied in section 1 above has all the possibilities that the Italian NP studied in chapter 3 has at the DS level. The differences, then, are only at the PF level.

Notice that in section 1 above, nothing crucial to my analysis (or to the implications for predication theory) rested upon the analysis of *of* as a preposition present from the base on. We realized above that *of* in these NPs is the null P – a common Case marker. Since Case Theory applies in the PF, we could allow NP right sisters of a head N to be base generated without the *of*. The base structure for the NPs of section 1 would then be as in:

(4–88)

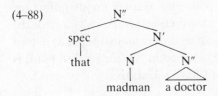

Once we reach SS, the structure in (4–88) needs to be mapped into a well-formed structure in PF. There are two ways that this can happen. One way is to add the null P *of*, to yield the type of NP studied in section 1 above.

(4–89)

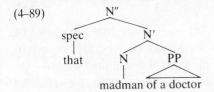

The other way is to restructure into a complex nominal.

(4–90)

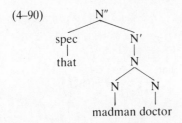

The rule mapping (4–88) into (4–90) would result in the deletion of the indefinite specifier *a*. This mapping would be an example of the Mapping Principle proposed in Marantz (1984b), whereby sisters in morphological structure must be concatenated in phonological structure.

Notice that with the above analysis I am arguing that the structure in (4–88) is the structure at DS and at SS. Since SS is the input level to LF and LF is the input level to Predicate Structure, (4–88) rather than (4–89) is the input structure for our NPs of section 1 to the Predicate Structure. This change in no way affects the conclusions of section 1, since we were careful there to make none of our arguments hinge upon the analysis of the *of* phrase as a PP in SS. What was crucial was that the material following the head N should be attached as a sister to N under N', and not as a sister to N' or as a sister to N". Thus the analysis in (4–88) changes nothing substantive from section 1.

Here let me take a moment to point out again a major difference between the American and British constructions. In British English the second element of our construction can be the pronoun *one* – thus it must be an N", not an N. Example (4–91) is good in British English but it is rejected by every American speaker I have asked (thus the asterisk):

(4–91)   *If he's a doctor, he must be a bit of a madman one, because he tells all his patients there's nothing wrong with them.

(Example (4–91) was offered to me by Andrew Radford (personal communication).) Notice that the fact that (4–91) is accepted in British English is consistent with the fact that (4–81) above is also accepted by British speakers.

Returning to our discussion of (4–88), we can see that the choice of mapping (4–88) into (4–89) or (4–90) would be free. However, in American speech, if the NP sister to the head N is definite, there is only one possible mapping: that into (4–90). Example (4–92)a, then, can be mapped only into the complex nominal in (4–92)b, and not into the NP in (4–93).

(4–92)a.

(4–93)   *that madman of George

I propose that the application of the mapping rule that takes (4–92)a into the complex nominal in (4–92)b is obligatory because there is no element that intervenes linearly between the head N of the overall NP and the head N of its sister NP in (4–92)a. Therefore, the terminal string of (4–92)a has the two head Ns adjacent before the mapping rule even applies, so it already has what we might consider the canonical form of a complex nominal. While in (4–88) the minimal intervenor *a* allowed two different mappings into PF, in (4–92)a the lack of an intervenor requires the complex nominal mapping.

We predict, then, that if an indefinite NP occurs as the right sister of the head N without a specifier of its own, the mapping into a complex nominal will also be obligatory. And it is.

(4–94)

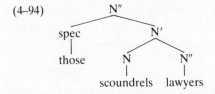

(4–95)   those scoundrel lawyers

(4–96)   *those scoundrels of lawyers

As with other types of complex nominals in English, the number of the complex nominal gets spelled out on the second element, rather than on both elements in (4–95). We see other types of complex nominals in (4–97), where the plural marker is on the second element.

(4–97)   some office desks (*some offices desks)
          many choir boys (*many choirs boys)
          five tool chests (*five tools chests)

We now have an explanation for the absence of plural NPs of the type studied in section 1 above: they are obligatorily mapped into complex nominals.

Given our analysis of these complex nominals, we expect that if the right NP sister to the head N in the base is a coordinated NP, even if no specifier appears, the mapping into a complex nominal will be blocked. This is because there is no way for the terminal string to be restructured into just two Ns in a row. And this is true.

(4–98)

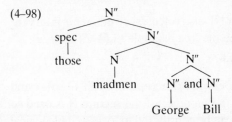

Example (4–98), if it could be mapped into a complex nominal, would be mapped into (4–99), with a singular first element of the complex nominal (see also (4–87)a versus (4–87)b).

(4–99)   *those madman George and Bill
(cf. the appositive: those madmen George and Bill)

The mapping rule into a complex nominal allows *a* to intervene between the two head Ns (as in (4–88), which is optionally mapped into (4–90)), but nothing else. Hence, the head N may have no sisters to its right that intervene between it and its subject role player.

(4–100)   *a wimp beyond belief professor

The ungrammaticality of (4–100) is totally expected, given that even the corresponding regular NP of section 1 disallowed modifiers of the head N in that position (see (4–40)b above).

(4–101)   *a wimp beyond belief of a professor

That is, as we saw at the end of section 1.3 above, there is a strong tendency for the NPs of the type studied in section 1 to have the predicate as linearly close to its subject role player as possible.

Given our explanation for (4–100), we expect that if the head N has a modifier that is so often used with that given head that they can be considered to form a single lexical item, the mapping into a complex nominal will not be blocked. And it is not.

(4–102)   that pain in the ass neighbor
that pain in the neck neighbor

And NPs of the type in section 1 also allow these post-head modifiers:

(4–103)   that pain in the ass of a neighbor

We also expect, then, that if the NP right sister of the head N has a left modifier, the mapping into a complex nominal will be blocked. And it is.

(4–104)   *that fool aging doctor

Again, the corresponding regular NP also rejects such elements intervening between the two head Ns (see the first example of (4–27) above).

(4–105)   *that fool of an aging doctor

(Once more, British speech differs here, accepting both (4–104) and (4–105).) On the other hand, if the modifier of the second N is used so often with that given N that they can be considered to form a single lexical item, the mapping rule should not be blocked. And it is not.

(4–106) that jerk [rookie cop] (cf. that jerk of a rookie cop)
that nervous Nellie [new mother] (cf. that nervous Nellie of a new mother)

There are other factors that affect the grammaticality of a resulting complex nominal. And all of them are mirrored in the corresponding regular NP studied in section 1 above. For example, the NP right sister to the head N rejects right sisters of its own head N to varying degrees, just as the NP in the *of* phrase in the NPs of section 1 does. Compare (4–107) to (4–26) above.

(4–107) *What a creep professor with tenure!
??What a creep teacher of physics!

Another restriction is that the first element resists having a modifying AP preceding it:

(4–108) *that terrific scoundrel lawyer

And the corresponding regular NP does, as well.

(4–109) *that terrific scoundrel of a lawyer

(Again, British speech accepts (4–108)–(4–109).) But whenever such an AP is accepted in the complex nominal, it is accepted in the corresponding regular NP.

(4–110) a real quack anesthesiologist
a lame duck president

(4–111) a real quack of an anesthesiologist
a lame duck of a president

The data in (4–100) through (4–111) establish that the restrictions on our complex nominals follow from restrictions on the corresponding regular NPs of the type studied in section 1. One might object to this generalization on the basis of examples like (4–112) compared to (4–113).

(4–112) that fool brother of hers

(4–113) *that fool of a brother of hers

(British speech accepts (4–113).) But the difference between (4–112) and (4–113) may be related to the fact that the NPs of section 1, always having an indefinite NP after the *of*, can be interpreted in two ways. One of those ways is with the NP after the *of* in its property sense. That is, (4–114) can mean that person who in his capacity as a priest is a rogue. (See the discussion of the semantics of (4–18) in sec. 1 above.)

(4–114) that rogue of a priest

Example (4–113), then, may fail on semantic grounds because it is not open to this interpretation: being a brother of someone is not the kind of capacity in which someone can be a fool. The set of brothers of a particular person is just too small a set to be open to this interpretation. However, we can say:

(4–115) that fool of a brother

to mean that person who in the capacity of being a brother is a fool (as well as to mean that person who is a brother and who happens to be a fool).

The complex nominal, on the other hand, does not require that two readings be associated with it. In fact, since the second element can be a proper name, which surely is not a property, the property reading is quite obviously not required.

(4–116) that madman John

Example (4–116) does not signify that person who in the capacity of being John is a madman. Instead, it signifies that John is a madman. Thus (4–112) is fine, since it signifies that that brother of hers is a fool.

In general, then, restrictions on the complex nominal follow from restrictions on the corresponding regular NP, although the corresponding regular NP has the added, and significant, restriction that the NP after the *of* must be indefinite and must be able to be understood in its property sense (although it is not limited to this sense).

The fact that the above restrictions on complex nominals are mirrored by the same restrictions on regular NPs is strong evidence that these complex nominals are derived from the corresponding regular NPs. And I refer the reader to Sproat (1985), who argues for a synthetic rather than lexical analysis of several types of compounds. Furthermore, Fabb (1984) has argued that only idiosyncratic processes belong in the lexicon. Therefore, if Fabb is correct, the productivity of our complex nominals would require that they be generated after the lexicon.

I conclude that the derivation of our complex nominals from the type of NP studied in section 1 is correct.

There are several big questions facing us now.

First, American English rejects definite NPs from the *of* phrase in the regular NPs of section 1.

(4–117) *that fool of the doctor

American English also rejects definite NPs other than proper names (plus titles) from our complex nominals.

(4–118)   *that fool the doctor

(4–119)   that fool Dr. Jeffers

But Italian accepts definite NPs in the *di* phrase of the NPs studied in chapter 3.

(4–120)   quel fesso del dottore
          'that dumbo (of the) doctor'

The question is why there is this difference in the two languages.

The answer to this question is a mystery to me. The problem is in the English, not in the Italian. That is, we have no reason to expect NPs of the form in (4–117) and (4–118) to be ungrammatical. And, in fact, as I pointed out above, complex nominals like (4–118) are accepted in British English, although they are rejected in American English. However, even British English rejects (4–117). Still, the contrast in acceptability in American English between (4–112) (*that fool brother of hers*) and (4–113) (**that fool of a brother of hers*) suggests that the filtering out of definites in the NPs after *of* is done in the LF. This seems to be a gap in the range of NP structures of English. In chapter 5, section 1 we will see that English does allow a definite NP following *of* to be the subject argument of a predicate head N all within the same overall NP. But in these examples of chapter 5 the head N is never one whose sense involves an evaluative judgment. Immediately below, I suggest that the reanalysis rule which forms complex nominals is obligatory when the head N is one whose sense involves an evaluative judgment. In a strict sense, this suggestion can be seen as an answer to the first question. However, then the question becomes one of why the reanalysis rule is obligatory when the head N is of a certain semantic type. And I have no answer to that question.

Second, we may ask why Italian lacks complex nominals of the type found in English.

(4–121)   *quel matto Giorgio
          'that madman George'

(4–122)   *quell'idiota elettricista
          'that idiot electrician'

(As with the English complex nominals, the reader must be cautioned to pronounce the examples in (4–121) and (4–122) without a pause after the first element of the complex nominal. Without a pause, these examples are bad in Italian. With a pause, they are good, but irrelevantly (for us) so, since they are then examples of appositives. See ch. 5, sec. 5.) The answer is, I believe, forthcoming.

In the Italian NP all evidence suggests that the *di* is present from the DS on (see ch. 3, sec. 2.2). The most pertinent evidence here is that inflected Ps, which are generated in the lexicon and are not the result of any morphosyntactic or morphophonological process (see Napoli and Nevis (1987)), occur in our NPs.

(4–123) quel fesso del dottore
         'that fool of the doctor'

These inflected Ps select N' rather than N'' complements. Thus we could not insert them at PF. Therefore, we have a *di* or its inflected form right from the start at DS.

Now there are two possibilities in Italian. One is that Italian does have synthetic processes for forming complex nominals. If so, then the presence of the *di* or its inflected form in SS would block any mapping rule in PF from the NP in (4–123) into a complex nominal.

The other possibility is that Italian does not have synthetic processes for forming complex nominals. I believe this to be the correct possibility, since compounding and complex nominal formation in Italian is idiosyncratic rather than productive. With this possibility there is simply no mechanism available in PF to map an NP like that in (4–123) into a complex nominal.

I would like to speculate for a moment about why Italian might not have developed a mapping rule for complex nominals similar to the English mapping rule. I suggest the answer is that the phrase-structure rules for Italian do not favor the canonical string needed for this kind of mapping rule – which is, in essence, a restructuring rule (of the branching relationships). That is, in English only right-branching modifiers of N follow N – and right-branching modifiers are much less frequent than nonbranching or left-branching modifiers. (For example, an A with a specifier is a more commonly found AP than an A with a following argument sister.) Therefore, in English a head N with a sister NP is most frequently going to be followed immediately by that sister with no intervening modifier. But in Italian modifiers of N may precede or follow N – and even modifiers that do not branch or that branch to the right can follow the head N. Therefore, in Italian a head N with a sister NP can very easily be separated from that complement by an intervening modifier, as in (3–24) of chapter 3, repeated here.

(3–24) quel cafone ripulito di Giorgio
        'that polished-up bumpkin George'

My proposal is that since the string [. . . N NP . . .] is not particularly favored in frequency by the PS rules in Italian but it is in English, the restructuring rule did not arise naturally in Italian whereas it did in English. (Notice that in both languages the possibility of a specifier and/or a modifier preceding the head N of the sister NP (that is, the contained NP) is high.)

A third question is how we can restrict our mapping rule so that it applies precisely when it should and not otherwise. This question, like the first, is hard to answer. But it is not a total mystery.

First of all, the mapping rule in question applies only when the head N of the regular NP is a predicate that allows only one role player. Thus it applies to (4–124) and (4–125), but not to (4–126).

(4–124) that [$_{N'}$ fool [$_{N''}$ a doctor]] ——▶
              that [$_N$ fool doctor]
         (cf. that fool of a doctor)
(4–125) the [$_{N'}$ little town [$_{N''}$ Framura]] ——▶
              the little [$_N$ town Framura]
         (cf. the little town of Framura)
(4–126) the [$_{N'}$ destruction [$_{N''}$ Rome]] —⁄—▶
              *the [$_N$ destruction Rome]
         (cf. the destruction of Rome
         the Huns' destruction of Rome)
         that [$_{N'}$ photograph [$_{N''}$ Bill's]] —⁄—▶
              *that [$_N$ photograph Bill's]
         (cf. that photograph of Bill's
         that photograph of Bill's of the London zoo)

We have argued already in section 1 above that the head N in (4–124) is a predicate. We will argue in chapter 5, section 1 that the head N in (4–125) is a predicate. And we have argued in chapter 1, section 2.3 that the head Ns in (4–126) are predicates. But the predicates in (4–124)–(4–125) are monadic, and those in (4–126) are not (see also ch. 1, sec. 1.5, where implicit arguments are discussed).

Certainly, since predicates are identified in Predicate Structure, which is read off of LF, our mapping rule must be from a structure no earlier than PS into phonological form.

Second, our mapping rule cannot apply to a predicative N whose internal srp could not be the external srp in a copular sentence.

(4-127) the [$_{N'}$ death [$_{N''}$ John]] ⟶̸⟶
                   *the [$_N$ death John]
      (cf. the **death** of John

      but not: *John is death. (in the relevant sense))

The third point is that our mapping rule applies obligatorily when the NP right sister to the head N is definite if the head N expresses an evaluative judgment. Otherwise the mapping rule is optional.

(4-128) *that fool of John
         that fool John

(4-129) the city of Sassari
         the city Sassari

Whether the identification of an evaluative term is in the lexicon or in LF, the distinction can certainly be made by the level of Predicate Structure (where I argue in ch. 5, secs. 2 and 5 that Predicate Structure is read off of LF), so our mapping rule faces no new problems here.

Before we leave this section, let me point out that I am not advocating a synthetic rather than lexical analysis of all complex nominals, but only of those studied here. Complex nominals in general in English display an exceedingly wide range of semantic relationships between the two items of the complex nominal. (See Levi 1978, from which some of the examples below are drawn.)

(4-130) a crank letter
         sand dune
         abortion vote
         leg man
         salary increase

The range of semantic relationships found between the two items of complex nominals is perhaps as great as the range of semantic relationships found between the two elements of nonverbal compounds. Selkirk (1982, p. 25) believes "it is a mistake to attempt to characterize the grammar of the semantics of nonverbal compounds in any way." She refers us to Downing (1977), who also recognizes the infeasibility of such a task. I heed their warning.

Our complex nominal, however, is quite restrictive in its possible semantic interpretations and is clearly derived from the corresponding NP in section 1.

I would like to close this section by noting that the complex nominal here poses no problem for the theory of predication put forth in chapter 2, since at PS it has precisely the same structure as the NPs studied in section 1 above.

3 Conclusion

The NPs studied in this chapter pose serious problems for many theories of predication, but they are perfectly consistent with the theory of predication presented in chapter 2.

English and Italian are not the only languages with this construction. It occurs in Spanish and in French. It also occurs, though with some additional constraints, in Japanese nominals containing an NP having the particle *no* (as Gen Isoe (personal communication) tells me). This phenomenon, then, is not some quirk of Italian and English. It is a common construction. And it offers strong support for my theory of predication.

5 A brief look at five more constructions

Works on predication have tended to handle only a small range of types of data. In chapter 2 we looked at the typical types of constructions analyzed in these works. In chapters 3 and 4 we examined NPs that to my knowledge have not been discussed previously with respect to the import of their analysis for predication theory. There are a variety of other constructions in both Italian and English which reasonably can be argued to involve the subject role player–predicate relationship and which traditionally have not been discussed in works on predication. In this chapter I briefly discuss only five such constructions (although there are many), all of which present problems for other theories of predication, but call for no changes in the theory of predication put forth in this book.

The discussions here are suggestive of possible analyses rather than in-depth studies (in contrast to the analyses of just a single construction in both chapters 3 and 4), and I hope to convince the reader only that these constructions deserve further examination with the issue of predication in mind. Thus, while the brevity of the analyses in this chapter may make them appear speculative, I offer them quite seriously as a program for future research.

1   NPs like *la città di Sassari*

NPs of the form *la città di Sassari* ('the city of Sassari') differ from the Italian NPs of chapter 3 and from the English NPs of chapter 4, sec. 1 in requiring that the NP following *di/of* within the overall NP be definite. Furthermore, the English counterpart NPs, such as *the city of Sassari*, optionally undergo restructuring to form complex nominals (as in *the city Sassari* – see the discussion of (4–129) at the end of ch. 4, sec. 2), whereas the NPs of the type studied in chapter 4 that have a definite NP right sister to the head N obligatorily undergo restructuring. The only difference I have been able to find between the two NPs in English that would account for their different behavior with respect to the formation of complex nominals is the sense of the head N: when the head N is one of an evaluative judgment, then restructuring is obligatory if the NP right sister of that head N is definite.

In chapter 3, section 3.1, however, we noted that NPs like *la città di Sassari*, in both English and Italian, have some syntactic properties in common with NPs like *quel matto di Giorgio* (that is, their syntactic inflexibility; see the discussion of (3–104)). In fact, as Dick Hudson (personal communication) has pointed out to me, they also have significant semantic properties in common. The NP following *di/of* in these NPs is taken to be a member of the set denoted by the head N. In this way we can see the head N as assigning a property (of set containment) to the NP following *di*. And sometimes in the English phenomenon, the NP following *of* fills the set denoted by the head N, as in:

(5–1)   *the three of us*

(called the "appositional use" in Jespersen 1905, but for which we could use the same tests employed in chs. 3 and 4 to show it is not syntactically an appositive). We, therefore, have another instance of the subject role player–predicate relationship within an NP, although this particular type of predication, the set relationship type, is very close to an identification or alternative description relationship, as discussed in chapter 1, section 1.3. In what follows the remarks hold equally for Italian and English, as the glosses of the Italian examples show.

(5–2)   La teoria della relatività ci affascina.
         'The theory of relativity fascinates us.'

(5–3)   Il concetto di giustizia deve sopravvivere.
         'The concept of justice must survive.'

The initial N in (5–2) tells us that relativity is a theory. That is, *teoria* is predicated of (*la*) *relatività*. The initial N in (5–3) tells us that justice is a concept. Again, *concetto* is predicated of (*la*) *giustizia*. But the structure of these NPs does not require this semantic relationship between the NP following *di* and its head N left sister. Instead, these are just regular NPs with the full range of possible semantic relationships between the head N and its sisters that we expect in all NPs. For example, in (5–4) *della relatività* characterizes the type of theories at issue, just as *blue* characterizes the type of shades in a regular NP such as *shades of blue*. And in (5–5), *della relatività* bears the theta role of theme with respect to the head N *distruzione*.

(5–4)   (una fra) le teorie della relatività
      '(one among) the theories of relativity'

(5–5)   la distruzione della relatività
      'the destruction of relativity'

Taking the NP in GF subject position in (5–2) as an instance of predication, we see that these NPs present the same problems for other theories of predication that the NPs studied in chapters 3 and 4 presented. And, just as with the NPs in chapters 3 and 4, neither of these types of NP is a problem for the theory of predication put forth in chapter 2.

2   Sentential complements of N

We have seen that an NP sister to a head N that is a predicate can be the subject role player of that predicate. We also have seen that NP sisters to a head N can have other relationships with the head N: they can be any argument of that head N and they can modify that head N. Since there is nothing special about the category NP as opposed to the category C″ that allows this versatility, we expect to find clausal sisters to a head N that have the same range of semantic relations toward the head N that nominal sisters have. And we do find some likely candidates, but they are extremely limited.

Many examples that at first seem to be instances of the subject role player–predicate relationship are, in fact, not. For example:

(5–6)   la bugia perfida che i linguisti bevano tutti la benzina
      'the treacherous lie that linguists all drink gasoline'

(5–7)   l'idea che Nicola possa vincere
      'the idea that Nicola may win'

In (5–6) one might posit that the clause is the subject role player of the head N and its modifying adjective. That is, that the proposition expressed in the clause is a treacherous lie. In (5–7) one might posit that the proposition expressed in the clause is a member of the set denoted by the head N. That is, the proposition that Nicola may win is hypothetical; it is an idea. Again, this looks like a predication relation. One could go further and contrast these examples to NPs such as:

(5–8)   la prova che le mosche sono mammiferi
      'the proof that flies are mammals'

(5–9)   la prova che Ugo ha presentato
      'the proof that Ugo presented'

In (5–8) the clause specifies what someone has proven. Thus the clause here is an argument of the head N but it is not the srp (which is an implicit argument here; see ch. 1, sec. 1.5). And in (5–9) the clause modifies the head N.

In support of the analysis of a predication structure in (5–6) and (5–7) one might use the observation made in Safir (1985, p. 69) – that DO clausal arguments of a head N cannot be separated from their head Ns in a copular construction. By this test the clauses in (5–6) and (5–7) could not be DOs.

(5–10) La bugia perfida fu che i linguisti bevano tutti la benzina.
    'The treacherous lie was that linguists all drink gasoline.'

(5–11) L'idea è che Nicola possa vincere.
    'The idea is that Nicola might win.'

Contrast (5–10)–(5–11) to (5–12), where we do have a clear DO clause:

(5–12) l'insistere che fosse un mio amico
    'the insistence that he was a friend of mine'

(5–13) *L'insistere era che fosse un mio amico.
    *'The insistence was that he was a friend of mine.'

However, with Safir's test (which he, actually, did not offer as a test, but only as an observation), we predict that the clause in (5–8) could not be separated from its head N, since this surely is a DO clause. Yet it can be so separated:

(5–14) La (sua) prova fu che le mosche sono mammiferi.
    'His proof was that flies are mammals.'

Safir's test, then, is inconclusive. So (5–6) and (5–7) could involve DO clauses, after all.

I contend, in fact, that neither (5–6) nor (5–7) provides an example of the subject role player–predicate relationship. Instead, they have a head N with a DO clause. We can see this by contrasting them to:

(5–15) la bugia perfida di Michele che i linguisti bevano tutti la benzina
    'the treacherous lie of Michele's that linguists all drink gasoline'

(5–16) l'idea di Elena che Nicola possa vincere
    'the idea of Elena's that Nicola might win'

In (5–15) *Michele* is the subject argument of the head N; in (5–16), *Elena* is the subject argument of the head N (see Cinque 1980 plus relevant discussion in ch. 1, sec. 2.3, and in ch. 3).

There are, however, examples of head Ns that take clause arguments where the clause could reasonably be analyzed as the subject argument of the head N and where the head N could reasonably be analyzed as predicative, so that its subject argument would be its subject role player. Consider (5–17), where (5–17)b was suggested to me by Raffaella Zanuttini (personal communication):

(5–17)a. Odia [il fatto che non potrà mai più insegnare la sintassi].
          'She hates [the fact that she can't teach syntax anymore].'
       b. Al contrario di me, lui è convinto [del fatto che Dio esista].
          'In contrast to me, he is convinced of [the fact that God exists].'

In (5–17)a what she hates is the proposition that she cannot teach syntax anymore, which I am characterizing as a fact. In (5–17)b what he is convinced of is that God exists, which I can characterize as a fact relative to his conviction, even though the use of the subjunctive here shows that I, the speaker, do not assert the truth of this clause. (See Napoli and Nespor 1976 for a discussion of how the speaker's and the GF subject's attitudes affect the mood of embedded clauses in Italian.) This function of *fatto* as characterizing its sister clause constitutes predication.

Notice further that *fatto* can take no other role players. Thus (5–17) has no counterpart to the examples in (5–15)–(5–16) above:

(5–18)   *il fatto di Tommaso che non posso insegnare
          *'the fact of Tommaso's that I can't teach'

So *fatto*, like the predicative head Ns of the NPs studied in chapters 3 and 4, takes only one role player: its srp.

Thus, once again we find an instance of the subject role player–predicate relationship inside an NP between the head N and its sister XP.

The analysis of the bracketed NP in (5–17) that takes the clause to be a sister to the head N is by no means uncontroversial (and see Matthews 1981, pp. 225 ff. for a quick but very useful analysis of the problems involved in determining structure here). As I have pointed out repeatedly, many have taken the position that N' can have a variety of sisters (not just conjuncts and specifiers) and even that N" can have a variety of sisters (not just conjuncts) under an immediate mother N" node. This is not the version of X-bar theory that I am using, as I have stated repeatedly. I am assuming a restrictive X-bar theory, in which X" has no sisters (other than conjuncts), and the only sister of X' is its specifier (or conjuncts). With this restrictive version of X-bar theory, the C" following the head N in all of (5–6) through (5–9) plus (5–12), and (5–

15) through (5–18) must be a sister of that head N (and this is the structure Chomsky (1986b, p. 81) assigns such NPs). For us the crucial NP to analyze the internal structure of, however, is only that in (5–17) – that is, the NP that involves the subject role player–predicate relationship.

Since many have assumed a less restrictive version of X-bar theory, however, I will consider the alternative analyses and show that they are not to be preferred. The discussion here will be very brief; for a justification of the tests used here, for more extended discussion, and for additional tests that one could use in comparing these analyses, see chapter 3, section 2.4 and chapter 4, section 1.2.4.

The analyses to consider are:

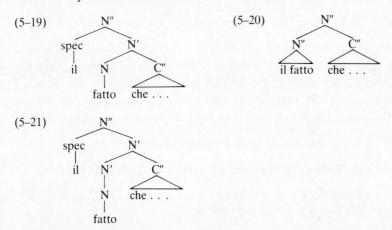

Example (5–20) is the type of structure given in Jackendoff (1977) for appositives to NP. This structure cannot be correct for our NPs, since a restrictive relative clause can follow the relevant clause, but restrictive relatives never can follow appositives.

(5–22)   Il fatto che i linguisti bevono tutti la benzina che quello stupido di
          Carmine vi ha detto deve rimanere un segreto.
          'The fact that linguists all drink gasoline that that idiot Carmine told you
          must remain a secret.'

Example (5–21) is the type of structure given in Jackendoff (1977) for restrictive modifiers of a head N. This structure cannot be correct for our NPs, since the clause does not function as a restrictive modifier of the head N. Notice that restrictive relative clauses cannot be separated from their nominal head in a copular construction, but the clause of (5–17) can be.

(5–23)   *La prova fu che Ugo ha presentato. [cf. (5–9)]
*'The proof was that Ugo had presented.'
Il fatto è che i linguisti bevono tutti la benzina.
'The fact is that linguists all drink gasoline.'

Example (5–21), therefore, is not the correct structure for NPs such as that in (5–17).

Example (5–19), then, is the only reasonable analysis of these NPs.

I conclude that head Ns which are predicates can take C″ sisters which serve as their subject role players.

One might object to the above analysis for English on the basis of the fact that we get sentences such as:

(5–24)   The fact upset John that Sam's wife was leaving forever.

(Italian resists extraposition of all sorts – thus there is no really natural counterpart in Italian to (5–24). See Valesio 1974 for a discussion of the failure of extraposition of relative clauses, Guéron 1980 for the failure of extraposition of PPs, and Cinque 1980 for both.) If one took a movement approach to the structure in (5–24), it would be generated from (5–25):

(5–25)   The fact that Sam's wife was leaving forever upset John.

But with this source the ungrammaticality of (5–26) is unexplained:

(5–26)   *That jerk came in of a doctor.
(cf. That jerk of a doctor came in.)

Recall that in chapter 4 (and in ch. 3 for the Italian examples) we accounted for the immovability of the *of* phrase in NPs such as that in (5–26) with an explanation that crucially used the fact that *a doctor* is the semantic head of this NP because of the predication relationship. We would therefore expect that the C″ in (5–25), being the semantic head of the NP in GF subject position, should, likewise, be immovable. Yet (5–24) is a good sentence.

There is, however, a movement analysis of (5–24) which would not be problematic in this way. And that is if the movement rule of extraposition did not take place before SS, but after SS in the PF (the phonological branch of the grammar), as a stylistic rule. There is good evidence against this analysis, though, in Culicover and Rochemont (1986).

I contend, therefore, that (5–24) offers one more piece of evidence in favor of the analysis of so-called extraposition sentences as base-generated inside the VP, as in Culicover and Rochemont (1986). Then

(5–24) is base-generated, and we can maintain the claim that the C″ inside the GF subject NP in (5–25) is immovable.

We must now, however, face other problems. If (5–24) is an instance of predication where the NP *the fact* in (5–24), for example, is a predicate and the C″ *that Sam's wife is leaving forever* is its subject role player, we have a violation of Proviso Two in (2–64) of chapter 2, in that the subject role player is separated from its predicate by a barrier (the V″ of the matrix clause) at SS.

There are at least two possible ways out of this problem. One is to analyze (5–24) as having a different semantic relationship between the NP *the fact* and the C″ *that Sam's wife is leaving forever* from that between the head N *fact* and its sister C″ in (5–25). Either the relationship in (5–24) is not one of predication, but of identification (and notice that the NP *the fact* in (5–24) is a definite NP, and as such resists being interpreted as a predicate, whereas in (5–25) only *fact* would be the predicate), or the relationship in (5–24) is one in which the C″ is the predicate and the NP *the fact* is its subject role player. For arguments in favor of the second possibility, see Culicover and Rochemont (1986). To defend this position, one would want to offer evidence that sentences like (5–24) and sentences like (5–25) are not semantically equivalent. I know of no such evidence. Furthermore, the extraposed clause in (5–24) is a closed clause (it contains no variables for role players), and thus it should not be open to an interpretation as a predicate (see ch. 1, secs. 1.1 and 4). (But in favor of the analysis of extraposed clauses as predicates, see Williams 1980.)

Another solution is to follow Guéron and May (1984) in having a rule in LF that constructs a head N-complement relation between the GF subject NP in (5–24) and the final C″. (Guéron and May's rule "reconstructed" the complement relationship, since they were assuming a movement analysis of extraposition structures. However, their claims about LF hold even if so-called extraposed structures are base-generated.) With this analysis we must allow Predicate Structure to be built off of LF; then the same Predicate Structure will be assigned to (5–24), the sentence with so-called extraposition, as to (5–25), the counterpart sentence without extraposition: in both the PS will have the C″ as a complement to the head N *fact*. Therefore, (5–24) and sentences like it will be no problem for Proviso Two, after all.

Yet another question comes up: that of whether or not this analysis (and Guéron and May's approach in general) is a violation of the

Projection Principle, as Ken Hale (personal communication) has pointed out to me. To answer this one needs to compare an explicit statement of the Projection Principle (see ch. 1, sec. 4) with a detailed account of precisely how the derivation outlined here would proceed. I suspect that this analysis can be consistent with the Projection Principle, particularly in light of the fact that Chomsky (1986b) sets subject arguments aside as not needing to be syntactically realized; thus they surely need not appear in only certain syntactic positions unless independently motivated principles affect their placement.

Since extraposition structures could form the basis for a much longer study (as the works of Guéron 1980, Guéron and May 1984, and Culicover and Rochemont 1986, among others, show us), I will not pursue this issue further here. Instead, keeping in mind the issues that both analyses must face, I will adopt the second analysis: the one that builds up Predicate Structure from LF and makes use of the complement constructing rule of Guéron and May. I do this for two reasons. First, the alternative solution calls for a semantic distinction between sentences like (5–24) and sentences like (5–25) that is significant and that I have been unable to find evidence for. Furthermore, the idea that a closed clause can be a predicate is simply counter to the entire development of the notion of predicate in chapter 1. And, second, we will see in section 5 below further evidence for complement-constructing rules in LF of the type proposed in Guéron and May. Thus the solution I am adopting here for sentences like (5–24) seems to be a mechanism needed for a range of other phenomena in the grammar.

I conclude that (5–19) is the correct structure for NPs of the type in (5–17) and that these NPs are another example of the predication relation. As such they constitute one more example of an instance of predication that is configurationally a problem for other theories of predication, but not for the one put forth in chapter 2.

Before I leave this section, let me point out two things. First, there is good evidence that the NPs in (5–6)–(5–7), as well as our NP in (5–17), have a head N with a sister clause. Thus these NPs can have a restrictive relative following the C″ – knocking out the structural analysis in (5–20). And these NPs can appear across the copula from the head N (as we saw in (5–10)–(5–11)) – knocking out the structural analysis in (5–21). Therefore, their analysis must be as in (5–19).

With (5–19) as the analysis of (5–6)–(5–7), we can now account for the data in (5–27):

(5–27) *la sua$_i$ idea che Nicola$_i$ possa vincere
       *'his$_i$ idea that Nicola$_i$ might win'

Sua in (5–27) c-commands and is coindexed with *Nicola*. With this reading (5–27) is a violation of part C of the binding theory. If, instead, the C" were attached outside N', we would not expect the ungrammaticality of (5–27).

The single syntactic structure in (5–19), then, is mapped into a range of semantic relationships (a situation we by now expect, given that the same situation was demonstrated for the NPs studied in chs. 3 and 4).

The second thing I would like to point out was brought to my attention by Andrew Radford (personal communication). In Italian (as in other Romance languages), certain nouns which, unmodified, typically take an indicative clausal complement, can, instead, take a subjunctive clausal complement if they are modified by an adjective with certain semantic properties. (For a discussion of the relevant semantic properties see Napoli and Nespor 1976.) For example, in (5–28)a we have an indicative clause, but in (5–28)b we have a subjunctive one:

(5–28)a. l'annuncio che Ugo non è riuscito . . .
         'the announcement that Ugo hasn't succeeded . . .'
      b. l'annuncio ridicolo e falso che Ugo non è riuscito
         'the ridiculous and false announcement that Ugo hasn't succeeded'

One might argue that if one could find a monadic noun which patterned as *annuncio* does in (5–28) (notice that *annuncio*, like *bugia* of (5–6), is not monadic – *l'annuncio di Maria che Ugo non è riuscito*, 'Maria's announcement that Ugo hasn't succeeded'), the fact that the adjective and not the head N determines the mood of the embedded clause would militate against my analysis of clauses like both that in (5–6) and that in (5–25) as being sisters to the head N.

On the contrary, however, such data are entirely expected with my analysis. As I argued in chapter 1, section 1.1, certain modifiers are parts of predicates. Therefore the predicate in the relevant examples would consist of the head N plus its modifying AP. The AP is, then, part of the predicate. Thus there is every reason to expect these APs to be able to affect the mood of any and all role-player clauses of the predicate (that they are a part of), whether those clauses be DOs or srp's or anything else.

3   The "create" examples

There is a third construction in English and Italian that involves the subject role player–predicate relationship, which I call the "create" examples. Let us start with one of the most common types, the *make* construction of English (but not so typical of Italian) found here:

(5–29)a. We made a fool (out) of Mary.
     b. We made an example of Virgil.
     c. We made a dress {out of/from/with} the silk.
     d. We made a mess of the dinner.

Here the NP following (*out*) *of*/*from*/*with* is the subject role player of the predicate *a fool*/*an example*/*a dress*/*a mess*. That is, the semantic relationship between *a dress* and *the silk* in (5–29)c, for example, is the same as that between these same words in (5–30), where (5–30)a is taken from Williams (1980, p. 211), who uses it as an example of the subject–predicate relationship.

(5–30)a. The silk made a fine dress.
     b. We used the silk for a dress.
     c. The silk became a fine dress.

And the selectional restrictions that hold in examples like those in (5–30) also hold in examples like those in (5–29). Thus clearly odd choices in one construction are odd in the other, as well (as in (5–31)a), but choices which are acceptable as metaphors in one are acceptable in the other (as in (5–31)b), as pointed out to me by Andrew Radford (personal communication).

(5–31)a. *We made a dress {out of/from} {the song/Sue's tears/June 14th/the gleam of Ralph's teeth}.
       (cf. *{The song/Sue's tears/June 14th/the gleam of Ralph's teeth} made a fine dress.)
     b. We made a quilt out of nothing at all – some scraps of material left over from all those dresses over the years.
       (cf. We used nothing at all to make a quilt – just some scraps of material left over from all those dresses over the years.)

Notice that while both *of* and *out of* are possible in (5–29)a, only *of* is possible in (5–29)d. Becky Brys (personal communication) suggests that *out of* favors a reading of physical transformation, so that if the predicate is not a physical object, *out of* is strange:

(5–32) The children made fun (*out) of the old man.
       They made light (*out) of the problem.

On the other hand *of* alone is not acceptable in (5–29)c, since the physical transformation is the essence of the predication here. This semantic factor is probably the reason the metaphorical fixed phrases of (5–33) require the *out*. Both of these examples were suggested to me by Becky Brys (personal communication).

(5–33)   You can't make a silk purse *(out) of a sow's ear.
         He makes mountains *(out) of molehills.

One might argue that a string like *make an example of* in (5–29)b can be analyzed as a complex verb (syntactically complex), since there are two passives corresponding to it, as seen in (5–34). (And see analyses of strings like *cut into slices* as complex verbs in Dowty 1979, Randall 1983, Simpson 1983a, and Hale and Keyser 1987 – who also argue that some depictives may be part of complex verbs, as in: *These dishes **stack wet** easily*.)

(5–34)   Virgil was made an example of.
         An example was made of Virgil.

But *the silk* cannot be the GF subject of any passive corresponding to (5–29)c.

(5–35)   *The silk was made a dress {out of/from/with}.

Thus the dual analysis of (5–29)b cannot be the basis for an explanation of the semantic relationships in (5–29).

A proponent of a theory of predication that requires the subject role player to c-command its predicate might try to analyze an example like (5–29)d with an *of* that is a Case marker rather than a real preposition. In this way *of the dinner* in (5–29)d would be a Case marked NP rather than a PP, so the subject role player would, after all, c-command its predicate. However, examples like (5–29)c, with *out, from,* and *with,* certainly could not be analyzed in this way: *out of, from* and *with* are undeniably prepositions. Thus in (5–29) the subject role player does not c-command its predicate.

Notice that the *make* construction in (5–29) is semantically close to the *make* construction with a so-called double object in (5–36)a and to the *make* construction in (5–36)b.

(5–36)a. We'll make you all zombies if you don't act good!
          That film director can make even the girl next door a famous star
          overnight.
      b. We'll make you all into zombies.
          The film director made the girl next door into a famous star.

In (5–36)a the first object is the subject role player of the second object, which is a secondary predicate. In (5–36)b the DO is the subject role player of the secondary predicate, which finds itself in a PP. Evidence for this analysis comes from agreement facts, as Greg Carlson (personal communication) has pointed out to me. Thus, if the srp is plural in (5–36), and if the secondary predicate is a nominal, the secondary predicate must also be plural, just as it must in the predication structure in (5–30)a:

(5–37)a. We'll make {them all/*him} zombies.
  We'll make {*them all/him} a zombie.
  [cf. (5–36)]
   b. {The boys/*The boy} made Mary good housekeepers.
  {*The boys/The boy} made Mary a good housekeeper.
  [cf. (5–30)a]

Thus we see that *make*, the verb that has been the object of much scrutiny in its causative use (*We made John cry*), occurs in a range of syntactic frames with secondary predicates where the subject role player of the secondary predicate is the GF subject (as in (5–30)a), or the DO (as in (5–36)a), or a prepositional object (as in (5–36)b) of *make*.

Once we have recognized (5–29) and (5–36) as instances of secondary predication, we can see that the examples in (5–38), which all involve an act of creation, are also instances of secondary predication. Furthermore, this kind of secondary predication occurs in both Italian and English. I will give the Italian examples, where their English gloss shows the same phenomenon.

(5–38)   Abbiamo ritagliato un vestito da quel pezzo di seta.
  'We cut a dress from that piece of silk.'
  Ha scolpito una statua di marmo di Carrara.
  'He sculpted a statue from the marble of Carrara.'
  La ragazzina ha formato una banana di pongo.
  'The little girl formed a banana out of the clay.'
  Le rondini disperate hanno fatto un nido con lo spago che abbiamo dato loro.
  'The desperate swallows made a nest with the twine we gave them.'

In these "create" examples the subject role player is the object of a preposition (that is, the silk becomes a dress, not vice versa) and does not, therefore, c-command its predicate.

As we expect at this point, these create constructions allow for other semantic relationships beside the predicate–subject relationship between the NP immediately following the create verb and the NP following the preposition.

(5–39)   We cut the dress with finesse.
We built the house with the latest construction techniques.
We sewed the jacket out of desperation.

In (5–39) the PPs are modifiers of the verb and, thus, part of the predicate.

The create examples in (5–29) and (5–38) are a problem for those theories of predication that require the subject role player to c-command its predicate and for the predicate to be bijacent to its subject role player. They are no problem, however, for the theory of predication put forth in chapter 2.

4   Another predication inside NP

Consider the sentences in (5–40).

(5–40)a.   Have I ever shown you these nude pictures of my grandfather?
  b.   Have I ever shown you these pictures of my grandfather nude?

In (5–40)a *nude* predicates of *my grandfather*, not of *pictures*. That is, pictures cannot be nude, but people can. Thus (5–40)a has the same reading as (5–40)b.

One might object to this analysis, since it is common to hear sentences like:

(5–41)   We love nude photographs.

In (5–41) the object of *photographs* is not overt, yet the AP *nude* is still acceptable. And in (5–42) *nude* can be taken to predicate of some missing object of *shots* or even of *Jessica*.

(5–42)   Jessica takes great nude shots.

In fact, we even hear sentences like:

(5–43)   Nude restaurants are the rage.

By (5–43) a speaker could mean that restaurants where people go or are served in the nude are the rage.

Still, (5–40)a means only that my grandfather is nude in the photographs and not that some unspecified other person is. And we can find instances where an AP left sister of a head N means something different depending on whether there is a right sister of that head N present:

(5–44)a.   These are some one-year-old shots.
  b.   These are some one-year-old shots of John.

Example (5–44)a taken without a context that makes clear what the shots are of means only that the shots themselves are a year old. But (5–44)b means either that the shots are one year old or, preferably, that these are shots of John as a one-year-old. Furthermore, sometimes an AP makes no sense with a given head N in the absence of another sister of that head N out of context.

(5–45)   I can't stand that old madhouse photo.

(5–46)   Would you like to see second-grade photos?

Examples (5–45) and (5–46) are decidedly strange. Yet (5–47) and (5–48) are fine.

(5–47)   I can't stand that old madhouse photo of Uncle Memo.

(5–48)   Would you like to see second-grade photos of Eva?

Example (5–47) mentions a photo of Uncle Memo in the madhouse; (5–48) mentions photos of Eva as a second grader.

Certainly the above are similar to the well-known analogous examples of modifiers like those in (5–49) (and see Hall 1973 and Tommola 1978):

(5–49)   a hot cup of coffee
          a racy book of short stories

Here one could argue that the cup itself is hot (from holding hot coffee) and the book itself is racy (from containing racy stories). And in other instances it is clear that it is not the coffee the A'' is modifying or even the cup, just as *nude* is not really modifying *restaurants* in (5–43). For example, Dwight Bolinger (personal communication) points out:

(5–50)   a quiet cup of coffee
          a warm cup of coffee

where neither cups nor coffee are what is quiet or warm, but the atmosphere surrounding the event of drinking the coffee. Thus Bolinger points out that *a warm cup of coffee* has a heart-warming connotation, whereas *a cup of warm coffee* is, perhaps, disgusting ("Yuck! Tepid coffee!") (see also Bolinger 1943 and 1952).

But we can also find:

(5–51)   a sugary cup of coffee

where the cup itself is not sugary no matter how sugary the coffee is, and the atmosphere also is not sugary. Here we must admit that *sugary* characterizes *coffee*.

I suggest that the XPs preceding the head N in (5–40)a, (5–44)b, (5–47), (5–48), and (5–51) are predicates taking the right sister of the head N as their subject role player. Again, these examples are problems for the c-command restriction on subject role players and for the bijacency requirement on predicates. And, again, they are no problem for the theory of predication put forth in this book.

5 Appositives

Appositives to NP predicate of that NP, as Rothstein (1983) has noted. Below I will use Italian examples, where the English gloss exemplifies the same properties. As in chapter 3, some of the examples here are obscene, and, occasionally, the English glosses are more mild than a literal rendition would be.

(5–52) Suo suocero, uno stronzo incredibile, viene stasera.
'Her father-in-law, an incredible slimeball, is coming tonight.'

(5–53) Sassari, una città della Sardegna, è bellina.
'Sassari, a city in Sardegna, is pretty.'

(5–54) Mia sorella, una persona molto capace, ricama motivi bucolici sul lino.
'My sister, a very capable person, is embroidering bucolic designs on the linen.'

(5–55) Il capo del dipartimento, il professor Lo Cascio, parla olandese.
'The head of the department, Professor Lo Cascio, speaks Dutch.'

Many have taken the position that appositives to NP form a constituent with the NP. As Emonds (1979) has shown, however, an analysis of appositive relative clauses that has them be daughters of S at SS is tenable. (I revise Emonds' analysis to be compatible with the X-bar theory of Chomsky 1986a, which I have adopted throughout this book. Thus I analyze appositives at SS as immediate daughters of I'.) And Stuurman (1983) compares Emonds' analysis favorably to the classic one of Jackendoff 1977. Emonds extends his analysis to parentheticals, as well. But many have noted that appositives like those in (5–52) through (5–55) above are similar with respect to intonation contour and function to both appositive relatives and parentheticals (see Safir 1985, 1986 and Matthews 1981 (who, however, suggests that apposition involves co-reference rather than predication), among many others). Appositives, unlike parentheticals, however, must be predicates, for not only are they NPs that could function as predicates in copular sentences, but they must be semantically appropriate as predicates to the NP they stand in apposition to:

(5–56)   *My sister, {a new idea/the last line on the page/a chill in the air/the funniest comic strip}, eats potato chips.

An interesting fact about Emonds' analysis of appositive relatives is that, even though it is so radically different from the traditional analysis, it can easily account for most of the same facts that the traditional analysis (with the appositive clause as a sister to N″, both under another N″) can account for. For example, Aoun, Hornstein, Lightfoot, and Weinberg (1987) claim that COMP cannot be deleted in appositive relatives because COMP is not properly governed by the head N of the NP the appositive modifies (or, in my analysis, predicates of). They assume the traditional analysis of appositive relatives. But their same explanation holds unchanged with Emonds' analysis.

I here adopt Emonds' analysis and, thus, the analysis of appositive relatives as predicates follows immediately. That is, appositive relatives cannot be modifiers if they fall outside the NP (see the discussion in ch. 1, sec. 1.4). Thus the fact that they assign theta roles entails that they be predicates. (And here we have the first instance in this book in which a clause – an open clause (with a variable for a role player) – is a predicate.)

I now propose to extend Emonds' analysis from covering appositive relatives only to covering examples like those given at the outset of this section. The structure of (5–52) at SS, then, would be as in (5–57).

(5–57)

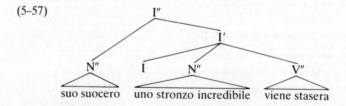

In (5–52) through (5–55) the appositive is to an NP which is in GF subject position. However, appositives can be to NPs in any GF. For example, in (5–58) the appositive is to the object of a P. (And this object of the P receives no theta role, a fact to which I return below.)

Clearly, one would not want to base-generate the structures in (5–57) and (5–58). I propose we follow Emonds' lead and generate appositives in the base as S-final adjuncts, as in the so-called Right Dislocation structure in (5–59).

(5–58)   Ho parlato con Elena, mia figlia, del tuo problema.
          'I talked with Elena, my daughter, about your problem.'

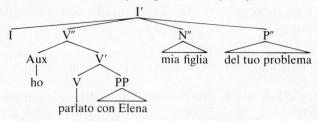

(5–59)   Suo suocero viene stasera, quello stronzo incredibile.
          'Her father-in-law is coming tonight, that incredible slimeball.'

One important issue that arises in my analysis of appositives and RD structures is exactly where these S-final adjuncts originate in DS. With my restrictive version of X-bar theory, I require them to be sisters to a head X only, so long as that X is N, V, A, or P. Otherwise, they could be sisters to to any projection of I(nflection) or C(omplementizer). I know of no evidence that cleanly determines the issue (but see the puzzles on binding facts presented in Safir 1986 and McCawley 1982). In the absence of such evidence, then, I will (arbitrarily) place these S-final adjuncts as sisters to I under I', although this arbitrary assumption will not be crucial to any of the analysis that follows.

One may object to the positing of RD structures as the source for appositives on the basis that not all RD structures sound good. In fact many RD structures sound far from good:

(5–60)   *Ho parlato con Elena del tuo problema, mia figlia.
          ??'I spoke with Elena about your problem, my daughter.'

However, appositive relative clauses in both English and Italian sound awful when they do not immediately follow the H″ they predicate of (where H=N, V, A, P). Yet Emonds generates them in S-final position anyway. He then accounts for the fact that they sound awful in S-final position by claiming that appositive relative clauses cannot be interpreted properly unless they immediately follow the H″ they predicate of.

We might, then, follow Emonds' lead and propose that all appositives must be adjacent to the H″ they predicate of in order to be properly interpreted. If this were true, we would expect similarities between the distributions of and the restrictions on interpretation of appositive relatives and appositives like those in (5–52) through (5–55). We find such similarities.

First, appositive relatives easily allow H″ to be a pronoun when the pronoun is phonologically strong in both Italian and English. Example (5–61)a was suggested to me by Raffaella Zanuttini (personal communication).

(5–61)a.   Proprio lui, che non ha mai voluto aiutarci, ha il coraggio di criticarci.
           'Precisely he, who never wanted to help us, has the audacity to criticize us.'
       b.   I want him, who never helps anyone, to wash the dishes tonight all by himself.

Likewise, our appositives can predicate of phonologically strong pronouns. Example (5–62)a was suggested to me by Raffaella Zanuttini (personal communication).

(5–62)a.   Proprio lui, un pigrone di prima categoria, ha il coraggio di criticarci?
           'Precisely he, a class A lazybones, has the audacity to criticize us?'
       b.   Then I asked him, the supreme pig, to help clean up.

But if the pronoun is phonologically weak, an appositive relative is ungrammatical in Italian and highly unusual in English.

(5–63)a.   *Voglio vedervi, che avete tutti studiato bene, all'esame domani mattina.
           'I want to see you [clitic pronoun], who have all studied well, at the exam tomorrow morning.'
           (cf. Voglio vedere voi, che avete tutti studiato bene, all'esame domani mattina.
           'I want to see you [tonic pronoun], who have all studied well, at the exam tomorrow morning.')
       b.   ?He, whom I met only yesterday, is coming to dinner.

Example (5–63)b improves with contrastive stress on the nominative pronoun *he* and a heavier pause before the appositive relative. That is, it improves as the pronoun is treated more and more like a phonologically strong pronoun.

And, as expected with our analysis, regular appositives do not predicate of phonologically weak pronouns in Italian, or, typically, in English.

(5–64)a.   *Voglio vedervi, i miei bravissimi studenti, al convegno domani.
           'I want to see you [clitic pronoun], my very good students, at the conference tomorrow.'
           (cf. Voglio vedere voi, i miei bravissimi studenti, al convegno domani.
           'I want to see you [tonic pronoun], my very good students, at the conference tomorrow.')
       b.   ?He, the bastard, left without a word.

Again, (5–64)b improves with added stress on *he* and a heavy pause before the appositive.

However, RD structures contrast with appositives, since they are acceptable in both English and Italian when they have antecedents that are pronouns of any type (weak or strong), including the pro of Italian (see Rizzi 1982 for much discussion of pro).

(5–65)   Voglio dargli un libro, a tuo fratello.
?'I want to give him a book, your brother.'
È uscito, il bastardo.
'He left, the bastard.'

(5–66)   He's gonna get a piece of my mind, that pompous nitwit.

The first example of (5–65) is from Sornicola (1981), who gives only attested data and who discusses (5–65) with and without a pause after *libro*. It is with a pause that we have the RD structure. I follow Sornicola in proposing that examples like (5–65) and (5–66) are good only if they are open to a functional analysis in which the S-final adjunct clarifies the preceding material by adding information which makes precise relationships relevant to the proposition it is adjoined to. The RD element in the first example of (5–65) has this function by letting us know whom the book is to be given to in contexts where this information is not made precise otherwise (see Sornicola 1981, pp. 187ff.). The first example of (5–65) is not appropriate in contexts where we know perfectly well already the referent of the clitic pronoun *gli* ('him') (note that (5–65) has a pause after *libro* – the remarks about context do not hold for the clitic doubling reading of (5–65), which has no pause). The RD element in the second example of (5–65) has this function by letting us know that the act of leaving was a bastard-like act. The RD element in (5–66) has this function by letting us know why the speaker wants to give him a piece of her mind: he is a pompous nitwit.

Ruwet (1982) has noticed this very same fact. He points out a distinction between phrases used as *classifiants* and those used as *nonclassifiants*. Appositives that immediately follow the H″ they predicate of are open to either interpretation. Thus in (5–57) her father-in-law may just happen to be a slimeball or he may be a slimeball by virtue of the fact that he is coming this evening. In (5–58), of course, Elena is my daughter, unrelated to whatever else she does.

But phrases in S-final position, that is, RD structures, must be *classifiants*. That is why (5–59) is good, but (5–60) fails. It is possible for her father-in-law to be a slimeball by virtue of his coming tonight, but it is not possible for Elena to be my daughter by virtue of my talking to her about your problem. The type of reading we get for (5–59), then, is similar to that for (5–67):

(5–67)   The chairman's gonna embarrass her about the review of her book, that heartless oaf.

Likewise, (5–60) contrasts to (5–68), in which the final phrase can easily be understood as a *classifiant*.

(5–68)   I spoke with Elena Furrow about your problem, the obstetrician who specializes in difficult pregnancies.

Thus neither (5–59) nor (5–60) is an example of an appositive, but of an RD structure.

I conclude that appositives of all types (both phrasal and clausal) must immediately follow the H″ they predicate of, just as we would have expected given our extension of Emonds' analysis to all appositives.

Second, as Emonds points out, H can be N, V, A, or P. That is, appositive relatives do not require NP antecedents (or, in my terms, NP srp's). Likewise, our appositives do not require NP subject role players.

(5–69)   He acted terribly, kept forgetting his lines.

(5–70)   It's too expensive, much more than I can afford.

(5–71)   He's into drugs, a state of mind I can't comprehend.

Example (5–69), with apposition to a VP, is from Matthews (1981, p. 226), and (5–70), with apposition to an AP, is a variation on another example in Matthews. In (5–71) we have apposition to a PP.

I conclude that appositives of all types originate as S-final adjuncts. Emonds accounts for the SS position of non-restrictive relatives by a movement rule which takes a DS-like (5–72) into an SS-like (5–74) by way of the intermediate stage in (5–73):

(5–72)   Too much sun made these tomatoes rot on the vine, and we paid a lot for them.

(5–73)   Too much sun made these tomatoes, and we paid a lot for them, rot on the vine.

(5–74)   Too much sun made these tomatoes, which we paid a lot for, rot on the vine.

The movement rule, just like all movement rules, would be restricted to moving a constituent only. And the movement rule that Emonds posits takes material and moves it rightward past the S-final clause in (5–72) to yield (5–73). (Here the VP moves rightward across the S-final clause.) The result is that all the material following an appositive relative clause must be a single constituent. The only way more than one constituent could follow an appositive relative clause would be if the movement rule which applies to (5–72) were to apply more than once in a single clause. For example, (5–75) contains two appositive relative clauses.

(5–75)   John, who was arrogant, and Mary, who was insensitive, were quite similar.

The source for (5–75) would be as in (5–76). (Here I give different structures from those of Emonds, since I am adopting the X-bar theory of Chomsky 1986a. Recall that I have placed these S-final clauses under I' arbitrarily.)

(5–76)

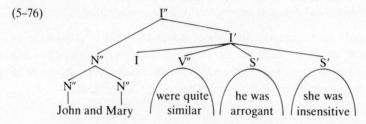

And the SS after two applications of the movement rule would be as in (5–77). (One application moves the V″ past the last appositive clause. The other application moves the second conjunct N″ past the first appositive clause.)

(5–77)

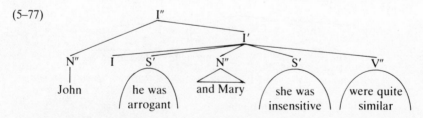

Appositive relative clause formation would yield (5–75), with the same constituency seen in (5–77).

If Emonds' analysis of appositive relatives were to be correct for all appositives, we would predict that appositives like those in (5–52) through (5–55) could be followed only by a single constituent. And this is so.

(5–78)   *?Ho dato a Gianni, quel fesso, un libro proprio ieri.
          *?'I gave John, that jerk, a book just yesterday.'

This analysis, of course, explains why appositives cannot be followed by material that belongs to the H″ that the appositive predicates of (see the discussions in chs. 3 and 4, especially those concerning (3–38) and (4–38)). The reason is that the appositive is not inside the H″. This analysis also explains why appositives cannot be stacked (see the discussion of (3–35) in ch. 3 and of (4–36) in ch. 4). The reason is that each appositive must immediately follow the H″ it predicates of – so only one appositive is allowed per H″.

The fact that appositives cannot be interpreted properly unless they immediately follow the H″ of which they predicate also accounts for the fact that appositives look as if they move with the H″ they predicate of.

(5–79)   Maria, una person intelligente, sembra aver capito.
          'Maria, an intelligent person, seems to have understood.'

I conclude that Emonds' analysis of appositive relative clauses is an empirically adequate analysis of all types of appositives. Thus the structures I gave above in (5–57) and (5–58) are the correct analyses at SS for such sentences. Let me repeat these here for convenience.

(5–57)

(5–58)

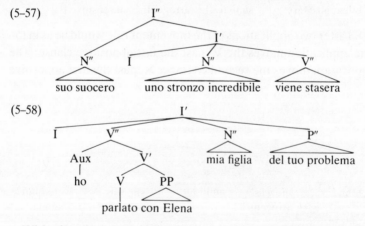

With the above analysis, we can see that appositives of all sorts, including appositive relative clauses, present significant questions for my theory of predication: in every example in which the H″ of which the appositive predicates is in the V″, a barrier of the H″ will separate it from the appositive at SS (this barrier being the V″ node itself). (And, of course, the structures in (5–57) and (5–58) present insurmountable problems for theories of predication that require a subject role player to c-command its predicate and a predicate to be bijacent to its subject role player.)

However, we have already noted in section 2 above that Predicate Structure must be formed off of LF rather than off of SS. So if sentences with appositives can be argued to have a different structure at LF from that at SS, and if, in particular, sentences with appositives can be argued to have a structure at LF in which no barrier of the H″ comes between it and the appositive, appositives will not present any problems for our theory of predication.

But an analysis quite close to the needed analysis has been argued for on independent grounds. Thus Safir (1986) argues, on the basis of binding puzzles, that, right up to the point of LF, appositive relative clauses are configurationally unattached to the proposition that their H″ appears in. Then in LF an attachment rule applies (to yield yet another level, which he calls LF′) to attach appositive relative clauses inside the H″ that they predicate of. His attachment rule does not single out appositive relatives, but instead will apply to any unattached element, where only athematic elements can be unattached. In this way he also handles parentheticals, which present problems for interpretation similar to those presented by appositive relatives (see also McCawley 1982, whose analysis is quite distinct).

It would be an easy matter to extend Safir's analysis to the full range of appositive types. However, what I would like to do is blend Emonds' with Safir's. That is, I follow Emonds in deriving appositives from S-final adjunct position and in allowing a movement rule which will wind up with the appositive immediately following its H″. Thus I accept the analyses at SS in (5–57) and (5–58). I propose that in the LF component of the grammar the appositives are then reattached inside their H″ (alla Safir 1986), with a rule similar to that proposed by Guéron and May 1984 for extraposed elements (see also the discussion of (5–24) above).

We now have a new question to face – which is how appositives, being inside the H″ at the time of Predicate Structure, are to be distinguished from modifiers. One possible answer is that they are not to be so distinguished. As we noted in chapter 1, section 1.4, it makes sense to distinguish between modification and predication in that a modifier contributes crucially to the determination of the referent of the entire phrase whose head it modifies, while a predicate does not play a part in the determination of the referent of the element it predicates of. But this distinction is still captured with my analysis, since appositives are outside the H″ at SS and remain outside the H″ during LF until the point of the relevant attachment rule that puts them inside the H″. Thus rules of LF that are sensitive to reference can make the proper distinction between predication and modification structures so long as they apply before the attachment rule.

On the other hand, as we mentioned briefly in chapter 1, section 4, there is no evidence presented in this book and no evidence I know of against the claim that the principles that apply to the coindexing of a predicate and its srp also apply to the coindexing of a modifier and the element it modifies (and many linguists have identified modification as an instance of predication – see the references mentioned in ch. 1). Thus the fact that in our analysis an appositive is inside the H″ at the time of the relevant coindexing is not problematic for us; we expect the same principles to hold here as would hold if the appositive were outside the H″. And they do.

As long as appositives are inside the H″ by the time of Predicate Structure, they will present no problems for the theory of predication offered in this book. However, if they are inside that H″ by the time of Predicate Structure, they will present problems for any theory of predication which requires that subject role players be maximal projections that c-command their predicates.

At this point we can note that RD structures, like appositives, are open to an analysis as predicates, as well. And, as Ruwet (1982) has pointed out, phrases that are *classifiants*, like those in RD structures, can appear in a number of positions:

(5–80)   Jean croyait alors, l'imbécile, que la terre est plate.
          'Jean believed then, the imbecile, that the earth is flat.'

In (5–80) *l'imbécile* predicates of *Jean*, yet it is not an appositive (since it does not occur immediately after *Jean* and it has only the *classifiant* interpretation, whereas appositives have both the *classifiant* and the *nonclassifiant* interpretations) nor is it an RD structure (since it does not occur in S-final position). I suggest that a similar re-attachment rule in LF (or, perhaps, the same one) that applies in appositives applies to these phrases and to RD phrases, so that they are inside the relevant H″ in LF.

Similar analyses may prove helpful for understanding a wide range of constructions involving material set off by pauses (see Matthews 1981 for a tantalizing group of examples), many of which turn out to fall together into the functional class of insults (see both Milner 1978 and Ruwet 1982). And, without justification here, I propose that such an analysis is viable for all secondary predicates set off by pauses which occur immediately following their srp or in S-final position. (Notice that precisely the secondary predicates set off by pauses in these two positions raised questions for us in various sections of chapter 2, particularly secs. 3, 4, and 5.)

While the above is schematic and certainly calls for a detailed analysis of precisely how the binding puzzles that McCawley and Safir have come up with will be resolved in my analysis of appositives and of the other similar structures alluded to above, I offer it without further support here, since an in-depth analysis of appositives of all types (plus of parentheticals and certain insults) would double the length of this volume. I hope only to have set up a promising program for future research.

6   Other constructions

There are many constructions beyond the five looked at in this chapter for which an analysis involving predication seems worth pursuing. For example, consider:

(5–81)   I am good friends with him.

Here *friends* is plural. But in (5–82) it is singular:

(5–82)   I am a good friend of his.

On the basis of agreement facts one might propose that *friends* in (5–81) predicates of a split srp: *I . . . him* (see the discussion of (5–37) above). We could go on from there to look for other evidence of predication. And, as with the constructions studied in sections 1 through 5 above, if this is a predication relationship in (5–81), it defies configurational approaches to predication.

Likewise, in a sentence like:

(5–83)   The first man landed on the moon in 1968.

pointed out to me by Greg Carlson (personal communication), *first* does not characterize the head N *man*, but rather characterizes this N in its role of landing on the moon, as in:

(5–84)   The first man to land on the moon did it in 1968.

I do not know whether we are dealing with an instance of modification or predication in this example, but in either case we are dealing with a theta assignment that cannot be accounted for with configurational approaches to modification or predication.

A third example is found in:

(5–85)   Mia has found a truly nice man in Alfred.

Here the DO could be argued to be a secondary predicate taking the object of the P as its srp.

I will not go on with these speculations, since the reader is, I hope, already making a list longer than my own.

7   Conclusion

In this chapter we have looked at five different constructions which I have offered as instances of predication. While the discussion here is cursory and many of the details necessary for a complete analysis are not included, we can see that the evidence given above is suggestive. The significant point for us is that all five of these constructions present serious problems for other theories of predication, but no problem for the theory of predication put forth in this book. And what is even more telling is that these five constructions point out differing problems for other theories, from problems for the c-command restriction, to problems for the bijacency restriction, to problems for the claim that subject role players be maximal projections, to problems for the claim that predicates be maximal projections. I conclude that configurationally based theories of predication are empirically inadequate in (almost) every way.

6 *An indexing theory encompassing anaphora and predication*

We have seen in this book a theory of predication that calls for coindexing between a predicate and its subject role player. In Binding Theory (as in Chomsky 1981) we find a set of conditions under which an item must or may not be coindexed with a c-commanding item. An item that must be so coindexed is an anaphor. The proposal I put forth in this chapter is that the principles developed in chapter two for predication coindexing hold also for anaphor–antecedent coindexing.

Before going into the discussion proper, let me point out that the desirability of a single set of coindexing principles for predication and anaphor coindexing follows from the work of Safir (1985). Safir argues that there should be only one kind of indexing in grammar. His main goal is to do away with the need for superscripting, and use only subscripting. He concentrates on the types of indices that "count" for the binding theory as formulated in Chomsky (1981). And he does not extend his position to predication indexing. This chapter, then, can be seen as an attempt to support Safir's Unity of Indexing Hypothesis by showing that predication coindexing and anaphor–antecedent coindexing, both being obligatory, are instances of one and the same set of indexing principles. If, on the other hand, predication coindexing were an entirely different kind of process from other coindexing processes, Safir's hypothesis would be disconfirmed and we would have to admit a more complicated set of coindexing principles to the grammar.

One might have an immediate objection to the grouping of predication coindexing with anaphor coindexing on the grounds that the latter but not the former involves referential indices. However, as Farmer and Harnish (1987) show with a range of different types of examples, anaphor coindexing does not call for coreference between an antecedent and its anaphor, after all. Thus such an objection would be based on a false premise. So far as I know, there is no *a priori* basis upon which to distinguish two types of indices here. The issue, rather, is whether or not the coindexing in each case obeys the same set of principles. And this is the issue I address in this chapter.

The parallels between predication coindexing and anaphor coindexing are striking. Notice first that all predication coindexing that we have discussed thus far takes place within the confines of a clause. At one point in the history of generative grammar, it was commonly believed that reflexive pronouns had to find clausemate antecedents. In fact, this belief was one of the primary motivations for rules like Raising into Object Position (as in Postal 1974). While many present grammatical theories indicate that a rule with the properties that Raising into Object Position has cannot belong to grammar, it is still equally clear that reflexive pronouns observe special restrictions on their collocation with respect to their antecedents. These restrictions are not, however, best stated in terms of clauses, but, rather, in terms of argument structure, as we will see below (and see Giorgi 1984).

Chomsky (1981) has argued that reflexive pronouns fall into a group of elements called anaphors, along with reciprocals and trace of NP movement. He has argued further that all anaphors must be bound within their governing category. For an item to be bound, it must be coindexed with a c-commanding element (see Reinhart 1976). This is part A of the binding theory.

I argue in the sections below that the principles of predication coindexing hold for anaphor–antecedent coindexing and should replace part A of the binding theory. In the final section I give a formulation of these unitary coindexing principles.

This chapter is not to be taken as a completed research project, nor is it intended to substitute for one. Instead, it is a natural extension of the ideas developed in chapter 2 of this book, but it is not a thorough development of many of the necessary details of that extension. Below I leave certain questions to the research of the many linguists now looking into anaphor binding. My hope here is to have contributed to this research by offering an alternative that demands further consideration.

1   Formulating the questions

A predicate needs to find a subject role player in order to be licensed (in the sense of Chomsky 1986b). An anaphor needs to find an antecedent in order to be interpreted. Therefore, I propose that the parallels are between predicates and anaphors, on the one hand, and subject role players and antecedents, on the other hand.

In section 2 I argue that both subject role players and antecedents of anaphors must be in A-positions, and that this restriction follows from the predication coindexing principles in chapter 2 and need not be stated as an extra restriction. An extended analysis of the Italian reciprocal is offered here, in support of the proposal that antecedents of anaphors must be in A-positions.

In section 3 I address the relevance of barriers to binding theory and I argue that, with regard to local anaphor binding, an antecedent may not be separated from its anaphor by any of its barriers, just as a subject role player may not be separated from its predicate by any of its barriers. I further show that this restriction combined with other parts of predication theory does away with the need for the restriction that an antecedent c-command its anaphor. In fact, I argue that the c-command restriction is empirically wrong, in any case. (I leave open the question of whether the notion of c-command is relevant for the binding of pronominals.)

Up to this point, the discussion will hold equally for both Italian and English. But now it becomes necessary to separate the two, since we find significant differences. I begin with a discussion of English and then move on to a discussion of Italian.

In section 4 I consider anaphors in English that fall within a theta domain. Predicates that fall within a theta domain are regulated by Proviso One. But we will see in section 4 that if we want Proviso One to account for anaphors as well as predicates, we must modify it by taking into account the new concept of argument ladders, as defined there. I argue that if an anaphor falls within the theta domain of a given lexical item, it must find its antecedent in the minimal available rung of the argument ladder to which it belongs. The concept of argument ladders does away with the empirically inferior concept of governing categories, at least in so far as governing categories have been claimed to be relevant for the binding of anaphors. (I leave open the question of whether the notion of governing category is relevant to the binding of pronominals.) I further argue that Proviso Two does not hold on long-distance anaphor binding.

In section 5 I look at anaphors in English that do not fall within a theta domain. I show that there are two types: those that occur as adjuncts and those that appear in GF subject position of tenseless clauses. These anaphors obey restrictions on their binding which are parallel to restrictions on primary predication. I then argue that predicates may not appear as sisters to Ps that are not theta-role assigners except in absolutive constructions, and that anaphors may not appear as the object of Ps unless the anaphor receives a theta role, and thus is closely semantically tied in to the other elements of the proposition it belongs to. I offer a single account for both of these facts.

In section 6 I look at Italian anaphors and compare them to the data on English in sections 4 and 5, concluding that one parameter that the grammars of individual languages make use of is how far up an argument ladder they allow an anaphor to look for an antecedent. This section draws heavily from the work of Giorgi (1984). In this section we will see a distinction between local anaphor binding and long-distance anaphor binding, where only the former obeys Proviso Two.

In section 7 I formulate coindexing principles that cover both predication coindexing and the binding between anaphors and their antecedents.

Section 8 points out some of the advantages of the new indexing theory proposed in section 7.

Throughout this chapter I consider anaphors that are phonetically audible. There are at least two types of anaphors that are not phonetically audible, however. One is the use of PRO in obligatory control structures. As Hornstein and Lightfoot (1987) argue, this PRO is an anaphor. And in chapter 2, section 9 we already saw that coindexing between anaphor PRO and its antecedent is subject to the principles of coindexing for predication structures. Thus anaphor PRO already has been seen to confirm the hypothesis of this chapter: that one set of coindexing principles holds for both predication and anaphor coindexing.

The other anaphor that is not phonetically audible is trace of NP movement. In chapter 2, section 13 we indicated, albeit briefly, that coindexing between anaphor trace and its antecedent is, likewise, subject to the principles of coindexing for predication structures. Again, we have already seen confirmation (or, at least, an indication of inquiry that promises to supply confirmation) of our hypothesis there.

The job of this chapter, then, is to demonstrate support for our hypothesis from the behavior of the phonetically audible anaphors.

2   Subject role players and antecedents of anaphors must be in A-positions

Chomsky (1981) takes his binding theory to be A-binding – that is, binding from an A-position (a potential theta position). This means that the antecedent of an anaphor must be in an A-position. I here assume Chomsky's position without argumentation. So far as I know, the only serious challenge to Chomsky's position with respect to the binding of anaphors is found in Aoun (1985). In section 2.1 below, therefore, I discuss Aoun's position at length. For now, let us assume that Chomsky is correct.

If anaphor coindexing and predication coindexing are really one phenomenon, as I am proposing in this chapter, we would then expect that subject role players of predicates could appear only in A-positions, just as antecedents of anaphors can appear only in A-positions.

Subject role players turn out, in fact, to appear only in A-positions because of independently needed restrictions on predication coindexing. Thus we need not state a separate restriction concerning A-positions. Let us see how.

First, if we have an instance of primary predication, the subject role player must be in GF subject position, which is an A-position.

Second, if we have secondary predication, the subject role player must not be separated from its predicate by any of its barriers (this is Proviso Two). Furthermore, if the predicate falls within the theta domain of H (where a theta domain, as I have defined it early in ch. 2, sec. 5, consists of all the arguments of a lexical item that receive their theta role via Direct or Compositional Theta Assignment), either the subject role player must appear in the lexical structure of H (by the version of Proviso One that is found in (2–77) and that applies for every H except noun), or the subject role player or the predicate must receive a theta role from H (by the version of Proviso One that is found in (2–79) and that applies for H=N). But Provisos One and Two together add up to requiring that a subject role player of a secondary predicate appear only in positions that are recognized as A-positions, regardless of the presence of a secondary predicate. Let us look at this point more closely.

If a subject role player is in GF subject, DO, IO, or object of a P where either the P is a theta assigner (the exceptional case) or where the P transmits a theta role so that its object gets a theta role via Compositional Theta Assignment, then the subject role player is, by definition, in an A-position. Therefore, what we need to look at are instances in which a subject role player appears in some other position.

The only remaining positions are objects of P where the object of the P does not get a theta role, and adjunct positions. We shall consider each separately.

First, subject role players never occur as adjuncts that do not bear a GF. Consider the adjuncts called appositives, for example. Just from looking at the data (and see the wide range of data in ch. 5, sec. 5), we see that no appositive can be the subject role player of a predicate. This fact follows from the principle of full licensing. Adjuncts must be licensed by elements that are independently licensed (that is, they must be licensed by elements that belong to a clause either because they fill a GF position or bear a theta role or modify such an element, etc.). Thus one adjunct cannot license another.

Second, consider a srp that is the object of a P and that is not L-marked. Object of P is, in fact, an A-position, so such a srp is, in fact, in an A-position. That is, being in an A-position is not the same thing as having a theta role. For example, both GF subject position and object of a P are A-positions, but both may be filled by non-arguments (see ch. 1, sec. 2.4 for arguments that not all objects of P receive a theta role).

Notice, however, that if the object of a P is not L-marked, then the PP would be a barrier for that object. So that object should not be able to be the srp for a predicate outside the PP (by Proviso Two), although it could be the srp for a predicate inside the PP. In general these predictions hold; such objects do not generally serve as srp's to predicates outside the PP, but they can to predicates inside the PP. (We will see below instances in which such an object is the srp for a predicate inside the PP.) However, there is one instance when such an object of a P can be the srp for a predicate outside the PP: that in which the predicate outside the PP is an appositive. We argued in chapter 5, section 5 that in LF appositives are moved from a position outside the X'' they predicate of to a position inside the X''. Then Predicate Structure, which is built off of LF, will see no barriers between the appositive predicate and its srp. So appositives are not problematic for our theory, after all.

A potential apparent counterexample to the generalization that srp's occur only in A-positions remains, however, in absolutes such as that in:

(2–88)   Arrivata Maria, la riunione ebbe inizio.
         'Maria having arrived, the reunion began.'

Here *Maria* plays no GF in the main clause. Therefore if the absolutive here can be argued to be non-clausal, *Maria* bears no GF in this monoclausal sentence and is not in any obvious A-position (except insofar as it is part of the absolutive). Yet *Maria* is the srp of the predicate *arrivata*, which would be a secondary predicate, given an analysis in which the absolutive is non-clausal.

There are at least two possible solutions to this problem. One is that the absolutive here is, in fact, clausal (as argued in Belletti 1981, who develops a small clause analysis) and therefore *Maria* has a GF after all (that of subject), and is in an A-position.

Another possibility is that absolutives are exceptional. We already saw in chapter 2, section 7 (with the principle of absolutive coindexing in (2–89)) that the srp of the predicate of an absolutive, where this predicate is a daughter of the minimal node Y that dominates all members of the absolutive, must be an XP which is also a daughter of Y. There is an obvious syntactic parallel between this position in an absolutive and GF subject position in a clause. And it may well be that this position in an absolutive must be filled by an argument and never by an inert element (such as the *there* of *there*-insertion sentences). In fact, the works of Stump (1981) and Napoli (1987a) would support this suggestion. Thus the relevant XP daughter of Y would constitute an A-position (parallel to GF subject position).

It is beyond the scope of this book, however, to delve further into the possible exceptional behavior of absolutives. The relevant point for us is that these absolutives may well not be problematic for my hypothesis, depending upon their proper analysis.

At this point, my argument that subject role players must be in A-positions is complete. But more interesting things now can be said.

First, in the instance in which a srp is the object of a P and is not L-marked, we pointed out above that the predicate cannot occur outside the PP because the PP will be a barrier for the subject role player – as in the sentence below, repeated from chapter 2 (and see the lengthy discussion of (1–89) in ch. 1).

(2–31)

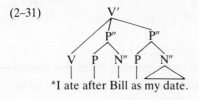

*I ate after Bill as my date.

Still, there is nothing to prevent a P from taking both the subject role player and its predicate as sisters. This is precisely the situation that defines a PP absolutive (see ch. 2, sec. 7). That is, there is nothing to prevent an absolutive from appearing as a PP that is not the argument of any lexical head. And this situation does occur, as both Ruwet (1982) and Napoli (1987a) have shown (see also the references on absolutives in ch. 2, sec. 7).

(6–2)   Nous avons visité Florence avec Pierre pour guide.
         We visited Florence with Pierre for a guide.

(Note that in these absolutives, in contrast to ones like that in (2–88) discussed above, the srp of the predicate in the absolutive is the object of the P that introduces the absolutive – thus it is an A-position regardless of the presence of the absolutive predicate.) We find that a subject role player can be the object of a P where it is not L-marked if it is the subject role player of an absolutive construction.

Based on the above data about srp's, we now have two predictions about antecedents of anaphors if, in fact, they are parallel to srp's. First, we predict that the antecedent to an anaphor may not be a non-argument object of a P where the anaphor is outside the PP. This is because the PP would constitute a barrier between the antecedent and its anaphor. This prediction holds in both Italian and English.

(6–3)   Osvaldo$_j$ è stato convinto da Gianni$_i$ del fatto che la propria$_{*i/j}$ casa è la più bella del paese.
         'Osvaldo has been convinced by Gianni that self's house is the nicest in the village.'

(6–4)   *Bill was introduced by Paul$_i$ to himself$_i$.

(Example (6–3) is from Giorgi 1984.) In chapter two, section 8, we saw that the object of a passive *by* phrase is not theta marked. Thus this object cannot serve as the antecedent for an anaphor, as (6–3) and (6–4) show. Of course, the Italian example in (6–3) raises many questions, since we have here an instance of so-called long-distance anaphora. I will discuss this phenomenon in section 6 below. The point for now is that an anaphor cannot take a non-argument NP as its antecedent, just as we would expect if the coindexing principles developed for predication also held for anaphor coindexing.

We also predict that the only exception to the above generalization will be in absolutives, where the antecedent of an anaphor inside the absolutive can be an NP daughter of the minimal node that contains all members

of the absolute (compare to the principle for absolute coindexing in
(2–89)). This is so.

(6–5)   With John always after himself about homework, we never have to nag
         him.
         With John so in love with himself, who needs a wife?

We have seen in this subsection strong support for the hypothesis that
predication coindexing and anaphor coindexing are ohe phenomenon,
based on shared restrictions on srp's and antecedents of anaphors. Before
I conclude this subsection, however, I would like to discuss one more
thing.

Anaphors and their antecedents typically occur within the same argument structure (although this is not necessarily so, as we will see in secs. 4
through 6 below). Since I have here assumed without argumentation
Chomsky's (1981) position that antecedents of anaphors must be A-
bound, let me offer some suggestive evidence that the distinction
between arguments and non-arguments as it relates to the notion of
barriers is relevant to referential dependence within a single argument
structure (that is, to the domain that most anaphor–antecedent binding
occurs in). This evidence follows from an observation and claim made by
Zubizarreta (1985), who discusses examples like the following:

(6–6)a.   Mary talked about his$_i$ mother to John$_i$.
     b.   *Mary went to his$_i$ farm with John$_i$.
     c.   Mary sang his$_i$ song to John$_i$ with Sally.
     d.   *Mary sang his$_i$ song to Sally with John$_i$.

Here, of course, *his* is not an anaphor. But the issue for us is what factors
are involved in our grammaticality judgments when we read (6–6)a&c as
allowing coreference between *his* and *John*, but (6–6)b&d as not allowing
it.

Zubizarreta notes that the fact that *John* does not c-command *his* in
(6–6)b&d has nothing to do with the ungrammaticality of these examples,
since *John* does not c-command *his* in the good sentences (6–6)a&c (and I
argue in sec. 3 below that the c-command restriction is empirically
inaccurate for the binding of anaphors, as well). Instead, she points out
that *John* is what she calls "an adjunct" in (6–6)b&d: it is a non-
argument. But *John* in (6–6)a&c is an argument of *talked/sang*. She
concludes that an argument of a given item cannot be referentially
dependent upon an adjunct of that same item. But notice that the
relevant non-arguments in (6–6) are contained inside PPs that serve as

282 An indexing theory encompassing anaphora and predication

their barriers. In our terms, we cannot have a barrier of an element come between that element and another which is referentially dependent on it. But this looks like just one more instance in which Proviso Two is applying.

Of course, as I said, the above is only suggestive, since anaphors do not, in fact, have to find their antecedents within the same argument structure that the anaphor belongs to. Yet it is interesting evidence that A-positions which are not cut off by barriers are the natural positions for allowing referential dependence. Therefore, A-positions are the natural positions for antecedents to anaphors.

In sum, subject role players and antecedents may appear in A-positions freely and in non A-positions under the identical (and exceptional) conditions. This fact follows if the coindexing between predicates and their subject role players is the same coindexing that occurs between anaphors and their antecedents.

It is worth pointing out now that in my theory both GF subject and object of P are A-positions which need not be filled by arguments. One might then expect that NP movement, which can freely move NPs into a non-theta-marked GF subject position, should also be able to freely move NPs into a non-theta-marked object of a P position. However, notice that if we have a non-theta-marked object of a P position, the PP will always serve as a barrier to the object of the P. Now if the trace of NP movement is an anaphor and if anaphor binding is sensitive to the principles of coindexing laid out in chapter 2 (including Proviso Two), as I argue in this chapter, then we have an explanation for why NP movement cannot, in fact, move an NP into a non-theta-marked object of a P. GF subject position, on the other hand, will not be separated by any of its barriers from elements inside the VP. So NP movement can apply freely into GF subject position. Therefore, the admission of object of P as an A-position that need not be filled by an argument adds no new problems for our grammar.

2.1   Aoun's theory and Italian reciprocals

Before leaving this section it is important to point out that Aoun (1985) extends the binding theory to binding from non A-positions. Aoun's strongest piece of evidence (in my opinion) for his argument that antecedents appear in non A-positions uses the analysis of Italian reciprocals offered in Belletti (1982). I am taking a position *contra* Aoun, then. Clearly, arguing against all of Aoun's evidence for his theory is well beyond the scope of this chapter. So I will here argue against Aoun's position by attacking only one part (what I believe is the strongest part) of the foundation upon which his theory rests: the analysis of Italian reciprocals. This digression will be long because the data are complex. However, it will be worth the reader's while both because Aoun's challenge to binding theory must be countered seriously and because interesting facts about the syntax and semantics of Italian, sometimes in comparison to English, will be brought out.

The word (*l'*)*altro* in Italian has at least four uses, just as its English equivalent (*the*) *other* does. One is simply as an adjective.

(6–7)   Preferisco l'altro libro.
        'I prefer the other book.'

Another is as an N in an NP that is elliptical, depending upon context for full interpretation.

(6–8)   Preferisco l'altro.
        'I prefer the other (one).'

The NP that *altro* heads can appear with any GF.

(6–9)   L'altro è fastidioso.
        'The other (one) is annoying.'

(6–10) Ho parlato con l'altro.
        'I spoke with the other (one).'

And the NP that *altro* heads can appear in a clause in which the NP *l'uno* is the GF subject.

(6–11) L'uno ammirava le foto dell'altro.
        'One admired the photos of the other.'

The fact illustrated in (6–11) is important to keep in mind, since we will see below that (*l'*)*altro* also occurs as part of a discontinuous sequence, what we will call the reciprocal, with the word *l'uno*. However, when (*l'*)*altro* is used as a reciprocal, it is an anaphor. That is, it must be bound within its governing category. (Actually, as we will see in sec. 4, governing category is not the relevant concept to anaphor binding. Instead, the concept of argument ladders is the relevant one. However, the discussion that follows would not be changed in any essential way if we were to talk about argument ladders. Thus I will continue here with the familiar concept of governing category.) In (6–11) we do not have the reciprocal use of (*l'*)*altro*; witness the fact that it can be free (that is, not bound) within its governing category.

(6–12)   L'uno ammirava le tue foto dell'altro.
         'One admired your photos of the other.'

As Cinque (1980) has shown, the possessive in Italian counts as the subject of an NP for the binding theory (and see M. Anderson 1983 for the same demonstration for English). Thus the governing category of (*l'*)*altro* in (6–12) is the NP *le tue foto dell'altro*. But (*l'*)*altro* is not bound within this NP. I conclude that the use of (*l'*)*altro* in (6–11) and (6–12) is not anaphoric, but is, instead, the same elliptical use found in (6–8) through (6–10).

Another use of (*l'*)*altro* that occurs in both Italian and English is that found in PPs and APs that begin with the word *l'uno*.

(6–13)   I ragazzi sono entrati l'uno dopo l'altro.
         'The boys came in one after the other.'

(6–14)   I ragazzi stettero seduti in panchina l'uno accanto all'altro.
         'The boys stayed seated on the bench one beside the other.'

(6–15)   I ragazzi stettero in panchina l'uno seduto accanto all'altro.
         'The boys stayed on the bench, one seated beside the other.'

These PP/APs modify not just an event (action/state) or a role player in that event, but some aspect of how a role player behaves with respect to the event. In this way they have much in common with the semantics of the real reciprocal construction, which we will examine below. However, they differ from the real reciprocal construction in several important ways. First, they can be semantically related (where I discuss below what this semantic relationship is) to any NP in a clause, whereas the reciprocal can be semantically related only to the subject role player, as we will see (and explain) when we turn to the real reciprocal below.

(6–16)   Ho spinto i ragazzi l'uno contro l'altro.
         'I pushed the boys one against the other.'

(6–17)   Il direttore ha parlato alle ragazze l'una dopo l'altra.
         'The director talked to the girls one after the other.'

(6–18)   Quel donnaiuolo è uscito con tutte le signorine, l'una dopo l'altra.
         'That woman-chaser went out with all the young women, one after another.'

In (6–16) the PP is semantically related to the DO. In (6–17) the PP is semantically related to the IO. In (6–18) the PP is semantically related to the object of the P, *con* ('with').

Second, they can be semantically related to an NP that a so-called floated quantifier is also related to, while real reciprocals cannot, as I will show and explain below in the discussion of reciprocals.

(6–19) I ragazzi sono tutti entrati, l'uno dopo l'altro.
        'The boys have all come in, one after the other.'

In (6–19) both *l'uno dopo l'altro* and *tutti* are semantically related to the NP *i ragazzi*.

Third, they can occur in any of the niches that parentheticals can occur in, whereas the real reciprocals cannot, as I will again show and explain below in the discussion of reciprocals.

(6–20) L'uno dopo l'altro i ragazzi sono entrati.
        'One after the other the boys came in.'

(6–21) I ragazzi, l'uno dopo l'altro, sono entrati.
        'The boys, one after the other, came in.'

We can see, then, that the use of (*l'*)*altro* in a PP/AP with an initial *l'uno*, like those in (6–13) through (6–21), is not the reciprocal use. It will be essential in our discussion below that we keep this use of (*l'*)*altro* distinct from the reciprocal use.

The fourth use of (*l'*)*altro* that occurs in both Italian and English is the reciprocal use. In this usage (*l'*)*altro* must occur with *l'uno*, just as the reciprocal (*an*)*other* in English must occur with either *each* or *one*.

(6–22) The boys love each other.

(6–23) The boys love one another.

However, the Italian and English reciprocals differ with respect to their syntactic properties: the Italian reciprocal must consist of the discontinuous sequence *l'uno . . . (l'*)*altro*, whereas the English reciprocal must consist of the continuous sequences *each other* or *one another*. (Italian does have a continuous sequence, *l'un l'altro*, but, as Belletti 1982 has shown, this is an adverbial that co-occurs with the reflexive/reciprocal clitic *si*. Thus this continuous sequence is not itself a reciprocal involving an anaphor and we will not discuss it further.) From this point on, I will discuss only the Italian reciprocal, since Aoun's theory of binding uses properties of the Italian reciprocal in ways crucial to his arguments. Still, many of the remarks that follow about the semantics of the Italian reciprocal hold for English as well as Italian. (Many of the literal English translations for the Italian sentences in this subsection are ungrammatical, often because of the fact that Case assignment in English requires strict adjacency of the Case assigner to the Case assignee (as Stowell 1981 shows), but Case assignment in Italian does not require strict adjacency, as I discuss in sec. 3 below with regard to (6–73) and following examples.)

Belletti (1982), looks at sentences like that in (6–24) and argues they have the syntactic structure given in (6–25).

(6–24)   I miei amici parlano l'uno dell'altro.
          the my friends talk the one about the other
          'My friends talk about one another.'

(6–25)

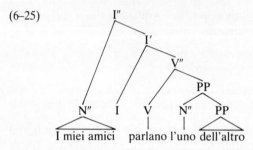

Thus the PP *dell'altro* is headed by the P that is selected by the verb *parlano* to introduce its theme argument (that is, Italians say *parlare di* ('speak of') and not **parlare su* ('speak on') or **parlare attorno* ('speak around'), etc.). Therefore, (*l'*)*altro* is an argument receiving a theta role (by Compositional Theta Assignment) from the head V. On the other hand, *l'uno* does not appear in the lexical structure of the head V; it is not an argument, it is an adjunct (to the PP, in Belletti's analysis).

Belletti argues convincingly that (*l'*)*altro* is an anaphor, and she contends that its antecedent is *l'uno* on the basis of evidence like the following.

(6–26)   Quei reporters ammiravano l'uno le foto dell'altro.
          'Those reporters admired one another's photos.'

(6–27)   *Quei reporters ammiravano l'uno le tue foto dell'altro.
          'Those reporters admired one your photos of the other.'

In (6–26) the NP *le foto dell'altro* does not have a possessive in its specifier position; therefore it is not a governing category for (*l'*)*altro*. Accordingly, (*l'*)*altro* can look outside this NP for its antecedent. But in (6–27) the NP *le tue foto dell'altro* has the possessive *tue* and is therefore the governing category for (*l'*)*altro*. Thus (*l'*)*altro* must be bound within the NP. But it is not. Therefore (6–27) is a violation of part A of the binding theory.

Since *l'uno* is an adjunct to PP, it is not in an 'A-position. Thus, if

Belletti's analysis is correct, elements in non A-positions can serve as the antecedents of anaphors. Aoun concludes from this that binding can be by non A-binders as well as A-binders.

Belletti further argues that in LF there is a Q-association rule that moves *l'uno* next to the NP it quantifies, leaving behind an empty node that is then an anaphor bound by the moved *l'uno*. In support of this claim she offers data like the following.

(6–28)   Mario ha sostenuto che i miei amici parlarono l'uno dell'altro.
       'Mario maintained that my friends spoke about each other.'

(6–29)   *I miei amici sostennero che Mario parlò l'uno dell l'altro.
       'My friends maintained that Mario spoke about one another.'

In the LF of (6–28) *l'uno* would appear beside *i miei amici* and can therefore serve as the antecedent for the reciprocal because it is within the governing category of that reciprocal. But in the LF of (6–29) *l'uno* would appear beside *i miei amici* and, therefore, it would not be within the governing category of the reciprocal, and, since the reciprocal requires a semantically plural antecedent, *Mario* is not an appropriate antecedent. Thus (6–29) is out because the reciprocal is not bound within its governing category.

Belletti's analysis is rather complex, so let me sum it up briefly. First, (*l'*)*altro* is an anaphor whose antecedent is *l'uno*. Second, in LF there is a trace in the original position that *l'uno* occupied, which is bound by the moved *l'uno* that is now positioned with the NP *l'uno* quantifies.

Belletti's analysis leads to a rather regrettable conclusion. She claims that *l'uno* is the subject of the phrase it is adjoined to. Thus in the relevant NP of (6–26), repeated here for convenience, *l'uno* is the subject of the NP.

(6–30)   l'uno le foto dell'altro

However, she also follows Cinque (1980) in claiming that for certain lexical classes of N, an NP in a *di* phrase which is a sister to the head N is the subject of that N. And *foto* falls in the relevant lexical class. Thus Belletti is led to claiming there are two subjects in (6–30), (*l'*)*altro* (which is the NP in the *di* phrase that is a sister to the head N *foto*) as well as *l'uno*. She recognizes this fact and takes the position that *l'uno* is only configurationally a subject, whereas (*l'*)*altro* in (6–30) is thematically a subject.

Belletti also fails to distinguish the PP/AP usage of (*l'*)*altro* discussed above with respect to (6–13) through (6–21). And this confusion leads to serious other problems in her analysis that we need not go into here.

Guéron (1985) follows Belletti with respect to the syntactic analysis of reciprocals, as in (6–25). However, she argues that the reciprocal is a small clause, with *l'uno* being the subject of the clause and (*l'*)*altro* being a pronominal rather than an anaphor. I believe Guéron's analysis is helpful with respect to the non-reciprocal usage of *l'uno* . . . (*l'*)*altro* exemplified in (6–13) through (6–21) (although I would disagree with her on the analysis of *l'uno*, which she claims is an anaphor). However, her analysis fails for the reciprocal construction for much the same reasons that Belletti's analysis fails, although it does have the advantage of not requiring a coindexing between *l'uno* and (*l'*)*altro*. In what follows I will point out problems only with Belletti's argument, but the reader can easily see how the issues discussed below also refute Guéron's small-clause analysis of the reciprocal.

I propose an alternative analysis. (*L'*)*altro* is an anaphor that requires a plural antecedent. *L'uno* is an adverbial similar to the so-called floated quantifiers, which are really also adverbials. (I employ here the functional term "adverbial," which is distinct from the category label of Adverb. See the discussion in ch. 1, sec. 1.1.) Let me demonstrate the explanatory value of this hypothesis.

First, the contrast between (6–26) and (6–27), repeated here for convenience, is easily explained since the NP *quei reporters* is the only appropriate antecedent for the anaphor (*l'*)*altro*.

(6–26)   *Quei reporters ammiravano l'uno le foto dell'altro.
         'Those reporters admired one another's photos.'

(6–27)   *Quei reporters ammiravano l'uno le tue foto dell'altro.
         'Those reporters admired one your photos of the other.'

In (6–26) the NP *quei reporters* falls within the governing category of (*l'*)*altro* (where the governing category is the whole clause here) whereas in (6–27) this NP falls outside the governing category of (*l'*)*altro* (where the governing category is the minimal NP containing (*l'*)*altro*). Thus (6–27) is a violation of part A of the binding theory.

Second, the contrast between (6–28) and (6–29) is easily explained and in the same way. Again, I repeat the examples for convenience:

(6–28)   Mario ha sostenuto che i miei amici parlarono l'uno dell'altro.
         'Mario maintained that my friends spoke about each other.'

(6–29)   *I miei amici sostennero che Mario parlò l'uno dell l'altro.
         'My friends maintained that Mario spoke about one another.'

I miei amici (being the only plural NP here) is the only appropriate

The A-position requirement   289

antecedent of *l'altro*. In (6–28) this antecedent falls within the governing category of the anaphor, but in (6–29) it falls outside.

The evidence that *l'uno* is an adverbial comes largely (and ironically) from Belletti herself. She notes that *l'uno* has much in common with so-called floated quantifiers. For one thing, we find contrasts with quantifiers that parallel the contrasts between (6–28) and (6–29). In the discussion that follows I will use the quantifier *tutti* ('all'). But I could as well have used the quantifier *ciascuno* ('each'), or *tutti* plus a cardinal number – as in *tutti e due* ('both'), or, for some speakers, *ognuno* ('every') (see Napoli 1974a).

(6–31)   Mario sostenne che i miei amici parlarono tutti dello stesso problema.
         'Mario maintained that my friends spoke all of the same problem.'

(6–32)   *I miei amici sostennero che Mario parlò tutti dello stesso problema.
         'My friends maintained that Mario spoke all of the same problem.'

In (6–31) the quantifier *tutti* can appear and is understood to be related semantically (in a way I will discuss below) to the plural NP *i miei amici*. But in (6–32) the quantifier *tutti* is out of place – in Chomsky's (1986b) terms, it is unlicensed – because there is no appropriate local plural NP that it can be related to semantically.

Given the contrast between (6–31) and (6–32), if my analysis is correct and *l'uno* is an adverbial quantifier, (6–29) is out both because the anaphor (*l'*)*altro* is not bound within its governing category and because *l'uno* cannot be related semantically to any local plural NP (where I will discuss this semantic relation below).

Belletti also notices that so-called floated Qs and *l'uno* have similar distributions, as seen in (6–33) through (6–36).

(6–33)   I miei amici ammiravano l'uno le foto dell'altro.
         'My friends admired the one the photos of the other.'

(6–34)   *I miei amici ammiravano le foto l'uno dell'altro.
         'My friends admired the photos the one of the other.'

(6–35)   I miei amici ammiravano tutti la foto di Maria.
         'My friends admired all the photo of Maria.'

(6–36)   *I miei amici ammiravano la foto tutti di Maria.
         'My friends admired the photo all of Maria.'

In (6–33) *l'uno* can appear to the left of the NP headed by the N *foto*. But in (6–34) we see that it cannot appear inside that NP between the head N and its PP sister. In (6–35) and (6–36) we see that *tutti* is admitted into and blocked from the same positions, at least linearly.

The similarity between *tutti* and *l'uno* in (6–33) through (6–36), however, is only apparent. Actually, the collocations of *l'uno* and *tutti* observe different restrictions that turn out to lead to the ungrammaticality of both (6–34) and (6–36).

The adverbial *tutti* is restricted to being a daughter either of the maximal projection or the single-bar level of the head of the predicate to which it is semantically related (again, we must wait till below for a discussion of this semantic relationship). We see this fact in (6–36), in the contrast between (6–37) and (6–38) below, and in the contrast between (6–39) and (6–40) below. (This is not true of adverbial *tous* in French, for at least some speakers – see Kayne 1975, who reports that some speakers can have *à tous* semantically related to a dative clitic. Thus the *tous* would be in a PP and would not be a daughter of any projection of the head of the predicate.)

(6–37)   Con Gianni e Paolo **tutti e due** studenti della geologia dell'Europa, avremo un bel gito informativo.
'With Gianni and Paolo both students of the geology of Europe, we'll have quite an informative little trip.'
Con Gianni e Paolo studenti **tutti e due** della geologia dell'Europa, avremo un bel gito informativo.

(6–38)   *Con Gianni e Paolo studenti della geologia **tutti e due** dell'Europa, avremo un bel gito informativo.

(6–39)   Sedettero **tutti** dietro a Gianni.
'They sat all behind Gianni.'

(6–40)   *Sedettero dietro **tutti** a Gianni.

That the initial absolute phrases introduced by *con* in (6–37)–(6–38) involve predication is shown in Ruwet (1982) for French and in Napoli (1987a) for English, where the arguments in both works go equally as well for the Italian construction. We can see that adverbial quantifiers like *tutti* must be daughters to the single- or double-bar level of the head of the predicate (in (6–37) *studenti*; in (6–39) *sedettero*).

L'uno, on the other hand, must be the left adjunct of a maximal projection that contains (*l'*)*altro* and that is a role player of the same predicate that the antecedent of (*l'*)*altro* is a role player of. (This restriction on collocation will be tied in to the semantics of the reciprocal in the discussion of semantics below.) This restriction accounts for the ungrammaticality of (6–34) in contrast to (6–33) above (repeated here for convenience), as well as the contrast in (6–41) versus (6–42) (example (6–42) is from Belletti 1982).

(6–33)   I miei amici ammiravano l'uno le foto dell'altro.

(6–34)   *I miei amici ammiravano le foto l'uno dell'altro.

(6–41)   Quei due amici apprezzano l'uno la fedeltà dell'altro.
'Those two friends appreciate one the faithfulness of the other.'

(6–42)   *Quei due amici apprezzano la fedeltà l'uno dell'altro.
'Those two friends appreciate the faithfulness one of the other.'

In (6–41) the NP *la fedeltà dell'altro* is a role player of the predicate *apprezzano*. And the antecedent of (*l'*)*altro* is the NP *quei due amici*, which is the subject role player of the predicate *apprezzano*. Therefore, *l'uno* can be the left adjunct of the NP *la fedeltà dell'altro*. But in (6–41) *dell'altro* is not a role player of any predicate (although (*l'*)*altro* is an argument of the lexical head *fedeltà*). Thus *l'uno* cannot be the left adjunct of the phrase *dell'altro*.

If the above statement of the restriction on the collocation of *l'uno* is correct, we expect that in a sentence with a V followed by a nominal followed by a PP (as in (6–41), if we remove the *l'uno* for a moment), where that V plus nominal form a multiple word predicate of which the object of the P is a role player of that predicate (unlike in (6–41)), then *l'uno* could be the left adjunct of such a PP. This expectation is fulfilled. (Example (6–43) is from Belletti 1982.)

(6–43)   Mario e Francesco non hanno mai avuto fiducia l'uno nell'altro.
'Mario and Francesco never had faith one in the other.'

In (6–43) the nominal *fiducia* is part of a multiple-word predicate (*non hanno mai avuto fiducia*), and the object of the (inflected) P *nell'* is a role player of that predicate (here the object of *nell'* gets a theta role by Compositional Theta Assignment). Thus *l'uno* can be the left adjunct of the phrase *nell'altro*. The contrast between (6–42) and (6–43) is explained in a simple manner with my analysis and thus should be considered strong support for my analysis. Belletti's analysis, on the other hand, needs to resort to the unfounded claim that Italian has reanalysis rules (and we have already seen in ch. 2, sec. 3 and ch. 4, sec. 2 that it does not – see the discussion following (4–121) in particular) in order to account for this contrast.

A similar example to (6–43) that has a multiple-word predicate ending in an adjective rather than a nominal is found in (6–44) (also from Belletti).

(6–44)   Quei due amici son rimasti fedeli l'uno all'altro.
'Those two friends remained faithful one to the other.'

Here the object of the (inflected) P *all'* is a role player of the multiple-word predicate *son rimasti fedeli*. Thus *l'uno* can be the left adjunct of the phrase *all'altro*.

It now follows from the fact that *l'uno* must be the adjunct of a role player of the predicate that the phrase initiated by *l'uno* can appear only in positions that role players can occur in. We now have an explanation for the fact mentioned above that the PP/AP modifier discussed in (6–13) through (6–21) above can occur in all the niches that allow parentheticals, while the real reciprocal phrase cannot. Thus, for example, in (6–45)a we see that the real reciprocal cannot appear between the GF subject and the VP, just as other role players in non-reciprocal sentences cannot occur there.

(6–45)a.   I ragazzi hanno parlato l'uno all'altro.
            'The boys spoke one to the other.'
          *I ragazzi, l'uno all'altro, hanno parlato.
          (cf. *I ragazzi a Maria hanno parlato.
            'The boys to Maria talked.')
      b.   I ragazzi sono entrati l'uno dopo l'altro.
            'The boys entered one after the other.'
          I ragazzi, l'uno dopo l'altro, sono entrati.
          (cf. Carlo, dopo Maria, è finalmente entrato.
            'Carlo, after Maria, has finally entered.')

Given the different restrictions on the collocations of *tutti* and *l'uno*, we predict that *tutti* can occur between an auxiliary and a head V (that is, attached under the single-bar level of the head of the predicate), whereas *l'uno* cannot. This is so.

(6–46)a.   I miei amici hanno tutti parlato dei loro problemi.
            'My friends have all spoken of their problems.'
      b.   *I miei amici hanno l'uno parlato dell'altro.
            'My friends have one spoken of the other.'

I will argue below that the difference in collocation facts between adverbials like *tutti* and the adverbial *l'uno* follows from the semantics of the two.

There is at least one other similarity between *l'uno* and adverbials like *tutti* that should be pointed out before we turn to the semantics of these adverbials. And that is that both of them must be semantically related to the subject role player of a predicate or to the DO if that DO is a clitic. (And, as I said above, this apparently is not so for French *tous* for at least some speakers, since Kayne (1975) reports *tous* semantically related to a dative clitic.) Consider the sentences below with the adverbial *tutti*.

(6–47)   *Ho descritto i miei amici tutti a Maria.
          'I described my friends all to Maria.'

(6–48)   Li ho descritti tutti a Maria.
          clitic
          'I described them all to Maria.'

(6–49)   *Ho descritto Maria ai ragazzi tutti.
          'I described Maria to the boys all.'

In (6–47) we see that *tutti* cannot be semantically related to a DO that is a full NP. In (6–48) we see that *tutti* can be semantically related to a DO that is a clitic pronoun. In (6–49) we see that *tutti* cannot be semantically related to an IO.

In (6–50) through (6–52) we see the same restrictions on *l'uno*.

(6–50)   *Ho descritto i ragazzi l'uno all'altro.
          'I described the boys one to the other.'

(6–51)   Li ho descritti l'uno all'altro.
          clitic
          'I described them one to the other.'

(6–52)   *Ho raccontato ai miei amici l'uno i problemi dell'altro.
          *Ho raccontato l'uno i problemi dell'altro ai miei amici.
          'I told to my friends one the problems of the other.'

One might object to my claim that both *tutti* and *l'uno* are blocked from being related to a full NP direct object on the basis of examples like the following, offered by Belletti.

(6–53)a. Ho incontrato i miei amici tutti davanti al cinema.
          'I met my friends all in front of the cinema.'
      b. Ho spinto quei bambini l'uno contro l'altro.
          'I pushed those boys one against the other.'

However, (6–53)b is not an example of the reciprocal construction, but instead of the PP/AP construction discussed above with respect to (6–13) through (6–21). To see this, note that the PP in (6–53)b can co-occur in the same argument complex (what we will define below in sec. 4 as an argument rung) with the adverbial *tutti*, but the reciprocal cannot (as we will see directly below).

(6–54)   Abbiamo tutti spinto quei bambini l'uno contro l'altro.
          'We all pushed those boys one against the other.'

Likewise, the *tutti* in (6–53)a is not the so-called floated quantifier *tutti*, but a Q which, like the *l'uno* of the PP/AP construction discussed in

(6–13) through (6–21) above, can introduce a phrase that functions as a modifier (here the PP *davanti al cinema*). Thus the Q *tutti* in (6–53)a can co-occur with the real adverbial *tutti* that we have been talking about all along.

(6–55)   Abbiamo tutti incontrato i nostri amici tutti davanti al cinema.
'We have all met our friends all in front of the cinema.' (Here all the friends are in front of the cinema.)

But the real adverbial *tutti* cannot co-occur in the same argument complex with another real adverbial *tutti*. Thus if we take (6–48) above and change the GF subject to a plural NP and add the real adverbial *tutti*, we get a bad result.

(6–56)   *Li abbiamo tutti descritti tutti a Maria.
'We have all described them all to Maria.'

Thus both the so-called floated Qs and *l'uno* must be semantically related to the subject role player or to a clitic DO. The fact that this unusual restriction is shared by both types of items is strong evidence that the *l'uno* of the reciprocal construction belongs to the same class of adverbials that so-called floated Qs belong to.

The adverbial analysis of the so-called floated Qs has the added advantage of not requiring any special mechanism to handle sentences with these Qs in which the GF subject is the impersonal *si* (see Napoli 1973), first noted by Kayne (1975, p. 63 n. 79) for French.

(6–57)   French: On est tous partis à la peche.
Italian: Si è tutti partiti a pescare.
'Everyone went fishing.'

If so-called floated Qs originated in GF subject position or even if they had to have all the properties of other QPs, it would be difficult to account for their association with *on* and *si* in (6–57). (Notice that we do not find *tous on* or *on tous*.) But if these so-called floated Qs are adverbials, their appearance in (6–57) is unproblematic.

It is now time to look at the semantic relationship between a so-called floated quantifier and the NP to which it is somehow tied. Then I will show that a similar semantic relationship holds between *l'uno* and the NP to which it is somehow tied.

Williams (1982) points out that so-called floated quantifiers cannot be quantifiers, in fact, since they do not show scope interactions that quantifiers located in specifier position of NP show. He suggests that floated Qs are adverbials "that 'modulate' the subject–predicate relation" (p. 284). Actually, adverbial Qs can modulate the relationship between a predicate and its clitic DO, as well, as we just saw above in (6–48). I will here adopt Williams' term 'modulate' and intend it to mean that the adverbial Q tells us that the relationship between the predicate and one of its role players is a complete-set one. That is, the predicate bears the same semantic relationship toward every member of the set denoted by the subject (or clitic DO) role player.

Other adverbial quantifiers modulate the relationship between a predicate and its relevant role player in a similar way.

(6–58)   Le donne hanno ciascuna ricevuto un fiore.
         'The women have each received a flower.'

(Example (6–58) is from Napoli 1974a.) Here *ciascuna* tells us that the relationship between the predicate and its subject role player is distributed across each of the members of the set to which the subject role player refers, picking out each relationship separately.

The same sort of modulation occurs with *l'uno*, but with an extra complexity. *L'uno* modulates the relation between the subject role player (or the clitic DO) and its predicate (just as so-called floated Qs do). But since the subject role player (or the clitic DO) is also the antecedent of the anaphor (*l'*)*altro*, the modulation of this relationship is with respect to how this relationship bears on the constituent which contains (*l'*)*altro* and to which *l'uno* is attached. To see this, consider the sentence below (also from Belletti 1982).

(6–59)   Quei ragazzi scrivono l'uno all'altro con regolarità.
         'Those boys write one to the other regularly.'

In (6–59) *l'uno* tells us that the relationship between the antecedent of (*l'*)*altro*, which is *quei ragazzi*, and the predicate *scrivono* as it bears on the PP *all'altro* is a distributive relationship. And since (*l'*)*altro* is an anaphor, this distribution is across the same set denoted by the antecedent of the anaphor – that is, *quei ragazzi*. Thus each boy wrote to at least one other boy in the same set.

Given the semantics of the adverbials we have been looking at, we can now see why *tutti* cannot co-occur with *l'uno*: their combination would render a sentence anomalous.

(6–60)   *I ragazzi hanno tutti parlato l'uno delle foto dell'altro.
         'The boys have all spoken one about the photos of the other.'

Tutti would modulate the relationship between the subject role player and the predicate to tell us that all the boys spoke about something. And since (*l'*)*altro* is an anaphor taking *i ragazzi* as its antecedent, we would have to see all the boys doing the same thing to all the boys. But *l'uno* would modulate this same relationship to tell us that each one in the set talked about at least one other one in the set. We cannot have both a complete set interpretation and a distribution across the set interpretation at once. Therefore (6–60) is anomalous.

Given the semantics of this use of *l'uno*, we can also explain another fact: neither possessive in (6–61) is acceptable (Belletti 1982 points out the unacceptability of the singular possessive, but the plural one is also unacceptable).

(6–61)   *I miei amici ammiravano l'uno le {sue/loro} foto dell'altro.
        'My friends admired one {his/their} photos of the other.'

Example (6–61) is out even if the possessive *sue/loro* is understood as coreferential with (*l'*)*altro*. This is, unlike reflexive or reciprocal anaphors in English, the Italian anaphor *l'altro* cannot be bound by a possessive. Belletti argues that this is because *l'uno* is the "designated" antecedent of (*l'*)*altro*. But since we already have seen that *l'uno* is adverbial, we must find another explanation for (6–61). And that answer follows immediately from two facts. First, the adverbial *l'uno* must be semantically related to the subject role player (or clitic DO) of the predicate (just as adverbials like *tutti* must). At the same time, *l'uno* must modulate the relationship between the antecedent of (*l'*)*altro* and the predicate as it bears on the phrase that *l'uno* is an adjunct of. But if *l'uno* must be semantically related in the same way to the subject role player (or clitic DO), and if it must also be semantically related to the antecedent of (*l'*)*altro*, then the antecedent of (*l'*)*altro* must be the subject role player (or clitic DO). Furthermore, if *l'uno* is to modulate the relationship between the antecedent and the predicate, then the antecedent must have a semantic relationship to the predicate. But the possessive in (6–61) does not have a theta role assigned by the predicate; it is not a role player of the predicate. Here the possessive has no direct semantic relationship to the predicate. Instead, it modifies the head of an argument of the predicate. So there is no direct relationship that *l'uno* could modulate between *sue/loro* and the predicate. In sum, (6–61) is out because of the semantic restrictions on *l'uno*. Thus we need not admit into our grammar anaphors that designate their antecedents (*contra* Belletti).

I conclude that *l'uno* is an adverbial like the so-called floated quantifiers.

Let me point out that *l'uno* and the so-called floated Qs agree for gender with the NP they modulate the relationship of to the predicate. The adverbial *ciascuno*, which is distributive in nature, is always singular, however, while the adverbials that are complete in nature, *tutti* and *tutti* plus a conjoined numeral, are plural. But *l'uno* can be singular or plural depending on the meaning.

(6–62)   Le ragazze sono tutte uscite.
         f.p.   f.p.
         'The girls have all left.'

(6–63)   Le ragazze hanno ciascuna comprato uno scaffale.
         f.p.   f.s.
         'The girls have each bought a bookshelf.'

(6–64)   Le ragazze hanno parlato l'una all'altra.
         f.p.   f.s.
         'The girls spoke one to the other.'

(6–65)   Le ragazze hanno parlato le une alle altre.
         f.p.   f.p.
         'The girls spoke in groups to each other.'

Furthermore, *l'uno* can have one gender while *l'altro* has another, as Belletti (1982) points out.

(6–66)   Paolo e Maria hanno parlato l'uno dell'altra di fronte a tutti.
         m.s. f.s.   m.s.   f.s.
         'Paolo and Maria spoke the one about the other in front of everyone.'

I conclude that *l'uno* is an adverbial and that *l'altro* is an anaphor taking the subject role player or a clitic DO as its antecedent.

The antecedent of the reciprocal anaphor *l'altro* in Italian, then, is in an A-position always (in fact, in GF subject or clitic DO position).

2.2   Conclusion

Antecedents of anaphors, like subject role players of predicates, must occur in A-positions. The only exception is in absolutives. This restriction on subject role players follows automatically from the predication coindexing principles developed in chapter 2. If the coindexing between an anaphor and its antecedent is the same coindexing as that between a predicate and its subject role player, the restriction that antecedents of anaphors must occur in A-positions follows from one and the same set of coindexing principles.

3   Barriers

We saw in chapter 2 that a subject role player cannot be separated from its predicate by any of its barriers. (For primary predicate coindexing, this fact follows from the fact that coindexing is always with the GF subject. For secondary predicate coindexing, this is Proviso Two.) If predicates and anaphors are really parallel, we then expect that an antecedent cannot be separated from its anaphors by any of its barriers.

In fact, this turns out to be true. We already have seen evidence to this effect in (6–3)–(6–4) above. Here I offer additional evidence:

(6–67)a. *John's mother loves himself.
    b. *Himself loves John.
    c. *La madre di Gianni$_i$ ama molto la propria$_i$ casa.
       'The mother of Gianni loves very much self's house.'
    d. *La propria$_i$ madre ama molto Gianni$_i$.
       'Self's mother loves very much Gianni.'

In (6–67)a the NP *John's mother* is not L-marked. Therefore it is a barrier for the NP *John's* contained in it. Thus *John's* is separated from the anaphor *himself* by one of its barriers and cannot bind it. In (6–67)b the antecedent *John* is separated from its anaphor by one of its barriers (the VP). Again, the coindexing is blocked. In (6–67)c&d we see parallel examples from Italian, due to Giorgi (1984). In (6–67)c the GF subject is not L-marked, so it forms a barrier for the contained NP *Gianni*, which therefore cannot serve as an antecedent for the anaphor *propria*. In (6–67)d the VP is a barrier for the DO *Gianni*, so, again, this NP cannot serve as an antecedent for the anaphor *propria*. (Actually, I will offer a different account of the ungrammaticality of (6–67)d later in this chapter.)

Of course, data like those in (6–67) are the typical data used to support the claim that a binder must c-command what it binds. Thus the traditional explanation for (6–67) is that *John('s)/Gianni* does not c-command *himself/propria*, therefore *John('s)/Gianni* cannot bind *himself/propria*.

One advantage of the c-command restriction over my barriers explanation for (6–67) is that with the c-command restriction we can rule out (6–67)a and (6–68) in the same way.

(6–68) *I described John's mother to himself.

In (6–68) the NP *John's mother* is L-marked by the V *described*; thus it is not a barrier for the contained NP *John's*. Therefore, my explanation for the failure of (6–67)a cannot carry over to explain the failure of (6–68). However, *John's* does not c-command *himself* in (6–68). Thus the traditional explanation for (6–67) holds equally well for (6–68).

While my theory cannot rule out (6–68) with the same explanation I have just offered for the ungrammaticality of (6–67)a, it does correctly rule out both sentences. Consider (6–68) closely. The anaphor here is within the theta domain of the V *described*. Therefore, if my predication theory is to be extended to anaphors and their antecedents, we predict by Proviso One (the relevant version here being (2–77)) that the antecedent of this anaphor must appear in the lexical structure of *described*. *John's* does not, however, appear in the lexical structure of *described*: it is neither an argument of this lexical head nor does it bear a GF with respect to this lexical head. Therefore, (6–68) is ruled out by Proviso One of my theory of predication. (Notice that (6–67)a&c are, likewise, ruled out. Thus these examples are redundantly marked ungrammatical.)

I contend, therefore, that the c-command restriction on the binding of anaphors is bogus. (And I leave open the question of whether it is a useful restriction on the binding of pronominals.) Evidence in favor of my contention is offered by instances of anaphor coindexing that are problematic for the c-command restriction but that are no problem whatsoever for my theory. For example, consider (6–69).

(6–69) As for himself, John loves baked beans.

The initial phrase sounds bad in any other position; thus a movement analysis of (6–69) is unfounded.

(6–70)a. *John, as for himself, loves baked beans.
     b. *John loves baked beans(,) as for himself.

Following the work we did in chapter 2, we know that the initial phrase here is attached as a sister to C″ (and we can have a filled specifier of the CP, as expected, as in: *As for John, how can he expect anyone to help him?*). Therefore, *John* does not c-command *himself* in (6–69). By the traditional binding theory, (6–69) should, therefore, be bad. But it is good, just as my theory would predict.

Furthermore, my theory predicts that anaphors in initial phrases like that in (6–69) can find their antecedent only in GF subject position, not in

DO or any other position, since an NP in any other position will be separated from the anaphor by one of its barriers. This prediction is true.

(6–71)   *As for himself, I love John.

The VP node acts as a barrier for the NP *John* in (6–71), thus *John* cannot be coindexed with the anaphor *himself.*

In (6–71) it is important to use a third-person reflexive, which typically obeys the various formulations people have proposed for anaphor binding, rather than a first- or second-person reflexive – which in many people's speech defies all such formulations, as is well known. For example, some people can say (6–72)a and (6–72)b, so it is no surprise that some people can say (6–72)c (in contrast to (6–71), which every speaker I have asked rejects). Example (6–72)c was pointed out to me by Andrew Radford (personal communication).

(6–72)a.   Q. How are you today?
            A. Fine. And yourself?
       b.   The nerve of the man! He dared to blame it on Mary and myself.
       c.   As for myself, four-letter words embarrass me.

The reader will note that my analysis of sentences like (6–69) requires a base-generated sister to C″. Throughout this book an important point has been to demonstrate that for the projections of N, V, A, and P, there is no evidence (at least not with respect to the kinds of phenomena examined in this book) that we need sisters at the X″ level or at the X′ level, other than conjuncts or specifiers. That is, both modifiers and arguments of N, V, A, and P are generated at DS as sisters to the N, V, A, and P. However, it is quite possible (and I believe that examples like (6–69) show that it is necessary) that the categories of I(nflection) and C(omplementizer) allow sisters at all the projection levels. (And see ch. 2, sec. 5 and ch. 5, secs. 2 and 5.) Thus my analysis of (6–69) is not inconsistent with the restrictive version of X-bar theory I have adopted here.

Returning to our refutation of the c-command restriction on binding, we find another problem offered by Italian. In order to understand the problem, we must first lay out some facts about Case assignment in Italian as compared to English. In Italian the adjacency requirement on Case assignment is blind to non-arguments, unlike in English.

(6–73)a.   Ho letto lentamente quel bel libro.
       b.   *I read slowly that fine book.

In (6–73)a the adverb *lentamente,* which is a non-argument, can intervene between the DO and its Case assigner. But in (6–73)b the adverb *slowly* cannot. To see that it is a question of Case assignment, rather than just some other problem of word order, contrast (6–73) to (6–74):

(6–74)a. la sua foto, ovviamente, di se stesso
     b. his photograph, obviously, of himself

(A context for (6–74) might be in response to the question, "What did Eddie Ego take on vacation with him?") Here we have the same word order as in (6–73) (that is: predicate–modifier–argument), but the predicate in (6–74) is an N and does not assign Case. Instead, the P assigns Case to its object. I conclude that Case assignment is blind to non-arguments in Italian but not in English.

On the other hand, Case assignment in Italian, while it does see arguments, still only weakly asserts an adjacency requirement, in contrast to English.

(6–75)a. ?Ho descritto a Mario il mio libro.
     b. *I described to Mario my book.

Example (6–75)b is totally out in English because the NP *my book* is not adjacent to a Case assigner and so fails to receive Case. But its Italian counterpart in (6–75)a is only marginally bad. Of course, in both languages heavy node shift can result in good sentences.

(6–76)a. Ho descritto a Mario il libro che sto scrivendo proprio ora.
     b. I described to Mario the book that I'm writing at this very moment.

Examples (6–76)a&b have a trace after the main verb, and Case is assigned to this trace in the normal way. But the contrast between this pair and (6–75)a&b tells us that (6–75)a&b do not involve a trace.

Now we find that if we have the word order seen in (6–75)a in Italian with an anaphor as the DO and its antecedent as the IO, the sentence has the same marginal grammaticality as (6–75)a. (Example (6–77) is from Belletti 1982, whose judgment my informants agree with.)

(6–77) ?Ho descritto a Mario se stesso.
     'I described to Mario himself.'

Example (6–77) is a problem for the c-command restriction on the binding of anaphors, since *Mario* here, being the object of a P, does not c-command the anaphor *se stesso*. With the c-command restriction we would expect (6–77) to be totally ungrammatical, but it is not. Example (6–77), however, is no problem for my theory, since it is consistent with

Proviso One: *se stesso* is within the theta domain of *descritto*, and *Mario* appears in the lexical structure of *descritto* (as an argument). Thus (6–77) is predicted with my theory to be only marginal, for reasons of Case assignment, entirely parallel to (6–75)a.

Other problems for the c-command restriction are offered by Giorgi (1984) with regard to so-called "long-distance anaphora" in Italian. (Giorgi concludes that c-command is irrelevant to long-distance anaphora, although she maintains a c-command restriction on what she calls "strict" anaphora. I discuss her position in section 6 below. See also Bouchard (1982), who argues that a reflexive that is not antecedent-governed is a pronominal, not an anaphor.) In (6–78) *propria* is an anaphor, yet it is not c-commanded by its antecedent:

(6–78)   La propria$_i$ salute preoccupa molto Osvaldo$_i$.
          'Self's health worries Osvaldo a lot.'
          La malattia della propria$_i$ moglie preoccupa molto Osvaldo$_i$.
          'The illness of self's wife worries Osvaldo a lot.'

Similar evidence against the c-command restriction comes up in the English so-called picture nouns. Larson (1987) offers:

(6–79)   Nude pictures of herself don't offend Mary.
          Stories about himself excite John.

Larson attributes the grammaticality of (6–79) to the fact that the verbs here are the so-called "psych verbs." He points out that in (6–80), where we do not have a psych verb, the anaphor coindexing is disallowed.

(6–80)   *Nude pictures of herself absolved Mary of the crime.

Larson accounts for the difference between (6–79) and (6–80) by adopting the analysis of psych verbs in Belletti and Rizzi (1986), whereby the GF subject of the psych verbs in (6–79) is base-generated as a sister to the psych verb, and thus in a position to be c-commanded by the antecedent (which is the DO) in (6–79). Then this NP is moved into GF subject position, but its trace is still properly bound by the DO of the verb.

This account, while it looks promising for the data considered in Belletti and Rizzi (1986) and in Larson (1987), is simply inadequate to handle all the relevant data. Thus the phenomenon in (6–79) occurs with non-psych verbs, as well. All my informants accept (6–81) and many accept (6–82):

(6–81)   Those nude pictures of himself cost John his job.

(6–82)   ?Those nude pictures of himself ruined John in his girlfriend's eyes.

No analysis of (6–81)–(6–82) is available in which the GF subject is in any position other than GF subject at all points in the derivation. Thus I take (6–79) and (6–81)–(6–82) as evidence against the c-command restriction on anaphor coindexing.

The reader at this point will have noticed, of course, that examples like (6–78), (6–79), (6–81), and (6–82) are problematic for my claim that the provisos on secondary predication hold for anaphor binding. I must beg the reader's indulgence here. In section 4 immediately below I turn to a discussion of not just these examples, but of a range of examples that are likewise problematic and that are all susceptible to a single explanation. I will argue there that Proviso One must be modified by making use of the concept of argument ladders (developed there). And I will argue further that Proviso Two holds only for local anaphor binding (where the distinction between local and long-distance binding is also developed there). For now, we can assume that my arguments in section 4 below will allow us to account for these examples without threatening the analyses already defended here. On this assumption I will now return to the issue of the c-command restriction and try to put it to rest for good.

The c-command restriction on anaphor coindexing is perhaps one of the most revered restrictions of recent linguistic theories, and I do not expect the reader of this book to abandon it lightly. But if one goes through the types of data typically used to support the c-command restriction (like those in (6–67) above), one will find that my theory consistently offers a viable alternative. And, as we have seen above, there are data that my theory easily handles that are problems for the c-command restriction (such as (6–69) versus (6–71), and (6–77)).

A proponent of the c-command restriction might point out pairs like the following (which were, in fact, pointed out to me by an anonymous reader of an earlier draft of this book, with the judgments given here):

(6–83)   Frank compared the men to each other.
         ??Frank's comparison of the men to each other.

(6–84)   Wanda warned the men about each other.
         ?Wanda's warning to the men about each other.

Here a DO can serve as the antecedent to an anaphor that is the object of a P in the first example of each pair. But in the second example of each pair, with a similar argument structure but a different syntactic structure, the object of a P cannot serve as the antecedent of an anaphor that is the object of another P. An obvious difference is that in the first example of each pair the antecedent c-commands the anaphor, but in the second it does not.

The anonymous reader who pointed out (6–83)–(6–84) to me also pointed out (6–85) (again, with the judgments here):

(6–85)   ?John wrote to Mary about herself.
         *John's letter to Mary about herself.

This reader attributed the difference here to the familiar claim that a V plus P can be reanalyzed as a complex V in English, but that an N plus P cannot. So if reanalysis applied in the first example of (6–85), the antecedent would c-command the anaphor. But under no analysis of the second example of (6–85) would the antecedent c-command the anaphor.

I have already argued at length in chapter 2, section 3 against the existence of a reanalysis rule taking a V plus P and forming a complex V in English. (And these arguments were in no way dependent upon my predication theory; a reanalysis rule simply makes wrong predictions about a range of data.) Thus I take both examples of (6–85) to have an antecedent inside a PP.

The question now is why there is a difference in acceptability in each pair in (6–83)–(6–85). The speakers I have asked agree with my anonymous reader that in all these instances the first example of each pair is preferable to the second, although they do not find as marked a difference as the anonymous reader reports. Thus they find the second example of (6–83) only slightly marginal and they accept the second example of (6–84). (A better example was offered to me by Barry Furrow (personal communication): *This is my last warning to you jerks about each other. You're gonna get each other in trouble for sure.*) And they feel that both examples of (6–85) are really quite marginal if not entirely ungrammatical.

Still, as I said, the first of each pair is preferred to the second. The reason, however, has nothing to do with c-command. Instead, if we replace the second example of each pair in (6–84)–(6–85) with an example in which the antecedent occurs in specifier position of NP (that is, in a position in which it would, in fact, c-command an anaphor inside the NP), we still feel a preference for the first example of each pair in (6–84) and (6–85) over these replacement examples:

(6–86)   Listen up! This is [your last warning about each other].
         *I'm going to sit down now and write [Mary's letter about herself].
         (cf. Both Mary and Jim have a right to know about the divorce. So I'm

going to sit down now and write Mary's letter about Mom and Dad's divorce. Then it'll be your turn to write Jim's letter about it.)

(Notice that there is no counterpart to the second example in (6–83) here, since this NP simply sounds terrible with *the men* in specifier position regardless of the presence of an anaphor.)

I do not know why these preferences arise. It is interesting to point out that a number of my informants accepted the second example of (6–86), just not with the reading in which the letter is to Mary. Instead, if the letter is going to be a forgery, where I write the letter and am going to pass it off as one that Mary wrote, for instance, the sentence is good. Thus the problem has to do specifically with *Mary* being interpreted as the goal argument – and has nothing to do with c-command. (I return to a discussion of theta roles as a factor in determining the ability of an NP to be an antecedent in sec. 6 below.)

There are, undoubtedly, other types of examples one could come up with to challenge my contention that c-command is irrelevant to anaphor coindexing. But I know of no examples that hold firm under close scrutiny.

I conclude that the c-command restriction on the coindexing of an anaphor and its antecedent is incorrect. Instead, restrictions needed for predication theory will account for all the cases that the c-command restriction was meant to cover without ruling out grammatical sentences like that in (6–69) and marginal sentences like that in (6–77) (which is just as good as (6–75)a, the sentence without an anaphor), and without calling for a movement analysis of psych-verb clauses (as in (6–79)).

It appears then that antecedents must not be separated by any of their barriers from the anaphors they bind (at least for local binding – see sec. 4 below). This is precisely what we would expect if the coindexing here were the same coindexing that occurs in predication structures.

4 Anaphors in theta domains in English

Up to this point the discussion has been intended to hold for both Italian and English. The discussion in this section, however, holds only for English, as does the discussion in section 5 below. I return to the consideration of data from Italian in section 6.

Secondary predicates may appear within the theta domain of a lexical head. (Recall that I use the term "theta domain" to include all the sisters and prepositional sisters of a lexical head. And only L-marked arguments, not other arguments, are within the theta domain of a lexical head.) When they do, their subject role player must appear in the lexical structure of that head. This is Proviso One (the relevant version being (2–77)) of our predication theory. We might expect, then, that whenever an anaphor falls within the theta domain of a lexical head, its antecedent must appear in the lexical structure of that head. Our expectation, however, holds only partially.

First, let us look at anaphors that fall within the theta domain of a V. If the V is the head of a predicate, then the antecedent of the anaphor must be an argument of the V.

(6–87)   Ralph [[enjoys] [himself]].

(6–88)   Ralph [[described] [me] [to myself] perfectly].

(6–89)   *Ralph [[told] [a story about Jane] [to herself]].

(6–90)   *Ralph [[said] [that I enjoyed himself]].

In (6–87) the antecedent is an argument of the V (and it is also the subject role player). In (6–88) the antecedent is an argument of the V (and it is also the DO). But in (6–89) the anaphor can find no antecedent. *Ralph* is inappropriate because of the clash of gender. Let us consider why *Jane* is unable to bind *herself*. We might ask whether either of the constraints on antecedents that we saw in sections 2 and 3 above are violated in (6–89). The answer is no. First, *Jane* is in an A-position (it is an argument of *story*), as all antecedents of anaphors must be. Furthermore, no barrier of the NP *Jane* comes between this NP and the anaphor, since the NP *a story about Jane* is L-marked (by the verb). I conclude that *Jane* cannot serve as the antecedent of the anaphor because it does not appear in the lexical structure of the head verb *told* that the anaphor is an argument of. The same is true of (6–90). Here *I* is not an appropriate antecedent because of the person clash. However, *Ralph*, which is in an A-position and which is not separated by any of its barriers from the anaphor, also is not a possible antecedent. This is because *Ralph* is not in the lexical structure of the verb *enjoyed*, whose theta domain the anaphor falls within.

Thus, we can conclude for English that when an anaphor falls in the theta domain of a verb that is the head of a predicate, its antecedent must appear in the lexical structure of that verb.

Likewise, when an anaphor falls within the theta domain of a verb that is the head of a VP which functions as a modifier, the antecedent of the anaphor must appear in the lexical structure of that V.

(6–91)   The girl [enjoying herself] smokes too much.

(6–92)   The psychiatrist [[describing] [Sue] [to herself]] makes a lot of mistakes.

(6–93)   *The doctor [[telling] [a story about Jane] [to herself]] is an old man.

(6–94)   *I met the girl [enjoying myself].

In (6–91) the NP *the girl* appears in the argument structure of the V *enjoying* (and is given a theta role by *enjoying* here via Theta Identification, discussed in ch. 1). In (6–92) the NP *Sue* is an argument of the V *describing*. But in (6–93) the NP *Jane* is not an argument of the V *telling*. And in (6–94) the NP *I* is not an argument of the V *enjoying*.

Anaphors that fall within the theta domain of V, then, behave as we expect given Proviso One.

Now let us look at anaphors that fall within the theta domain of an A that is the head of a predicate. Again, we find that the antecedent of such an anaphor must appear in the lexical structure of that A.

(6–95)   Ralph is [fond of himself].

(6–96)   *I consider Sue [fond of myself].

(6–97)   *I think Ralph is [fond of myself].

In (6–95) *Ralph* is an argument of the A *fond* (and it is also its subject role player), so it can serve as the antecedent. But in (6–96) *I*, although it is in an A-position and although it is not separated from the anaphor by any of its barriers, cannot serve as the antecedent. This is because *I* is not in the lexical structure of *fond*. Likewise in (6–97) *I*, although it is in an A-position and although it is not separated by any of its barriers from the anaphor, cannot bind the anaphor. This is because *I* is not in the lexical structure of the A *fond*, whose theta domain the anaphor falls within.

Turning to anaphors in the theta domain of an A where the A″ functions as a modifier, we find that the antecedent once more must appear in the lexical structure of the A.

(6–98)   I like anyone [fond of himself].

(6–99)   *I like anyone [fond of myself].

In (6–98) *anyone* appears in the argument structure of *fond* (where (6–98) is parallel to (6–91) above). But in (6–99) *I* does not appear in the argument structure of *fond*.

Thus an anaphor that falls within the theta domain of an A must find an antecedent that appears in the lexical structure of that A, just as Proviso One would require.

So far so good. Our anaphors are behaving in a pattern entirely parallel to predicates.

Now let us turn to anaphors that fall within the theta domain of an N where the N is the head of a predicate. Suddenly we find problems for the neat parallelism we have been seeing thus far.

(6–100) Catherine$_i$ is an advocate of {herself/*her(s)$_i$}.

(6–101) The drug rendered Catherine$_i$ an enemy to {herself/*her$_i$}.

(6–102) John$_i$ considered Catherine an equal to {(?)himself/him$_i$}.

In (6–100) and (6–101) *Catherine* is an argument of the N *advocate/ enemy*, so it can be an antecedent for the anaphor. But in (6–102) *Catherine* is not an appropriate antecedent, both because of the gender clash and because of the semantics. Thus even (6–103) is odd:

(6–103) ??John considered Catherine an equal to herself.

The problem with (6–103) is that it is hard to figure out what on earth the speaker could mean by this sentence. We see, then, that in (6–102) the anaphor cannot find an appropriate antecedent among the arguments of the N *equal*. We might expect that in such a situation no anaphor would be possible. And certainly every speaker I asked accepted the regular pronoun in (6–102). But, surprisingly, many also felt the anaphor was possible (and all felt it was no worse than marginal) with *John*, which is not an argument of *equal*, as its antecedent. Notice that *John* is in an A-position and is not separated by any of its barriers from the anaphor. Thus this example is consistent with Proviso Two, but it makes us question Proviso One, as stated in (2–77).

But recall that in chapter 2, section 5 we saw that a weaker version of Proviso One was necessary for predicates that fall within the theta domain of an N. In fact, we said that if such a secondary predicate were theta marked by the N, its subject role player would have no restriction on it other than that imposed by Proviso Two (see (2–79)). We are finding, then, that anaphors which fall inside the theta domain of an N also appear to have weaker restrictions on where they can find their antecedents than do anaphors that fall within the theta domain of other types of lexical heads. While we have yet to determine what those restrictions are (and while I will argue below that the differences between coindexing with secondary predicates/anaphors that fall within the theta domain of N and coindexing for those within the theta domain of other categories are only apparent and not real, after all), we can see that once more a parallel between anaphors and secondary predicates emerges.

Another example in which the lack of an appropriate antecedent among the arguments of the head N allows an anaphor to look outside the N's argument structure for an antecedent is seen in:

(6–104) Meredith accepted the betrothal of herself to Ralph because she didn't have any choice.

Here *betrothal* is the relevant N. But if there is a genitive present that is a semantically appropriate antecedent, the coindexing is blocked:

(6–105) *Meredith$_i$ accepted Mother's betrothal of herself$_i$ to Ralph because she didn't have any choice.

The contrast between (6–104) and (6–105) brings to mind the familiar pattern that we have seen used to support the notion of SUBJECT in GB, often with the so-called picture nouns (see Gruber 1967).

(6–106) I like (those) photographs of myself.

(6–107) *I like Bill's photographs of myself.

(6–108) I showed Bill photographs of himself (as a baby).

(6–109) *I showed Bill Sally's photographs of himself.

Here we see that the antecedent of the anaphor in (6–106) and (1–608) can appear outside the argument structure of the N *photographs*. But if there is a genitive in the NP, this coindexing is blocked, as we see in (6–107) and (6–109). The blocking effect is found even when the genitive is not in specifier position:

(6–110) *I like those photographs of Bill's of myself (on stage).
         (cf. I like those photographs of Bill's of me on stage.
         I like those photographs of Bill's of the children in their Sunday clothes.)

Given our definitions of srp in chapter 1, we can see that in all examples in (6–100)–(6–110) where an anaphor that falls within the theta domain of an N can look outside the argument structure of that N for an antecedent, either the N lacks an explicit srp (as in (6–104), (6–106), and (6–108)) and/or there is no argument of the N that could possibly be an appropriate antecedent for the anaphor due to other semantic factors (as in (6–102) – witness the marginality of (6–103) – and in (6–104)).

It is important to recognize that the lack of an appropriate antecedent must be due to general semantic considerations, and not just to gender or number or person clash (i.e., not just to feature clash).

(6–111)   *John considered Catherine an advocate of himself.

Here *himself* and *Catherine* clash for gender. Yet, since there is nothing odd about someone's being an advocate for herself, *Catherine* is not blocked from being an antecedent on general semantic grounds. Therefore, the anaphor cannot step outside the argument structure of the N *advocate* to find an antecedent. (The same is true of the person clash in (6–107).)

We now have two questions in front of us and their answers turn out to be related. First, why should Ns be different from Vs and As with respect to the requirements we find on the antecedent of an anaphor that falls within the theta domain of the lexical head? Second, exactly what are the requirements on the antecedent of an anaphor that falls within the theta domain of an N?

In answer to the first question, I believe that Ns do not really differ in any definitional or categorical way from Vs and As regarding anaphor coindexing. Instead, I believe that it is easier to find examples where an anaphor in the theta domain of H can look outside the argument structure of H for an antecedent when H is an N rather than a V or an A, simply because NPs are so frequently the arguments of other lexical items. That is, what we are dealing with here are interrelated argument structures. If an N heads an NP that is an argument of some V, for example, then all arguments of the N are, formally, part of an argument (the NP) of that V. So one argument structure is inside the other argument structure.

I propose that we look at it in terms of lexical ladders, where each rung of a ladder is defined by a theta assigner. All the items that appear in the lexical structure of a lexical item H are on the lexical rung defined by H (that is, all the arguments of H and all the elements that bear a GF toward H are on the lexical rung defined by H). If H″ is an argument of another theta assigner or bears a GF toward another theta assigner, call it H*, then the rung defined by H* is the next rung up in the ladder. If H*″ is an argument of another theta assigner or bears a GF toward another theta assigner, call it H**, then the rung defined by H** is the next rung up in the ladder. And so forth.

We can then see that typically an anaphor that is on a rung of a lexical ladder (in most cases this means an anaphor that is an argument of some

H) must find its antecedent on the same rung. However, if there is no explicit srp of H and/or there is no argument or GF of H that is semantically appropriate as an antecedent, then the anaphor may look up to the next rung in the lexical ladder to find an antecedent.

Notice that it is lexical structures that matter, regardless of whether the relevant theta assigner is a predicate or a modifier:

(6–112)   I like the girl looking at photographs of herself.
        *I like the girl looking at photographs of myself.

(6–113)   I dislike any boy fond of photographs of himself.
        *I dislike any boy fond of photographs of myself.

In (6–112) the anaphor is an argument of *photographs*, but there is no explicit srp here. The anaphor can therefore look up to the next rung in the lexical ladder, that defined by the V *looking,* which acts as a modifier to the N *girl* here. And it successfully finds an argument of *looking* to act as its antecedent. Therefore, it cannot go beyond this lexical rung to any higher rung (and that is why the second example of (6–112) is bad). The same situation precisely holds in (6–113), with the difference that here the modifier is headed by an A (*fond*), rather than a V.

The reader will of course recognize that the traditional explanation within GB for facts like those above involving anaphors that are found within NPs is that of governing categories. The idea is that the minimal NP or clause that contains a governor for X″ and a s u b j e c t accessible to X″ is the governing category for X″. So if an NP has a genitive NP in specifier position (which will qualify as an accessible s u b j e c t), then an anaphor within that NP cannot look outside the NP for an antecedent because the NP is the governing category of the anaphor.

The data in (6–112), however, cannot be explained by appealing to governing categories. In (6–112) the modifying VP, *looking at photographs of herself,* is not a governing category for the anaphor. The NP *the girl looking at photographs of herself* is not, either, since this NP does not have a subject argument. With the traditional GB approach, then, we have no explanation for the failure of the second sentence of (6–112).

In order to salvage the governing category explanation, we might try to argue that the modifying phrase *looking at photographs of herself* in (6–112) is a C″, rather than a V″. This would then be some form of a relative clause and the antecedent of the anaphor would be the variable in GF subject position of the relative clause. The second sentence of (6–112) would then be ruled out because the antecedent of the anaphor is not within the governing category (the C'' of the relative clause) of the anaphor.

Whether or not such an analysis of (6–112) could be maintained, however, we would still have to deal with (6–113). In (6–113) the AP *fond of photographs of myself* is not a governing category for the anaphor. Nor is the NP *any boy fond of photographs of ANAPHOR*. Thus the governing category of the anaphor is the entire sentence. We therefore have no explanation for the failure of the second sentence in (6–113).

Furthermore, if I am correct that the relevant factor is one of lexical ladders, then the phenomenon we have been looking at should not, in fact, be limited to only anaphors that are within the theta domains of Ns. Instead, this phenomenon should occur with anaphors that are within the theta domains of Ps or As or Vs, also, so long as the PP or AP or VP is in the lexical structure of some other lexical item, typically as an argument.

I do not know of clear-cut instances in which VP is the argument of some other lexical item (although this is, in fact, Zubizarreta's 1985 analysis of certain complements of causatives and perception verbs in Romance – see the discussion in ch. 2, sec. 10). However, we have seen instances in which APs and PPs are the arguments of a V (see ch. 1, sec. 3), as in:

(6–114)   Ralph considers Mary nice.

Here the AP *nice* is an argument of *considers*. Now if we have an anaphor inside the AP complement of *considers,* we find that it must not go outside the lexical structure of the head A to look for an antecedent unless there is no argument or GF of that A that is semantically appropriate as an antecedent.

(6–115)   *Ralph considers Mary fond of himself.

(6–116)   Ralph considers Mary inferior to himself.

In (6–115) a person can certainly be fond of herself, and therefore *Mary* is not semantically inappropriate as an antecedent for an anaphor within the AP. Thus the anaphor cannot look outside the lexical structure of the A for its antecedent. But in (6–116) a person cannot be inferior to herself, and therefore *Mary* is semantically inappropriate as an antecedent for an anaphor within the AP. Thus the anaphor can look outside the lexical structure of the A for its antecedent.

However, in both (6–115) and (6–116) the governing categories for the anaphors should be the same. Therefore, a governing category solution to anaphor coindexing simply fails to make any distinction between (6–115) and (6–116) and cannot account for the difference in coindexing possibilities here.

A parallel situation arises for PPs. So in (6–117) the secondary predicate *as after anyone in pants* is an argument of the V *depicted*, as is the secondary predicate *as into jazz* in (6–118):

(6–117) Ralph depicted Mary as after anyone in pants.

(6–118) Ralph depicted Mary as into jazz.

Since someone cannot be after herself in the sense of (6–117) (although someone can be after herself in the sense of nagging herself), we expect that an anaphor inside the PP here can look outside the lexical structure of this PP for an antecedent. But since someone can easily be into herself in the sense of (6–118), we expect that an anaphor inside the PP here cannot look outside the lexical structure of this PP for an antecedent. And, in fact, some speakers accept (6–119), but no one I asked accepted (6–120).

(6–119) ?Ralph depicts every woman as after himself.

(6–120) *Ralph depicted Mary as into himself.

Again, a governing category solution could not make the required distinction between (6–119) and (6–120). But a lexical ladder solution can.

I conclude that governing categories have nothing to do with the binding of anaphors. Instead, the key to the matter is lexical ladders, as I have explained already. Let me state this proposal formally:

(6–121) *Anaphor Coindexing* (a first approximation): An anaphor must take an antecedent from the minimal available rung of its lexical ladder.
Definition: A rung is available if it has some argument or GF other than the anaphor and there is nothing in the sense of the lexical head that defines that rung that would prevent one of its arguments or GFs from being coindexed with the anaphor.

As Andrew Radford (personal communication) has pointed out to me, if we were to look at each lexical rung as a kind of lexical cyclic domain, then (6–121) is simply saying that anaphor coindexing is cyclic in some sense.

Proposal (6–121) is quite clearly inaccurate: it both allows for more anaphor coindexing possibilities than actually occur and disallows some that do occur. We will modify it accordingly in section 6 below. The relevant point for us here is that the concept of lexical ladders is helpful in analyzing the data we have seen thus far.

It is important to note that lexical ladders are not made up strictly of arguments. (In this way the notion of lexical ladder is distinct from the notions of T-domain and T-government in Chomsky 1986b.) GF positions that appear in the lexical structure of a word and that are not assigned theta roles can appear on the rung defined by that word. This is important, since I will use the notion of lexical ladders in the principle below for indexing predicates with their subject role players as well as for anaphor coindexing. And, as we pointed out in chapter 2, section 5, the subject role player of a secondary predicate that falls in a theta domain can appear in the lexical structure of the lexical head whose theta domain the predicate falls within, either as an argument of that lexical head or as having a GF with respect to that lexical head. We will also see below that modifiers are treated as though they belong to the rung defined by the lexical head X, where the minimal phrasal node that contains that modifier is X″.

We have now answered both of the questions we asked above. First, Ns are not really special (witness (6–116) and (6–119)); they only appear to be so at first because they so often head NPs that are arguments of some other lexical head. Second, Ns do not in fact call for any individual statement of coindexing for anaphors that fall within their theta domain. Instead, (6–121) will handle all anaphors that fall in a theta domain of any category head.

As I said above, we will find in the sections below that it is necessary to modify (6–121). However, even at this point, we might try to find a single statement that will do what Proviso One (as stated in (2–77)) does for predication and at the same time do what (6–121) does for anaphor coindexing.

There is, in fact, only one major difference between Proviso One and Anaphor Coindexing in (6–121). And that is that predicates must find their subject role players on the minimal rung of the ladder they belong to, while anaphors can keep on looking up the ladder, depending on availability.

I do not know why this difference exists. Certainly there are differences between anaphors and predicates. For example, anaphors that appear in a theta domain are always arguments, but predicates that appear in a theta domain are rarely arguments. Instead, such predicates are typically adjuncts. If this fact were the key to the difference between Proviso One and Anaphor Binding, we would expect that predicates which are, in fact, arguments would behave like anaphors. However, they do not. For example, the noun *diagnosis* can take a predicate as an argument:

(6–122) Jeff cried at the diagnosis of Mary as a schizophrenic.

(6–123) Jeff cried at Mary's diagnosis as a schizophrenic.

The noun *diagnosis* also need not syntactically realize all of its arguments:

(6–124) Jeff cried at the diagnosis.

(6–125) Jeff cried at Mary's diagnosis.

We might expect that if the argument which is a predicate is realized but no other argument is syntactically realized, the predicate can look up to the next rung of the lexical, or argument, ladder to find a subject role player. But it cannot.

(6–126) Jeff hated the diagnosis as a schizophrenic.

When faced with a sentence like (6–126), my informants have fallen into three groups. Group A says that (6–126) is an ungrammatical sentence. Group B says that (6–126) feels incomplete because we do not know who has been diagnosed as a schizophrenic – it could be Jeff or anyone else. And Group C goes the way we would expect and says that (6–126) is good with the only interpretation being that Jeff has been diagnosed as a schizophrenic.

Thus it would look as if our expectations are met by Group C. However, they are not, really. Consider

(6–127) The doctors disagreed with the diagnosis as a schizophrenic.

Group A rejects (6–127), just as it rejected (6–126), but some people felt a slight improvement in (6–127) over (6–126). Group B accepts (6–127) and says that the diagnosis is most probably of someone other than the doctors, but it could be of any single one or all of the doctors, too. And Group C accepts (6–127) with the same interpretation that Group B assigned it. If Group C had really been following a principle like that of Anaphor Coindexing in (6–121) above, the only interpretation should have been that in which the doctors have been diagnosed as schizophrenics.

I believe that (6–126) and (6–127) are, strictly speaking, ungrammatical. The only reason speakers accept them at all is that they are readily interpretable on analogy with sentences like:

(6–128) Jeff hated the diagnosis of schizophrenia.
The doctors disagreed with the diagnosis of schizophrenia.

I conclude that predicates must find their subject role players on their own rung (just as Proviso One states) of the argument ladder they belong to. This is the first difference we have seen between the binding of predicates and the binding of anaphors.

At this point we can look back at problematic examples that arose in section 3 above. Consider again (6–78)–(6–82):

(6–78) La propria$_i$ salute preoccupa molto Osvaldo$_i$.
'Self's health worries Osvaldo a lot.'
La malattia della propria$_i$ moglie preoccupa molto Osvaldo$_i$.
'The illness of self's wife worries Osvaldo a lot.'

(6–79) Nude pictures of herself don't offend Mary.
Stories about himself excite John.

(6–80) *Nude pictures of herself absolved Mary of the crime.

(6–81) Those nude pictures of himself cost John his job.

(6–82) ?Those nude pictures of himself ruined John in his girlfriend's eyes.

In (6–79)–(6–82) the anaphor falls within the theta domain of *pictures*, but there is no argument or GF of *pictures* other than the anaphor. Thus by Anaphor Coindexing in (6–121), we expect the anaphor to be able to find an antecedent in the next-higher rung – that defined by the matrix verb. In (6–79)–(6–82) the results are as expected, given (6–121).

The problem is that the antecedent here is within the VP, which acts as a barrier. Thus (6–79), (6–81), and (6–82) are violations of Proviso Two.

Looking at (6–78) we find another violation of Proviso Two, although here the anaphor is not in a theta domain and the N it specifies does not have an argument structure. Still, it would appear that all Ns act as though they define a rung of the argument ladder and that their specifiers belong to their rung. (See also M. Anderson (1983), who points out that all possessives of NP act as subjects for the binding principles, regardless of whether or not they have theta roles. And see Pustejovsky (1985) and Torrego (1986) for evidence that possessives which are not thematic have, nevertheless, a significant effect on whether or not extraction from within the NP is possible.) Thus (6–78) would be another instance in which an anaphor looks up to the next-higher rung to find an antecedent.

Although I argued in section 3 above that a movement analysis of sentences with psych-verbs does not help here (given that we still would be left with no account of (6–81)–(6–82)), I believe that Belletti and Rizzi (1986) and Larson (1987) are correct to point out the significance of the lexical choice of the verb for the possibility of an anaphor properly contained in GF subject position being coindexed with an antecedent inside the VP. Let us make use of the thematic prominency hierarchy of Giorgi (1984), in which agent is more prominent than experiencer, which is more prominent than theme and the other theta roles. We can see that in (6–78), (6–79), and (6–81) the antecedent of the anaphor is arguably an experiencer, while the GF subject (the NP the anaphor is properly contained within) is not an agent and not an experiencer – and therefore must be lower on the prominency hierarchy than the antecedent of the anaphor. In other words, the antecedent of the anaphor is the most prominent argument of the next-higher rung of the argument ladder.

In fact, Giorgi (1984) argues that whenever an anaphor does not find a local antecedent, it must take the most thematically prominent argument of a higher rung of the argument ladder as its antecedent. I contend, instead, that the restriction is that such an anaphor must find only an agent or an experiencer as an antecedent, as we will see below. (Actually, Giorgi frames her claim in terms of governing categories and complete functional complexes (which she takes as the relevant distinction between local and long-distance binding) – and see Giorgi (1987). But in my terms her claim would amount to the above. I return to a comparison of Giorgi's and my positions in sec. 6 below.)

In (6–82) the antecedent of the anaphor is also quite possibly an experiencer, while the GF subject is not an agent but, perhaps, an instrument or even a theme.

Now we have already noted that in all these sentences a barrier of the antecedent (the VP node) intervenes between it and the anaphor, in violation of Proviso Two. However, Proviso Two cannot simply be dismissed in light of examples such as (6–67) and (6–71), discussed above.

I propose that **when the antecedent is on a higher rung of the argument ladder than the anaphor, so long as the antecedent is the agent or experiencer argument of its rung on the argument ladder, Proviso Two can be overlooked**.

Notice that Proviso Two must be maintained when the antecedent and the anaphor belong to the same rung of an argument ladder. Thus, for example, we could rule out (6–67)b without Proviso Two if every anaphor were required to find an antecedent that is an agent or an experiencer.

(6–67)b. *Himself loves John.

Here *John* is a theme. However, even if the DO is an experiencer – as happens with psych-verbs – a sentence with the structure in (6–67)b is ruled out:

(6–129) *Himself worries John.

Furthermore, it is common to find in the literature on reflexives examples in which a reflexive takes a theme on its own rung as its antecedent. Proviso Two, then, correctly rules out both (6–67)b and (6–129). Also, no requirement on the theta role of the antecedent can help explain contrasts like (6–69) versus (6–71) (since the relevant theta roles here are both nonagents and nonexperiencers), whereas Proviso Two nicely accounts for them.

I conclude that Proviso Two holds when an anaphor and an antecedent belong to the same rung of the argument ladder. (And I am taking a modifier phrase'like *as for X″* to belong to the rung of the X head of the X″ it modifies.) Let me call anaphor binding on a single rung LOCAL ANAPHOR BINDING. Let me call all other anaphor binding (where an antecedent belongs to a higher rung on the argument ladder than the anaphor) LONG-DISTANCE ANAPHOR BINDING. We can then say that Proviso Two holds for local anaphor binding. And we can say that the theta role constraint (that an antecedent be an agent or an experiencer) holds for long-distance anaphor binding. (We will return to a discussion of the theta role constraint in sec. 6 below, where I will argue that it should not be stated as a discrete constraint, but, rather, it should fall out from the proper definition of argument ladders.)

Before leaving this section let me point out that sentences with *seem* do not present any particular problem for my theory. In a sentence like:

(6–130) John seems to himself to be invincible,

the predicate is the discontinuous string *seem to be invincible* (see ch. 1, sec. 1.3). We therefore have only one argument rung in this sentence (although we have two clauses). Therefore, the anaphor in (6–130) is entirely expected.

5   Anaphors outside theta domains in English

Many anaphors fall outside theta domains. When a predicate falls outside a theta domain, there are two restrictions on its coindexing: if the predicate is primary, its subject role player must be in GF subject position; if the predicate is secondary, its subject role player must not be separated by any of its barriers from the predicate and it must fall within the domain of the primary predicate that it is secondary to.

In this section I will look at anaphors that fall outside theta domains and test whether their binding restrictions mirror the coindexing of predicates that fall outside theta domains.

5.1   Emphatic reflexives

One type of anaphor that falls outside a theta domain is the so-called emphatic reflexive. Since I cannot here go into a detailed analysis of all the uses of the emphatic reflexive, I will consider only that use which clearly involves an anaphor that is not in a theta domain: that is, the emphatic reflexive in floated position. Thus I will not consider emphatic reflexives that immediately follow the nominal they are bound by.

(6–131)   The president is coming himself!
The president convinced us himself!

Such an anaphor cannot usually be bound by a DO:

(6–132)   *We put the president in our car himself!

(Example (6–132) is good, but with the "alone" reading, not the emphatic reading.) Nor can it be bound by an IO:

(6–133)   *We gave the president a kiss himself!

Nor can it be bound by the object of a preposition:

(6–134)   *I looked behind the president for guards himself!

Instead, floated emphatic reflexives typically find an antecedent only in GF subject position. However, this fact should not be taken as definitional. Instead, an emphatic reflexive can take an antecedent that is a srp of a predicate, whether that srp is in GF position or any other.

(6–135)a.   I consider the president entirely responsible himself.
b.   With the president coming himself, we can count on a large crowd.

(Example (6–135)a was offered to me by Andrew Radford (personal communication). See Postal 1974 for further examples of this sort (but a different account of them).)

The question now is whether the antecedent must be on the same argument rung that the floated emphatic reflexive is attached to. So, consider:

(6–136)a.   That the president came himself convinced us (I can tell you that)!
     b.   *That the president came convinced us himself!
     c.   *The president announced that I was coming himself after he had already announced that the Vice-President was coming!

The emphatic reflexive can be attached to an embedded clause, as in (6–136)a. But if the emphatic reflexive is attached to the matrix clause, it cannot look into an embedded clause to find its antecedent, as we see in (6–136)b, even when the embedded clause is on a lower rung of the same argument ladder that the matrix verb defines a rung of. And if the emphatic reflexive is inside an embedded clause, as in (6–136)c, it cannot look into a higher clause to find an antecedent, regardless of the existence of an argument ladder.

We can see that a floated emphatic reflexive must take a srp as its antecedent and it must be locally bound. In this way, floated emphatic reflexives observe coindexing restrictions that are close to those that primary predicates observe.

5.2   Anaphors in GF subject position

Another anaphor that falls outside a theta domain is one that appears in GF subject position of an infinitival:

(6–137)   Bill wants [himself to win].

(6–138)   The boys want [each other to win].

(6–139)   The boys seemed [t to understand].

In (6–137) the NP *himself* is not a sister node to the verb *want*; instead, the C″ *himself to win* is a sister to the verb *want*. Therefore, the NP *himself* is not in a theta domain. (It does receive a theta role, but from the verb *win*, whose theta domain it is not located in.) Likewise, the anaphor *each other* in (6–138) is not in a theta domain, and the trace of NP movement (which is an anaphor, in the sense of Chomsky 1981, 1982) in (6–139) is not in a theta domain.

If anaphors are parallel to predicates, we expect that such an anaphor will behave like a predicate. Notice that anaphors in this position must find the GF subject of the next-higher clause as their antecedent.

(6–140)   *Jack said Sue wants himself to win.

(6–141)   *Mary told the boys that Sue wants each other to win.

(6–142)   The boys$_i$ seem to me$_j$ [t$_{i/*j}$ to understand].

In (6–140) and (6–141) we see that the antecedent for such an anaphor cannot be found two clauses up. In (6–142) we see that the antecedent for such an anaphor cannot have a GF other than GF subject.

It seems that anaphors in these positions are parallel to primary predicates, since they require that their antecedent be in the GF subject position. A difference, however, is that the antecedent of the anaphors above is found in the next higher clause, whereas the subject role player of a primary predicate is always found in the same clause as the predicate. This difference, of course, follows from the fact that the anaphors in (6–137) through (6–139) are in the GF subject position of their own clause themselves. Therefore, their antecedent has to be elsewhere. And it turns out that their antecedent is the minimal available GF subject around, which turns out to be the minimal available srp around.

The difference here between anaphors and predicates is reminiscent of the difference we saw in section 4 above. Whereas secondary predicates must find their subject role player in their own rung of the argument ladder, anaphors must find their antecedents in the minimal available rung of the argument ladder. And now we see that whereas primary predicates must find their subject role player in GF subject position of their own clause, anaphors that do not appear in a theta domain (other than specifiers of N, which behave as though they are in a theta domain – see the discussion of (6–78) at the end of sec. 4 above) must find their antecedents in the minimal available srp position.

While in this section we have looked only at anaphors in GF subject position of infinitivals, the same kind of data are found for anaphors in GF subject position of other tenseless clauses, as in the complements of causatives (see Rothstein 1983, p. 96) and in the Accusative-*ing* construction (see Reuland 1983).

(6–143) John made [himself cry].

(6–144) John counted on [himself winning].

We have therefore seen at least two instances in which anaphors which do not fall in a theta domain behave in a similar manner to primary predicates: the floated emphatic reflexive of section 5.1 above and anaphors that appear in GF subject position of tenseless clauses.

5.3   Anaphors as objects of P

We have seen in sections 5.1 and 5.2 above anaphors which do not appear in theta domains. They are in adjunct position (as in sec. 5.1) or in GF subject position of a tenseless clause (as in sec. 5.2). We also saw in section 4 with Italian (as in (6–78)) that anaphors in specifier position of N behave as though the N defines a rung to which they belong, regardless of whether or not that N has an argument structure. This is true also for English (and see M. Anderson 1983):

(6–145)   The boys borrowed each other's books.

Thus anaphors in specifier position behave as though they are in theta domains. (Notice that this fact can be seen as support for my position in ch. 1, sec. 2.3 that possessives are generated in sister position to the head N.)

The only remaining place to look for an anaphor that is not in a theta domain is as the object of a P that is not a theta assigner and where the object of the P does not receive a theta role via Compositional Theta Assignment, either. So our next question is, do anaphors occur in this position?

Before we answer this, let us try to see what we expect the answer to be on the basis of the behavior of predicates. We find that predicates never occur inside PPs unless they are accompanied by the object of the P and they predicate of that object. This may be partly because the objects of Ps are typically things (in the sense of Jackendoff 1983), but predicates are events. However, I think the main reason has to do with the function of Ps.

As we saw in chapter 1, section 2.4, Ps are relational items. They relate their object to the proposition they are located in or to some other proposition that is brought to mind by the context and other pragmatic factors. If the object of the P is a role player in the proposition the PP is located in syntactically, then the P has either almost no semantic function (being, perhaps, only a Case assigner), or functions to (help) tell which role player that object is, or (in the rare case) the P is itself a predicate. But if the object of the P is not a role player in the proposition the PP is located in, the PP functions as a modifier to (some part of) that proposition.

It is in the latter case that the object of the P is not in a theta domain. Therefore, it is this latter case (in which the PP is a modifier) that concerns us here. And in this case the PP is semantically insular: it sets off all the material in it as a unit which functions semantically as a whole with respect to the rest of the proposition – and no item within the PP can be singled out to participate in some semantic rule with respect to a position outside the PP. (This idea is relatable, of course, to Aoun's (1985) proposal that PP is a governing category.) I propose that this is the real reason why predicates do not appear as the object of a P. A predicate cannot be alone on a semantic island. It has to find a subject role player in order to be licensed. So if a predicate finds itself inside a PP that functions as a modifier, it must also find its subject role player inside that PP. The result is that, whenever we have a predicate inside a PP, we have an absolutive construction.

Let us now consider anaphors. Although an anaphor contrasts with a predicate in being appropriate as the object of a typical P (being a thing, rather than an event), anaphors require an antecedent. So anaphors simply cannot be semantically independent of the proposition they belong to in the way that objects of non-theta-assigning Ps typically are.

I predict, therefore, that an anaphor will appear as the object of a P only if it receives a theta role.

There are, in fact, suggestive data that anaphors cannot freely occur as the object of Ps where they do not receive a theta role. It has been noted repeatedly and with varying explanations that objects of P are sometimes anaphors and sometimes pronominals even when their antecedent is local (see Chomsky 1981, pp. 289–90, Guéron 1984, Aoun 1985, pp. 68–9, among many others, including particularly Dwight Bolinger, in class lectures at Harvard, winter 1972, and elsewhere). The question for us is whether the choice of anaphor or pronoun depends upon whether the object of the P receives a theta role.

We do, in fact find contrasts like those below.

(6–146) John$_i$ is into {himself/*him$_i$} too much. (We have to encourage him to try to be more sociable.)

(6–147) John$_i$ looks after {himself/*him$_i$}.

(6–148) Bill {brought/carried} some books with {*himself/him}.
The box has books in {*itself/it}.
The list includes my name on {*itself/it}.
The dame stood looking about {her/*herself}.

(The first three examples in (6–148) are from Gruber 1965). In (6–146) *into* is a theta-assigning P, and the anaphor is the only choice for its object. In (6–147) the object of *after* receives a theta role compositionally from *look* (after), and an anaphor can appear here (and, in fact, must). But in (6–148) the objects of the Ps receive no theta role and an anaphor cannot occur here. These PPs are modifiers and here are part of the predicate of their clause.

We can conclude from the above that if an object of a P receives no theta role, it cannot be an anaphor. This explains (6–148). If an object of a P receives a theta role, and if it is coindexed with a local NP (where a local NP is one on the same rung of the argument ladder), then it must be an anaphor. This explains the ungrammaticality of the pronominals in (6–146) and (6–147).

Other less obvious examples of this same point can be found. Guéron (1984) has noted sentences in which either an anaphor or a pronominal is possible, as in (6–149).

(6–149)   John$_i$ pulled the blanket over {himself/him$_i$}.

She attributes the possibility of both an anaphor and a pronoun following *over* in (6–149) to the possibility of two syntactic analyses for this sentence. On one analysis, the V has what Guéron calls "the transfer property." The V in this analysis assigns a theta role to the object of the P (where the PP is not a sister to the V, but a sister to V′, since Guéron adopts Kayne's (1984) binary branching hypothesis), and the anaphor emerges. On the other analysis the string *the blanket over X″* forms a small clause, where the object of the P receives no theta role since the PP is itself a predicate. The pronoun emerges in this analysis.

I would contend, instead, that the anaphor is a possibility in (6–149) because it is possible to see a close semantic tie in the words *pull the blanket over*. These words can be viewed in two ways. In one way the PP *over X″* is simply a location, and the X″ object of *over* receives no theta role. Accordingly, we find the pronoun here. In the other, *pull . . . over* is viewed as a single action of covering, where the item covered is the object of *over* and the instrument used for covering is the object of *pull*. On this reading the object of *over* is the theme argument of the multiple-word discontinuous predicate *pull . . . over*. It therefore receives a theta role, and, accordingly, we find an anaphor here. Notice that if the object of *over* received a theta role, we would expect that it could be the subject role player of a predicate that falls within the theta domain of the verb. And for many speakers it can. Example (6–150) was offered to me by Ken Hale (personal communication).

(6–150)   I pulled the blanket over Jack as the one most in need of protection.

There is a great deal of similarity between Guéron's and my explanations of (6–149). Guéron attributes the presence of the anaphor in object position of the P here to theta-role assignment to the object of that P from the V. I, similarly, claim that the object of the P in (6–149) receives a theta role from the multiple-word predicate. Guéron assigns two syntactic structures to an example like (6–149), and she adopts the small-clause analysis. I, however, assign only one syntactic analysis to (6–149), not involving a small clause, but I attribute the choice of anaphor or pronominal to the fact that a speaker can semantically analyze the words *pulled . . . over* either as a unit (denoting a single action) or not.

As I said above, Guéron attributes the possibility of an anaphor in (6–149) to a property of the V – the transfer property. Verbs of action which assign the theta role of theme to their object and goal or source to their prepositional object and agent to their subject have the transfer property, according to Guéron. But if Guéron were right, *pull* could do this to any prepositional object. That is, the transfer property is associated with a given verb. Yet *pull* rejects an anaphor as the object of the P in (6–151).

(6–151)   John$_i$ pulled the wagon beside {*himself/him$_i$}.

And in place of *beside* in (6–151) we could put a range of locative Ps, finding the same acceptability judgments regarding the anaphor and pronominal. In order to salvage her analysis Guéron would have to claim that *pull* has the transfer property only when the P with it is *over*. But then her analysis would be a terminological variant on my own.

In my analysis, (6–151) is expected. We see the *beside X″* here as simply marking location. That is, we do not have the option of viewing *pull . . . beside* as a single action (in contrast to *pull . . . over* in (6–149), where the action is one of covering). The object of the P here, then, is not closely tied in semantically to anything else in the proposition. Thus an anaphor as an object of this preposition would be semantically insulated from the rest of the proposition. Therefore, an anaphor is impossible in (6–151).

In chapter 2, section 3 we discussed the idea, posed by many in different guises (see the citations in ch. 2), that pseudo-passives are possible only if the P forms a possible semantic word with the verb. I argued there that the possible semantic word hypothesis could not correctly account for the data on predication and that the semantic unit idea is divorced from the hypothesis of reanalysis (which also fails as an explanation for the behavior of predication). However, it does seem true that whenever we find a pseudo-passive, the preposition is closely tied semantically to the verb (even though the converse is not true: that is, we can have prepositions which are closely tied semantically or even lexically or structurally selected by the verb without allowing a grammatical pseudo-passive). Now notice that (6–149) has a corresponding pseudo-passive for at least some speakers, whereas (6–151) does not, as Andrew Radford (personal communication) has pointed out to me (the following examples are his):

(6–152)   The blanket was pulled over.

(6–153)   *The wagon was pulled beside.

Thus (6–152) offers support for my claim that *over* is, in fact, closely semantically tied to *pull* in (6–149). But (6–153) tells us nothing about whether or not *beside* is closely semantically tied to *pull* in (6–151).

As further support for my claim that it is how we view a string of words and therefore which items we take to be predicates and which to be arguments that determines whether an anaphor is an option as the object of a P, consider (6–154).

(6–154)   John$_i$ hid the book behind {?himself/him$_i$}.

In isolation, speakers I asked judged the pronominal to be highly preferable to the anaphor in (6–154). However, in an appropriate context, the preference disappeared.

(6–155)   John$_i$ quickly hid the book behind {himself/him$_i$} so that his mother wouldn't realize he still had it.

I suggest that the intensification of the furtiveness here allows us to see the string *hid . . . behind* as a single action performed by John to himself. With this semantic analysis, the object of the P is an argument of the multiple-word predicate and an anaphor is appropriate. On the other hand, we always have the option of viewing the PP as merely a location – so the pronoun is also appropriate.

I conclude that the crucial factor in the choice between anaphor and pronominal in (6–149) through (6–155) is whether or not the object of the P bears a theta role.

Guéron also offers the examples in (6–156) and (6–157) as evidence that it is the transfer property of the V that is crucial to the possibility of an anaphor.

(6–156)   We gave Bill those pictures of {us/each other}.

(6–157)   We envy Bill those pictures of {us/*each other}.

According to Guéron, since *give* has the transfer property, but *envy* does not, the small clause (in Guéron's analysis) following *Bill* in (6–157) does not permit binding over its boundary.

My analysis of anaphor binding nicely handles (6–156): *each other* can be bound by *we* because *we* occurs on the first available rung of its argument ladder. However, (6–157) is a problem.

Still, I think (6–157) is open to an explanation with my analysis if we allow ourselves some flexibility in how we define the rungs of an argument ladder. Notice that there is a crucial difference between how we interpret *Bill* with respect to the NP *those pictures of X"* in (6–156) and its interpretation in (6–157). In (6–156) *Bill* received the pictures, as a complete non-role player with respect to them. That is, *Bill* had no relationship to the pictures, so far as this sentence tells us, prior to the giving. Bill's only stated relationship to the pictures is by way of the giving. However, in (6–157) Bill owns or took or somehow else relates to the pictures, independently of our envying him. In this sense, we can see the NP *Bill* as controlling our interpretation of the agent argument of *pictures*. We could say that *Bill* binds the specifier of the NP, so that *Bill* and *those* are coindexed. And, therefore, the head N *pictures* has two arguments on its rung: the anaphor and the specifier *those* (coindexed with *Bill*). The result is that *each other* does not find an antecedent within the first available rung of its argument ladder (which has its own rung, given that there is another argument of *pictures* present there), so (6–157) fails with an anaphor.

In support of the claim that *Bill* in (6–157) controls the interpretation of the specifier of the NP headed by *pictures*, notice the strangeness out of context of an agent argument inside the NP headed by *pictures*.

(6–158) ??We envy Bill Jack's pictures of the elephant.

(6–159) ?*We envy Bill those pictures of the elephant of Jack's.

Examples (6–158) and (6–159) are decidedly odd. What is strange here is the interpretation. Without a context, we do not immediately imagine why someone might envy Bill for some relationship Jack has to certain pictures. We typically envy people because of something we see them having some kind of close relationship with, such as possession, but not limited to possession:

(6–160) I envied Mary her mother's good looks.

Since Mary may benefit from her mother's good looks (perhaps by winding up beautiful like her mom), (6–160) makes sense.

The analysis of (6–157) is not without its problems (the exact mechanism that allows coindexing between *Bill* and *those* being something that demands scrutiny – and see Williams (1985) for the proposal of a similar coindexing rule in the analysis of different data). However, it has some advantages, too. For instance, if we allow NPs that our sentence tells us have an actor-type relationship toward a head N to be considered as controlling some argument that belongs to the rung of the argument ladder defined by that head N, we can easily explain the following facts.

Many verbs can be construed as active or causative, as Guéron (1984) argues (and see the works cited by Guéron). Thus Guéron offers examples such as the following, where in (6–161) we see the active sense of *give* and in (6–162) we see the causative sense of *give*.

(6–161)   My mother gave me a book for my birthday.

(6–162)   The war gave Mailer a book.

Then Guéron points out examples such as (6–163), which is ambiguous between the two readings.

(6–163)   Nixon gave Mailer a book.

We find that on the active reading of (6–163) we get an anaphor in a sentence like (6–164), but on the causative reading we get a pronominal.

(6–164)a.   (active) Nixon$_i$ gave Mailer a book about himself$_i$.
      b.   (causative) Nixon$_i$ sure did give Mailer a book about him$_i$.

This is as we would predict, since Nixon on the active reading has an actor relationship toward the book independently of the giving. That is, he had the book first or he could not have given it to Mailer. Thus the NP *Nixon* in the active reading can be viewed as controlling the agent argument of the N *book*, perhaps by being coindexed with the specifier *a*. Then the anaphor *himself* would find an antecedent (the *a* coindexed with *Nixon*) on its own rung of the argument ladder.

But in the causative reading Nixon has no actor relationship toward the book. He may not even know about the book. His only relationship toward the book that we are told of here is expressed by way of the PP *about him*. So the NP *Nixon* cannot be interpreted as controlling the agent argument of *book*. Therefore, if we had an anaphor as the object of the P *about*, this anaphor would find no antecedent on its own rung – and would therefore be limited to finding only an agent or an experiencer from some higher rung as its antecedent. But on the causative reading, *Nixon* is not an agent, but perhaps a theme or an instrument. Thus an object of *about* that is coreferential with *Nixon* cannot be an anaphor. We therefore expect the pronominal in (6–164)b.

Let me point out that *Mailer* in (6–164)b is a beneficiary with respect to *gave*, and not an agent or an experiencer. However, if every lexical head that has an argument structure has a most thematically prominent argument, then *Mailer* must be the most thematically prominent argument of *gave* here. We can now find an empirical difference between Giorgi's (1984) claim and my own. Giorgi's analysis (which claims that the anaphor in long-distance anaphor binding 'must take the most thematically prominent argument as its antecedent) would lead us to expect *Mailer* to be an acceptable antecedent of an anaphor as the object of *about* (or, at least, would give us no explanation for why *Mailer* could not be such an antecedent). (Actually, since Giorgi uses the notion of governing category to distinguish boundaries for anaphor binding, she would see only one domain for anaphor binding in (6–164) on any reading – and therefore her analysis would give us no explanation for why *Mailer* could not be such an antecedent.) But my analysis would lead us to expect that *Mailer* could not be the antecedent to such an anaphor.

In fact, when I presented speakers with the sentences in (6–164) and asked whether an anaphor object of *about* could be understood as coreferential with *Mailer,* I found interesting responses. First, on the causative reading (in which Nixon's behavior gave Mailer cause for writing a book about Mailer), everyone I asked rejected an anaphor coreferential with *Mailer* in favor of a pronominal, although they all disliked both choices and said they would try to express the idea differently. Their preferences then would support the idea that the antecedent must be an agent or an experiencer, rather than the most thematically prominent argument. However, on the active reading (in which Nixon handed over to Mailer a book that was about Mailer), many people could accept both the anaphor and the pronominal here, again expressing a general dislike for both choices.

This result is not predicted by either a prominency restriction or my restriction on agents and experiencers. It is as though on the active reading the speakers are treating the sentence as involving only one rung, but on the causative reading they are treating it as involving two rungs (and see relevant remarks in Guéron 1984). I conclude that so far as these data go, they are partially supportive of the idea that long-distance anaphora requires an agent or experiencer antecedent rather than the most thematically prominent argument antecedent.

Finally, let me suggest that the type of explanation given for (6–157) might be used fruitfully to account for the semantics of sentences such as that in (6–165), discussed in Williams (1985).

(6–165)   John submitted Harry to Sue's scrutiny.

Williams says that Harry "binds" the patient argument of *scrutiny*. Jackendoff (1987b) says this binding takes place in conceptual structure. In my analysis an NP coindexed with *Harry* would belong to the rung defined by *scrutiny*, and *Harry* would belong to the rung defined by *submitted*.

While much of the above deals with rather delicate semantic distinctions and rather ill-defined (with respect to their precise nature) extensions of the theory I have presented in this book, I believe that we can firmly conclude that anaphors cannot appear as the objects of Ps unless they either receive a theta role or are closely semantically tied in to the other elements of the proposition of the clause in which their PP is located.

In this way, anaphors and predicates are, once again, very similar: neither can be semantically isolated from the clause they appear in.

5.4   Conclusion

I conclude that anaphors that do not fall in theta domains behave in a manner parallel to predicates that do not fall in theta domains. This parallelism should be captured by a theory of indexing that treats predication indexing and anaphor indexing as a unitary phenomenon. Section 7 will offer such a theory. But first let us turn our attention more closely to long-distance anaphor binding by looking at some issues of anaphora in Italian.

6   Long-distance anaphora in Italian

In many languages anaphors and their antecedents need not appear on the same rung of an argument ladder (as we have seen for English in sec. 4 above) or even in the same clause. Among these languages are Latin, Eskimo, Japanese, Icelandic, Norwegian, and others (see Mey 1970, Ernout and Thomas 1972, Kuno 1973, Thráinsson 1976, Hellan 1981, S. Anderson 1982, and Koster and Reuland 1987 and the references there). Given that a predicate must find its srp within the same clause the predicate is located in, the fact that anaphor binding is not clause-bound in these languages and others presents a potentially serious threat to my proposal that predication coindexing and anaphor coindexing can be handled by a single set of principles. Surely an investigation of non-clausebound anaphora in these languages with my proposal in mind is called for. Such an investigation, however, cannot be reasonably attempted within the confines of this chapter.

I will, however, look at non-clausebound anaphor binding in Italian, with comparisons with English (where the phenomenon occurs but with less frequency and more restrictions). And I hope that the discussion in this section can lay the groundwork for fruitful discussion of the relationship between predication coindexing and anaphor coindexing in the other languages that exhibit non-clausebound anaphor binding.

A review of the conclusions we have reached thus far in this chapter is in order before we can go on to look at new data.

First, in section 4 we arrived at the following first approximation of a principle for anaphor coindexing:

(6–121) *Anaphor Coindexing* (a first approximation): An anaphor must take an antecedent from the minimal available rung of its lexical ladder.

(Note that I use the terms "lexical ladder" and "argument ladder" interchangeably.)

This principle needs revision and must eventually replace Proviso One.

We also noted that Proviso Two (the barrier proviso) does not hold on long-distance anaphor binding, but only on local anaphor binding, where local anaphor binding is on a single rung of an argument ladder and long-distance anaphor binding is all other anaphor binding.

On the other hand, we noted that for long-distance anaphor binding in place of Proviso Two we find the restriction that the antecedent of the anaphor be the agent or experiencer argument of the antecedent's rung. The evidence for this restriction in section 4 was based solely on English data.

Giorgi (1984) has offered an alternative way of viewing anaphora in Italian. She proposes that instead of viewing all anaphors as belonging to a single class, where the issue would be one of whether the antecedent was local or nonlocal, there are two classes of anaphors. She calls one class "strict" anaphors – and these anaphors require an antecedent within their governing category. That is, strict anaphors obey Part A of Chomsky's binding theory. Giorgi claims that Italian has two strict anaphors: *se stesso* ('himself'), and *proprio* ('self's'). She further claims that English has only strict anaphors.

The second class of anaphors for Giorgi is long-distance anaphors – which can take antecedents outside their governing category. The restriction on these anaphors is that they be P-bound within their modal domain. An anaphor is P-bound if it is coindexed with the thematically most prominent argument of some lexical head and if the anaphor is either an argument of that lexical head or contained within an argument of that lexical head. And, finally, @ is the modal domain for % if and only if @ is the minimal thematic argument containing % and a subject accessible to % and @'s INFL is marked [-dep]. An INFL is [-dep] if it is in the indicative mood.

What Giorgi's proposal comes close to in my terms (but still differs from in a range of ways) is the claim that if an anaphor is not locally bound, (a) its antecedent must be on some higher rung of its argument ladder; (b) its antecedent must be the most prominent argument of its own rung; and (c) the anaphor must be contained in a subjunctive or tenseless clause.

Giorgi claims that there are two long-distance anaphors in Italian: *sè* ('himself'), and *proprio* ('self's').

Notice that *proprio*, according to Giorgi, belongs to both classes: it is both strict and long-distance.

There are several important differences between my approach and Giorgi's. I list here some of them. The items on the list are not always discrete, but I list them in this way because I want to make discrete remarks below about each of them.

(1)   Giorgi sees two classes of anaphors, where strict anaphors obey Part A of the binding theory but long-distance anaphors do not; I see only one class of anaphors – with varying domains for binding for all anaphors.

(2)   Giorgi sets up the modal domain as the relevant domain for binding of long-distance anaphors. I set up the argument ladder as the relevant domain for the binding of all anaphors.

(3)   Giorgi does not require an anaphor to find an antecedent in the first available rung of the argument ladder, but my first approximation of an anaphor binding principle (that in (6–121)) does.

(4)   Giorgi notes the importance of INFL's dependency on non-clausebound anaphora. My theory has yet to incorporate the insight behind this claim.

(5)   Giorgi claims that P-dominance is important; I claim that the antecedent in long-distance anaphor binding must be an agent or an experiencer.

I will now discuss these differences in order.

With respect to (1), the classification of anaphors into two different groups (rather than seeing all anaphors as belonging to one class, with a range of possibilities for the domain of binding) has several effects. One is that Giorgi must claim that English has only strict anaphors. But English, like Italian (as we will see below), allows anaphors which are not bound within their governing category.

(6–166) The men think photographs of themselves are ugly.

(Example (6–166) was offered to me by an anonymous reader of an earlier draft of this book.) Giorgi is forced to make the claim that anaphors embedded in GF subject position can behave as though they are long-distance anaphors, even though they are really strict anaphors (and see Manzini 1983). However, anaphor binding which goes across the governing-category node in English is not restricted to anaphors embedded in GF subject position only:

(6–167) Who would want such wrath to be brought down upon himself?

(Example (6–167) is a variation on an example offered to me by Dwight Bolinger (personal communication, 1973).) Other examples which are probably more familiar to the reader abound:

(6–168)a. Ted knew that it would be a story about himself.
Ted feared that there would be a photo of himself hanging in the post office.
   b. Those artists actually stood there and insisted that the philanthropist should buy each other's work rather than their own.

(See Ross (1970) for a discussion of more such examples. And see Napoli (1979) for additional examples taken from newspapers.) Thus Giorgi would have to allow at least four escape hatches, so to speak: sister position to a noun which heads an NP in GF subject position (as in (6–166)); object of a P position (as in (6–167)); the position following the copula or some other appropriate verb in an *it*-copula or *there*-insertion sentence (as in (6–168)a); and the specifier of all these positions (which I have not exemplified, but which the reader can easily confirm), PLUS the specifier of DO (as in (6–168)b).

Essentially, an anaphor seems to be able to be long-distance bound in any position except DO (that is, direct object of a verb) and GF subject of a tensed verb. In fact, no anaphors ever appear as GF subject of a tensed verb in English or Italian (at least not in the speech of any native English or Italian speaker I have asked – but see Manzini 1983). But anaphors do appear as direct objects. I contend that the real restriction is the following:

(6–169) *DO Restriction*: An anaphor in DO position must be locally bound.

(Recall that my definition of local binding (6–169) requires an anaphor filling DO position to be bound by another element on the same rung of its argument ladder.) That is, all anaphors have the potential to be locally or long-distance bound, except when they occur in DO position, where they must be locally bound.

Certainly this restriction begs for an explanation, and I would like briefly to suggest one. My explanation depends on an analysis of event structure as analyzable into sub-events (as in much of the recent work in lexical semantics), where the most embedded (in a lexical sense) sub-event could be called the central event of the whole overall event and its single participant could be called the central participant. Hale and Keyser (1987) develop such a picture of event structure for causation events. For example, an event such as John's breaking a pot can be analyzed as containing the central event of the pot's breaking. (This idea of lexical analysis is not new, of course. We have seen its syntactic analogue in some of the various approaches to generative semantics of the 1960s.) I contend that an extension of this lexical analysis to non-causation events can allow us to view the object of any transitive verb as being the central participant of the overall event.

An item in DO position, then, would be a central participant on an argument rung where *per force* there is another role player present on that same rung (in GF subject position). So the potential for local binding is present. I suggest that (6–169) follows from a more general principle which requires anaphors that are central participants to be locally bound if there is potential for local binding. (Notice that the potential for local binding will not always be present, as when a central participant is the GF subject of an intransitive verb.) This approach predicts that if a given predicate places its central participant in IO position, for example, then an anaphor filling object of that P position would have to be locally different predicate places its central participant in object of a P position, an anaphor filling object of that P position would have to be locally bound.

Testing the predictions and exploring the ramifications of this explanation for the DO Restriction in (6–169) would take us far beyond the bounds of both this chapter and this book. It is an area I intend to research.

But even if I were to have offered no explanation for (6–169), the reader should consider the DO Restriction seriously. Let me point out that I am replacing an arbitrary restriction of Giorgi's (that the escape hatch be only certain positions), which turns out to be an arbitrary restriction on virtually every position except DO, with a possibly arbitrary (if my central participant account should be shown to be incorrect) restriction of my own on a single position. From a theoretical point of view, then, (6–169) is the superior restriction, since it captures a generalization (that the DO position is the special position) that Giorgi's restriction fails to capture.

Another effect of Giorgi's division of anaphors into two classes is that we can see no relationship between the anaphors *sè* and *se stesso*. According to her, the first is long-distance and the second is strict – but there is no explanation for why they should slice the pie up in this way. However, I believe there is a close relationship between the two which must be recognized in order to account for their behavior.

Notice first that *stesso* can be used in two other positions besides with *sè*. One position is adnomially with a lexically full N to mean "same" or in an elliptical NP to mean "same":

(6–170) La stessa ragazza di ieri viene stasera.
'The same girl as yesterday is coming tonight.'
La stessa di ieri viene stasera.
'The same (one) as yesterday is coming tonight.'

Another position is with a pronoun or postnominally with a lexically full N to function as an intensifier:

(6–171) Lui stesso viene.
'He himself is coming.'
Il presidente stesso viene.
'The president himself is coming.'

The intensifier use of *stesso* here parallels the use of the emphatic reflexive in English (and see sec. 5.1 above). (See Giorgi (1984) for arguments that *lui stesso*, as in the first sentence of (6–171), is not an anaphor.)

I propose that there are only two anaphors in Italian: *proprio* and *sè*. *Se stesso* is a combination of *sè* plus the *stesso* found in other contexts. The addition of *stesso* to *sè* intensifies the anaphor, telling us that the referent of the anaphor is the same not just of some other NP, but of some structurally close NP – that is, of some NP we have just mentioned (similarly to the use of *stesso* and *same* in both English and Italian in a variety of contexts). The choice of *sè* or *se stesso*, then, would depend on whether or not the antecedent is structurally close. If it is, the choice is *se stesso*. If it is not, the choice is *sè*.

One prediction of the above analysis is that if an anaphor falls in DO position it will be only *se stesso* and never just *sè*, since an anaphor in DO position must take a local antecedent (as stated in (6–169)), so it will take the GF subject, which is structurally close, as its antecedent. This is, in fact, the case. For Giorgi, on the other hand, the fact that *sè* never occurs in DO position is an arbitrary restriction.

The real catch of the above proposal, of course, is the determination of what counts as "structurally close." I doubt that anyone would object to my claim in the above paragraph that a GF subject is structurally close to a DO. But is an object of a P, for example, structurally close to a GF subject? Is an object of a P structurally closer to a DO than to a GF subject? Is closeness to be defined in terms of the linear terminal string or in terms of a path through the tree, such as in the work of Kayne (1984)?

There is slight evidence that it is the path notion of Kayne's that is relevant to determining closeness for these anaphors. Let me present that evidence. Giorgi (1984) offers the following sentence, which my informants doubt they would use in speech, although they can imagine it in a text and they judge it grammatical.

(6–172) Gianni ha ricondotto Maria a se stessa con una lunga terapia psicoanalitica.
'Gianni brought Maria back to herself with a long psychoanalytical therapy.'

Here *se stessa* takes the DO as its antecedent – and the DO is the closest available antecedent both linearly and pathwise. We expect, then, that *sè* in this same position would be unacceptable, and, in fact, it is.

(6–173) *Gianni ha ricondotto Maria$_i$ a sè$_i$ con una lunga terapia psicoanalitica.

Now if we take a structure like that in (6–172) and we have an anaphor that is coreferential with the NP in GF subject position, we find that while both *se stesso* and *sè* are judged grammatical, *sè* is preferred.

(6–174) Gianni$_i$ ha ricondotto Maria a {se stesso/sè$_i$} con il suo affetto paziente.
'Gianni brought Maria back to himself with his patient affection.'

Here *Maria* is closer to the anaphor both linearly and pathwise. In (6–175) I have circled the nodes on the path to the DO, and I have boxed the nodes on the path to the GF subject.

(6–175)

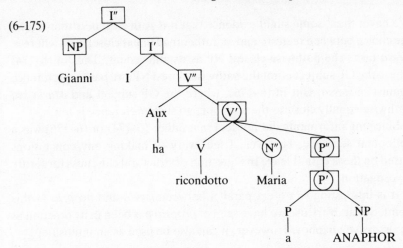

Now compare to (6–174) the sentence below, which my informants judge to be awkward, but agree is grammatical.

(6–176) Gianni₍ᵢ₎ ha mentito a Maria su di {se stesso/sè₍ᵢ₎}.
'Gianni lied to Maria about himself.'

Here the preference for *sè* which was found in (6–174) disappears. Speakers find both anaphors equally acceptable. And here, while *Maria* is linearly closer, it is pathwise the same distance (i.e., the same number of nodes) from the anaphor as the NP in GF subject position is, if we ignore the I′ node, whose branching results in no addition of audible material.

(6–177)

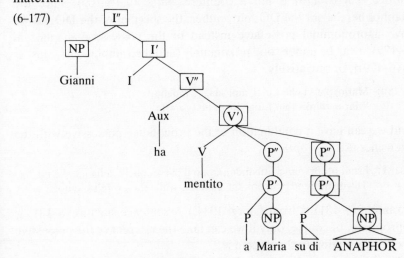

We have, then, some slight evidence that it is path closeness that affects the choice between *se stesso* and *sè*, rather than linear closeness – where *se stesso* takes the pathwise closest NP as its antecedent. Thus in (6–174) where the GF subject is not the pathwise closest NP, we have a preference against *se stesso*. But in (6–176), where the GF subject and *Maria* are pathwise equally close to the anaphor, no such preference is felt.

Since my informants did not feel that either (6–174) or (6–176) was a colloquial sentence, however, I feel wary of making any conclusions based on these data. I leave the question of structural closeness for future investigation.

It is interesting to note a parallel between *stesso* and *proprio* at this point. So far every use we have seen of *proprio* has been in its function as a possessive anaphor. However, it can also be used as an intensifier.

(6–178)　È proprio intelligente.
　　　　　'She's precisely intelligent.'
　　　　　È proprio un furbo.
　　　　　'He's precisely a trickster.'

Now recall that when *proprio* is used as a possessive anaphor, it can be bound locally or at a distance (which is why Giorgi classifies it as both a strict and a long-distance anaphor).

(6–179)　Mario$_i$ pensa che Luigi$_j$ ami la propria$_{i/j}$ moglie.
　　　　　'Mario$_i$ thinks that Luigi$_j$ loves his own$_{i/j}$ wife.'

(Notice that (6–179) is not a counterexample to (6–169), since the anaphor here is not the DO, but, rather, the specifier of the DO.) If we have a pronominal possessive instead of the possessive anaphor in (6–179), it can be understood proximately (and then ambiguously, just as in (6–179)), or obviatively.

(6–180)　Mario$_i$ pensa che Luigi$_j$ ami sua $_{i/j/k}$ moglie.
　　　　　'Mario$_i$ thinks that Luigi$_j$ loves his $_{i/j/k}$ wife.'

And we can have a combination of the pronominal possessive with the intensifier use of *proprio*.

(6–181)　I suoi propri amici abbandonarono il paese, quelli della moglie no.
　　　　　'His own friends forsook the country, while (his) wife's did not.'

(Example (6–181) is from Giorgi 1984.) A sentence such as (6–181) is appropriate, of course, only if we can take the referent of the possessive as old information to the discourse.

The interesting point is that if we combine the intensifier *proprio* with the pronominal possessive in a sentence in which the pronominal possessive has a linguistic antecedent, we find that the antecedent must be the structurally closest one possible. Thus if this possessive occurs as the specifier of the DO, then only the GF subject of the same clause can be taken as the antecedent. Contrast (6–182) to (6–179)–(6–180) above:

(6–182) Mario$_i$ pensa che Luigi$_j$ ami la sua propria·$_{i/j/*k}$ moglie.
'Mario$_i$ thinks that Luigi$_j$ loves his own·$_{i/j/*k}$ wife.'

And if we have a single clause sentence in which the GF subject is pathwise more distant than the DO from a possessive on the object of a preposition, my informants give a first reading in which the antecedent is the closer NP, although some eventually judge the sentence ambiguous.

(6–183) Mario$_i$ ha ricondotto Luigi$_j$ alla sua propria$_{??i/j}$ moglie.
'Mario$_i$ brought back Luigi$_j$ to his own $_{??i/j}$ wife.'

On the other hand, if the GF subject and some object of a P are pathwise equidistant from a possessive on the object of another P, we find clear ambiguity.

(6–184) Mario$_i$ ha mentito a Luigi$_j$ su della sua propria$_{i/j}$ moglie.
'Mario$_i$ lied to Luigi$_j$ about his own$_{i/j}$ wife.'

The parallels between (6–182) through (6–184) (with possessives and the intensifier use of *proprio*) and (6–172) through (6–176) (with the anaphor *sè* and the intensifier *stesso*) are remarkable and lend support to the idea that a notion of structural closeness operates on certain combinations of intensifiers and other elements in Italian. However, while the judgments on (6–173) and (6–182) (those involving an anaphor or possessive in DO or in the specifier of DO position) are strong, the judgments on (6–183) and its parallel (6–174), and on (6–184) and its parallel (6–176) are not so strong. I therefore offer these data as indications for future research rather than as the basis for any strong conclusions at this point.

In sum, we have seen that instead of there being two classes of anaphors, there is really only one – with varying possibilities for the domain of binding, depending on factors other than the lexical choice of the anaphor.

Let us turn now to point (2) above. Giorgi sets up the modal domain as the relevant domain for long-distance anaphor binding, while I set up the argument ladder as the relevant domain. One might argue that sentences such as (6–179) above, repeated here for convenience, give immediate support to Giorgi's theory over my own:

(6–179) Mario$_i$ pensa che Luigi$_j$ ami la propria$_{i/j}$ moglie.
'Mario$_i$ thinks that Luigi$_j$ loves his own$_{i/j}$ wife.'

In section 4 we said that each rung of an argument ladder is defined by a lexical head, where items that bear a GF or theta role toward that lexical head and modifiers that are sisters to that lexical head or some projection of it are on the rung of that lexical head. Each rung of a lexical head is related to the next higher rung by the fact that the lexical head that defines the lower rung is the head of some argument or GF or modifier of a higher lexical head – which then defines the higher rung. And so on. With this definition of argument ladder, the GFs and arguments and modifiers of a V are not on an argument ladder with any higher elements, unless the V‴ itself bears a GF or theta role with respect to some other lexical head. Now in (6–179), *propria* is on the rung defined by *moglie*. And the next rung up the ladder is defined by *ami*. But since the V‴ of the embedded clause is not the argument of any other lexical head, the argument ladder stops here. Thus *propria* is not on an argument ladder with *Mario*, but only with *Luigi*. I therefore have no way to account for the fact that *Mario* is a possible antecedent for *propria* (setting aside the whole question of optionality of anaphor choice in (6–179) for now). On the other hand, the entire embedded clause is within the P-domain of *Mario*, so Giorgi's theory has no problem accounting for (6–179).

I believe, however, that sentences like (6–179) show not that modal domains and P-domains are the relevant notion here, but that the definition of argument ladder must be extended to allow a ladder to be formed in just those cases in which the clause defined by a primary predicate is an argument of or bears a GF toward or modifies some higher lexical head. With that extended definition of argument ladders, we find that both *Mario* and *Luigi* occur on the argument ladder with *propria* in (6–179). Thus, while I have not yet offered any evidence that my approach is superior to Giorgi's, I have at least modified my definition of argument ladder in such a way that I can now account for sentences like (6–179).

There are other data, however, that suggest that it is the argument ladder and not modal domains or P-domains that is relevant to long-distance anaphor binding. Those data come from the examination of anaphors inside adverbial clauses. Giorgi predicts that the antecedent of a long-distance anaphor which is located in an adverbial clause cannot find its antecedent in the clause the adverbial modifies, but only in some superordinate clause. This is because the adverbial clause could not be P-bound by any argument in the clause of the element the adverbial modifies. My theory, on the other hand, would allow anaphor binding with an antecedent inside the clause that the adverbial modifies.

Once again, the data at first seem to support Giorgi's theory over my own. Consider the sentence below, from Giorgi (1984).

(6–185)   Quel dittatore$_i$ pensava che il popolo$_j$ sarebbe stato molto più felice se i libri di storia avessero parlato di sè$_{i/*j}$ e delle sue geste.
'That dictator$_i$ thought that the people$_j$ would have been much more happy if the history books had talked about himself$_{i/*j}$ and his gestures.'

Here *sè* is an anaphor which finds no available antecedent on its own rung. *Sè* is in an adverbial clause which modifies the clause that *il popolo* is situated in. Yet *sè* cannot take *il popolo* as an antecedent, but only the NP *quel dittatore*, which is located in a superordinate clause. Similar data concerning the anaphor *proprio* are also presented by Giorgi, and she points out that similar facts have been reported for long-distance anaphor binding in Japanese (by Kuroda 1965) and in Icelandic (by Maling 1981). Giorgi concludes that the data in (6–185) must be as they are because of the principles which govern such binding – that is, because the adverbial clause falls outside the P-domain of *il popolo* in (6–185).

I do not have an explanation for the failure of binding between *il popolo* and *sè* in (6–185). However, this failure cannot be due to any universal principle on the binding of anaphors, because precisely such a binding is allowed in English:

(6–186)   John got angry when a picture of himself appeared in the paper.

(This sentence was brought to my attention by the same anonymous reviewer of an earlier draft of this book that gave me (6–166) above.) Furthermore, as Giorgi (1984) herself notes, the acceptability of binding in these structures even in Italian "varies according to the degree of 'involvement'" of the GF subject of the clause immediately containing the adverbial clause. She offers the following sentence, which she marks with a single question mark, and which my informants find marginal to acceptable.

(6–187)   ?Gianni$_i$ fu informato che il capo si era innamorato della propria$_i$ moglie.
'Gianni was informed that the chief was in love with self's wife.'

Giorgi points out that the marginality (rather than full acceptability) of

(6–187) may be due to the fact that the embedded clause here is in the indicative mood. And she contrasts this sentence to (6–188) below, where the emotional involvement of the relevant GF subject is low and the sentence is quite unacceptable.

(6–188) *Gianni$_i$ fu ucciso in quanto il capo si era innamorato della propria$_i$ moglie.
'Gianni was killed because the chief was in love with self's wife.'

The fact that the involvement of the potential antecedent is relevant to the binding possibilities here brings to mind similar work of others. Many have noticed (Napoli 1973, 1979, Thráinsson 1976, von Bremen 1984, Kameyama 1985, Kuno 1986, Maling 1984, Sells 1987) that anaphors that find their antecedents outside their clause often are logophoric. As Clements (1975, p. 141) states, the antecedent of a logophoric element is the one "whose speech, thoughts, feelings, or general state of consciousness are reported." Just such anaphors are studied in Napoli (1973, briefly, 1979 in depth), who looks at a phenomenon that is not common to most Italian speakers. It is exemplified here:

(6–189) La signora lascia che io giaccia presso di sè.
'The woman allows that I lie near herself.'

However, even though Napoli's study is of a usage that is confined to a limited group of speakers, this study is worth taking note of here, since the results she arrives at are strikingly similar to the results Giorgi (1984) arrives at in her study of all long-distance anaphor binding in Italian. Like Giorgi, Napoli notes that the involvement of a potential antecedent increases the likelihood of acceptability of across-clause binding. Like Giorgi, Napoli notes that the anaphor must be in a subjunctive or an infinitival clause (that is, in a clause with a [+dependent] INFL). Like Giorgi, Napoli notes that the thematic role of the antecedent is relevant (where Napoli argues that the antecedent must be an agent or experiencer). And, like Giorgi, Napoli finds that ambiguity may arise, where a local NP or a non-local NP or even more than one non-local NP can be taken as possible antecedents for the anaphor.

I would argue that the fact that the involvement of the antecedent affects the likelihood of acceptability of long-distance binding in Giorgi's example (6–187) and in Napoli's (1979) study offers support to my proposal above. We need to extend the definition of argument ladders to allow an item inside a lower clause to be on a rung of the same argument ladder that some item in a higher clause is on just when the lower clause is an argument of or bears a GF toward or is a modifier of some item in the higher clause. That is, the psychological involvement of the antecedent toward the lower clause in sentences such as (6–187) and (6–189) helps to allow us to see the elements in the lower clause as belonging to the same argument ladder that the antecedent belongs to.

As further support of this extended definition of the argument ladder, let me point out that not all embedded clauses are arguments of or bear a GF toward or modify some item in a higher clause. For example, consider relative clauses. Restrictive relative clauses modify their head. But appositive relative clauses predicate of them rather than modify (see ch. 5, sec. 5). I therefore predict that an anaphor inside a restrictive relative clause can look outside the clause for an antecedent – since the relative clause is part of an argument ladder. But an anaphor inside an appositive relative clause cannot look outside the clause for an antecedent – since the appositive relative clause is not part of any larger argument ladder. This prediction is correct. Examples (6–190)–(6–191) are from Giorgi (1984):

(6–190) La salute di quelli che amano la propria$_i$ moglie preoccupa molto Osvaldo$_i$.
'The health of those who love self's wife worries Osvaldo a lot.'

(6–191) Gianni$_i$ pensa che Mario$_j$ che t$_j$ ama la propria$_{*i/j}$ moglie sia intelligente.
'Gianni thinks that Mario, who loves self's wife, is intelligent.'

In (6–190) we have a restrictive relative clause, and the anaphor *proprio* can be bound by an antecedent outside the relative clause, just as I would predict. But in (6–191) we have an appositive relative clause, and the anaphor here can be bound only by the trace (which is a variable, being the trace of wh-movement) inside the relative clause, again just as I would predict. These data offer support for the notion of argument ladder as I have defined it, but are problematic for Giorgi's proposal (and see her footnote 19).

Let us now turn to point (3) above: Giorgi allows for more than one possible antecedent in a given sentence, whereas my (6–121) limits an anaphor to taking the first available antecedent (that is, the antecedent on the minimal available rung). Here, Giorgi is clearly right for Italian – and (6–121), which was arrived at after the examination of English data, is clearly right for English. Thus in (6–179), repeated here for convenience, we find two possible antecedents in Italian:

(6–179) Mario$_i$ pensa che Luigi$_j$ ami la propria$_{i/j}$ moglie.
'Mario$_i$ thinks that Luigi$_j$ loves his own$_{i/j}$ wife.'

But English long-distance anaphor binding requires that the minimal available antecedent be the binder (where we must recall that incompatibility of gender, person, and number features is not enough to block availability – availability instead depends upon the pragmatic and semantic feasibility of coindexing in the indicated positions – see the discussion leading to (6–121) above).

(6–192)   *Tad knew that Sheila had claimed that it would be a story about himself.
(cf. Sheila claimed that it would be a story about herself.)

(Example (6–192) is from Ross 1970, who offers several other similar examples.)

Now recall that predication coindexing is limited to the minimal rung of the argument ladder to which the predicate belongs. And since we are heading toward an eventual conflation of the principles of anaphor binding witĥ the principles of predication coindexing, we should there-fore view the restriction common to predication coindexing (in both Italian and English) and to anaphor binding in English as the standard restriction, with the domain of binding for the Italian anaphor as the special case. I propose, then, to amend (6–121) as follows:

(6–193)   *Anaphor Coindexing* (a second approximation): An anaphor must take an antecedent from the minimal available rung of its argument ladder. Exception: In Italian the minimality restriction is not observed.

We now come to point (4) above: Giorgi claims that for non-clausebound anaphor binding, the clause that contains the anaphor must have an INFL that is marked [+dependent]. This is equivalent to requiring the clause to be infinitival or subjunctive. We have already seen that such a requirement does not hold for English, since only a few of the examples we have given with non-clausebound anaphor binding in English have an infinitival or subjunctive embedded clause. Fur-thermore, it does not always hold even in Italian, as we saw above in (6–190), where an anaphor inside an indicative restrictive relative clause found an antecedent outside the relative clause.

I conclude that the fact that typically in Italian non-clausebound anaphor binding occurs only when the anaphor is in an infinitival or subjunctive clause is not evidence for a restriction on the modality of the embedded clause. Rather, these data suggest that the typical modality of these clauses is a symptom or the result of some other factor that is the truly relevant factor to anaphor binding. What we need to do, then, is find a factor in common between the Italian and the English examples with non-clausebound anaphor binding.

But such a common factor has already been pointed out. To see this, consider the predicates that occur in the clause of the antecedent in the English examples we have seen with non-clausebound anaphor binding. They are *think* and *want* in (6–166); *knew*, *feared*, and *insisted* in (6–168); and *got angry* in (6–186). And in the only Italian example we have in which the embedded clause is not subjunctive or infinitival, the predicate in the clause of the antecedent is *preoccupa* ('worries'). What we have here are predicates which call for psychological involvement of one of their arguments with respect to their clausal argument. That is, all of these examples really involve logophoricity in Clements' (1975) sense. Thus the contrast between (6–187) and (6–188) is not some minor side issue, but is, in fact, at the heart of the matter.

The reader may object to my claiming so blithely that a verb like *knew* in (6–168) calls for the involvement of one of its arguments with respect to the clausal argument. However, I presented English speakers with the pair below and asked them for example contexts in which they might use one rather than the other.

(6–194)   Ted knew that it would be a story about him.

(6–195)   Ted knew that it would be a story about himself.

One of the most common remarks I got was that (6–195) would be most likely to be used "emphatically" in a situation in which Ted was "upset" or "surprised" at the contents of the story. These speakers are clearly indicating contexts in which Ted is involved with respect to the embedded clause. However, (6–194) did not call to mind such colorful contexts. I conclude that the examples with *knew* support my contention that psychological involvement is the key here.

And let me point out that Dwight Bolinger (in class lectures, Harvard, 1972–3) offered several examples of sentences in which the choice of an anaphor or a pronominal in object of a P position depended on the psychological involvement of the antecedent. For example, consider:

(6–196)   The woman clasped the child to her.

(6–197)   The woman clasped the child to herself.

Bolinger argued that the emotional intensity of the second sentence was greater, so that it would be more likely to be chosen if the child had just been spared a terrible fate or the woman had not seen the child for a long while, etc. The contrast between (6–196) and (6–197) is distinct from but related to the contrasts we saw in section 5.3 above, where an anaphor in object of P position was allowed only if we could view it as being an argument of some predicate. Here the anaphor is allowed if the antecedent has an intense emotional involvement toward the anaphor. We could say that the intensity of the emotional involvement extends the range of arguments, in a sense, of the predicate in (6–197).

In sum, what we need in order to describe these data accurately is not an arbitrary restriction on modality. Rather, we must recognize the regrettably unformalizable and subjective factor of psychological or emotional involvement. I therefore propose that we leave unchanged for the moment the principle of anaphor binding as stated in (6–193), and instead **amend our definition of argument ladders to allow an item in one clause to be on the same argument ladder as an item in a higher clause only if some argument of the higher clause is emotionally involved with respect to the lower clause (or, perhaps, only when some item in the lower clause is logophoric with respect to some item in the higher clause).**

Finally, let us consider point (5): Giorgi claims that the antecedent of a long-distance anaphor (using her term) must be the thematically most prominent argument of its argument rung (using my term). I claim, instead, that the antecedent must be an agent or experiencer. In fact, in every relevant example Giorgi gives, the antecedent is an agent or an experiencer. The really significant difference here between Giorgi's and my claims, then, is that hers allows her to use the notion of P-dominance, and thus to set up modal domains. If in fact modal domains were the proper domains for this binding, Giorgi's theory could capture generalizations that mine could not. However, we have already seen that modal domains are not the proper domains. Thus the question of whether it is P-dominance or a limitation of the theta role of the antecedent to only agent or experiencer becomes less interesting from a theoretical point of view.

I believe, however, that there is still interesting evidence that the restriction should be stated as limiting the theta role of the antecedent to only agent or experiencer. That evidence comes from the fact we have just seen above: the emotional involvement of the antecedent is relevant to the binding possibilities. But it is agents and experiencers whose psychological or emotional states a predicate tells us about – not themes or instruments or other role players (see Sells 1987). Thus it is not a question of which argument is thematically most prominent, but a question of which argument's emotional state the predicate tells us about. Therefore, the proper restriction is that the antecedent in non-clausebound anaphor binding must be an agent or experiencer.

We could add this restriction as a condition on anaphor binding in (6–193):

(6–198) Condition I: If the coindexing is across clause boundaries, the antecedent must be an agent or experiencer.

However, I suspect that Condition I above is unnecessary. That is, I suspect that Condition I could (and should) fall out as a natural consequence of the way we define argument ladders. Consider the fact that an item in one clause will not be on the same argument ladder with an item in another clause unless there is an argument in the higher clause which is emotionally involved with respect to the lower clause. (That is, our extension of the original definition of argument ladders was shown above to be needed only under these conditions.) So if one could show that whenever we do have items in different clauses belonging to a single argument ladder, if the lower clause contains an anaphor free inside that clause, then the emotionally involved element of the higher clause will always turn out to be the antecedent of that anaphor, then Condition I above could be dispensed with. While I have not yet arrived at a formulation of the definition of argument ladders that will make such an entailment, a proper formulation will, I believe. Therefore, I will proceed below on the assumption that Condition I need not be stated after all, but will always turn out to hold, given a proper definition of argument ladders.

In conclusion, the anaphor binding principle developed in section 4 for English (that is, (6–121)) can cover the instances of non-clausebound anaphor binding in both English and Italian with only minor modifications (as in (6–193)), including an extended definition of the concept of argument ladder.

The question now is whether this anaphor binding principle can be rewritten as an indexing principle which will suffice for both subject–predicate coindexing and antecedent–anaphor coindexing. That question is addressed in section 7.

7   Indexing theory

In this section I offer a single set of coindexing principles that will cover both predication and anaphor indexing. Let us first take an inventory of what must be included in the principles.

In section 2 we argued that both subject role players and antecedents of anaphors must be in A-positions except in absolutives. However, as was pointed out there, these facts follow from other principles of the indexing theory, so we need not have any stipulation as to A-positions.

In section 3 we saw that the antecedent of an anaphor cannot be separated by any of its barriers from its anaphor, and in section 4 we saw that this restriction was limited to local anaphor binding. Since all predication coindexing is local, this restriction is the counterpart to Proviso Two on predication coindexing, and it must be stipulated in the indexing principles.

In section 4 we saw that in English an anaphor must find its antecedent on the minimal available rung of its argument ladder. We also argued that predicates must find their subject role players on the minimal rung of their argument ladders. This is the counterpart to Proviso One on predication coindexing, and it must be stipulated in the indexing principles. Italian anaphors, however, need only find an argument anywhere on their argument ladder, as we saw in section 6. Since predication coindexing in both Italian and English is limited to the minimal rung of the argument ladder containing the predicate and since English anaphor binding is also so restricted, I have treated Italian anaphor binding as the special case. Thus we need a condition or exception specific to Italian (and other languages which exhibit similar binding facts) on this indexing principle.

We also noted in section 6 that if anaphor binding is across clause boundaries, the antecedent must be an agent or an experiencer. I raised there the question of whether this fact might fall out as a consequence of the proper definition of argument ladder, and I decided to proceed on the assumption that it would. That is, I am assuming that the phenomenon of logophoricity extends an argument ladder. Thus we need not incorporate this restriction into our indexing principles.

Notice that an anaphor or a predicate will not be on an argument ladder unless it is located in a theta domain. Therefore, our new indexing principle will not have to mention the location of the anaphor/predicate with respect to theta domains (in contrast to Proviso One).

In section 5 we showed that anaphors outside theta domains (as with the adjunct emphatic reflexive and with anaphors in GF subject position of tenseless clauses) must take an antecedent that is a srp of some predicate. This restriction is similar to that on primary predicates with the following difference: a primary predicate must find its subject role player in GF subject position of its own clause, but an anaphor that is an adjunct or in GF subject position of a tenseless clause must take an antecedent that is the srp of the minimal available rung of the argument ladder. This restriction, then, would be the counterpart of the principle of primary predication coindexing in (2–6) of chapter 2 and must be stipulated as part of our indexing principles.

We are now ready to state our indexing theory.

(6–199) *Definitions*:
A *dependent* is a predicate or an anaphor.
A *parent* is an item coindexed with a dependent.
A *primary dependent* is a primary predicate or an anaphor that is not in a theta domain. Primary dependents are a proper subset of the set of dependents.

(6–200) *Indexing Theory*:
Apply these principles in order as presented.
I   Coindex a dependent with a member of the minimal available rung of its argument ladder.
Exception: If the dependent is an Italian anaphor, the minimality condition does not hold.
Availability is determined thus:
A rung is always available for a dependent that is a predicate.
A rung is available for a dependent that is an anaphor only if that rung has an argument or a GF other than the anaphor and there is nothing in the sense of the lexical head that defines the rung that would prevent one of its arguments or GFs from being coindexed with the anaphor.
II Coindex a primary dependent with the GF subject or a srp on its argument rung.
III Coindex a free dependent with some other element.
IV No barrier of a parent may come between a parent and its dependent if both the parent and the dependent belong to the same rung.

Principle (I) will apply only to dependents that are on argument ladders. That is, it will apply to anaphors that are not primary dependents and to secondary predicates that fall in a theta domain. If a dependent finds (I) applicable, then it will skip (II) (since (II) will automatically be inapplicable). And it will skip (III), since the dependent already will have undergone (I), so it will no longer be free. However, the coindexing will still obey (IV).

If a dependent is not on an argument ladder, then (I) is inapplicable. That is, primary dependents and secondary predicates which do not fall in theta domains will skip (I) and pass right on to (II). At this point if a dependent is primary (that is, if it is a primary predicate or an anaphor that is not in a theta domain), (II) will apply. Then (III) will be inapplicable, and, of course, (IV) will still be observed.

If, instead, this dependent is not primary (that is, if it is a secondary predicate that falls outside a theta domain), it will then pass right on to (III), and be coindexed with any other element. But the indexing that results must obey (IV). Thus, in essence, (IV) is the only restriction on the coindexing of a secondary predicate outside a theta domain.

8   Advantages of the indexing theory

The indexing theory offered in (6–200) has several advantages over other theories of predication and over Chomsky's (1981) theory of binding.

First, it is empirically more adequate, as this whole book shows.

Second, it properly captures the fact that indexing relationships are semantic in nature. That is, they are sensitive to the lexical and logical form properties of a sentence. Thus, purely configurational notions like "c-command," "governing category," "maximal projection", and "bijacency" are not mentioned in this theory and should not be, since they are irrelevant to the semantic phenomenon of indexing.

Third, by lumping predicates and anaphors together in one class, we no longer have to see predicative NPs as exceptions to the binding theory (see Safir 1985, p. 170). Instead, predicative NPs behave just like anaphors.

Fourth, by seeing the indexing of anaphors and predicates as a single phenomenon, we have an explanation for why these indexing relationships turn out to be so similar. Beyond all the similarities already mentioned above, there is also the similarity mentioned earlier, in chapter 2 – that neither anaphors nor predicates require their antecedents/subject role players to be maximal projections, or even constituents, or even uninterrupted strings in the syntax. Thus both anaphors and antecedents present the well-known phenomenon of split antecedents (*contra* the claim of many; see Giorgi 1984). Examples (6–201) and (6–202) are from Green (1973).

(6–201) John$_i$ gave Mary$_j$ a picture of themselves$_j$ which was taken in Tivoli.

(6–202) John$_i$ told Mary$_j$ that physicists like themselves$_j$ were underpaid.

(6–203) John$_i$ argued with Mary$_j$ over whether it was appropriate for the child to see each other's$_{ij}$ films.

I do not find (6–201) acceptable myself; however, I do accept (6–202). And, obviously, there are speakers who accept (6–201), such as Green. Example (6–203) is my own concoction, but speakers I have asked accept it and interpret it in the relevant way. In all three examples the antecedent of the anaphor is the discontinuous string, *John . . . Mary*.

An example of the same phenomenon involving predication is that below, already discussed in chapter 2, section 14.

(2–159) I don't walk my children home from school as a responsibility, but as a treat.

Here the predicates *as a responsibility* and *as a treat* take the whole preceding string minus *not* as their subject role player. That is, the srp is not a constituent or even a continuous string. (For similar examples involving binding theory, see Farmer and Harnish (1987).)

Examples like (6–201)–(6–203) and (2–159) raise a barrage of questions about the indexing principles and may well be used to show that the indexing principles as stated in (6–200) are inadequate. But the point I want to make is not that (6–200) must be revised (which, undoubtedly, it eventually must be), but rather that whatever inadequacies of or puzzles for indexing theory exist, they exist with counterparts for both anaphors and predicates. Thus indexing theory finds serious support in these puzzles: indexing theory captures the generalization that anaphora and predication are one phenomenon.

References

Abney, Steven 1986. "Functional elements and licensing." Paper presented at the 1986 GLOW Conference, Gerona, Spain

d'Addio, Wanda 1974. "La posizione dell'aggettivo italiano nell'gruppo nominale," in Mario Medici and Antonella Sangregorio, eds., *Fenomeni morphologici e sintattici nell'italiano contemporaneo*, pp. 79–103. Rome: Bulzoni

Akmajian, Adrian 1970. "Aspects of the grammar of focus in English." Unpublished doctoral dissertation, MIT

Alinei, Mario 1971. "Il tipo sintagmatico *quel matto di Giorgio*," in Mario Medici and Raffaele Simone, eds., *Grammatica trasformazionale italiana*, pp. 1–12. Rome: Bulzoni

Anderson, Mona 1979. "Noun phrase structure." Unpublished doctoral dissertation, University of Connecticut

1983. "Prenominal genitive NPs," *The Linguistic Review* 3: 1–24

Anderson, Stephen 1971. "On the role of deep structure in semantic interpretation," *Foundations of Language* 6: 387–96

1977. "Comments on the paper by Wasow," in Peter Culicover, Thomas Wasow, and Adrian Akmajian, eds., *Formal syntax*, pp. 361–77. New York: Academic Press

1982. "Types of dependency in anaphors: Icelandic (and other) reflexives." Paper presented at the 1982 GLOW Conference, Paris

Aoun, Youssef 1985. *A grammar of anaphora*. Cambridge, MA: MIT Press

Aoun, Youssef and Dominique Sportiche 1983. "On the formal theory of government," *The Linguistic Review* 2: 211–36

Aoun, Youssef, Norbert Hornstein, David Lightfoot, and Amy Weinberg 1987. "Two types of locality," *Linguistic Inquiry* 18 (4): 537–78

Bach, Emmon 1977. "Comments on the paper by Chomsky," in Peter Culicover, Thomas Wasow, and Adrian Akmajian, eds., *Formal syntax*, pp. 133–56. New York: Academic Press

Baker, Mark 1987a. "Theta theory and the syntax of applicatives in Chichewa." Unpublished ms., McGill University, Montreal

1987b. *Incorporation: a theory of grammatical function changing*. Chicago: University of Chicago Press [forthcoming]

Baltin, Mark 1978. "Toward a theory of movement rules." Unpublished doctoral dissertation, MIT

Barwise, Jon and John Perry 1983. *Situations and attitudes*. Cambridge, MA: Bradford Books, MIT Press.

Belletti, Adriana 1981. "Frasi ridotte assolute," *Rivista di grammatica generativa* 6: 3–32

1982. "On the anaphoric status of the reciprocal constructions in Italian," *The Linguistic Review* 2 (2): 101–37

1986. "Unaccusatives as Case assigners," Lexicon Project Working Papers no. 8. Cambridge, MA: Center for Cognitive Science, MIT

Belletti, Adriana and Luigi Rizzi 1981. "The syntax of *ne*: some theoretical implications," *The Linguistic Review* 1:2

1986. "Psych-verbs and theta-theory." Unpublished ms., MIT

Bolinger, Dwight 1943. "The position of the adverb in English – a convenient analogy to the position of the adjective in Spanish," *Hispania* 26: 191–2

1952. "Linear modification," *PMLA* 67: 1117–44

1958. "Stress and information," *American Speech* 33: 5–20

1972. *Degree words*. The Hague: Mouton

Bouchard, Denis 1982. "On the content of empty categories." Unpublished doctoral dissertation, MIT

von Breman, Klaus 1984. "Anaphors: reference, binding, and domains," *Linguistic Analysis* 14: 191–229

Bresnan, Joan 1978. "A realistic transformational grammar," in Joan Bresnan and George Miller, eds. *Linguistic theory and psychological reality*, pp. 1–59. Cambridge, MA: MIT Press

1982a. "Control and complementation," *Linguistic Inquiry* 13: 343–434

1982b. "The passive in lexical theory", in Joan Bresnan, ed., *The mental representation of grammatical relations*, pp. 3–86. Cambridge, MA: MIT Press

Burzio, Luigi 1986. *Italian syntax: a government-binding approach*. Dordrecht: Reidel Publishing Co.

Chierchia, Gennaro 1985. "Formal semantics and the grammar of predication," *Linguistic Inquiry* 16: 417–43

Chomsky, Noam 1970. "Remarks on nominalization," in Roderick Jacobs and Peter Rosenbaum, eds., *Readings in English transformational grammar*, pp. 184–221. Waltham, MA: Ginn and Co.

1972. "Deep structure, surface structure, and semantic interpretation," in Noam Chomsky, ed., *Studies on semantics in generative grammar*, pp. 62–111. The Hague: Mouton

1977. "On Wh-movement," in Peter Culicover, Thomas Wasow, and Adrian Akmajian, eds., *Formal syntax*, pp. 71–132. New York: Academic Press

1981. *Lectures on government and binding*. Dordrecht: Foris Publications

1982. *Some concepts and consequences of the theory of government and binding*. Cambridge, MA: MIT Press

1986a. *Barriers*. Cambridge, MA: MIT Press

1986b. *Knowledge of language*. New York: Praeger

Chomsky, Noam and Morris Halle 1968. *The sound pattern of English*. New York: Harper and Row

Cinque, Guglielmo 1980. "On extraction from NP in Italian," *Journal of Italian Linguistics* 1/2: 47–99

Clark, Romane 1970. "Concerning the logic of predicate modifiers," *Nous* 4: 311–35

Clements, George N. 1975. "The logophoric pronoun in Ewe: its role in discourse," *Journal of West African Languages* 2: 141–77

Croft, William 1986. "Categories and relations in syntax: the clause-level organization of information." Unpublished doctoral dissertation, Stanford University

Culicover, Peter and Michael Rochemont 1986. "Extraposition." Unpublished paper, University of Arizona at Tucson

Culicover, Peter and Wendy Wilkins 1986. "Control, PRO, and the projection principle," *Language* 62: 120–53

Davidson, Donald, 1970. "The individuation of events," in Nicholas Rescher, ed., on behalf of the editorial committee, *Essays in honor of Carl G. Hempel,* pp. 216–34. Dordrecht: Reidel Publishing Co.

    1975. "The logical form of action sentences," in Donald Davidson and Gilbert Harman, eds., *The logic of grammar,* pp. 235–45. Encino, CA: Dickenson Publishing

Davis, Lori 1986. "Remarks on the theta criterion and Case," *Linguistic Inquiry* 17: 564–8

Davison, Alice 1980. "Peculiar passives," *Language* 56: 42–66

Demonte, Violeta 1986. "C-command, prepositions, and predication in Spanish." Paper presented at the 16th Linguistic Symposium on Romance Languages, Austin, Texas (March 1986)

Dik, Simon 1968. *Coordination: its implications for the theory of general linguistics.* Amsterdam: North-Holland

Donegan, Patricia and David Stampe 1983. "Rhythm and the holistic organization of language structure," in John F. Richardson, Mitchell Marks, and Amy Chukerman, eds., *Papers from the parasession on the interplay of phonology, morphology, and syntax,* pp. 337–53. Chicago: Chicago Linguistic Society

Donnellan, Keith 1966. "Reference and definite descriptions," *Philosophical Review* 77: 203–15

Downing, Pamela 1977. "On the creation and use of English compound nouns," *Language* 53: 810–42

Dowty, David 1979. *Word meaning and Montague Grammar.* Dordrecht: Reidel Publishing Co.

    1980. "Grammatical relations and Montague Grammar." Unpublished paper, Ohio State University

Emonds, Joseph 1976. *A transformational approach to English syntax.* New York: Academic Press

    1979. "Appositive relatives have no properties," *Linguistic Inquiry* 10: 211–42

    1985. *A unified theory of syntactic categories.* Dordrecht: Foris Publications

Ernout, P. and D. Thomas 1972. *Syntaxe latine.* Paris: Klinksieck

Erteshik, Nomi 1973. "On the nature of island constraints." Unpublished doctoral dissertation, MIT

Fabb, Nigel 1984. "Syntactic affixation." Unpublished doctoral dissertation, MIT

Farmer, Ann 1984. *Modularity in syntax.* Cambridge, MA: MIT Press

Farmer, Ann and Robert Harnish 1987. "Communicative reference with pronouns," in Jef Verschueren and Marcella Bertuccelli-Papi, eds., *The pragmatic perspective,* pp. 547–65. Amsterdam and Philadelphia: John Benjamins

Fillmore, Charles J. 1968. "The case for case," in Emmon Bach and Robert Harms, eds., *Universals in linguistic theory,* pp. 1–88. New York: Holt, Rinehart, and Winston

Firbás, Jan 1962. "Notes on the function of the sentence in the act of communication," *Journal of Studies of the Philosophical Faculty of the University of Brnq,* Series A, no. 10

Fodor, Janet Dean 1970. "The linguistic descriptic of opaque contexts." Unpublished doctoral dissertation, MIT

Gazdar, Gerald, Ewan Klein, Geoffrey Pullum, and Ivan Sag 1982. "Coordinate structure and unbounded dependencies," in Michael Barlow, Daniel Flickinger, and Ivan Sag, eds., *Developments in generalized phrase structure grammar: Stanford working papers in grammatical theory,* vol. 2, pp. 38–68. Bloomington, IN: Indiana University Linguistics Club

Geach, P. T. 1950. "Russell's theory of descriptions," *Analysis* 10: 84–88

1968. *Reference and generality,* emended edition. Ithaca: Cornell University Press

George, Leland 1980. "Analogical generalizations of natural language syntax." Unpublished doctoral dissertation, MIT

van Gestel, Frank C. 1986. *X-bar grammar: attribution and predication in Dutch,* Dordrecht: Foris Publications

Giorgi, Alessandra 1984. "Toward a theory of long distance anaphors," *The Linguistic Review* 3: 307–61

1987. "The notion of complete functional complex: some evidence from Italian," *Linguistic Inquiry* 18: 511–18

Giurescu, Anca 1972. "Osservazioni su un tipo di gruppo nominale dell'italiano contemporaneo," in Giuseppe Petronio, ed., *Scritti e ricerche di grammatica italiana,* pp. 215–19. Trieste, Italy: Edizioni LINT

Givón, Talmy 1978. "Definiteness and referentiality," in *Universals of Human Language,* vol. 4: *Syntax,* pp. 291–330. Stanford, CA: Stanford University Press

Green, Georgia 1973. "Some remarks on split controller phenomena," in Claudia Corum, T. Cedric Smith-Stark, and Ann Weiser, eds., *CLS* 9: 123–38

Grimshaw, Jane 1986. "Nouns, arguments, and adjuncts." Unpublished ms., Brandeis University

Gruber, Jeffrey 1965. "Studies in lexical relations." Unpublished doctoral dissertation, MIT

1967. [Unpublished, untitled paper on child language (referred to in Ross 1970 below), MIT]

Guéron, Jacqueline 1980. "On the syntax and semantics of PP extraposition," *Linguistic Inquiry* 11: 637–78

1984. "Locative small clauses and the definiteness effect." Unpublished ms, University of Paris VIII

1985. "Inalienable possession, PRO-inclusion and lexical chains," in Jacqueline Guéron, M. Obenauer, and J.-Y. Polloch, eds., *Grammatical representation*, pp. 43–86. Dordrecht: Foris Publications

Guéron, Jacqueline and Robert May 1984. "Extraposition and logical form," *Linguistic Inquiry* 15: 1–32

Guerssel, Mohamed 1986. "On Berber verbs of change: a study of transitivity alternations," Lexicon Project Working Papers no. 9. Cambridge, MA: Center for Cognitive Science, MIT

Guerssel, Mohamed, Kenneth Hale, Mary Laughren, Beth Levin, and Josie White Eagle 1986. "A cross linguistic study of transitivity alternations," in *Papers from the Regional Meetings* 21 (2): 48–63, Chicago Linguistic Society, 1985

Gunnarson, Kjell-Ake 1986. "Predicative structures and projections of lexical dependence," *Linguistic Inquiry* 17: 13–48

Haegeman, Liliane 1984. "Remarks on adverbial clauses and definite NP-anaphora," *Linguistic Inquiry* 15: 712–15

Hale, Kenneth, and Samuel Jay Keyser 1986. "Some transitivity alternations in English," Lexicon Project Working Papers no. 7. Cambridge, MA: Center for Cognitive Science, MIT

1987. "A view from the middle," Lexicon Project Working Papers no. 10. Cambridge, MA: Center for Cognitive Science, MIT

Hall, Robert A., Jr. 1973. "The transferred epithet in P. G. Wodehouse", *Linguistic Inquiry* 4: 92–94

Halliday, M. A. K. 1967a. "Notes on transitivity and theme in English, Part 1," *Journal of Linguistics* 3: 37–81

1967b. "Notes on transitivity and theme in English, Part 2," *Journal of Linguistics* 3: 199–244

1970. "Language structure and language function," in John Lyons, ed., *New horizons in linguistics*, pp. 140–65. Harmondsworth: Penguin Books

Hawkins, Jack, 1978. *Definiteness and indefiniteness: a study in reference and grammaticality prediction*. Atlantic Highlands, NJ: Humanities Press

Hellan, Lars 1981. "On anaphora in Norwegian." Unpublished ms., University of Trondheim, Norway

Higginbotham, James 1983. "Logical form, binding, and nominals," *Linguistic Inquiry* 14: 395–420

1985. "On semantics," *Linguistic Inquiry* 16: 547–94

Higgins, Francis Roger 1979. *The pseudo-cleft construction in English*. New York and London: Garland Publishing, Inc.

Hook, Peter and Mohabbat Singh Man Singh Chauhan 1987. "The perfective adverb in Bhitrauti," *Word* [forthcoming]

Hopper, Paul 1979. "Aspect and foregrounding in discourse," in Talmy Givón, ed., *Syntax and semantics 12*, pp. 213–41. New York: Academic Press

Hopper, Paul and Sandra Thompson 1980. "Transitivity in grammar and discourse," *Language* 56: 251–99

Hornstein, Norbert 1984. *Logic as grammar*. Cambridge, MA: MIT Press

Hornstein, Norbert and David Lightfoot 1987. "Predication and PRO," *Language* 63: 23–52

Hornstein, Norbert and Amy Weinberg 1981. "Case theory and preposition stranding", *Linguistic Inquiry* 12, 55–91

Huang, C.-T. J. 1982. "Logical relations in Chinese and the theory of grammar." Unpublished doctoral dissertation, MIT

Jackendoff, Ray 1972. *Semantic interpretation in generative grammar*. Cambridge, MA: MIT Press

    1977. *X' syntax: a study of phrase structure*. Cambridge, MA: MIT Press

    1983. *Semantics and cognition*. Cambridge, MA: MIT Press

    1987a. "The status of thematic relations in linguistic theory," *Linguistic Inquiry* 18: 369–412

    1987b. "Adjuncts." Unpublished ms., Brandeis University

Jaeggli, Osvaldo 1986. "Passive," *Linguistic Inquiry* 17: 587–622

Janda, Richard 1980. "On a certain construction of English's," in Bruce Caron *et al.*, eds., *Proceedings of the sixth annual meeting of the Berkeley Linguistics Society*, pp. 324–36. Berkeley: Berkeley Linguistics Society

Jespersen, Otto 1905. *Growth and structure of the English language*. New York: Free Press, 1968, edn (first published 1905)

    1924. *A modern English grammar*. London: Allen & Unwin

Kameyama, Megumi 1985. "Zero anaphora: the case of Japanese." Unpublished doctoral dissertation, Stanford University

Kayne, Richard 1975. *French syntax*. Cambridge, MA: MIT Press

    1981a. "Binding, quantifiers, clitics, and control," in Frank Heny, ed., *Binding and filtering*, pp. 191–212. Cambridge, MA: MIT Press

    1981b. "ECP extensions," *Linguistic Inquiry* 12: 93–134

    1981c. "On certain differences between French and English," *Linguistic Inquiry* 12: 349–72

    1984. *Connectedness and binary branching*. Dordrecht: Foris Publications

Kean, Mary-Louise 1981. "Explanation in neurolinguistics," in Norbert Hornstein and David Lightfoot, eds., *Explanation in linguistics*, pp. 174–208. London: Longman

Keenan, Edward and Leonard Faltz 1978. "Logical types for natural language," *Occasional Papers in Linguistics*. Los Angeles: UCLA

Kitagawa, Yoshihisa 1985. "Small but clausal," *CLS* 21

Koster, Jan and Eric Reuland (eds.) 1987. "Long distance anaphora." Unpublished ms. [containing 17 articles on a variety of languages]. Groningen, The Netherlands: Dept. of Linguistics, Groningen University

Kuno, Susumu 1973. *The structure of the Japanese language*. Cambridge, MA: MIT Press

    1986. "Anaphora in Japanese," in S. Y. Kuroda, ed., *Papers from the first SDF workshop in Japanese syntax*, pp. 11–70. Dept. of Linguistics, University of California–La Jolla

Kuroda, S.-Y. 1965. "Generative grammatical studies in the Japanese · language." Unpublished doctoral dissertation, MIT

Larson, Richard 1987. "On the double object construction," Lexicon Project Working Papers no. 16. Cambridge, MA: Center for Cognitive Science, MIT

Lasnik, Howard 1984. "Random thoughts on implicit arguments." Unpublished ms., University of Connecticut at Storrs [referred to in Roeper 1987]

Lepschy, Anna Laura and Giulio Lepschy 1979. *The Italian language today.* London: Hutchinson & Co. [first published in 1977]

Levi, Judith 1978. *The syntax and semantics of complex nominals.* New York: Academic Press, Inc.

Levin, Beth 1985. "Lexical semantics in review," Lexicon Project Working Papers no. 1. Cambridge, MA: Center for Cognitive Science, MIT

Levin, Beth and Malka Rappaport 1986. "What to do with theta-roles," Lexicon Project Working Papers no. 11. Cambridge, MA: Center for Cognitive Science, MIT

Levin, Nancy 1978. "Some identity-of-sense deletions puzzle me. Do they you?" in Donka Farkas, Wesley M. Jacobsen, and Karol W. Todrys, eds., *Papers from the fourteenth regional meeting of the Chicago Linguistic Society*, pp. 229–40. Chicago: Chicago Linguistic Society

Lieber, Rochelle 1983. "Argument linking and compounds in English", *Linguistic Inquiry* 14: 251–85

McCawley, James 1982. "Parentheticals and discontinuous constituent structure," *Linguistic Inquiry* 13: 91–106

    1983. "What's with *with,*" *Language* 59 (2): 271–87.

McConnell-Ginet, Sally 1982. "Adverbs and logical form: a linguistically realistic theory," *Language* 58: 144–84

Maling, Joan 1972. "On 'gapping and the order of constituents'," *Linguistic Inquiry* 3: 101–8

    1981. "Non-clause-bounded reflexives in Icelandic." Unpublished ms., Brandeis University

    1983. "Transitive adjectives: a case of categorial reanalysis," in Frank Heny and B. Richards, eds., *Linguistic categories: auxiliaries and related puzzles*, pp. 253–89. Dordrecht: Reidel Publishing Co.

    1984. "Non-clause-bounded reflexives in modern Icelandic," *Linguistics and Philosophy* 7: 211–41

Manzini, Maria Rita 1983. "On control and control theory," *Linguistic Inquiry* 14: 421–56

Marantz, Alec 1984a. *On the nature of grammatical relations.* Cambridge, MA: MIT Press

    1984b. "Tagalog reduplication is affixation, too." Paper presented at the winter LSA, Baltimore, Maryland

Matthews, P. H. 1981. *Syntax.* Cambridge: Cambridge University Press

Mey, J. 1970. "The cyclic character of Eskimo reflexivization," *AL* 13: 1–31

Miller, Barry (1988). "Predicate argument structure and the lexicon: Tagalog as a case study." Unpublished doctoral dissertation, University of Michigan

Miller, George and Phillip Johnson-Laird 1976. *Language and perception*. Cambridge, MA: Harvard University Press

Milner, Jean Claude 1978. *De la syntaxe à l'interprétation. Quantités, insultes, exclamations*. Paris: Editions du Seuil (series "Travaux linguistiques")

Myhill, John 1984. "A study of aspect, word order, and voice." Unpublished doctoral dissertation, University of Pennsylvania

    1985. "Pragmatic and categorial correlates of VS word order," *Lingua* 66: 177–200

Napoli, Donna Jo 1973. "The two *si*'s of Italian: an analysis of reflexive, inchoative, and indefinite subject sentences in modern standard Italian." Unpublished doctoral dissertation, Harvard University [Distributed by IULC in 1976]

    1974a. "The no crossing filter," *CLS* 10: 482–91

    1974b. "Una breve analisi dei verbi modali *potere* e *dovere*," in Mario Medici and Antonella Sangregorio, eds., *Fenomeni morfologici e sintattici nell'italiano contemporaneo*, pp. 233–40. Rome: Bulzoni

    1975. "A global agreement phenomenon," *Linguistic Inquiry* 6: 413–35

    1978. "A look at some adverbs and prepositions in Italian: evidence for syntactic analogy," *Montreal working papers in linguistics* 10: 191–218

    1979. "Reflexivization across clause boundaries in Italian," *Journal of Linguistics* 15: 1–28

    1981. "Semantic interpretation vs. lexical governance: clitic climbing in Italian," *Language* 57: 841–87

    1983. "Comparative ellipsis: a phrase structure analysis," *Linguistic Analysis* 14, 675–94

    1985. "Verb phrase deletion in English: a base-generated analysis," *Journal of Linguistics* 21: 281–319

    1987a. "Subjects and external arguments/clauses and non-clauses", *Linguistics and Philosophy* [forthcoming]

    1987b. "Predication inside NPs in Italian: a case study for a theory of predication," in Jean Pierre Montreuil and David Birdsong, eds., *Proceedings of the Sixteenth Linguistic Symposium on Romance Languages*, at Austin Texas, March, 1986. Dordrecht: Foris Publications [forthcoming]

    1988. Review of *Italian syntax: a government-binding approach*, by Luigi Burzio (Dordrecht: Reidel Publishing Co., 1986) in *Language*

Napoli, Donna Jo and Marina Nespor 1976. "Negatives in comparatives," *Language* 52: 811–38

    1986. "Comparative structures in Italian," *Language* 62: 622–53

Napoli, Donna Jo and Joel Nevis 1987. "Inflected prepositions in Italian," in Arnold Zwicky and Ellen Kaisse, eds., *Phonology Yearbook*, vol. 4, pp. 195–210

Napoli, Donna Jo and Emily Rando 1979. *Syntactic argumentation*. Washington, DC: Georgetown University Press

Nespor, Marina and Irene Vogel 1982. "Prosodic domains of external sandhi rules," in Harry van der Hulst and Norval Smith, eds., *The structure of phonological representation* Part I, pp. 225–65. Dordrecht: Foris Publications

Newmeyer, Frederick 1975. *English aspectual verbs*. The Hague: Mouton

O'Grady, William 1982. "Remarks on thematically governed predication," *Linguistic Analysis* 9: 119–34

Peterson, Peter 1981. "Problems with constraints on coordination," *Linguistic Analysis* 8: 449–60

Poser, William 1982. "Lexical rules may change internal arguments," *The Linguistic Review* 2: 97–100

Postal, Paul 1974. *On raising: one rule of English grammar and its theoretical implications*. Cambridge, MA: MIT Press

Pullum, Geoffrey 1982. "Syncategorematicity and English infinitival *to*," *Glossa* 16: 181–215

Pustejovsky, James 1985. "Studies in generalized binding." Unpublished doctoral dissertation, MIT

Pyle, Howard 1915. *The wonder clock, or four and twenty marvelous tales, being one for each hour of the day* ("embellished with verses by Katherine Pyle"), New York: Harper and Brothers

Randall, J. 1983. "A lexical approach to causatives," *Journal of Linguistic Research* 2: 3

Rando, Emily and Donna Jo Napoli. 1978. "*There* sentences in English," *Language* 54: 300–13

Rappaport, Malka 1983. "On the nature of derived nominals," in L. Levin, M. Rappaport, and Annie Zaenen, eds., *Papers in lexical–functional grammar*, Bloomington, IN: Indiana University Linguistics Club

Rappaport, Malka, Beth Levin, and Mary Laughren 1987. "Levels of lexical representation." Unpublished ms. printed by the Lexicon Project of the MIT Center for Cognitive Science [forthcoming in *Lexique*]

Reinhart, Tanya 1976. "The syntactic domain of anaphora." Unpublished doctoral dissertation, MIT

Renzi, Lorenzo and Laura Vanelli 1975. "*E un ingegnere/è ingenere* (e anche *fa l'ingegnere*)," *Lingua Nostra* 36 (3): 81–2

Reuland, Eric 1983. "Governing-*ing*," *Linguistic Inquiry* 14; 101–36

van Riemsdijk, Henk 1978. "On the diagnosis of wh-movement," in S. J. Keyser, ed., *Recent transformational studies in European languages*, Linguistic Inquiry Monograph 3, pp. 189–206. Cambridge, MA: MIT Press

Rizzi, Luigi 1982. *Issues in Italian syntax*. Dordrecht: Foris Publications

Roeper, Thomas 1987. "Implicit arguments and the head–complement relation," *Linguistic Inquiry* 18: 267–310

Roeper, Thomas and Muffy Siegel 1978. "A lexical transformation for verbal compounds," *Linguistic Inquiry* 9: 199–260

Ross, John R. 1970. "On declarative sentences," in Roderick Jacobs and Peter Rosenbaum, eds., *Readings in English transformational grammar*, pp. 222–72. Waltham, MA: Ginn and Co.

Rothstein, Susan 1983. "The syntactic forms of predication." Unpublished doctoral dissertation, MIT [distributed by IULC in 1985]

Rouveret, Alain and Jean-Roger Vergnaud 1980. "Specifying reference to the subject: French causatives and conditions on representations," *Linguistic Inquiry* 11: 97–202

Ruwet, Nicolas 1972. *Théorie syntaxique et syntaxe du français.* Paris: Le Seuil
  1982. *Grammaire des insultes.* Paris: Le Seuil
  1987. "Les verbes météorologiques et l'hypothèse inaccusative," in Claire Blanche-Benveniste, Andre Chervel, and Maurice Gross, eds., *Mélanges à la mémoire de Jean Stefanini* [forthcoming]

Safir, Kenneth 1983. "On small clauses as constituents," *Linguistic Inquiry* 14: 730–35
  1985. *Syntactic chains.* Cambridge: Cambridge University Press
  1986. "Relative clauses in a theory of binding and levels," *Linguistic Inquiry* 17: 663–90
  1987a. "The syntactic projection of lexical thematic structure," *Natural Language and Linguistic Theory* [forthcoming]
  1987b. "Evaluative predicates." Unpublished ms., Rutgers University

Schachter, Paul 1977. "Constraints on coordination," *Language* 53: 86–103

Schein, Barry 1982a. "Small clauses and predication." Unpublished ms., MIT
  1982b. "Non-finite clauses in Russian," in Alec Marantz and Timothy Stowell, eds., *MIT Working Papers in Linguistics*, vol. 4

Selkirk, Elisabeth 1977. "Some remarks on noun phrase structure," in Peter Culicover, Thomas Wasow, and Adrian Akmajian, eds., *Formal syntax*, pp. 285–316. New York: Academic Press, Inc.
  1982. *The syntax of words,* Linguistic Inquiry Monograph 7. Cambridge, MA: MIT Press

Sells, Peter 1987. "Aspects of logophoricity," *Linguistic Inquiry* 18: 445–79

Simpson, Jane. 1983a. "Resultatives," in L. Levin, M. Rappaport, and Annie Zaenen, eds., *Papers in lexical–functional grammar.* Bloomington, IN: IULC
  1983b. "Aspects of Walpiri morphology and syntax." Unpublished doctoral dissertation, MIT

Solan, Lawrence 1977. "On the interpretation of missing complement NPs" Unpublished ms., University of Massachusetts, Amherst

Sornicola, Rosanna 1981. *Sul parlato.* Bologna, Italy: Il Mulino

Speas, Margaret J. 1986. "Adjunctions and projections in syntax." Unpublished doctoral dissertation MIT

Spooren, W. 1981. "Over de verschillen tussen uit breidende en beperkende bijzinnen en de rol er van in Jackendoff's argumentatie voor de Uniforme Drie Niveauhypothese." Unpublished ms., Instituut De Vooys, University of Utrecht, The Netherlands [cited in van Gestel]

Sproat, Richard 1985. "On deriving the lexicon." Unpublished doctoral dissertation, MIT

Stockwell, Robert, Paul Schachter, and Barbara Hall Partee 1973. *The major syntactic structures of English.* New York: Holt, Rinehart, and Winston

Stowell, Timothy 1981. "Origins of phrase structure." Unpublished doctoral dissertation, MIT

Strawson, P. F. 1950. "On referring," *Mind* 59: 320–44

Stump, Gregory 1981. "The formal semantics and pragmatics of free adjuncts and absolutes in English." Unpublished doctoral dissertation, Ohio State University

Stuurman, Frits 1983. "Appositives and X-bar theory," *Linguistic Inquiry* 14: 736–44

1985. *Phrase structure theory in generative grammar*. Dordrecht: Foris Publications

Swanson, Pina 1969. "Sintagma preposizionale come modificatore del nome," in *La sintassi*, pp. 387–400. Rome: Bulzoni

Talmy, Leonard 1985. "Force dynamics in language and thought." Papers from the 21st Regional Meeting of the Chicago Linguistic Society, ed. William H. Eilfort, Paul D. Krocher, and Karen Z. Peterson, *CLS* 21: 293–337

1986. "Lexicalization patterns: semantic structure in lexical forms," in Timothy Shopen, ed., *Grammatical categories and the lexicon*. Cambridge: Cambridge University Press

Thomason, Richmond and Robert Stalnaker 1973. "A semantic theory of adverbs," *Linguistic Inquiry* 4: 195–220

Thomson, Judith Jarvis 1977. *Acts and other events*. Ithaca, NY: Cornell University Press

Thráinsson, Hoskuldur 1976. "Reflexives and subjunctives in Icelandic," *Proceedings of NELS* 6: 225–39

Tommola, Jorma 1978. "Expectancy and speech comprehension," in Viljo Kohonen and Nils Erik Enkvist, eds., *Text linguistics, cognitive learning and language teaching*, no. 22 of Suomen sovelletun kielitieteen yhdistyksen (AF in LA) julkaisuja, pp. 49–70. Turku: Finnish Association for Applied Linguistics

Torrego, Esther 1986. "On empty categories in nominals." Unpublished ms., University of Massachusetts at Amherst

Valesio, Paolo 1974. "L'estrazione della relativa. Implicazioni italiane," in Mario Medici and Antonella Sangregorio, eds., *Fenomeni morfologici e sintattici nell'italiano contemporaneo*, pp. 339–56. Rome: Bulzoni

Wiggins, D. 1970. "The individuation of things and places," in M. J. Loux, ed., *Universals and particulars*, pp. 307–39. New York: Anchor Books, Doubleday & Co.

Williams, Edwin 1977. "Discourse and logical form," *Linguistic Inquiry* 8: 101–39

1979. "Passive." Unpublished ms., University of Massachusetts at Amherst

1980. "Predication," *Linguistic Inquiry* 11: 203–38

1981a. "Argument structure and morphology," *The Linguistic Review* 1: 81–114

1981b. "On the notions 'lexically related' and 'head of a word'," *Linguistic Inquiry* 12: 245–74

1982. "The NP cycle," *Linguistic Inquiry* 13: 277–95

1983a. "Against small clauses," *Linguistic Inquiry* 14: 287–308

1983b. "Semantic vs. syntactic categories," *Linguistics and Philosophy* 6: 423–46

1984a. "*There*-insertion," *Linguistic Inquiry* 15: 131–53

1984b. "Grammatical relations," *Linguistic Inquiry* 15: 639–73

1985. "PRO and Subject of NP," *Natural Language and Linguistic Theory* 3 (3): 297–315

Woisetschlaeger, Erich 1983. "On the question of definiteness in 'An old man's book'," *Linguistic Inquiry* 14: 137–54

Zubizarreta, Maria-Luisa 1985. "The relation between morphophonology and morphosyntax: the case of Romance causatives," *Linguistic Inquiry* 16: 247–90

1986. "Levels of representation in the lexicon and in the syntax." Unpublished ms., University of Maryland and University of Tilburg

Zwicky, Arnold 1985. "Heads," *Journal of Linguistics* 21: 1–29

Index of names

Index of subjects

absolutives, 54, 103, 112, 120, 124–27, 276, 278–81, 290, 297, 323, 348
  absolutive coindexing, 126, 163
adjuncts, 4, 25, 63, 82–84, 88, 103, 117, 120, 121, 128, 144, 148–50, 156, 157, 159, 160, 162, 177, 178, 269, 275, 278, 281, 286, 315, 321, 349
adverbials, 10–13, 24, 26, 32, 55, 83, 115, 116, 125, 127, 130, 135, 285, 288–98, 340–43
  see also floating quantifiers, modifiers
agreement
  subject–verb, 151, 152, 167, 197–99, 210, 271
  gender and/or number, 188, 189, 197–201, 223, 225, 258, 297, 310, 344
anaphors, 2, 36, 37, 42, 60, 61, 132, 133, 136, 152, 153, 168, 211, 273–351
  anaphor coindexing, 313, 344, 347
  long distance anaphora, 275, 276, 280, 302, 303, 317, 318, 329–47
  see also reciprocals
appositives, 96, 175–78, 218–19, 234, 242, 247, 251, 261–71, 278
arguments, 6–80, 81–165, 273–351, 181–83, 187
  arguments and A-positions, 275, 277–82, 286, 287, 297, 298, 306–8, 348
  argument ladders and rungs, 120, 275, 283, 293, 303, 310–18, 330–50
  argument versus role player, 6, 13, 31
  attraction into an argument network, 74, 80
  implicit arguments, 23ff., 68–71, 80, 133, 243, 249
  see also anaphors, theta theory
aspectual verbs, 18, 19, 74, 129, 161, 318

barriers, 5, 87, 109–13, 122, 124, 128, 133, 150, 152–54, 156, 160, 163, 228, 268, 269, 275, 277–82, 298–308, 316, 317, 319, 331, 348

c-commands, 85, 86, 94–100, 115–17, 130, 137, 160, 164, 171, 206, 215, 227, 255, 257–61, 269, 270, 272–75, 281, 298–305, 350
control, 16, 23, 24, 61, 68, 71, 73, 84, 85, 131, 136, 137, 148, 276
copula
  as a grammatical word, 9, 33, 56, 61, 88, 110, 129
  as head of a predicate, 61

direct object restrictions, 333–38

events (notions of, event lexical item, event structure), 6–80; see also 106, 107, 119, 151, 284, 322, 334
  central events, 48, 49, 334
  central participant in an event, 48, 49, 334, 335

floating quantifiers, 135, 285, 288–97
functional criterion, 73, 75, 76, 80, 123

governing category, 273, 275, 283, 286–89, 311–13, 317, 323, 329, 330, 333, 350

i-within-i constraints, 37–39, 138, 139, 230
identification, 16, 17, 91, 92, 247, 253
indexing principles, 349–50
  see also predication

L-marking, 109, 110, 122, 123, 133, 144, 149, 155–57, 207, 208, 228, 229, 278–80, 298, 299, 305
  see also arguments, barriers
lexical heads/lexical items, 6, 14, 25–26, 29–32, 53, 60, 66, 72, 79, 84, 173, 220, 238
lexical ladders, see argument ladders
licensing, 63, 120–23, 128, 129, 145, 162, 212, 274, 278, 289, 323

mediation, 144–47, 154–57, 161
Minimality Condition, 110, 111, 153

368

modifiers, 3, 11–13, 20–22, 30–35, 55, 62, 67, 72–76, 90, 91, 94, 102, 105, 113, 123, 128, 132, 133, 135, 158, 162, 165, 173, 176–83, 187–89, 192, 193, 199, 201, 202, 219–21, 224, 227, 238, 242, 243, 249, 251, 259, 260, 262, 269, 270, 272, 284, 294, 296, 301, 306, 307, 311, 314, 322, 323, 340, 341, 343
   see also adverbials, floating quantifiers

passives, 67, 90, 91, 118, 257
  by phrase, 41, 55, 72, 101, 129–35, 221, 280
  -en as agent, 24
  impersonal passives, 24
predicate (notion of), 6–80, 81–165, 246–272, 273–351; *see also* 184, 186–202, 215, 216, 222–27, 233, 234
  complex predicate, 207–8, 229
  head of a predicate, 8, 14, 23, 26, 27, 29–34, 44–52, 55–58, 67, 74, 77, 79, 81, 88, 90, 91, 112, 121, 123, 161, 290, 306–8
  natural predicate or possible semantic word, 97, 98, 325
  predicate within a complex nominal, 234–41
  predicate versus lexical head, 6, 13, 27–30
  primary predication, 88, 129, 163
  Proviso One, 111, 119, 121, 126, 130, 144, 145, 147, 152, 155, 156, 158, 163, 206, 228, 275, 277, 299, 302, 303, 306–18, 348
  Proviso Two, 112, 123, 124, 126, 130, 152, 155, 156, 158, 160, 163, 164, 206–8, 228, 229, 253, 275–78, 282, 298, 303, 308, 316–18, 331, 348
  secondary predication, 89, 95, 109; *and see* Proviso One, Proviso Two
prepositions, 64, 65, 84, 94, 101, 125, 136, 149, 150, 179–82, 277, 278, 322
  as heads of predicates, 46–48, 52, 56, 106, 228, 323
  as parts (but not heads) of predicates, 32, 51, 52, 83, 259
  as defective categories, 57
  in the English phrase *that crook of a chairman*, 215–16, 220–22, 227
  in the Italian phrase *quel matto di Giorgio*, 170–73, 194, 195
  insularity of PP, 127, 128, 153, 322, 323
  particular Ps: *of* as a null P, 31–34, 41, 47, 57, 102, 105, 171, 172, 182, 183, 215, 216, 221, 227, 235, 257; *after*, 52–54; *with*, 47–49, 73

Principle of Coincidences, 29, 31, 62, 67, 79, 81, 140
Projection Principle, 19, 49, 73, 74, 80, 84, 86, 254
  Extended Projection Principle, 68, 70, 73, 141, 254
psych verbs, 302, 303, 316–18

reciprocals, 275, 282–98
  see also anaphors
restructuring (or reanalysis)
  in LF, 253, 254, 269–71
  in the syntax, 15, 65, 96–100, 103, 106, 130, 137, 150, 291, 304, 325
  into a complex nominal (in the PF), 235–44, 246, 247
Right Dislocation structures, 262–66, 270
  see also appositives
role players (concept of), 6–80, 81–165, 246–72, 273
  see also arguments, predicates

semantic relations/semantic roles, 6, 16, 25–27, 29, 30, 45, 51, 52, 90, 189
small clause, 84, 87, 103, 151, 152, 206, 279, 288, 324–26
specifiers, 2, 3, 11–14, 26, 32–43, 67, 90, 91, 155, 168–170, 172, 179, 184–85, 202–6, 211, 212, 216, 218, 222, 223, 229–30, 233, 304, 322, 327, 328, 333
structural (or syntactic) versus semantic heads, 78, 79, 193–202, 225, 226, 233, 252
subject role playes and subject arguments, 6–80, 81–165, 246–72, 273–351; *see also* 171, 184, 186–202, 206–8, 215, 218, 222–30, 234–41
  subject role players versus external arguments, 137–44, 164, 206, 227

T-government, 111, 112, 161, 314
theta theory, 6–80, 81–165; *see also* 178, 179, 192, 218, 220, 262
  Theta Criterion, 72, 80, 84–86
  theta domain, 42, 109, 112, 206–8, 228, 229, 275, 277, 299, 305–30, 348–50; *see also* Proviso One *under* predicate
  Theta Assignment: Compositional, 64–66, 76, 79, 90, 94, 100, 109, 110, 129, 136, 156, 277, 286, 291, 322, 323; Direct, 64–66, 76, 79, 90, 109, 277; External, 66, 67, 72, 75, 79, 90, 109

X-bar theory, 2–4, 40, 42, 82, 88, 110, 117, 127, 164, 165, 168, 173, 178, 179, 219, 220, 250, 251, 261, 267, 300